Systematic Theology

VOLUME II

Systematic Theology

~

VOLUME II

The Works of God

ROBERT W. JENSON

OXFORD
UNIVERSITY PRESS

OXFORD
UNIVERSITY PRESS

Oxford   New York
Athens   Auckland   Bangkok   Bogotá   Buenos Aires   Calcutta
Cape Town   Chennai   Dar es Salaam   Delhi   Florence   Hong Kong   Istanbul
Karachi   Kuala Lumpur   Madrid   Melbourne   Mexico City   Mumbai
Nairobi   Paris   São Paulo   Shanghai   Singapore   Taipei   Tokyo   Toronto   Warsaw

and associated companies in
Berlin   Ibadan

Copyright © 1999 by Robert W. Jenson

First published in 1999 by Oxford University Press, Inc.
198 Madison Avenue, New York, New York 10016

First issued as an Oxford University Press paperback, 2001

Oxford is a registered trademark of Oxford Univeristy Press, Inc.

Library of Congress Cataloging-in-Publication Data
Jenson, Robert W.
Systematic theology / Robert W. Jenson
2 v.   cm.
Includes bibliographical references and index.
Contents: v. 1. The triune God; v. 2. The Works of God
ISBN 0-19-508648-1 (v. 1); ISBN 0-19-508649-x (v. 2); ISBN 0-19-514599-2 (pbk.)
1. Theology, Doctrinal.   I. Title.
BT75.2.J45   1997
230—dc20   96-5507

1 3 5 7 9 8 6 4 2

Printed in the United States of America
on acid-free paper

Preface

The volume here offered is the second of two. Certain peculiarities of the work's general organization suggest that a few paragraphs of renewed orientation may be useful.

The entire first volume was devoted, after prolegomena, to the doctrine of God. Several traditional topics that in most systems appear later under other headings appeared already in that volume. According to a conviction systematically determinative for the present work, Christology, pneumatology, and the soteriological interpretation of Christ's life, death, and resurrection belong to the telling of God's own story.

Now in this second volume we come to the works of God *ad extra*, as the tradition has labeled them, though the phrase is here understood somewhat less expansively than is traditional. We come to acts of God directed to a reality other than himself, considered thematically in their otherness, and so to the doctrines of creation, of the church, and of the final Kingdom. It must be admitted that the distinction between these matters and those chosen to be covered in volume 1 is at some points tenuous; but organizing the work on the plausible principle that finally *all* Christian teaching in one way or another tells God's own story would of course have obliterated the point.

The order of this volume's parts among themselves is a matter of tactics; each of their six possible combinations would have its conceptual and expository advantages. I simply decided, after making the rather drastic changes in familiar order that shape volume 1 and its relation to volume 2, to abide for the rest by more accustomed sequences. Thus in volume 2 we follow what is usually taken to be the natural sequence of the Bible and the creeds, misleading though also that assumption can in some ways be.

I should here, between the two volumes of my work, confess an increasing awareness of indigence. Martin Luther's farewell says it all: " *Wir sind Betler. Das ist verum.* " Writing volume one—and then reading it!—has insistently shown me how much I have left out or not understood. The truth of the gospel is simple and mind-boggling and above all abundant. Everything I have read or heard since beginning to write, and every moment of reflection, has revealed some new matter or consideration or contention that demands to be included in this book but cannot be if I am ever to finish. Since a preface can be revised until the last minute, I can mention as example an event that happened when I thought I was done with ecclesiology: Blanche Jenson and I spent ten days in Helsinki with the theologians there, with Tuomo Mannermaa and his associates, and I came back realizing that I had to rewrite and expand much of the part dedicated to it.

Thus every day it has become clearer to me why the *Kirchliche Dogmatik* and the *Summa theologiae* are so long and even so were not finished. It has been my doubtless superficial determination to be brief—relatively—and—God willing—to finish. That you are reading this tells you that I have been and that he has been.

Finally, early in the first volume I remarked that "It is the fate of every theological system to be dismembered and have its fragments bandied in an ongoing debate." I intended the remark as an offering of my own system for such treatment. But in the time since, I have become more aware of how thoroughly this work dismembers its predecessors and uses the fragments in strange ways, and of the offense and puzzlement this can be for disciples of, say, Thomas or Barth or Palamas or Luther. I can only say, "Sorry. But that is how it goes when mere humans try to do theology."

Contents

PART IV

THE CREATION

FIFTEEN

The Act of Creation

I

The Bible begins with a straightforward doctrinal proposition: "In the beginning God created the heavens and the earth." Genesis 1:1 should be so translated since it is, almost certainly, to be read as the *caption* of the following narrative,[1] both summarizing and introducing it.[2]

The proposition became a rule of faith in Israel. A text from II Maccabees is often cited: "Look at the heavens and the earth . . . and acknowledge that God made them."[3]

The primal church simply maintained the Jewish doctrine. Indeed even "maintained" is too energetic a verb; in the New Testament the doctrine is not so much asserted as assumed[4] and used to warrant other assertions. Thus the missionary proclamation cited in Acts' story of Paul and Barnabas at Lystra includes their

---

1. Genesis 1:2–2:3.

2. That this is the correct reading and translation, rather than that of such versions as the New Revised Standard, has surely been demonstrated for good and all by Claus Westermann, *Genesis, Biblischer Kommentar Altes Testament*, ed. Martin Noth, Hans Walter Wolff (Neukirchen-Vluyn: Neukirchener Verlag des Erziehungsvereins, 1968), ad. loc. The recent preference for translations that make Genesis 1:1 a dependent clause derives from residual prejudices of a now antique form of critical exegesis that tended always to look for the "real" meaning of texts in some stage of the tradition before and outside the structure of the canonical text and then to intepret the canonical text to fit.

3. II Maccabees 7:28.

4. Thus the difference between Creator and creature is an immediate classification; Romans 1:25, Hebrews 14:13. "Creator" can be just a variant for "God"; I Peter 4:19, 3:19. "Creature" can be used for "everything;" Romans 8:19–39, Colossians 1:23, and "human creature" (*anthropine ktisis*) can serve for the always troublesome notion of "human being"; I Peter 2:13. "Beginning of creation" means simply absolute beginning; Mark 13:19. In I Timothy 4:3 , being created by God means being good and useful.

confession that Israel's God "made the heaven and the earth and the sea and all that is in them" not for its own sake but to show wherein the gods of paganism, who make no such claim, are by contrast unworthy of worship.[5] Or again, the passage in Hebrews, "By faith we understand that the worlds were prepared by the word of God," interprets not the worlds but faith.[6]

The New Testament does make one new assertion about creation: that it is done for the sake of Christ and so, since he also antedates it, "through" him.[7] But also this teaching is in direct consequence from Judaism. Contemporary Judaism, fully in accord with *Genesis*, as we shall see, taught that "[i]t was for us that you created the world."[8] The church, in its claimed continuity with Israel,[9] appropriated also this aspect of Jewish teaching: "The world was made for the church's sake."[10] When Christ appears in Colossians as mediator and goal of creation, it is as "the head of . . . the church" that he has this position.[11]

One passage both gathers many aspects of the primal church's belief and has a more deliberate dogmatic ring. Against polytheism, Paul cites a christological expansion of the Jewish confession of one God: "There is one God, the Father, from whom are all things and for whom we exist, and one Lord, Jesus Christ, through whom are all things and through whom we exist."[12] Yet even here Paul's purpose is not to enforce the idea of creation itself or to develop it christologically, but to ward off any temptation to take the pagan gods seriously except as occasions of temptation: since all real things but the biblical God are his creatures, all alleged gods other than the one must be either figments or if real then creatures who pose as gods and so become demons.

From about the middle of the second century the situation changed, as the church confronted gnostic and other modes of denial that the being responsible for this world deserves to be called God. Mediterranean paganism in its decadence experienced the world in the way Martin Luther would reduce to a famous dictum: that one who observes the actual management of this world and judges by any usual moral standard must conclude "either that God is not or that God is wicked."[13] The escapes available to paganism were nihilism, Stoic resignation, or a desperate hope that the power responsible for this world is not truly God. Only the last default could tempt Christians theologically; so Justin Martyr contended with Marcion, who, says Justin, taught that we should "think of another God," the God revealed in Christ, "as greater than . . . the Creator."[14]

---

5. Acts 14:4–18
6. Hebrews 11:3.
7. The New Testament witness to the christological qualification of creation is conveniently assembled by Colin E. Gunton, *Christ and Creation* (Grand Rapids: Eerdmans, 1992), 22–30.
8. II Esdras 6:55.
9. Pp. 170–172, 191–196.
10. Hermas, *Vision* ii.4.1. The limits of such appropriations will be discussed in a later chapter.
11. Colossians 1:15–20.
12. I Corinthians 8:6.
13. *De servo arbitrio* (WA 18), 784: "aut nullum esse Deum, aut iniquum esse Deum."
14. *First Apology*, 29.

This conflict was one of those in which the church was moved to its second- and third-century proliferation of rules of faith and creeds.[15] Therefore confession that the God revealed in Jesus and the Creator are the same, now indeed made for its own sake, is a staple of these formulas, regularly appearing as the first doxology of the Father. So the rule of faith given by Irenaeus in the second century: "The church . . . has received the faith from the apostles and their disciples: in one God, the all-ruling Father, who made heaven and earth."[16] Notably, these doctrinal statements reiterate the biblical and Jewish proposition with little or no conceptual elaboration, against directly contrary views current in the culture.

II

Plainly, our next task must be to inquire what "God creates" means in Scripture, since the church's doctrine simply appropriates the biblical proposition. Lexical investigations are here of little help, because Scripture reserves the verb translated "creates" (*barah*) for this one use; "creating" is something only God does.[17] We are directed to context; fortunately this is all we need, since the meaning of "God created" in Genesis 1:1 must in any case be determined by the narrative that follows.

Developing the concept of creation by exegeting the Genesis account is of course no new strategy. We will proceed through a series of propositions, in this and the next sections.

The first proposition: that God creates means there is other reality than God and that it is really other than he. The most obtrusive feature of the priestly creation narrative is the drumbeat rhythm of the six days; indeed this is the chief means by which this subtly reflected document, the product of a rhetorically sophisticated theology, does its teaching. Primary among the insistent rhythms is "And God said 'let there *be* . . . ,' and there *was* . . . ,"[18] with its variants.

The point needed and needs such insistence. In the world's religions the dominant understanding of our being and the being of our world is that it derives from deity by *emanation* of one sort or another. By this interpretation either there finally is no reality other than the divine, or insofar as it is other it is illusion or degradation. We should note that modern secularist interpretations of the world's derivation do not break this pattern but merely exacerbate either the world's divinity or its worthlessness, or in postmodernism both at once.

Once the church was thoroughly involved with various versions of this interpretation present in the gentile world, it became difficult also for the church

---

15. The immediately following of course summarizes to the point of caricature. For the nuances and additions necessary to a properly historical presentation, see Leo Scheffczyk, *Schöpfung und Vorsehung*, vol. 2, fasc. 2a of *Handbuch der Dogmengeschichte*, ed. Michael Schmaus, Alois Grillmeier (Freiburg: Herder, 1963), 30–50.

16. *Against All Heresies*, i.10.1.

17. The notion that creatures should or could be "co-creators" is, if "create" is intended to mean what it does in Scripture, simply oxymoronic.

18. *Yehi . . . Weheyi . . .*

to resist it.[19] The Arian controversy itself was a narrowly successful struggle to expel antique paganism's emanationism from at least the church's innermost christological thinking.

The emanationist temptation has continued throughout the church's history; I will note only two instances. For at least the Western church, the teaching of the fourth Lateran Council of 1215 may be taken as the dogmatic definition of creation: "There is only one true God . . . , the one principle of the universe, creator of all things visible and invisible . . . , who by his almighty power simultaneously at the beginning of time made all creatures from nothing, whether visible or corporeal, angelic or earthly."[20] Definition was found necessary because of Platonist thinkers who blurred the distinction of God and creatures, and reappearing gnostic groups who regarded the otherness of creation as evil.[21] And at the time of this writing, academically and church-politically powerful "feminist/womanist/mulierist theology" oddly supposes that any "dualism" of God and creature is "patriarchal."

Proposition two: there is other reality than God because he speaks. The rhythm has a second beat: "God *said*, let there be . . ." The motif of world-origin by making, direct or delegated, is clearly present in the priestly writer's conceptual repertoire but in the canonical text is subordinated to creation by speaking.[22] By the time of our text's writing, it was a rule of faith in Israel: "By the word of the Lord the heavens were made. . . . For he spoke, and it came to be; he commanded, and it stood firm."[23] God, we must formulate, *speaks the world into being.*

The notion that God or the gods evoke other reality by speaking is not in itself unique to Israel.[24] What is particular to Israel is the *sort* of word God speaks to bring the world to pass: he issues a command. Nevertheless, given the theological history, we need to linger with the sheer notion of creation by word.

Theology, we have seen, has often failed to understand the *Logos* as God's utterance and has substituted the notion that he is God's concept.[25] The *Logos* is said to proceed from the Father as the Father's act of knowing himself;[26] creation through the *Logos* is then interpreted as an immanent act of the Father's will, to actualize ideas that belong to what he knows in knowing the Son. In knowing himself in the Son, God knows what he can do, including what he can initiate

19. A nice instance of a converted intellectual's inability to free himself at this point was the celebrated Marius Victorinus in the fourth century; see Scheffczyk, *Schöpfung*, 60.

20. *Constitutiones*, 1. de Fide Catholica.

21. Scheffczyk, *Schöpfung*, 81–82.

22. That "And God said, let there be . . ." is creation by speaking but "And God said, let the earth bring forth . . ." is not hardly convinces, important though the "secondary causation" implied by the second formula may be in itself.

23. Psalm 33:6–8.

24. To this, Westermann, *Genesis*, 52–57.

25. So, for example, Thomas Aquinas, *Summa theologiae*, i.34.1: "It is as 'word' signifies a concept of the intellect, that 'Word' is properly predicated in God."

26. Ibid., i.27.2.

other than himself. Thus he knows the possibilities of creatures as these are ideas in the divine self-concept; creation is then the decision that all or some of these be instantiated.[27]

This theologoumenon stems finally from Origen's pioneering speculations and is appropriate in some contexts. But as the primary description of how God creates, it subverts Genesis' account. It has even been argued that it displaces Christ from his New Testament role in creation: not the *person* Christ has the function but Plato's Ideas, relocated in a "mind of God" that only after the fact is identified with Christ.[28]

Of classic theologians, it is perhaps Martin Luther who most straightforwardly corrected the usual interpretation. Commenting on Genesis, he reports the ordinary exegesis and rejects it as at odds with its text. Then he proceeds: "Moses uses the term *amar*, which simply denotes the spoken word. . . . By a mere word that he speaks God makes heaven and earth from nothing."[29] This exegesis includes a decisively biblical understanding of the *Logos* himself: even the word that is "in the divine being" is "an uttered word by which something is ordered and enjoined."[30]

God's act to create is certainly an act of intellect and will, as the majority tradition has said; but it is the kind of such act that is not enclosed within the subject but takes place as communication.[31] Already the Word that is a triune person is God's *Utterance* in his triune life; in the first volume we belabored this point. Now we must further insist: therefore the Word by which God creates is not silent within him but is his *address*, and is creative in virtue of the specific character of this address. Thus we arrive at our next proposition.

This is: God *commands* the world to be, this command is obeyed, and the event of obedience is the existence of the world. A second subrhythm of our passage is, "God said, *let* there be . . . And there was . . ."[32] It is this character of God's creating Utterance that is peculiar to Israel.[33] God creates the world by utterance of a moral intention for other beings than himself; "[b]y your will they existed

27. Ibid., i.14.8; 19.4. The general teaching is ecumenical. So Lutheran scholasticism as epitomized by Johann Baier, *Compendium theologiae postivae* (1695), i.iii.17–18: "Causam exemplarem creationis constituunt ideae singularum creaturarum in intellectu divino expressae. . . . Causam impulsivam creationis in bonitate Dei sola quaerimus."

28. So Colin E. Gunton, *A Brief Theology of Revelation* (Edinburgh: T. & T. Clark, 1995), 42–45. Wolfhart Pannenberg, *Systematische Theologie* (Göttingen: Vandenhoweck & Ruprecht, 1991), 2:41–42, gives a brief history of the notion's vicissitudes and concludes "in interpreting the Son's mediation of creation, theology must give up (the notion)."

29. *Ennaratio in Genesis* (WA 42), 13:13.

30. Ibid., 15.

31. Basil the Great's splendid commentary *almost* breaks through at this point. *Homilies on the Hexaemerson*, ii.7: "When we speak of voice or speech or command in connecton with God, we do not think of the divine word as a sound projected by the organs of speech; . . . we suppose that the determination of the will is expressed in the form of a command."

32. Basil the Great, *Hexaemeron*, ii.7: "God said, 'Let there be light.' And the command was itself the deed."

33. Westermann, *Genesis*, 56.

and were created."[34] Thus his creating of the world is agency of the same sort as the *torah* by which he creates Israel.[35]

Here too we may note Luther's exegesis. Already the "divine thought" that "remains in God . . . but is nevertheless a distinct person" is an "inner command." It is then by *this* "uncreated Word" that the "created word" is evoked, the created word of obedience and worship that every creature is[36]—and to this last contention we must of course return.

Israel understood the reality of the world on the pattern of her own reality: just as she depends on the Lord's moral utterance, so does the world. A psalm evokes the parallel with all desirable clarity: "He sends out his command to the earth, and his word runs very swiftly. . . . He makes his wind blow, and the waters flow. . . . He declares his word to Jacob, his statutes and his judgments to Israel."[37] Both the creation and Israel live "by every word that comes from the mouth of the Lord."[38]

That Israel interpreted the world and its origin on the pattern of her own self-understanding is nothing peculiar to Israel. All cultures have seen the universe in their own images and its foundation in the images of their beginnings. What is specific to Israel's understanding of universal origins is not this general pattern but the material understanding of her own reality that Israel in fact has.

A fourth proposition: all the preceding holds in the present tense. Stories such as Genesis 1–11 tells are here as elsewhere aetiological; they are told to certify life and the world as we now find and live them.[39] In Genesis, they are indeed meant to be taken realistically as narratives of past events, but their purpose is still to illumine permanent structures of life. This holds also for the first of these stories,

---

34. Revelation 4:11.

35. Does God then "cause" the world to be, in any now likely sense of "cause"? Reinvigorated English-language "theism," often somewhat oddly related to the Christian faith it claims to defend— a truly bizarre case is Richard Swinburne, *The Christian God* (New York: Oxford University Press, 1994)—has brought with it a remarkable resurgence of "first efficient cause" arguments for the reality of God. So and impressively, Craig in William Lane Craig and Quentin Smith, *Theism, Atheism and Big Bang Cosmology* (Oxford: Clarendon Press, 1993), 3–76, 92–107, 141–160. Almost he persuades me that the so-called *kalam* argument for the necessity of a first cause is valid. Smith, an "atheist"—who is of course entirely unpersuaded—concludes their volume of debates: the differences between them come "down to the question: Is the intelligible explanation of the universe causal or acausal?" The difficulty is to know whether *either* rubric covers the actual biblical assertion, that *obedience* to God's *speech* is "the explanation of the universe."

36. *Ennaratio in Genesis*, 13.17. It should be noted that Luther's position is *not* that of his nominalist education. The nominalists continued the understanding of creation as an imminent act of intellect and will; they merely made the divine act of will contingent over against the divine intellect, and so arbitrary. Luther understands creation as effected not by an imminent act of will but by an uttered public word and so as effected by a word with rational content.

37. Psalm 147:16–20.

38. Deuteronomy 8:3.

39. The sort of Old Testament exegesis that found aetiologies everywhere and thought it was finished when it had done so is of course now discredited. But the quite specifically aetiological character of that part of the biblical narrative in which God's partner is the world and the human race as such is surely plain.

the story of creation. Therefore there is a sense, treacherous though its assertion has often been, in which Genesis makes the world's dependence on God be independent of the difference between one moment of created time and another. The world would not *now* exist did not God *now* command its existence. Again we may cite Luther: "This is what the philosophers[40] do not know, that all perdurance is wholly from the power of the Word of God."[41]

A distinction between creation and "preservation" or between initial and "continuing" creation has been rightly used to warrant that there was a first existence of creatures at a zero point of time. But such distinctions can have no other metaphysical or religious significance. The world is no less dependent on God's creating word in any moment of its existence than it was at the beginning. God's creating word no more waits upon its auditor now than at the beginning.

Thus Thomas Aquinas set his discussion of "preservation" under the motto of Hebrews 1:3: "He sustains all things by his powerful word." Then he defined: "God's conservation of things is not by any new act, but by a continuation of the act by which he grants them being"; nor is this "continuation" either a process from or a temporal elongation of the creating act.[42] Whatever difference the existence of creatures, once they are there, may make to God's "continuing" creative work, their role cannot make his command any less immediate now than "in the beginning."[43] So Philip Melanchthon: "God is present to his creation, not as the God of the stoics, but as a free agent sustaining his creature."[44]

Two recurring problems of the theology of creation emerge from the foregoing observations. The first: it has often been supposed that the doctrine of creation is a part of Christian teaching shared with the otherwise unbelieving. Recently this has just as generally been denied. But there must be a moment of truth in the former opinion, for all cultures do in fact tell just such primal aetiological stories as appear in Genesis 1–11, and around much the same set of motifs. How are we to understand this?

What is common to all the race, and emerges in the need to tell aetiological stories of primal times, is, we may suggest, a set of *worries*. Thus the fragility of the physical circumstances in which human life is possible is felt by all cultures;

---

40. Meaning, of course, Aristotle and theologians who followed him too closely.

41. *Ennaratio in Genesis*, 26.

42. *Summa theologiae*, i.104.1. We may note that the Franciscans were even more radical at this point; for Duns Scotus the distinction between creation and preservation is only conceptual. See Scheffczyk, *Schöpfung*, 100. For Karl Barth, on the other hand, it is vital to distinguish creation and providence as metaphysically different relations; so *Kirchliche Dogmatik* (Zürich: Evangelischer Verlag, 1950), III/3:1–13. An investigation of the connections of this insistence within Barth's System would take us too far from the concerns of this chapter.

43. Colin Gunton, *Theology through the Theologians* (Edinburgh: T. & T. Clark, 1996), 146: "The stability and reliability of the world . . . depends not on some intermediate being or beings—the point of Berkeley's polemic against the concept of substance—but directly on God." Gunton's chief contention in this essay is that while there can be no *intermediaries* between Creator and creation, creation must be understood as *mediated* if the actuality of the creature is to be maintained. Perhaps this concern is satisfied in the following.

44. *Loci theologici* (1559), 639.

and stories are everywhere told about the bare aversion of universal catastrophe. Or again, encounter with peoples whose speech cannot be understood is always a threatening puzzle. In Israel, as elsewhere, stories like those of Genesis 1–11 are told to bring such anxieties to word and so make them bearable, that is, to certify reality as it is now experienced.

Among the universally felt fragilities of existence, one is metaphysical. Not only is our human world ambiguous and threatening in certain dominating but contingent features, so also is the precondition of our human history, the world in its mere givenness prior to all our action in it: there is a sort of absolute worry. We have already cited Heidegger citing Leibniz: "Why is there anything at all? Why not just nothing?"

The ambiguities of such things as diverse languages or the perennial conflict of herdsmen and cultivators can be illumined by stories involving human actions and motivations. The problematic character of the world as such cannot, since the world is the presupposition of all human action. Therefore it is not so much fragility or ambiguity that must here be grasped as it is mystery in the full sense.

To bring the mystery of the world's existence to a narrating word, we are compelled to make logically odd narratives, that in one or another way begin, "When everything was still nothing . . ." To recount the beginning of a connected series of events, we have to start by telling how things were at that beginning, and just so make some reference to the state of affairs before it; but in the present case the beginning to be recounted is that before which there was no state of affairs. Genesis begins its narrative in just this peculiar way, with its second verse.

The oddity of narrating an absolute beginning raises the second problem: Can such a narrative be truly historical? Can the fact stated by "God creates the world" be an event and sequence of events? Must not the proposition, despite its form, instead be read as the statement of a timeless relation?

The great *mythic* stories of origin cause no problem here. Myths intend not to narrate any particular events but rather to evoke something that happens in all events, and they show this by the rhetoric of their storytelling. The origin they tell is logical and ontological, not temporal. Is not then the story in Genesis after all to be read as myth? There has been continuous pressure on Christian theology to read it that way, whether or not under the overt label.

Origen, for example, was clear about what the church taught and about what he therefore wished to teach: "First of all, that God is one, who created and ordered all things, and who when there was nothing made the universe to be."[45] But in the course of explicating the doctrine, he describes God as intrinsically "creative power," and then sees a puzzle. For "to think that such divine power was ever . . . idle would be absurd."[46] This seems to demand that God always creates, and therefore that there always are creatures.[47] Origen pondered a variety of

---

45. *First Principles*, 9.13–14.
46. Ibid., 66.1–3.
47. Ibid., i.4.5.

ways in which there could always be a world even though the world has a beginning, and to his usual credit seems to have been satisfied by none.

Through the history of theology, whenever the mutual definition of time and eternity by mere negation has reached gnostic stringency, Origen's argument has reappeared, often in nearly his words. Thus the nineteenth-century "mediating" theologian Richard Rothe: if one thinks of creation as having a beginning, "one must think of God as not being Creator before the advent of creation, which contradicts the concept of God."[48] And indeed, unless the love out of which God creates is the specific inner-triune actuality of the triune God, if it is a simple unitary love for creatures, then creation must be eternal since the love is. In modern theology, the pressure to think of creation as a standing relation has perhaps intensified; the recent "process" theology offered an instance of simple capitulation.

The tendency is opposed by our fifth proposition: the creature, simply in that it is creature, has an absolute beginning. Genesis' story is not a myth, for it does not in fact tell us anything about what things were like when there were no things. Its "tohu webohu" is not an antecedent nothingness-actuality like the Great Slime dismembered by Babylonian Marduk, nor yet an eternal egg or womb or pure potentiality of primal matter. The fathers were clear about this: "The heretics say, 'But there was also the darkness . . . over the deep.' Again new occasions for myth . . . ! 'The deep' is not a fullness of antithetical powers, as some fantasize, nor is the darkness an original and evil force arrayed against the good."[49] Genesis' reference to emptiness and formlessness, and the darkness and "waters" of chaos, is not to a *presupposition* of creation but to the *inconceivable beginning* of creation, made inconceivable by the absence of presuppositions. Augustine reads Genesis precisely: "You have made all times; and before all times only you are, nor does time antecede itself."[50]

Were the nothingness of Genesis 1:2 a describable antecedent of creation, then God's act to create the world would be like Marduk's a victory over this nothingness or, as in other myths, its impregnating or digesting or other action upon it. But although the language of the myths provided Israel with literary and perhaps ritual motifs with which to celebrate creation, and doubtless stands genetically behind some of Genesis' imagery, the mythic assertions themselves are avoided, since a jealous God can brook no competitive primal powers.[51]

At the beginning of creation there is nothing and the "ruach of God." If this phrase were to be translated "wind from God," as some modern versions do, again the narrative would be mythic. But in translating so, the translators show their prejudice for what a piece of language may have meant before its canonical place-

---

48. *Dogmatik* (Heidelberg: J. C. B. Mohr, 1870, posthum.), 1.135.
49. Basil the Great, *Hexaemeron*, ii.4.
50. *Confessions*, 11.14.17.
51. So Basil, *Hexaemeron*, ii.2, rejects interpreting the unformed world of Genesis 1:2 as preexistent *prima materia*: "But if matter is without origin, it must be of equal honor with God."

ment. Whatever may have been said or meant in traditions from which the priestly writer drew, it is quite inconceivable that the shapers of the canonical text, at their theologically sophisticated time in Israel's history, can have written *ruach Elohim* and not clearly intended "God's Spirit"; nor do we here have any reason to take earlier stages of tradition for our object.[52]

Does Genesis then teach the dogmatic tradition's creation "out of nothing *(ex nihilo)?"* Judaism anyway read it so. The passage cited earlier from Maccabees continues: "and not from anything." This exegetical tradition too was continued by the church. The Maccabees passage or its source seems in fact to be quoted, if with antique freedom, by one of the earliest known rules of faith: "First of all believe, that there is one God who . . . made the universe to be from not being."[53] Such language then appears in Irenaeus,[54] Origen,[55] and others.

According to Genesis, at least as Judaism and the church have read it, "before" there is the creature there is God and nothing. Nor is this nothing of a kind that can be the antecedent condition of something. God speaking is the creature's only antecedent condition: as Philip Melanchthon formulated, "When things were not, God spoke and they began to be."[56]

III

Proposition the sixth: reality other than God not only has a beginning but also has an end,[57] in that it has a goal. Also this end must be either nothing or God. And the end, unlike the beginning, might indeed be a sort of real nothing, a nothing*ness.* Creatures once given, it would not violate the difference of Creator and creature to think of creatures' end as entry into a sort of created negativity, into what Karl Barth untranslatably called *das Nichtige.*[58] But the end sighted in

52. Basil the Great, *Hexaemeron*, ii.6: The best reading of *pneuma theou* in Genesis 1:2 is "Holy Spirit," for the Scriptures "do not speak of any other Spirit of God but the Holy Spirit who perfects the divine and blessed Trinity." Martin Luther, *Ennaratio in Genesis*, 8: "But I prefer to understand here the Holy Spirit. For a wind is a creature, of which there then were none. . . . And the great consensus of the church is that here the mystery of the Trinity is hinted." Augustine, *De civitate Dei*, viii.11, supposes that Plato may have had Genesis translated to him and taken *pneuma theou* for the element *aer*, through insufficient acquaintance with Scripture's diction.

53. Hermes, *The Sepherd, Mandates*, i.1: To avoid misunderstanding, it should be noted that Judaism has not always abided by this founding insight. Medieval philosophical rabbinism, and the mysticism that grew from it, followed the suggestion of the neoplatonism whose concepts it had adopted, and taught that before God created there were God and a subsistent indeterminism. It is a nice irony that thereby it repristinated a departure from Israel's faith that had tempted Christianity centuries before, and had been rejected.

54. *Against All Heresies*, iv.20.2.

55. *Peri Archon*, i.3.3; ii.1.4.

56. *Loci communes* (1559), 638: "Deo dicente, cum res non essent, esse coeperunt."

57. Basil the Great, *Hexaemeron*, i.3: "What has a temporal beginning must necessarily have a temporal ending."

58. See to this Robert W. Jenson, *Alpha and Omega* (New York: Thomas Nelson, 1963), 33–37.

Genesis is not *das Nichtige*, for in Genesis, being is good, and the creature has being.

This is established by another beat of the narrative's insistent rhythm. If "God said" is the downbeat, then "it was *good*" is the upbeat. The word that creates, we have noted, is a command; it aims at something. And the Creator not only commands but judges that the command is obeyed. In Genesis, God's judgment that the creature is good belongs to the story of creation itself; creatures exist *in that* God determines that they are good.

Hebrew *Tov*, like English "good," suggests "good *for* . . ."; it works within a framework of purposes. Thus according to Genesis creatures exist in that God finds them good for his purpose with them—which of course means that he does have a purpose with them. Why is there anything at all? Genesis' answer so far may be stated: the world is in that it is commanded to be and in that its obedience is accepted by the speaker as serving the intent of his command.

Moreover, it is also clear what, according to Genesis in its canonical placement, the world's purpose is. Israel made and used aetiological primal stories in her own way. Israel's way was to tell them within a total narrative whose determining event is not itself a primal event but an event within history: the Exodus. The genealogies of Genesis 1–11, so boring to modern readers, belong to the very point of those chapters:[59] they establish the continuity of events from the beginning to Abraham and the other patriarchs. But already the patriarchal story is, as we have noted,[60] a prelude. The patriarchal history tells how God was the God of Israel before there was Israel: before God created Israel by deliverance from Egypt, Israel preexisted in God's promise that there would be Israel.

The history of Israel's own coming into being is a history of promise, of the leapfrogging succession of promise, fulfilling—or penultimately unfulfilling—event, and new promise.[61] It is into history so conceived and told that Genesis incorporates also the beginning of the world. What Israel certifies for the present by *its* story of the universal origin is the universal scope and unconditional validity of JHWH's promises and of his faithfulness to those promises: the Lord can keep the promises he makes because all things are his creatures and so in his hand. So Jeremiah, at a time when this faith was severely tested: the idols of the nations "are worthless, a work of delusion. . . . Not like these is the Lord, the portion of Jacob, for he is the one who formed all things, and Israel is the tribe of his inheritance."[62]

Or we may say, what the creation-narrative certifies for the present is the universal scope of the Exodus: there is, Genesis claims, nothing more ontologically fundamental than this event. Or again, the Resurrection having occurred, the church goes on to say that what the creation-narrative certifies for the present is

---

59. Westermann, *Genesis*, 8–24.

60. 1:49.

61. This is of course the great insight of Gerhard von Rad, which remains foundational for any serious theological understanding of the Old Testament.

62. Jeremiah 10:15–16.

the universal scope of the Resurrection: for Paul it is a single concept that God "gives life to the dead and calls into existence the things that do not exist."[63]

Thomas wrote the beautiful sentence: "In [God's] hand were all the ends of the world: . . . when his hand was opened by the key of love, the creatures came forth."[64] If only it be always remembered that God's love is triune and so spoken, that is the whole truth of this chapter.

A seventh point gathers up those made so far in this section: the world God creates is not a thing, a "cosmos," but is rather a history. God does not create a world that thereupon has a history; he creates a history that is a world, in that it is purposive and so makes a whole.[65] The great turnings in God's history with his creation, at the call of Abraham, the Exodus, the Crucifixion and Resurrection and the final Judgment, are not events within a creation that is as such ahistorical; they are events of the history that is created. Even the biblical account of the absolute beginning is itself a narrative; the six days of Genesis do not recount first an absolute beginning on the first day and then what happens to the creation on subsequent days; the whole story of one week tells the one absolute beginning.[66] The "beginning" is not accomplished until the works of the six days are there.

The loss of this insight is the great historical calamity of the doctrine of creation.[67] And it is indeed the loss of something once possessed, for near the beginning of theology Irenaeus of Lyon cast a grand vision in which initial creation and redemption and fulfillment were dramatically united moments of God's one creative work, shaped and moved by his one intent to save.[68] But thereafter the doctrines of creation and redemption were developed with less and less reference to one another, and the notion of a total dramatically unified divine action was obscured.[69] Perhaps the key diagnostic question is whether redemption is under-

63. Romans 4:17. I must call attention to the remarkable exegesis of this passage by Jean-Luc Marion, *God without Being*, tr. Thomas A. Carlson (Chicago: University of Chicago Press, 1991), 86–94; e.g., "The call does not take into consideration the difference between nonbeings and beings: the nonbeings are called inasmuch as they are not beings, the nonbeings appear, by virtue of the call, as if they were."

64. *In sententiarum*, prol. Called to my attention by Henri de Lubac, *The Mystery of the Supernatural*, tr. Rosemary Sheed (New York: Herder & Herder, 1967), 299–300.

65. From a wholly different starting point, Carver T. Yu, "Stratification of the Meaning of Time," *Scottish Journal of Theology* 33:31–32: "Time emerges as the directional-relational aspect of the structure of reality. That means the universe as a whole is a coherently correlated structure, and the correlation takes a historical form."

66. This was the nearly unanimous position of the fathers. Basil the Great, *Hexaemeron*, i.6: "In order that we might be taught that the world came into being at once and timelessly by the will of God, the phrase is used, 'In the beginning he created.'" The position taken here is sometimes said to threaten the separate reality of the creature. Since creation here is not attributed to an imminent act of divine will but to God's *utterance*, the opposite is the case. As I assert in trinitarian form hereafter, only in the situation of the word from one person to another is reliable otherness posited.

67. Scheffczyk's admirable history of the doctrine, *Schöpfung*, is in its tone a sort of sustained lamentation of the loss.

68. Gustaf Wingren, *Man and the Incarnation : A Study in the Biblical Theology of Irenaeus*, tr. Ross Mackenzie (Edinburgh: Oliver & Boyd, 1959).

69. Scheffczyk, *Schöpfung*, 54–66.

stood to fulfill initial creation or merely to restore it; theology has too much tended to the latter.[70]

IV

Observation eight must be the haste with which Genesis moves from the sheer "big bang" to the creation of living beings and its then lavish expenditure of days on their sequential creation. The biblical doctrine of creation is centrally a doctrine of the creation of life, of beings which, as the standard modern definitions have it, maintain themselves by metabolizing materials from their environment and reproduce their like. That is, creation is imperatively directed to those creatures that are teleological in their own being, that manifest and are sustained by striving, by pursuit of a determinate end. The world is not a dead apparatus in which a few living beings happen to find themselves; it is a garden and pasture of living beings, which the cosmic and atomic and chemical systems make possible—and this is true even if the tiny speck Earth is the only home of life in the vast system.

The canonical text of Isaiah preserves explicit doctrine from the days of Israel's greatest theological consciousness. A gloss on the prophet's proclamation lays down two propositions in immediate succession. The first: "He did not create it a chaos"; it has purposeful order. The second stipulates that purpose: "He formed it to be inhabited."[71]

Genesis then ontologically distinguishes one set of living creatures. In the sixth day, the rhythm is broken. After the land animals are in place by a command and verification on the usual pattern, an additional action is announced with a portentous new locution: "Let us make . . ." This out-of-rhythm act is the creation of humanity, "male and female." The priestly narrative gives this creature three distinctions: humans are "in the image" of the Creator; they are to "have dominion" over the other creatures; and, as emphasized in an earlier connection, the Creator does not merely create them by his word but turns to address that word directly to them.

These out-of-sequence creatures remain creatures. They are made on the same day with the other land animals, to whose general sort they thus belong. Even the address that God makes to them begins as a blessing of animal fertility that repeats one given earlier.[72] Genesis locates their distinction not in elevation beyond the status of creature, nor even in endowments of their species, remarkable as these may turn out to be, but strictly in the three marks noted.[73]

---

70. E.g., at the historical center, Anselm of Canterbury, *Monologion*, 15.

71. Isaiah 45:18.

72. Augustine inquires why the blessing is specifically repeated for humankind, *De Genesi ad litteram*, iii. 13: "The blessing had to be repeated for the case of man, lest someone should say that there was any sin in the task of begetting children, as there is in lust itself or in fornication or in immoderate indulgence even in marriage."

73. Augustine, *De Genesi*, vi.12: "For so it is written, 'God made from earth the wild animals of every kind.' If then he formed both man from earth and the beasts from earth, what has man that is superior in this connection, unless that he specifically is created in the image of God?"

The first of these is exegetically difficult; probably the best interpretation reads the Hebrew usually translated "image" simply as "counterpart."[74] In any case, the text provides its own commentary with the other two specifications. Humans are to exercise "dominion" among the creatures. That is, they are to be the Creator's representatives to his other creatures, and in that sense to be his counterpart. Most decisively, God does not merely establish this dominion but does so by *addressing* them. The impersonal blessing of fertility turns in their case into a personal speech of commission. The Creator begins a conversation with these new creatures, and *so* they are his counterpart.

Humans, we may say, are those animals whose creation is not merely that God speaks *about* them but that he also speaks *to* them. Humans are those creatures who exist in that they are mentioned in the triune discourse *and* are called to join it. Humans are those creatures who not only exist by words that state God's moral will, but are given to hear and reply to those words. We may turn to Peter Brunner, whom we have cited at decisive junctures before: "In that God in the creation of man addresses him as 'You' [*Du*], God opens a history with man, that is constituted by the address of God and the answer of man."[75] And we must, of course, return at length to these creatures, that is, to ourselves.

---

74. Westermann, *Genesis*, 203–218.

75. "Der Ersterschaffene als Gottes Ebenbild" (1952), *Pro Ecclesia* (Berlin: Lutherisches Verlagshaus, 1962), 1:92.

SIXTEEN

The Character of Creation

I

Two tasks are posed by the previous chapter, which we may conveniently take up under this title. First, at several points the question of God's motive in creating emerged. The matter is of such religious importance that it must have its own discussion; the following two sections are devoted to it. Second, the previous chapter has implicitly laid down a series of theological mandates. Fulfilling them will occupy the remainder of the chapter.

II

Two classical questions intertwine in the question of God's motive in creation. One we discussed earlier: Would the Son have become incarnate had humankind not sinned?[1] The question is usually posed about the motive of the Incarnation, and that is how we then treated it, but of course it is about the motive of creation also. If there might have been creation but no Incarnation because there contingently had been no sin, then it is not the *incarnate* Son for whom God eternally intends the world. And if the incarnate Son is not the reason for the world, what is?

The other question may seem esoteric but is not: Does God create for the creatures' sake or for his own? The tradition was summarized by the first Vatican Council: God creates "out of his goodness" and "to manifest his perfection."[2] We want immediately to say not only that both propositions are true but that they are somehow equivalent. Irenaeus provides a beautiful aphorism to that effect: "The glory of God is the living human person; the life of a human person is the vision of God."[3] But how can that work out?

---

1. 1:71–74.
2. Session iii,i.
3. *Against All Heresies*, iv.20.7: "Gloria dei vivens homo; vita autem hominis visio dei."

The option that God creates simply for our sake, out of "sheer love," is tempting and in modernity has been often chosen, with plausible arguments. So, for example, the nineteenth-century Lutheran Gottfried Thomasius: the teaching "usual since Anselm, that the glory of God is the final end of creation,[4] seems to me to confuse the outcome with the founding purpose. For the creation is indeed a glorification of God . . . but what moves him to create is not this glorification of himself, that he does not need, but love alone."[5]

Despite its seeming piety, the move is disastrous. Its dominance in popular theology is doubtless one cause of late modernity's degradation of deity into a servant of our self-help. The tradition had taught that God was the final cause of creation;[6] that is, that what the creature is for is God, so that the creature's good is determined by God's antecedent moral character. Much modern popular theology, however, has evaded that antecedent determination and so been at liberty to suppose that God is so "unconditionally loving" or "accepting" or something of the sort that whatever we take to be our good must be what he created us to be. The twentieth-century English theologian P. T. Forsyth rebutted such sentimentality with wholly traditional language: "If he slew us we should praise His holy name. It is a question not of His utility to us but of ours to Him."[7]

Yet neither does the simply contrary doctrine, that God creates for his own satisfaction, seem quite appropriate to the gospel. We may turn to Jonathan Edwards for guidance through this dilemma, which his Puritan-Calvinist tradition had minutely and painfully analyzed.

God, Edwards begins, must be the final purpose of all his own acts, since he is the source of all good and therefore is the proper final object of any person's "regard," and so also of his own.[8] But the God who is thus both subject and object of final regard is triune; therefore Edwards's analysis does not stop with this apparent choice for one horn of the dilemma.

The "glorious attributes of God," Edwards continues, "*consist* [emphasis added] in a sufficiency to certain acts and effects."[9] Therefore, in that God supremely values himself he identically values those acts and effects. But given the nature of this God's triune being, his acts are acts of communication, and their effects therefore knowledge, in the biblical sense that unites cognition and love. Therefore, in supremely valuing himself God supremely values other persons' knowledge and love of himself. But since God is himself the supreme value, to

4. E.g., Baier, *Compendium theologicae positivae* (1693), i.ii.23: "The final end of creation is the glory of God's wisdom, goodness and divine power; an intermediate end is the good of humanity."

5. *Christi Person und Werk: Darstellung der evangelisch-lutherischen Dogmatik vom Mittelpunkte der Christologie aus* (Erlangen: Dreichert, 1886), 144.

6. Thomas Aquinas, *Summa theologiae*, i.44.4, that "God is the final cause of all things:" "Every agent acts with some end in view. . . . But it is not appropriate to the first agent to act in view of acquiring some end; but rather he intends only to communicate his own perfection."

7. P. T. Forsyth, *The Principle of Authority* (London: Independent Press, 1952) 387.

8. *Dissertation Concerning the End for Which God Created the World*, i.i.3–5.

9. Ibid., i.ii.1.

know and love him is to be infinitely blessed. Therefore, in infinitely valuing himself God equivalently values our blessedness.[10]

The converse must also hold, if the dilemma is to be resolved: in infinitely valuing us God infinitely values himself. This proposition is dangerous: it seems to threaten the distinction of Creator and creature. Yet if it is not asserted, Edwards has still simply chosen one horn of the dilemma.

In an earlier connection we noted that according to Edwards our knowledge and love of God are a "conformity" to God. We now add that this conformity is to God's knowledge and love of himself. Moreover, God's ability to communicate himself is infinite, so that the conformity of the saints' knowledge and love of God to his own knowledge and love of himself can and will increase to infinity. But God *is* knowledge and love. Therefore the "good that is in the creature comes forever nearer . . . to an identity with that which is in God." Finally, it is only from our point of view that the identity is never reached; "In the view . . . of God, who has a comprehensive prospect of the increasing union and conformity through eternity, it must be . . . perfect unity." From God's point of view, the creatures who are supremely valued by God, "considered with respect to the whole of their eternal duration, . . . must be viewed as being . . . one with him," so that his "respect to them finally coincides . . . with respect to himself."[11]

If Edwards were a unitarian, this doctrine would pantheistically dissolve the boundary of Creator and creature. But Edwards unpacks it onto the doctrine of Trinity. As the union of God and creature becomes "more and more . . . perfect," what this means is that it becomes "nearer . . . to that between God the Father and the Son."[12]

"The adequate communication of the Father's goodness" simply as such is eternally accomplished in the Son. But "the Son has also his own inclination to communicate himself, in an image of his person that may partake of his happiness: and this was the end of the creation, even the communication of the happiness of the Son of God. . . . Therefore the church is said to be the completeness of Christ."[13] Thus the motive of creation, more precisely located, is a moment in the triune *perichoresis*, in which the *Logos*, the inner-triune Communication, is himself one who communicates.

And the final goal of creation is thus at once God and his creature united in Christ, the *totus Christus*. Edwards was a already a master of post-Enlightenment second naiveté: "There was, [as] it were, an eternal society or family in the Godhead, in the Trinity of persons. It seems to be God's design to admit the church into the divine family as his son's wife."[14] "Heaven and earth were created that the Son of God might be complete in a spouse."

---

10. Ibid., i.ii.1–4; i.iii.
11. Ibid., i.iii.
12. Ibid., ii.vii.
13. *Miscellanies*, 1004.
14. Ibid. 741.

Moreover, Edwards thus arrives at an answer also to the first of our intertwined questions: precisely the work of *redemption*, just as it occurs in the actual event of Christ, is the purpose of creation.[15] "As to this . . . world, it was doubtless created to be a stage upon which this . . . work of redemption should be transacted."[16] The writer of that sentence might have been Karl Barth two centuries later, and we turn now to him—though again we could as well have turned to Irenaeus, who sixteen centuries earlier wrote, "Since the Savior was preexistent, it was necessary that what was to be saved come to be, lest the Savior be pointless."[17]

It was Barth's chief concern throughout his mature work[18] that Christ's death and Resurrection for sinners is not to be construed as a "wretched expedient . . . in view of the failure of a plan . . . that had originally a different intention and form."[19] On the contrary, creation is to "prepare the sphere in which the institution and history of the covenant takes place . . . and the subject that is to be God's partner in this history";[20] and the content of this eternal covenant is Jesus Christ just as he appears in the Gospels.[21] God's eternal decision is made "exactly as it is fulfilled and revealed in time."[22] In a bluntly explicit formula: "Because *servatio*, therefore *creatio*."[23] Indeed, when God declares his creation good, it is in view of *both* sides of its destiny, its glorious salvation and the sin from which it needs saving.[24]

As before, this work agrees with Barth at this point. The great problem posed by this agreement can no longer be evaded.

III

If the creation is good, and if what it is good for is Jesus' Resurrection, then there is a sense in which also the Crucifixion must be an intermediate good; there cannot be a Resurrection of someone who has not died. And if the Crucifixion is for sin, there must even be some—conceptually and morally nearly unmanageable—sense in which the fallenness of the creation is again an intermediate good. Such doctrines as that of Paul Tillich, that creation and fall are the same relation,[25] are wrong but not preposterous.

15. *Dissertation*, ii.iii-v.

16. *A History of the Work of Redemption*, Doctrine.ii.i.

17. *Against All Heresies*, iii.22.1.

18. Robert W. Jenson, *Alpha and Omega: A Study in the Theology of Karl Barth* (New York: Thomas Nelson, 1963).

19. *Kirchliche Dogmatik* (Zürich: EVZ-Verlag, 1933–1967), IV/1:68.

20. Ibid., III/1:107.

21. Ibid., IV/1:57.

22. Ibid.

23. Ibid., III/3:91.

24. Ibid., III/1:422–430. Jonathan Edwards can be incautious indeed, *Miscellanies*, 710.app.: "The fall of the devils was wisely permitted and ordered to give occasion for a redemption from that evil they should introduce."

25. *Systematic Theology* (Chicago: University of Chicago Press, 1957), 2:29–44.

One thing must, however, be made plain from the start: with the following suggestions no theodicy is proposed. It is in any case not possible within the system here presented to "justify the ways of God to men"; and assuredly we may not do it by decreeing that sins and evils are in fact blessings so that God deserves no blame for allowing them. As has often been observed, someone so utterly in control as the biblical God is supposed to be—in the flat language here traditional, someone at once "omniscient" and "omnipotent"—cannot lack responsibility for what in fact happens, for the bad as for the good, *including* the boundary-conditions within which sometimes the bad may be necessary for the sake of the good, *and* including our standards of judgment of good and bad.[26]

Various expedients have been devised to relieve God of moral opprobrium for the evils in his creation, and some of these are indeed necessary or helpful. Thus the common and in itself obvious argument that since God is personal there must be a distinction between what God actively wills and what he merely permits is necessary if God is not indeed to appear, as to Luther's rationalist, a sheer Malevolence. So also is Augustine's reflection illuminating, that since evil is pure negativity it can have *no* cause, and so not God as its cause: "We should not seek any efficient cause of the evil will; for [a cause of evil] would not work by effecting but by 'defecting'."[27] Perhaps even the idea may in some contexts be appropriate, that it is sometimes good to allow evil within a given situation, so that if we knew the total creation-situation as does God we would see that the actual world is the best *possible* world.[28]

But such devices have force only when paired with some account of where evil does then come from. Since Scripture says that divine approbation belongs to the creating act itself,[29] the only possibility is that evil results from the action of creatures once they are there; and that is the general assertion of the orthodox tradition. The traditional proposition is obviously true in some everyday sense; nobody "made" Eve or Adam obey the serpent, or, if the devil is a fallen angel, "made" him rebel. And the disasters that befall fallen humanity are indeed nobody's fault but its own.

The difficulty is that the same considerations that show how creaturely freedom is possible at all also close off any attempt to justify God's ways in our eyes by blaming creaturely free will for evil. The considerations that show how there can be both the biblical God and free choices by creatures also show that we cannot say, "Creatures chose evil, and so it was not God who chose it."[30]

---

26. It is of course possible to justify God's ways by denying that he is both omniscient and omnipotent. The question is whether such a god is worth justifying; he, she, or it is anyway not the God of Israel. A recent classic of this tactic is Brian Hebblethwaite, *Evil, Suffering, and Religion* (Bria, New York: Hawthorn Books, 1976).

27. *De civitate Dei*, xii.7: "non enim est efficiens sed deficiens."

28. This is of course a caricature of the position developed in Leibniz's *Essais de Theodicée*. Voltaire's demolition of Leibniz in *Candide* is great humor but not argumentatively very stringent.

29. Pp. 13–14.

30. For a classic instance of the move, Philip Melanchthon, *Loci communes* (1559), 644: "Thus God is not the cause of sin. . . . For the causes of sin are the will of the devil and the will of man."

The usual invocation of creatures' free will to exculpate God supposes that God once created and then somehow retreated, so that at least some things that happen within creation, those dependent on creatures' "free will," he merely, as it were, observes. But that, as we have seen, is not at all the relation between Creator and creature. Yet if in no present instant does anything happen outside the deliberate act of God, how can some things be the responsibility of our wills? Are we not, as is regularly inquired, then mere "puppets?"

The solution proper to Christianity has in various ways been perceived by all the more profound of those who have seriously pondered the question: God's sovereignty of human and other events does not foreclose human freedom precisely *because* God's will is absolute, so that between God and creatures choosing is not a zero sum situation.[31] If you and I must decide a certain matter, there is an obvious—though even in this case limited—sense in which to the extent that you make the decision I do not and vice versa. But just because God's will is absolute, there is no such competition between his will and mine, no arithmetic within which a decision by me is one less for him to make or vice versa.[32]

Thomas Aquinas worked this out with lapidary precision. He first lays down a general principle: "Because the divine will is supremely efficacious, it not only must be that what God wills to happen does happen, but that it happens in the *way* in which he wills it to happen. Thus God wills some things to happen by necessity and some contingently," and that then is how they severally happen.[33] Thomas then applies this to God's willing of those events that are contingent because they depend on human choice. If God "moves" a human will to incline to some object or action, that will necessarily so inclines. Nevertheless, if God, in accord with the nature of what he in this case moves, wills also that this inclination be itself a *free* "movement," then that is the sort of movement it is.[34]

If there is the biblical God, there can be free creaturely choices only and precisely because God's will is so entirely of another sort than ours that he not only can will us to choose this rather than that, but that our choice be in itself uncoerced by his. But just so—and that is the present point—neither then do our choice and responsibility obviate his; precisely when we freely choose, we fulfill his choos-

---

Melanchthon is clearer than most about what this entails: Thus ibid., 647: "If the proposition is established, that God does not cause or will sin, it follows that sin is contingent, that is, that not all things happen necessarily." Since Melanchthon here identifies being willed by God and happening necessarily, and does not make the elegant scholastic distinction I will note in a moment, he thus takes Erasmus's side against Luther, in the debate on which Luther said the whole Reformation movement finally depended.

31. Augustine, *De praedestinatione sanctorum*, xi.22: "Ideo enim haec et nobis praecipiuntur, et dona Dei esse monstrantur; ut intelligatur quod et nos ea facimus et Deus facit ut illa faciamus."

32. Augustine, *De gratia et libero arbitrio*, i.7–8. Augustine begins with human choice to accept grace itself: "Et Dei donum est, et liberum arbitrium." But then he continues to such created virtues as chastity: "Neque enim praeciperentur, nisi homo haberet propriam voluntatem, qua divinis praeceptis obediret. Et tamen Dei donum est."

33. *Summa theologiae*, i.19.8. Also *Questiones de veritate*, 23.5.

34. Ibid., i-2.10.4.

ing. We may close with Augustine: "The Almighty works in the hearts of men even the movement of their will, thereby to work through them whatever he himself chooses."[35]

The stringent implication of the foregoing considerations—often, to be sure, avoided also by theologians who otherwise advance them—is that all theodicies must eventually fail, whatever wisdom they may yield on the way. The evil and sin in God's creation will always be reason to deny him;[36] Luther's rationalist will always have arguments for his conclusion. If we join the creeds against nihilism on the one hand and gnostics on the other, or against contemporary fusion of the two, our confession of a good Creator is and will remain a great "nevertheless," a defiance of what we would otherwise conclude. We may, however, explore the "nevertheless" from within.

Could God have made a world without sin and evil? We must suppose he could have, but then must immediately admit we hardly know what either the question or the answer may mean.

We can cast fictitious scenarios. A world grounded in Plato's and Aristotle's divinity would be a world containing at worst imperfections, the incompletions of what is endlessly on the way to its good.[37] A world caused by the deity of mere theism might be a single transparent entity, unambiguously related to a unitary meaning, whether positively or negatively. A world that was the body or conceptus of the great Mother would be prior to any distinction of good and evil, and in it we would not be worrying these matters. But all these deities are not, and their correlated worlds therefore are not merely nonexistent but are strictly impossible; for the actual God could not make any of them, and the actual God cannot not be God.

Father, Son, and Spirit are the actual God. We may of course note another abstract possibility: this God could have been Father, Son, and Spirit otherwise than as the crucified Jesus and *his* Father and Spirit. But immediately we must, as this work has several times insisted, embrace our inability to fill in that "otherwise." Just so, we must also acknowledge ignorance of what a world created by an "otherwise" triune Trinity might have been like, at least with respect to the possibility of suffering and default: we can have no idea whether such a world would have been "better" or indeed what "better" could mean in this context.

The actual life of the triune God with us is a true drama, and therefore conflicted and twisting. Since this drama is God's, its conflict is infinite, the conflict of death and life. Since this drama is God's, its twists and turns are infinite, the twists and turns of inexhaustible creativity. The actual world is the God-commanded stage and supporting players to this drama; we should therefore not be surprised to find it glorious but also painful and even self-conflicted. Surely,

---

35. *De gratia*, xxi.42: "Agit enim Omnipotens in cordibus hominum etiam motum volutatis eorum, ut per eos agat quod per eos agere ipse voluerit."

36. In modernity, to deny his existence or with Ivan Karamazov to "turn back the ticket."

37. As the world of Kingdom will in fact be!

to know this is already to know more "justification" of God's creating act than we could without knowing it have dreamt of discovering.[38]

The most intellectually notable school of American theology to date, the New Divinity of Jonathan Edwards's immediate disciples, both stated the truth with unparalleled audacity and clarity and showed how one may go one step too far. Samuel Hopkins wrote of God's eternal will:

> The sin of man shall, in every instance of it, be the occasion and made the means of the manifestation and display of the glorious character and perfections of God, which could not have been made . . . in so great a degree in any other way. . . . This is not owing to the nature . . . of sin, considered in itself—for it tends to directly the contrary, to dishonor him . . . but to his power, wisdom and goodness, by which he is able and disposed to overrule all the rebellion against him.[39]

Further: "The counsel of God's own will determined whether there should be any such thing as sin . . . and how much of this should exist—even just so much as should praise him, and no more." But then the step over the edge: the existence of sin and God's will to overcome it "are so united and blended together, the one implying the other, that all . . . form a perfectly wise plan."[40] It is the mutual "implying" and the rational "plan" that we dare not assert.

Would any one sin or any one of history's horrors have had to happen? No. Would the world have been another world without any particular selection of these? No. For sins and for horrors we can only repent and weep. *Nevertheless* we may give the last word to Maximus Confessor, a man better acquainted with horror than most, and to the story of Jesus: "The one who knows the mystery of the cross and the tomb, knows the reasons of things. The one who is initiated into the infinite power of the Resurrection, knows the purpose for which God knowingly created all."[41]

Maximus's knowledge is that of *initiates*, into a mystery-event. Those who are baptized into Christ's death and say "Amen" to the Eucharist's prayers and behold the Fraction of the bread that is Christ's body, these are the ones who know the goodness of the creation, also as it is plotted by Christ's suffering, and so also, somehow, as it is plotted by the sin for which he suffered and the evil that he suffered. The great "nevertheless" cannot finally be resolved from the conceptual outside; but it can be liturgically inhabited.

---

38. Wolfhart Pannenberg, *Systematische Theologie* (Tübingen: Vandenhoeck & Ruprecht, 1993), 3:684: the theodicy problem is "not to be mastered by merely theoretical clarifications. For that also the actual history of redemption is needed. The history of redemption concerns the future of the world, which will be at once its end and its clarification."

39. *The Works of Samuel Hopkins* (Boston: Doctrinal Tract and Book Society, 1865), 3:728.

40. Ibid., 729.

41. *Centuries* (PG 90), 1108A–B.

IV

We referred to theological mandates implicitly enforced by the previous chapter; these appear when the chapter is read with the first volume of this work in mind. For it is the general outcome of the first volume: any work of God is rightly interpreted only if it is construed by the mutual roles of the triune persons.[42] This must first of all be true of creation.

We may take our model from John of Damascus: the Father "creates by thinking, and what is thought is worked out as it is carried on by the Logos and perfected by the Spirit."[43] Creation is said to become actual as it is "worked out." This work is done between all temporal dimensions by the three persons God is: God the Father is the sheer given of creation; God the Spirit is the perfecting Freedom that animates creation; God the Son is the mediator of creation.

Being a creature is a specific relation to God, specified by the propositions of the preceding chapter. But the God in question is Father, Son, and Spirit. To make our first and fundamental step, we need merely to remember that these three subsist only in their relations to each other. Thereby we arrive at the idea of *envelopment*: to be a creature is to be in a specific way bracketed by the life of the triune persons. We are "worked out" *among* the three.

The central proposal of this section is then just the converse: for God to create is for him to *make accommodation* in his triune life for other persons and things than the three whose mutual life he is. In himself, he *opens room*, and that act is the event of creation.

We call this accommodation in the triune life "time." It is an old and central insight, that creation is above all God's taking time for us; the point is primally established in Augustine's *Confessions*,[44] where the effort to understand God's creating turns out to have as its material content but one question: "What is time?"[45] The answer here proposed: created time is accommodation in God's eternity for others than God.

We have again arrived at God's *roominess*. The next chapter will directly discuss the nature of time and of the divine "distention" that, in Augustine's language, makes time. Here it remains to display God's room-making act as a triune act. For it is a mutual implosion of the agencies of Father, Son, and Spirit that opens created time within God's eternity.

There is other reality than God, and it is really other. But we have seen that the only fully reliable otherness is that of persons, engaged in a discourse that is not merely between "Thou" and "I," that is not merely in the first and second persons. The word, "Let there *be* . . ." can truly be spoken only in *dramatic* dis-

---

42. To this whole matter, Colin E. Gunton, "The Doctrine of Creation. The End of Causality?" now in *Theology through the Theologians* (Edinburgh: T. & T. Clark, 1996), 129–150.

43. *The Orthodox Faith*, 6.6–8.

44. *Confessiones*, xi.

45. Ibid., 14.17.

course. The Trinity is such a conversation, the only one that can never collapse into dialogue or monologue, because the three who make its poles *are* the conversation. Creatures occur as in this discourse others are commandingly mentioned or addressed beyond the three who conduct it. So and only so there are entities that truly are and are truly other than God.

The Father is Creator as he is the God of Israel and therein, as we have seen, the personhood of the Trinity as such. He is this person, the person as which the one God is personal, insofar as he is the sole Source, *arche*, of the Son and the Spirit. Thus he is the absolute *Antecedent* of all possible other reality, and so also of the space that opens to accommodate us in the triune life.

Theology has often speculated that the Father's originating of the Son and the Spirit is itself the condition of the possibility of the Trinity's originating of a world. So Athanasius taught that the divine nature is "generative" *because* it is identical with the Father-Son relation, and that just therefore God can be the source of reality other than himself; or again that the Father can be a source generally because his own being is to be the source of the Son.[46] The insight is reappropriated in recent theology: "The Father's Creator-goodness, by which he grants existence to his creatures, . . . is not other than the love with which the Father eternally loves the Son."[47]

If we formulate the creating utterance of God as: "Let there be . . . ; and that is good," we may think of the Father's particular accent as: "Let there *be* . . . ; and that is good." It is the sheer fact of positing being that is his specific role.[48]

The Spirit is *Spiritus Creator* as he frees the Father from retaining all being with himself, and so frees what the Father initiates from being the mere emanation it would have been were the Father God by himself. That is, the Spirit is Creator precisely as he overcomes the possibility that the world's religions mostly assume is actualized, that other being than the divine source is divinity's mere prolongation. We may think of the Spirit's particular word in the creating conversation as: "*Let* there be . . . ; and that is good."

God and only God is the creature's future. God the Spirit is God's own future and so draws to and into the triune converse those for whom the Trinity makes room. God can be the creature's future, without absorbing the creature, in that God is not a monad: we can be brought into his life while becoming neither Father nor Son in that the Spirit brings us. God can himself be the purpose of his own act to create without absorbing his creation, in that God who is God's own future is another person than God as the one who has this future.

Finally, one must ask what precisely the Son mediates, as mediator of creation. The suggestion here made: he mediates between the Father's originating

---

46. Peter Widdicombe, *The Fatherhood of God from Origen to Athanasius* (Oxford: Clarendon, 1994), 146–174.

47. Wolfhart Pannenberg, *Systematische Theologie*, 2:36.

48. John Zizioulas, *Being as Communion* (Crestwood: St. Vladimir's Seminary Press, 1985), 41: "We ascribe the being of God to his personal freedom. In a more analytical way this means that God, as Father and not as substance, perpetually confirms through 'being' his *free* will to exist. And it is precisely his trinitarian existence that constitutes this confirmation."

and the Spirit's liberating, in that his trinitarian identity as the crucified and risen Jesus determines the content of their mutuality. Because it is the risen Jesus whom the Father eternally initiates, the Father's initiating is open to freedom; because it is the crucified Jesus whom the Spirit by raising him eternally frees, the Spirit's liberating can be the liberation of an actuality. Were there not the crucified and risen incarnate Son, then—all else impossibly remaining the same—the Spirit's word would be the infamous "Let go and let be," and the Father's would be "That is mine." An other than God that can exist by the Father's actual initiating and by the Spirit's actual liberating, mutually determined in their content by the Son, can only be this Son's personal and impersonal dramatic context.

The Son's particular word in the creating conversation may therefore be formulated: "Let there be . . . ; *and that is good.*" The Son speaks the actuality, the givenness by the Father, of the purposiveness that the creature has by the Spirit.

Or more abstractly, we may say that the Son mediates the Father's originating and the Spirit's liberating, thereby to *hold open* the creatures' space in being. The relation of the creature to the Creator, by which the creature is, holds in the present tense of created time without thereby being a timeless relation, in that one of the three, the Son, has his own individual entity *within* created time, in that he is himself one of those among whom and upon whom creatures' participation in God's story is being "worked out." The envelopment of our time by God is itself accomplished in the course of our time.

As the Father's love of the Son as other than himself is the possibility of all otherness from God, and so of creation, so the Son's acceptance of being other than God is the actual mediation of that possibility. It is only fair now to cite Gottfried Thomasius favorably: "Creation occurred for this reason through the Son, that creation was to be in creaturely and finite fashion what the Son in eternal and infinite fashion is in relation to the Father."[49] In the twentieth century: "To the Father's turning to the Son corresponds the Son's self-distinction from the Father. . . . Here originates the otherness . . . of created being."[50]

We must repeat the great saying of Maximus: "The one who knows the mystery of the cross and the tomb, knows the reasons of things. The one who is initiated into the infinite power of the Resurrection, knows the purpose for which God knowingly created all." God speaks a moral command to create the world. The moral command that he speaks is the Son. And the Son is in fact Jesus of Nazareth. Therefore the story of Jesus, as the story of this one man's moral will, is the content of the command "Let there be . . . ," by which the creation comes into being and perdures. The story told in the Gospels states the meaning of creation.

Perhaps we may summarize: The Father commands, "Let there be . . ." The Son, who is himself this commanding word insofar as the Father hears therein his own intention, is given to be the meaning of the creature; within creation he

49. *Christi Person und Werk*, 143.
50. Pannenberg, *Systematische Theologie*, 2:37.

is the creature as intended by and for God. And the Spirit, as the intrusive liveliness of this exchange, intrudes also on the creature who is now an item in the exchange, so that the creature is not merely in fact and statically intended for God but lives for God.

It is God's Trinity that allows him to create freely but not arbitrarily. His act of creating is grounded in the triune life that he is but just so is not necessary to him. He can be the essential ground of the creature without the creature being any sort of extension or conclusion of his being, because the love that is the ground of creation would without creation be fully actual in the triune life. God does not first become active and relational when he creates; just so creating is *both* appropriate and unnecessary for him.

SEVENTEEN

Time, Created Being, and Space

I

The heart of Western teaching about creation derives from Augustine. To him we owe the great insight that for God to have creatures is first and foremost to take time for them. And as Augustine probed that insight he created an interpretation of time itself, and so of created being, that has been for both good and ill a chief determinant of all Western theology, as indeed of Western thought generally. Our next step must be critique but also reappropriation of the eleventh book of Augustine's *Confessions*.[1]

Augustine rightly drew his interpretation of time from his doctrine of God. Unhappily, his recurrent conceptual unitarianism[2] manifests itself with special force just here: God is understood as sheer simultaneous Presence. Augustine begins his discussion with the invocation, "You, God, *are* eternity."[3] When he then comes to define eternity, it is as a single moment that is "always the present."[4]

---

1. One cannot now discuss this text without mentioning the magisterial commentary by James J. O'Donnell, *Augustine: Confessions* (Oxford: Clarendon, 1992), vol. 2, even though this interpretation differs from his at several points.

2. Currently, Augustine is vehemently defended against such critique as this by pointing to the trinitarian richness of his piety, as this appears in his sermons and commentaries and in such works as *De civitate Dei*, and as it indeed must be reckoned with in any general appreciation of his thought. The critique of Augustine that appears here and in volume 1 has strictly to do with his propositional teaching within certain realms of discourse, as these have in fact determined subsequent Western theology within those same realms. Augustine did unfortunately say the things that critics like me report, and what he said has had the ill consequences likewise reported, and we cannot honestly pretend otherwise.

3. *Confessiones*, xi.1.1.

4. Ibid., 14.17: "praesens autem si semper esset praesens nec in praeteritum transiret, non iam esset tempus sed aeternitas."

In this book of the *Confessions*, Augustine's undifferentiated concept of static divine simplicity determines many analytic moves, as it often does when he juxtaposes God and time directly.

If God is being, the being of God determines what it means also for temporal things to be. If then God is simple Presence, future things and past things cannot have being *as* past or future but only as they are somehow present. So the decisive proposition of Augustine's interpretation of time: "It is not entirely appropriate to say, 'There are . . . past, present, and future.' It would be better to say, 'There are . . . the presence of past things, the presence of present things, and the presence of future things.'"[5]

Past or future things, according to Augustine, have no being *as* they are past or future, but only insofar as they are somehow present. This is not problematic relatively to Augustine's divine Presence, for whom everything is anyway there at once.[6] But the question here is about time as itself creation, that is, about the past and future of creatures for themselves, whose present is not infinitely encompassing.

Moreover, the nonbeing for creatures of past and future as past and future may even, on Augustine's principles, imply the nonbeing for them also of the present. Augustine laid it down: "If the present remained always the present and did not pass into being past, it would not be time but eternity." But just so he had immediately to ask, "If the present, in order that there be time, must pass into the past, how can it be said to be at all?"[7] Here is the point of the most notorious—if perhaps somewhat playfully proposed—argument of book 11: it seems there can be a finite present only as an instantaneous transition from future to past, and so as a purely geometrical point between them, which then must itself be temporally null.[8]

Thus throughout his discussion Augustine is pressed to the verge of answering "What is time?" with a flatly Neoplatonic "Nothingness." Yet as a reader of the Bible he cannot accept this outcome. He finds his solution in the ontology of a particular creature, the human soul: since the soul is a finite image of the infinite Presence, past and future things must, somehow , be presently there for it.

But they cannot be present for it in the same way as for God. What has being is, to repeat, "the presence of past things, the presence of present things, and the presence of future things." This works out differently for infinite and finite consciousness: while for God it means that things are present to him in their proper entity, for us it must initially mean simply that there "are neither future things

---

5. Ibid., 20.26: "praesens de praeteritis, praesens de praesentibus, praesens de futuris."

6. *De civitate Dei*, xi.21: God "comprehends" future, present and past things "all in a changeless and sempiternal present."

7. Ibid., 14.17.

8. Ibid., 15.20: "If we think of a temporal entity that cannot be divided into even the most minute parts, . . . this alone can be called '*the* present.' But such a moment is so immediately carried from the future into the past that it is utterly unextended, for if it were extended it would be divisible again into past and future. The present thus occupies no space of time."

nor past things."[9] Past and future things, insofar as they are other than the finite soul, really are past and future for it, and so are what is *no* more or is *not* yet. On Augustine's principles it seems this must mean that for the finite soul they simply are not.

Augustine sees just one escape from this conclusion: past and future must be there for the soul as they are grasped *within* the soul in the soul's own essential presentness. The passage just cited continues: "Therefore they must be in the soul, and I can see no other place for them. . . . The presence of past things is memory, the presence of present things is immediate apprehension,[10] the presence of future things is expectation." The escape is that memory, immediate apprehension, and expectation are themselves, regardless of their contents, all present acts of consciousness.

Thus the intrinsic temporality of creatures occurs as such only *within* creatures of one sort, souls made in the image of the divine Presence. Augustine then adopts a corresponding category under which to bring time: it is a "stretching out," *distentio*, of the soul 's present act to make interior accommodation for past and future. As my "present intention" draws expected things through itself so that they become remembered things,[11] "the act itself is stretched out in memory . . . and expectation."[12]

Created time for Augustine finally depends for its extension on a space within created images of divine Presence, who would most straightforwardly reflect their Archetype as temporally located but dimensionless points, but are "stretched out" to let them encompass past and future despite their finitude. In few products of intellect are profound insight and obvious muddle so mingled as in Augustine's doctrine of time.[13]

II

In the subsequent history of Western thought, two general interpretations of time have then been available. One, in various adaptations, descends from Augustine: time is the inner horizon of human experience. The other is in a general way Aristotelian: time is the metric of external physical movement provided by a standard such movement.

For Aristotle, the motion of the heavenly bodies provided the standard measure of the world's processes; just so this motion was approximated to eternity, and the heavens became mediators of divinity. Augustine demythologized the heavens by relocating time in the soul—the question is whether he did not thereby mythologize the soul.

---

9. Ibid., 20.26.
10. *Contuitus.*
11. Ibid., 27.36.
12. Ibid., 28.38.
13. Hegel would, I suppose, provide the chief competition.

The Aristotelian understanding of time has anyway not been able to be suppressed. One reason is the internal incoherence of the Augustinian alternative. Augustine agrees with Aristotle that time is not motion as such but is rather a standard by which to measure motion.[14] But the soul's distention cannot really provide such a metric, since the specious present of immediate apprehension can always, as Augustine himself points out, be differently marked off from past and future, so that its "length" is arbitrary—so that indeed its length is potentially null[15]—while the reach of memory and expectation of course varies from instance to instance. In fact Augustine still subliminally assumed an Aristotelian external time line on which the soul is located and on which its extensions are measured— just as we have had to assume such a metric in order even to describe his teaching.

Indeed what Augustine seems at bottom to have assumed is the Platonic picture of the turning wheel of time with the geometric still point of eternity at its center. As a Christian he could not be content with this picture; he cut the circle and stretched it out as a line, to model the biblical understanding of reality as history. But he continued to think of the point of eternity as equidistant from all temporal points. Many puzzles within Western discourse about time result from this oxymoronic root metaphor, of a point perpendicular to a straight line yet equidistant from all points on it.

Thus Western thinking regularly gives up the Augustinian interpretation of time and recurs to Aristotle, whenever the world external to the soul must be dealt with in its temporality or even when the soul and its experience become themselves temporal objects of reflection. Yet the Aristotelian doctrine is also unsatisfying: it does not account for what is after all the experientially decisive feature of our dealing with time, unveiled for good and all by Augustine: that we find our experience antecedently and constitutively—"transcendentally"—shaped by it.

The two interpretations regularly appear paired in their mutual inadequacy, even as unreconciled interpretations of time offered by recent cosmological physics.[16] On the one hand, there is the time of classic relativity theory. It can account

---

14. Ibid., 24.31.

15. Ibid., 15.20.

16. The theological bits of Stephen Hawking's popular presentation in *A Brief History of Time* (New York: Bantam Books, 1988) depend on the distinctions discussed in the next paragraphs. When we construe the history of the universe in classically relativistic fashion, we are, according to present information and calculations, led back to a beginning of the universe in an initial "big bang." Within classic relativity theory, this event appears as a "singularity" where the mathematics of relativity theory cannot apply, so that we have no theory by which to connect the event to an antecedent cause—note that what is here encountered is not a "gap" in scientific explanation. On this reading, the universe appears simultaneously to have a beginning and to have no nontheologically stipulable cause. Hawking does not wish to acquiesce in such epistemic ascesis, and thinks it might be avoided if a "quantum theory of gravity" could be developed—a thing that admittedly has not yet been done. If we could "discuss the very early stages of the universe" in terms of such a theory, also the sheer inception of the universe from nothing would be predicted by laws timelessly—if that is the word—valid for that universe, thus leaving no explanatory function for the proposition that an agent other than the universe creates it.

for the time we actually inhabit, in which there are irreversible causal sequences; relations in this time can be like those between points on a line, and so be distinct from those in space, which posit more than one dimension.[17] Real time is compatible with our transcendental experience of time. And in it the universe, by current observations and calculations, has a beginning that can be thought of as itself an event, "the big bang," and one susceptible of—though far from requiring—such explanation as that God wills it.

On the other hand, application of quantum mechanics to the first minimoment of the big bang might, some theorists hope, reveal there a time that has no such compatibility with the transcendental shape of our experience, or with a doctrine of initial creation. Two moments of this time, called "imaginary" time, are like points on a map, so that which way the arrow points depends on from which side the two moments are viewed; this time is indeed a "fourth *dimension*" indistinguishable from the other three.[18]

When we construe the beginning moment of the universe in imaginary time, we are not—or so it appears—obliged to account for it otherwise than by physical laws (if such they can here be called) that simply obtain for this same universe, since the big bang cannot in this construal be traced back to a first moment, to a "singularity" for which they do not apply. What quantum cosmology thus perhaps says—that the universe's own laws predict its existence—is what Thomas says is distinctive of God. This cosmology, should it be asserted as physically true and not merely convenient for certain calculations—and sheer assertion, it

---

For a relatively lucid description of the situation in speculative physics, see Chris J. Isham, "Quantum Theories of the Creation of the Universe," *Interpreting the Universe as Creation*, ed. Vincent Brümmer (Kampen: Kok Pharos, 1991), 37–64. William Lane Craig and Quentin Smith, *Theism, Atheism and Big Bang Cosmology* (Oxford: Clarendon Press, 1993), 279–337, one a "theist" and the other an "atheist," between them demolish the arguments of Hawking's book. But Smith, 301–337, thinks it possible to reconstruct the argument from the more technical writings in which Hawking lays down the desiderata and possibilities of quantum cosmology. In Smith's reconstruction, the quantum theory of gravity sketched by Hawking would, if actually produced, yield a probability-curve of the universe's coming to be. But as Isham, 63, points out, as it is in general hard to know what a probabilistic statement is supposed to mean when applied to a single thing, it is the more problematic when the single thing is the universe.

17. The relation between these conceptions of time and the conceptions of time labeled, in some more strictly philosophical debate, A-theory and B-theory is not clear, at least to me. A-theories insist on the irreducibility of tensed language—or language using devices to the same purpose—and perhaps also propose the reducibility of B-determinations to A-determinations. B-theories insist that A-determinations can be reduced to expressions using no tenses but only the "B-series" constructed by the relation "earlier(later) than." What *is* clear is that theology must take the side of the A-theorists. To the debate itself, and for presentation of what seem overwhelming strictly analytical arguments for A-theory, Richard M. Gale, *The Language of Time* (London: Routledge & Kegan Paul, 1968), esp. 37–102.

18. Another way of putting this is to say bluntly, with Frank J. Tipler, "The Omega Point as Eschaton," unmarked paper: "In quantum cosmology . . . *there is no time!* The universal wave function Psi(h,F,S) is all there is, and there is no reference to a 4–dimensional M or a 4-dimensional metric g in the wave function."

seems, is all that could ever be contemplated—would relapse to the theology of the Greeks,[19] for whom the cosmos was divine. Whether science itself could then continue is an interesting question.

One is anyway moved to ask: Which time, "real time" or "imaginary time," is the *really* real time?[20] For the two are metaphysically contrary: only real time can be experienced, since real time is the condition of any possible experience. Instantly an inveterate dichotomy of metaphysical tempers presents itself: that real time is the time of the world as necessarily experienced will suggest to some that it is the "really" real time, and the very same consideration will suggest to others that it is not.

Neither temper can be satisfied by itself. When Immanuel Kant defines time as the enabling horizon of specifically personal experience[21] we are immediately convinced. Time is what we inwardly experience in experiencing anything at all. Yet when popular cosmological writings describe time as a sheer fact of the world outside us, a feature of its architecture, we are just as immediately convinced. Something that subsisted only for us or that could be fully assimilated into our inwardness would not be what we ineluctably mean by "time."

Surely our primal intuition of time is that it must possess the characters of *both* Augustine's "time" and Aristotle's "time," of both "real" time and "imaginary" time. Time is precisely the *horizon of experience*, with both nouns demanding full weight. A resolution suggests itself: that time is indeed, a la Augustine, the "distention" of a personal reality, and that just *so* it provides creatures with an external metric of created events.[22] That is: the "stretching out" that makes time is an extension not of finite consciousness but of an infinite enveloping consciousness.

God makes narrative room in his triune life for others than himself; this act is the act of creation, and this accommodation is created time. Thus as we "live and move and have our being" in him, the "distention" within which we do this is an order external to us, which therefore can provide a metric that is objective for us. Yet we are within the divine life as *participants* and so experience this metric as a determining character also of our existence as persons.

---

19. Which is what Tipler has explicitly done, ibid., 17: "In this sense, we can say that the Omega Point 'creates the physical universe,' but there is another sense in which the Omega Point and the totality of everything that exists physically can be said to create themselves." For the Omega Point in his theory is exactly Aristotle's Prime Mover.

20. Although Hawking, *A Brief History* , 137, says that whether one construes the initial state of the universe in real time or in imaginary time depends on what calculations are to be made, this is disingenuous or confused, and he is in fact no more immune to this metaphysical choice than the rest of us. Quite transparently he hopes that there is a metaphysically deeper time and that "imaginary" time is it, precisely on account of difficulties this makes for what he takes to be the notion of creation. Smith, *Big Bang*, 321–337, is in similar if philosophically more sophisticated case: he argues that his reconstructed version of Hawking is a good explanation of the existence of the universe precisely because it does not require a cause of the universe. This perhaps does not quite beg the question, but surely comes close.

21. *Kritik der reinen Vernunft* (1781–1799) (Transzendentale Ästhetik, 2. Abschn.), ed. R. Schmidt (reprint, Hamburg: Meiner, 1956), 74–79.

22. This is undoubtedly a Hegelian sort of solution—and why not?

Time is *both* the inner extension of a life, as for Augustine, *and* the external horizon and metric of all created events, as for Aristotle. For time is a "distention" in the life that is God and just so is the enveloping given horizon of all events that are not God.

It is in this matter as in others: Augustine's doctrine of divine simplicity made it impossible for him to acknowledge in God himself the complexity of the biblical God, and he compensated by contemplating that complexity, which as an ardent student of Scripture he could not avoid, in the created images of God. But the triune God is not a sheer point of presence; he is a life among persons. And therefore creation's temporality is not awkwardly related to God's eternity, and its sequentiality imposes no strain on its participation in being.

We are now also able to make a choice earlier postponed. The life of God is constituted in a structure of relations, whose referents are narrative. This narrative structure is enabled by a difference between whence and whither, which one cannot finally refrain from calling "past" and "future," and which is identical with the distinction between the Father and the Spirit. This difference is not measurable; nothing in God *recedes* into the past or *approaches* from the future. But the difference is also absolute: there are whence and whither in God that are not like right and left or up and down, that do not reverse with the point of view. Since now we find that what we know as time is located within and enabled by this structure, the last inhibition is surely removed. It indeed better suits the gospel's God to speak of "God's time" and "created time," taking "time" as an analogous concept, than to think of God as not having time and then resort to such circumlocutions as Barth's "sheer duration."

God takes time in his time for us. That is his act of creation.

III

God, we said, is a fugue, a conversation, a personal event. If the being of God may so be described, what is it for creatures to be? What is it to inhabit the accommodation in God that is created time? And if God is being, then the being of God must determine what it means also for temporal things to be. How does that work out?

Our primary answer to the first question has already been given. In the context of creation, the specification of God's being as conversation is privileged. We must therefore say: to be, as a creature, is to be mentioned in the triune moral conversation, as something other than those who conduct it.

Western intellectual history has for the most part continued the Greek tradition for which "to be" meant to have form and so to appear and be seen, whether with the body's or the mind's eye.[23] But there plainly is another possibility: that

---

23. The at once clearest and deepest exposition of the following matter known to me is a regrettably neglected article by Franz K. Mayr, "Philosophie im Wandel der Sprache," *Zeitschrift für Theologie und Kirche* 61 (1964):439–491.

to be is to be *heard of*;[24] and it is this interpretation that is demanded by the doctrine of creation. Within such an interpretation, instead of apprehending immediately encountered realities as "phenomena," "things that appear," we will apprehend them as "*legomena*, "things that are spoken of." Things are as we hear of them, from third parties or themselves. And if beings are apprehended in their being itself, this is apprehended "from the speech and address of . . . God."[25]

But what then, if we make this move, is it to be *as* a creature , that is, as a real being that is not God? In the first volume, we adopted Thomas Aquinas's decisive maxim: a creature's difference from God, in respect of its being, is that its existence is other than its essence, that in what it is—if it is—there is no reason for it to be. We must now follow this out a bit further. In the process, we may slightly relocate Thomas's teaching.

Thomas construes the dependence of creatures on the Creator as creatures' relation to a primary efficient and final "cause" of their being;[26] in our less flexible modern language, to what is at once the cause of their being and the reason for their being. Thomas also accepts the Neoplatonic[27] rule as valid without exception: "Every agent produces effects that are similar to itself in that respect in which it acts as agent."[28] Therefore, when we say "God is" and "This tree is," our use of "is" cannot, according to Thomas, be simple equivocation; since God is the cause of creatures' being, that God is and that creatures are cannot be sheerly incomparable facts. Creatures' being must be somehow "similar" to God's being.

Yet neither, says Thomas, can any predicate, including "being," be univocally predicated of God and creatures.[29] The difference of Creator from creatures is, again, that there are in God no real distinctions between the fact that he is and what he is, or therefore between aspects of what he is. But all our language gets its purchase on its referents by exploiting just such distinctions in them[30]— "Jones," we say, "is good," modeling a difference between substance and accident. Therefore, the sentence "God is good" lacks the sort of purchase on its subject possessed by the sentence "Jones is good," and the predication made by the two sentences must be in some way equivocal.

It is at this point[31] that Thomas's famous doctrine of analogy appears.[32] A word is used analogously, Thomas stipulates, when it is used simultaneously of differing referents but neither univocally nor merely equivocally. This properly

24. Mayr, ibid., following Heidegger, argues that this interpretation was present in the earliest Greek speculations.

25. Mayr, ibid., 456.

26. *Summa theologiae*, i.44.

27. To Thomas's Neoplatonism, Klaus Kremer, *Die neuplatonische Seinsphilosophie und ihre Wirkung auf Thomas von Aquin* (Leiden: Brill, 1966).

28. Ibid., i.4.3: "Omne agens agat sibi simile inquantum est agens."

29. For somewhat deeper analysis than the following, Robert W. Jenson, *The Knowledge of Things Hoped For* (New York: Oxford University Press, 1969), 75–79.

30. *Summa theologiae*, i.3.4; 13.1.

31. The question about the possible "analogy" or "univocity" "of being" has of course traditionally been raised not here but in the doctrine of God. The assumption is that we know what it is

happens when a word is used simultaneously in a primary sense and in one or more other senses that are dependent on it: so a horse may be "healthy" and climates, diets, teeth, and so on, be also "healthy" insofar as they are causes, symptoms, and so on, of the horse's health.[33]

God is primary efficient and final cause of creatures. A word like "good" must therefore be capable of simultaneous use of God and creatures; and now we can say that this use is analogous. Its meaning with primary reference to God is then "first archetypical causation of what in creatures we call goodness," and with dependent reference to creatures is the experienced created quality as such. *All* predicates properly used at once about God and creatures are, according to Thomas, analogous in this way. Therefore "being" used simultaneously of God and creatures must, as *we* use it, mean in the case of God "first archetypical causation of created being" and in the case of creatures just "being."[34]

With most words used simultaneously of God and creatures, the account just given suffices;[35] moreover, if we use such words of creatures without simultaneous reference to God, they may or may not be used analogously. But "being" is used *only* within metaphysical discourse, of which the difference between Creator and creature is in Christian theology the first axiom. Therefore "being" is used only analogously. Which is to say that being itself must be such as to compel analogous use of language when evoking it, that "God is" and "this creature is" are irreducibly at once incomparable and comparable facts.[36]

So far Thomas's doctrine of analogy. What we must now note is that Thomas's discourse in this context is, despite great originality over against the inherited metaphysical tradition otherwise, nevertheless still firmly situated within the apprehension of being as *shape* that *appears*. The comparability of God's being and creatures' being is a *similitudo*, a *resemblance* of archetype to ectype;[37] it is

---

for things in general to be, and must inquire, first, whether this concept of being can at all be used of God or is perhaps made merely equivocal in the attempt, and then, if it can be used of him, whether this use is univocal or analogous. Since in my judgment inquiry about what it is for God to be, and inquiry about how "being" is to be understood, can only be pursued *simultaneously*, I did not take up the analogy of being in its traditional place. The chapter on God and being was engaged at once in discovering what God is in that he is and what it means for anything to be. But now, as we inquire what then it means for creatures to be as creatures and so not as God, we do encounter the "analogy-problem."

32. To the following, Ralph M. McInerny, *The Logic of Analogy; An Interpretation of St. Thomas.* (The Hague: Nijhoff, 1961); Robert W. Jenson, *Knowledge*, 58–89, and further literature there.

33. This is the same, of course, as Aristotle's "equivocity with reference to one."

34. Note that in the case of analogy to God and creatures, the order of being and the order of knowing run oppositely.

35. To the following, Jenson, *Knowledge*, 85–89.

36. And that is further to say that there is, in a famous if much misused phrase of twentieth-century theological polemics, not only analogical language but an *analogia entis*, an "analogy of being." To the discussion and controversy between Karl Barth and Erich Przywara, see now Bruce L. McCormack, *Karl Barth's Critically Realistic Dialectical Theology: Its Genesis and Development 1909–1936* (Oxford: Clarendon, 1995), 319–322, 383–391.

37. E.g., *Summa theologiae*, i.4.3.

that "all created things are *images* [emphasis added] . . . of their first cause."[38] And the *in*comparability of God's being and creatures' being—as of God's goodness and our goodness, and so on—is an imperfection of this imaging.[39]

But if God's creating word is an actual utterance and not an unspoken mental form actualized by will, the matter cannot be construed quite in this way. Creatures have being precisely as God transitively says "Let there be . . ." Therefore whatever God himself means by "be" is exactly what it means for a creature to be; indeed the utterance "Let there be . . ." is itself the positive relation of creature to Creator, is itself the comparability of the fact that God is and that others than God are. Therefore insofar as "being" says something *about* God or creatures, "being" must after all be univocal rather than analogous.

And yet there must be some break between "God is" and "Creatures are"; the force of Thomas's insight remains. Perhaps we may adopt categories from J. L. Austin[40] and suggest: "x is" is univocal in its "locutionary sense," in what it says about x, but equivocal in its "illocutionary force," in what is done when it is said. Just so the utterance is indeed constituted in a kind of analogicity, which may indeed be finally much like that posited by Thomas.

An utterance's illocutionary force is the particular act performed when it is said, and there are many sorts of such acts. We may ask: When we say "God is," what do we *do?* And we should answer: we acknowledge our entire dependence on a primary cause and reason of our being. But we may also ask: When *God* says, "God is," what does *he* do? And then we must answer: in the infinite perichoresis of the triune life, he declares himself both as the one who is sufficient reason for his own being and as the one who has that reason. Or again, when we say, "Creatures are," we give thanks, but when God says, "Creatures are," he creates. It is such propositions that state the incomparability between the fact that God is and the fact that we are.

But now it is time and perhaps past time to end this train of thought. We have again fallen into using "God" without explicit trinitarian unpacking. We must ask what a creature is as it answers to each of the divine persons in the creating discourse.

IV

It is by virtue of the Father's particular triune role that the creating command is "Let there *be* . . ." Insofar as creatures are initiated by the role of the Father, their being is their mere existence, on which we then must here focus as narrowly as possible. We must interpret creaturely being as it answers to the simple occurrence of the triune being, and that is, in the concluding language of the previous volume, to the fact of the triune fugue.

---

38. *Summa contra gentiles,* iii.19.
39. E.g., ibid., i.13.5.
40. *How to Do Things with Words* (New York: Oxford University Press, 1965).

We must therefore here abstract from the semantics of the divine conversation and so think only of its sheer musicality. To be a creature in specific relation to the Father is to be a motif in the orchestration that occurs when God's musicality opens *ad extra*. We might say: the Father hums a music "of the spheres," the tune of the creating triune conversation, and precisely so and not otherwise there are the "spheres." Nor is it merely that there are creatures who are then harmonious with each other; to be a creature *is* to belong to the counterpoint and harmony of the triune music.

The previous paragraph is likely to be read as metaphor, and indeed as metaphor run wild. It is not so intended, or not in any sense of "metaphor" that is alternative to "concept."[41] Such words as "harmony" are here conscripted to be metaphysically descriptive language more malleable to the gospel's grasp of reality than is, for central contrary example, the language of "substance" in its native Aristotelian or Cartesian or Lockean senses. That we are used to the metaphysical concepts of Mediterranean pagan antiquity and its Enlightenment recrudescence does not mean they are the only ones possible; there is no a priori reason why, for example, "substance"—which after all simply meant "what holds something up"—should be apt for conscription into metaphysical service and, for example, "tune" should not.

We may again follow the lead of Jonathan Edwards.[42] Living at the height of the Enlightenment, he found in Newtonian and Lockean science a grand vision of universal dynamic harmony, in itself perfectly correlate to the harmony that is the very being of the triune God. But to appropriate Newton's vision in this fashion, he had to undo the metaphysics with which the usual Enlightenment identified it.

His target was "mechanism," the notion that "bodies act upon each other" as if they were agents,[43] as this notion provided the vulgar Enlightenment's general picture of reality. A universe that was significantly like a great machine would not have the *sort* of dynamic order that answers to the harmonious life of the triune God; and indeed Edwards clearly saw that Christianity could not long coexist with a mechanist worldview. Nor did he think Christianity needed to, since mechanism was, he judged, a mere conceptual blunder, an anachronism that resulted

---

41. This may be the place to insist on a vital point against most recent "metaphor" theology. Its practitioners want to have it both ways. Sometimes it is important for them to note that metaphor is a universal function in all language. This of course is a truism, and when we think of "metaphor" in this way, there is no opposition between "metaphor" and "concept." But then the key step in their *theological* arguments is that they pit metaphor *against* concept: we have, they say, "only" metaphors for God. It is perhaps safe to say that what most theologians now have in mind when they speak of metaphor is trope that is not concept; it is for this reason that I am so leary of "metaphor."

42. To the following, see Robert W. Jenson, *America's Theologian: A Recommendation of Jonathan Edwards* (New York: Oxford University Press, 1988), 23–49.

43. *Scientific and Philosophical Writings*, ed. Wallace Anderson, *The Works of Jonathan Edwards*, vol. 6 (New Haven: Yale University Press, 1960), 216.

from reading the antique conceptuality of substance onto terms in the formulas of modern science.

Unthinkingly applied to the terms of scientific propositions, the old notion of substance had become the Cartesian or Lockean "something" that was supposed to *exercise* the characters that we experience in a body or that science for experienced reason attributes to it. Edwards applied Occam's razor: he excised this godlet as the moot but nevertheless conceptually disordering unneeded posit that it is. When we, for example, touch something "solid," there is no need to posit an "x" that *causes* this experience; rather, "body and solidity are the same."[44] With respect to the proceedings of everyday experience and science, the supposition that the world is composed of matter-substances is merely empty; "the case is the same" if we suppose this or if we do not.[45] But for religion and civil society the mechanistic supposition must be actively deleterious.[46]

Edwards's position, he insisted, does not "deny that things are where they seem to be . . . or the science of the causes or reasons of corporeal changes." Whatever meaning words like "body" or "matter" or "motion" have in the Newtonian laws themselves is exactly what he wants these words to be taken to mean.[47] And on causation he shares the position of David Hume: a cause is any event that appears in the protasis of a true proposition of the form "If . . . happens, then . . . will happen." A cause does not "make" its effect happen; nor need there be any other occult connection between them.[48] Gravity, for central example, is not an agency operating mysteriously at a distance; it is simply an instance of the regularity of reciprocal motion and resistance that *is* the reality of body[49]—Edwards can even say, "The essence of bodies is gravity."[50]

Edwards's interpretation of our knowledge of the world was thus phenomenalist and operationalist. But unlike many others who have held such positions, he had an answer to the question: Is there then nothing *to* the play of phenomena? There is, he said, and it is "God himself, in the immediate exercise of his power."[51]

The play of phenomena is the play of the mandating thoughts of God; their law-like coherence is the coherence of that thinking.[52] At his most youthfully speculative, Edwards could identify space, the field of physical phenomena, with the field of God's consciousness:[53] God thinks movements and resistances in

44. Ibid., 211.

45. Ibid., 215: "The certain unknown substance which philosophers used to think subsisted by itself, and stood underneath and kept up solidity and all other properties" is in the new science properly "nothing but solidity itself."

46. Jenson, *America's Theologian*, 141–168.

47. Ibid., 353.

48. *Scientific and Philosophical Writings*, 180–181.

49. Ibid., 234–235, 377–380.

50. Ibid., 234.

51. Ibid., 214.

52. Jenson, *America's Theologian*, 27–34.

53. Newton had done something similar, but by simply calling space and time God's "sensorium," Newton blurred the line between Creator and creation; Edwards's formulation preserves it.

universally mutual harmony, and that is the "substance" of the physical world[54]—
if, as Edwards says, we "must needs" use that word. Just so, the world described
by Newton's physics and Locke's Newtonian psychology[55] is a finite harmony
appropriate to the infinite triune harmony that is God himself.

Some of Edwards's propositions are dangerous as they stand in his text: to
say that "God himself, in the immediate exercise of his power" is the creatures'
sole support and coherence, were we to take the proposition without trinitarian
differentiation, would surely threaten the distinct reality of creation. But if we
take "God" in such references of the Father specifically, then everything we have
so far said about creation must move us to affirm his speculations, *as* one triune
aspect of the truth about creatures.

Edwards has in any case cleared the way for the assertion first to be made: as
the harmony of the divine consciousness is finally musical, so the harmony of
creation, *sheerly as such*, is musical. And since the very being of creation is this
harmony, to be a creature is, in this respect, to be harmonized, to fit in an endlessly complicated web of mutually appropriate relations—which is of course
increasingly the vision of the sciences, insofar as their practitioners allow themselves to see it.

V

What, a second time, is it to be a creature? It is in virtue of the Spirit's triune role
that the creating command is "*Let* there be . . ."—that it is a liberating word.
Insofar as creatures occur by the Spirit's triune agency, their being is therefore
their contingency, on which we must again focus as narrowly as possible. That is,
we must here interpret creaturely being as it answers merely to the freedom of
the divine decision in which it is enveloped. We may say: to be a creature is, in
this respect, to be freed.

The modern impediment to this insight is again, of course, the usual Enlightenment's mechanism, now to be considered in this other connection. Every medium
of what in the modern world "everyone knows" installs it in our minds that according to "science" all events could in principle be predicted using "the laws of
nature." Even most scientists, who know better in their practice, continue to
assume in everyday metaphysics that someone who knew all physical laws and
the total state of the universe at some moment could predict all future events.

The creation, we are taught unthinkingly to suppose, is a realm in which determinism rules. If we then nevertheless take our own experience of freedom seriously, we are forced to interpret that experience as an intrusion into the created
order by another order, which is necessarily then an order of *uncreated* reality.[56] It
is this seeming necessity that lies behind the renewed blurring of the line between

---

54. Jenson, *America's Theologian*, 20–21, 28–34.
55. To Edwards on Locke, Jenson, *America's Theologian*, 29–34.
56. Paradigmatically and foundationally, Immanuel Kant, *Kritik der reinen Vernunft*
(Transzendentale Dialektik, 2. Hauptst.), 522–529.

the Creator and created personhood in so much nineteenth-century theology. And yet the initial supposition is a mere prejudice. Why not instead take our indubitable experience of freedom as a conclusive refutation of mechanism?[57]

A beautiful passage in Augustine's *City of God* can point our way. Cicero, wrote Augustine, "a great and learned man, who had pondered human life much and acutely," thought he had to choose between affirming human freedom and affirming divine foreknowledge, and in love for humanity chose the former, thereby blaspheming God.[58] But Christians have a better understanding of the dynamics of events, so that "holding to God's foreknowledge does not compel us to abandon freedom of the will nor holding to freedom of the will compel us to deny that God knows what is to come."[59] For "the only efficient causes of events are willing causes, that is, causes in this respect like the Spirit of life."[60] According to Augustine, the freedom by which we as persons participate in the divine life is the very Spirit that evokes all "life," all the dynamic processes of creation.

It is of course around the possibility of miracle—and so of the Resurrection—and of prayer that Christian concern for creation's freedom circles. If we affirm miracles and petitionary prayer, there are two ways of accounting for them. We may assume the deterministic character of natural process and account for prayer and miracles by describing limitations of natural law and locating God's freedom in the "gaps"[61] between these boundaries. Or we may take the reality of prayer and miracles as itself a metaphysical axiom; we may construct a believing interpretation of natural events that is from the start and in its entirety an interpretation by the triune role of the Spirit who is Freedom.[62]

In Scripture it is true of all creatures: "When you take away their breath, they die. . . . When you send forth your spirit, they are created."[63] The universe or a galaxy or a quark or the reader of this text all occur in that they are enabled by the Freedom that God is for himself and then for others. In Scripture, all the

57. Stephen M. Barr, "The Atheism of the Mind," *First Things* 57 (Nov 1995):52: "It is a prediction of materialism that human beings can have no free will." This is because materialism "involves only two possibilities, the regularity of deterministic laws or the randomness of stochastic laws. There is no room for the tertium quid that is free will. But this prediction of materialism is falsified by the data of our own experience: we actually exercise free will, and thereby know it to be other than either determined or random."

58. *De civitate Dei*, v.9.

59. Ibid., 10.

60. Ibid., 9.

61. Rendered, one must suppose, permanently infamous by Dietrich Bonhoeffer's scorn.

62. The always interesting speculations of George E. Murphy seem still undecided between going the one way or the other. So, e.g., "The End of History in the Middle," *Works* 5 (1995), no. 2. In this article, Murphy strives to make characterization of Jesus' Resurrection as an anticipation of the Eschaton, in the manner of Wolfhart Pannenberg, scientifically intelligible. He does so by combining Frank Tipler's theory that all lives, as bundles of information, are conserved in the total process of the universe, and will, if certain boundary conditions of cosmic process in fact obtain, be "raised" as the universe is transmuted into one universal communal intelligence at "the big crunch," with the possibility that "advanced potentials," which if they exist reverse cause and effect in time, could be the means of an occurrence of this resurrection ahead of its event.

63. Psalm 104:20–30.

dynamics of the created world, the events in which it constantly becomes what it was not yet, are understood to represent the creative actuality of the Spirit.

It is precisely these dynamics that mechanism conceives deterministically. Even abstracting from theological insight, the conception is certainly false. It is now well understood that the carriers of change within dynamic systems are events that individually can only be conceived either as spontaneous or as random.[64] Thus, for example, when there "is a twenty percent probability of snow," no one can say whether reality will fill the long odds; nor is this a limitation of our knowledge, for improvements in meteorology will only improve determination of the odds. Of the multitude of possible outcomes from the irradiating and agitating of Earth's prebiotic soup, each outcome with its own infinitesimal probability, one was the appearance of protein-nucleotides. And not the most completely informed maker of predictions[65] could then have known more than the possibility and colossal improbability of the event. The mechanics of survival described by Darwinism evidently do sometimes filter some mutations that in fact appear, but no lawlike principle dictates those appearances.[66]

If there were not God or if there were some monadic God, we would just have been describing the *randomness* of created events. Since there is the Spirit as one of the Trinity we have been describing the *spontaneity* of created events. The difference between regarding the dynamics of the world-process as random and regarding them as spontaneous may not be significant for empirical research,[67] but it is decisive for our life as creatures in creation. If the dynamics of creation are a spontaneity, then events happen not mechanically but voluntarily, just as Augustine said. If this spontaneity is opened by the Spirit, then when we confront any actual or possible event we confront someone's freedom. And believers claim to know that someone.

Nor do we thereby invoke a "God in the gaps." We have not located the liberating agency of Christ's Spirit in regions supposedly not covered by scientific description; what is attributed to the Spirit is a universal feature of the world precisely *as* scientifically described.[68]

64. For the most succinct presentation of these matters known to me see George E. Murphy, "The Third Article in the Science-Theology Dialogue," unpublished paper available from writer.

Present understandings of dynamic process may of course change—though it is hard to see what the alternatives might be. Should theology not therefore avoid assuming current science? Perhaps, but this work emulates rather the priestly savants who constructed Genesis 1, who took the risk and came out pretty well.

65. Not even even an *omniscient* scientist could do it, so long as he or she was not also omnipotent, that is, unless his or her omniscience amounted to what the Bible calls foreknowledge.

66. Thus Darwinism offers no explanation whatever of the actual history of species—an obvious point usually missed or deliberately obscured in public instruction.

67. We have of course no way to know that before trying out the second interpretation, perhaps as a guide in the formulation of hypotheses.

68. So, with respect to the emergence of life, Murphy, "The Third Article": "When we state the matter in this way, we can see that claiming the Spirit's involvement in the low-probability emergence of life is not simply a god of the gaps idea. It is part of a total belief in the Trinity's activity in all natural and scientifically describable processes."

Therefore prayer, to come to the religious point, is simply the reasonable thing to do. For the process of the world is enveloped in and determined by a freedom, a freedom that can be addressed. What is around us is not iron impersonal fate but an omnipotent conversation that is open to us. We can meaningfully and sensibly say, "Please let it rain," because rain will or will not happen in a spontaneity with whom we can and may discuss or even argue the matter. And we can make such addresses in hope and trust, for it is the crucified and risen Jesus whose Spirit is this freedom of all events.

Through the modern period, such robustly petitionary prayer has declined in the church. This is the result not of enlightenment but of superstition. The decline rests in part on a notion of God that makes it seem absurd to tell God what he "already" knows about our needs, or to expect such telling to alter determinations supposedly made in changeless impassibility; the whole first volume of this book labored to overcome this doctrine. Insofar as the decline rests also on the vulgar Enlightenment's deterministic misunderstanding of natural process, we can be free also from this hindrance. Precisely the scientifically accountable actual course of events can and so must theologically be understood as a history occurring within God's Freedom.

As for miracles, the true problem is therefore not whether they are possible, but how we are to distinguish them from events in general. We may cite a founding thinker of modern Catholicism, Maurice Blondel: "Each phenomenon is a particular case and a unique solution. . . . There is, no doubt, nothing more in the miracle than in the least of ordinary facts. But also there is nothing less in the most ordinary fact than in the miracle." That we are shocked into seeing this is the very intent of the miracle.[69] Thomas Aquinas laid it down: "If we speak with reference to God and his power, there are no miracles."[70]

What we may at this point recognize is that *all* actual events in their spontaneity are "done immediately by God, only in harmony and proportion,"[71] the harmony given by their envelopment in God's own harmonious life. As so often in the present complex of thought, Jonathan Edwards has the decisive insight. The ordering of all events is their coherence by logical and musical appropriateness within God's thinking of them; events lying outside the more usually expected order of events differ only as they are "done in the most general proportion, not tied to any particular proportion, to this or that created being, but the proportion is with the whole series of [God's] acts and designs from eternity to eternity."[72] Or in a contemporary statement: miracles "are occasions when normal physical regularities are modified by a more overt influence of the underlying basis of all beings. . . . [This] modification will show finite things in their true relation to their infinite ground. It will

69. *Action: Essay on a Critique of Life and a Science of Practice* (1893), tr. O. Blanchette (Notre Dame: University of Notre Dame Press, 1984), 365.

70. *Summa theologiae* , i.105.8: "Nihil potest dici miraculum ex comparatione potentiae divinae."

71. Jonathan Edwards, *Miscellanies*, 64.

72. Ibid.

not be an arbitrary breaking of rational and self-contained laws. Thus miracles have their own internal rationality, which can probably only be perceived by us when the totality of the cosmic process is completed."[73]

The events we call miracles are as ordered as any others; to see that order we must only look to their place within the whole of God's history with us, rather than to any smaller or abstracted part of it.[74] For it is the final truth here to be grasped: the stories told by, for example, cosmological physics or evolutionary narrative, or by such a proposition as "Water always runs downhill," or by a history of England or a religious history of humankind, are not other stories than the story of salvation, or even its fixed presuppositions, but rather are each merely one or another abstracted aspect of it. If miracles can be regarded as events that violate some rule, this is only by reference to such a subordinate partial ordering of events. From all of which it does not, of course, follow that purported miracles have in fact occurred.

VI

What, a third time, is it to be a creature? It is in virtue of the Son's triune role that the creating command is a word with definite content. Therefore insofar as creatures are determined by the *Son's* role in the triune conversation, their being is their material determination by the moral will of God, on which again we must now focus as narrowly as possible. That is, we must interpret creaturely being strictly as it answers to *what* is morally said in the divine conversation that mandates it. We will then say: to be a creature is, in christological respect, to be a revelation of God's will. In the more dramatic and therefore more accurate language we found in Luther, to be a creature is to be a "created word" from God.

We will not here proceed as we did in the previous two sections. The question of God's revelation in creation and of our knowledge of God from creation has historically acquired such importance and complication as to require its own chapter. The way in which creatures are words that speak for God must be the foundation of that chapter, and its discussion will appear there.

Here we will take up only one—perhaps initially surprising—aspect of the matter. We saw that as the specific personal history that Jesus the Son is, as the moral content of the divine conversation, the Son mediates the Father's originating and the Spirit's liberating with one another. *That is*, he is the specious present of the divine life. But the horizon of presence, of what is present to us at any time, is what we call space. Thus we earlier said that the Son "holds open the space" for creatures to be.

---

73. Keith Ward, *God, Chance and Necessity* (Oxford: One World, 1996), 83.

74. Martin Luther, *Ennaratio in I. Cap. Genesis* (WA 42), vi.18: "Si autem non omnes causas in creatura primitius condita praefixit, sed aliquas in sua voluntate servavit, non sunt quidem illae, quas in sua voluntate servavit, ex istarum quas creavit necessitate pendentes, non tamen possunt esse contrariae, quas in sua voluntate servavit, illis, quas sua voluntate constituit. . . . Istas ergo sic condidit, ut ex illis esse illud, cuius causae sunt, sit, sed non necesse sit; illas autem sic abscondit, ut ex eis esse necesse sit hoc, quod ex istis fecit, ut esse possit."

As we began with time, we end with space. For God to create, we said, is for him to take time for us. But it must surely also be said, that for God to create is for him to make space for us.[75] Perhaps merely to preserve a certain symmetry of presentation, we will begin a new section for the matter.

VII

In interpreting the reality of time, we could not avoid the language of space. Time, we said, is the room God makes in his eternity for others than himself. But what do we mean by speaking of "room"?

The metaphysical tradition has tended to interpret time in terms of space, pointing to the need to use spatial language when speaking of time. But of course we also need to use temporal language to speak of space: a distant point is where we now are not but could be in the future, and so on. Christian theology must interpret the mutuality signalled by these linguistic phenomena the other way around from the inherited metaphysical tradition. Time is not what happens in space; space is the horizon of the present tense, that is, of one aspect of time, of what is all there for us at once.[76] Augustine did not notice that not only do the "presence of the future" and the "presence of the past" in consciousness demand a "distention" of consciousness but that so does presence itself. Space is the distention within which things can be now there for us.

The removal of certain distinctions between time and space by relativity theory—and indeed already by the first beginnings of modern science[77]—precisely reflects the theological fact: God does not create spatial objects that thereupon move through time; he creates temporal-spatial objects, that is, in a more precise language, he creates histories. We must only avoid the suggestion of popular appropriations, which in calling time a fourth "dimension" tend to use "dimension" in a pictorial sense, thus obliterating time's distinction from space.[78]

Immanuel Kant analyzed space as the a priori experience that is the condition of our locating objects of experience outside ourselves,[79] that is, of distinguishing them from ourselves. Space, we may perhaps push Kant to say, is the a priori of otherness. So far as this goes, surely it corresponds to our intuition.

---

75. I hope that the following may, at least in part, reassure Colin E. Gunton, whose—for the most part flattering—critique of my trinitarianism appears in a revised edition of his *The Promise of Trinitarian Theology*, 2nd ed. (Edinburgh: T. & T. Clark, 1997), 118–136.

76. Thomas Aquinas, *Summa theologiae*, i.8.2: "Sicut se habet tempus ad successiva, ita se habet locus ad permanentia."

For a succinct presentation of the difference between time and space, in contemporary philosophical idiom, Gale, *Time*, 201–212. Very succinctly indeed, 201: "There is no temporal field of vision corresponding to a spatial field of vision, since events which are earlier and later than each other by definition do not coexist."

77. When theorists began to put temporal quantities in formulas and equations so that they could, like spatial quantities, be squared or divided or otherwise manipulated.

78. As, of course, quantum cosmology seems actually to do.

79. E.g., *Kritik der reinen Vernunft*, 70–71.

Yet here, as with time, the intuition divides. When Kant then claims that space simply is *not* "a determination . . . that pertains to objects themselves,"[80] we cannot but turn and sympathize with thinkers who have wondered what Kant can then mean by "objects."

What with time was the end of reflection can here be a beginning. Time, we came to see, cannot be satisfactorily interpreted except as a "distention" in God's life. If space is the horizon of time's present tense, it must be interpreted as a feature of that same distention. Thus if space is the form of consciousness that enables distinguishing other reality from oneself, we must say that this distinction is first made by God. God opens otherness between himself and us, and so there is present room for us.

We have already argued that and why those accommodated as participants in the divine life do not thereby become persons of that life. Space, we may say, is the form of God's own experience of this otherness, which experience, of course, enables it. It is therefore not merely because of the limitations of our finitude that we inevitably imagine God as "beyond" or "above" us, using what we are likely misleadingly to call "metaphors" or "mere" pictures; it is simply the reverse of the fact that we are beyond for God.

It is an ancient maxim: "God is his own space."[81] The maxim is meaningful only if God does posit an other than himself from which he is at a *distance*, so as himself to be a *space*, only, that is, if there are creatures. Since there are in fact creatures, their otherness from God establishes that God is one place, and creation is spatially located by not being *at that* place. God is one place and creatures another, and just and only so there is created space.

We now first think of space as the extension within which creatures are distinguished from each other. Space here is experienced as an aspect of the universe's architecture: an objectively given three-variable coordinate system by which I am located at point $x^1/y^1/z^1$, you at point $x^1/y^1/z^2$, and so on.[82] A dilemma appears here similar to that which characterized our intuition of time: we want space to be *both* an a priori of consciousness and a sort of container within which we and all our consciousnesses are to be found.

The resolution has been anticipated: space can be at once an a priori of our consciousness and a structure within which we locate ourselves, because it is an aspect of God's enveloping conscious life. Were there only one point, that is, were there no space, the universe's multiplicity and variation would be illusion. But the universe could be thus simple only if it were not finally other than the one Origin, only if the emanationist possibility were actual. The great motto of the Upanishads, "You are that," where any "you" and any "that" can satisfy these variables, identifies all created beings with one another in that it identifies them all with the divine. This threat is overcome in that God sets us as other

80. *Kritik der reinen Vernunft*, 70.
81. John of Damascus, *The Orthodox Faith*, 13.11.
82. We of course can mathematically generate "spaces" with as many and different sorts of axes as we like. But we cannot fit any but this one to experience.

than himself, in that our accommodation in him has the present dimension of separateness.

We may now recur to the Son's mediation of creation. The Father's love of the Son is, we have seen, the possibility of creation. Insofar as to be a creature is to be other than God, we may say that the Father's love of the Son as other than himself is the possibility of creation's otherness from God. And the Son's acceptance of being other than God is the condition of that possibility's actualization.[83] Moreover, we now also see why we had to say that time was the "room" God made for us in his life: did not God set us other than himself, did he not make space between him and us, all time would just be *his* time and there would be no "accommodation" in him.

And finally, we must inquire into the relation between God himself and the space he makes for us. God is his own place. What then is the relation of God, as his own place, to the space he makes in time for creatures? If he is not to be an absent, deist God, he must be present to creatures in their space. How is that?

According to Thomas Aquinas, "Wherever something is at work, that is where it is," at least in the sense of "where" here appropriate.[84] In the case of persons, Thomas unpacks this into presence "by power" and presence "to" consciousness. And in the case of the person God, he is present with all creatures "by power in that they are subject to his rule" and is also present with all creatures "in that all things are naked and open to his sight."[85]

Thomas's teaching exploits a quite straightforward analogy: there is a plain sense in which my space is the presentness spread before me as I go about any task or as I enter converse with some person or group; space is the place then available to my agency and for the sake of that agency open to my immediate apprehension. Just in this way the creation is a place open to God; the distance he sets between him and us is our placement *before* him as objects of his will and knowledge. And *within* creation, turning back to the Damascene, "That place is called God's place that more fully participates in his energy and grace."[86]

VIII

Finally we must register two facts. The one is matter, which takes up and defines space. And the other is consciousness, which takes up no space but nevertheless occurs temporally and so is located in space, in God's case as the space he is for himself.

About matter, we may call on Edwards for the needed insight, for the last time in this context.[87] With material "substances" eliminated, he is free to specify

83. Among contemporary theologians, see above all Wolfhart Pannenberg, *Systematische Theologie* (Göttingen: Vandenhoweck & Ruprecht, 1991), 2:34–59.

84. *Summa theologiae*, i.8.1.

85. Ibid., i.8.3.

86. *The Orthodox Faith*, 13.17–18.

87. For the following, Jenson, *America's Theologian*, 26–32.

"body" as identical with solidity or "resistance" itself, resulting from "the immediate exercise of God's power, causing there to be indefinite resistance in that place where it is."[88] Uniform motion is then "the communication of this resistance, from one part of space to another successively";[89] and accelerated motion, gravity, is basically the same phenomenon as solidity. Thus matter is constituted in a harmony of God's spatial ordinations, of his lively separatings of creatures from himself and each other.

Any creation of the triune God, no matter how different from the actual creation, would be in some way material. That is, in it creatures would be made available to one another as other than one another, in a structure of such presentations set by God's command. We must note this particularly to prepare for the final part of this work, for also the new heaven and the new earth will be God's creatures.

As for consciousness, it is so obvious that it sometimes seems to be a puzzle. But there is nothing to solve: we cannot and should not try to define or analyze consciousness, since we know it better than we know anything by which we might try to explicate it. Thus the fact of consciousness is the same as the fact of being itself, of sheer givenness. This is the—precarious and almost irresistibly misleading—moment of truth in modern idealisms: to be given is necessarily to be given for a consciousness or to be that consciousness.

We can perhaps alleviate some of that temptation. If being is conversation, then consciousness is the sheer fact of being one pole of some personal communion. This is not a definition or derivation, since it is circular. Or we can say: "consciousness" is just a somewhat misleading label for the sheer fact of being a person; and to that fact we will shortly devote an entire chapter.

Assuredly consciousness cannot be derived from anything else, as scientistic ideologues decree it must be. The formulas of biology—or chemistry or physics—cannot "explain" it, since it is not mentioned by any variables that appear in them:[90] all attempts to "reduce" the fact of consciousness to neurological or otherwise biological or chemical events are merely logical blunders of a remarkably crude variety. From these two paragraphs on, we will therefore simply assume—as indeed we have already been doing—that God and we, and whatever other creatures God may designate, are consciousnesses and that we know what we mean when we say that.

---

88. *Scientific and Philosophical Writings*, 215.
89. Ibid., 216.
90. Keith Ward, *God, Chance and Necessity*, 147, surely has it right. Quoting the Darwinian ideologue Richard Dawkins that consciousness is "the most profound mystery facing biology," he responds, "It is more than that. . . . It is a mystery that biology can never solve, because it is not a biological mystery."

PART V

THE CREATURES

EIGHTEEN

The Image of God

I

Explicit attention must now be given—indeed, three chapters of it—to that peculiar creature who appears at the end of the priestly creation narrative and is the chief matter of the following Jahwistic narrative. The tradition has made the one phrase "image of God" a comprehensive rubric under which to discuss the uniqueness of this creature. One may cite for example the classic Lutheran scholastic Johann Gerhard: "Man is made in the image and similitude[1] of God, which distinguishes him from all other corporeal creatures."[2] One might wish some other notion had been given this comprehensive function, but it is too rooted in the tradition now to be displaced.

It was their general appropriation of the "image"-metaphysics of late antiquity that led the fathers to give so much scope to language that indeed appears in Scripture but plays there a quite minor role.[3] Antiquity's speculation began in aesthetics, where "image" denotes the relation of a work of art to its archetype. As noted earlier, to be an image is not to be the archetype, but nor is it to be other than the archetype: the statue of a god is not the god personally[4] but is neverthe-

---

1. Whether "image" and "similitude" are to be distinguished in the Genesis passage here quoted, and whether, if they are, the distinction has any theological weight, is controverted between and among the "Catholic" and "Reformation" positions I will here shortly relativize, and therefore need not further concern us.

2. *Loci theologici* (1610), ii.8.13.

3. In the New Testament, more or less relevant appearances of *eikon* are Romans 8:29; I Corinthians 11:7; 15:49; II Corinthians 3:18; Colossians 3:10; in none of these passages is *eikon* irreplaceable. In the Old Testament, there is really only the Genesis passage itself, that is, to be sure, central for the Scriptures' anthropology if not for its language.

4. This was, of course, in part because the ancient gods were not reliably personal.

less not simply other than the god. Thus the aesthetic relation of imitation, between prototype and ectype, is thought to be a mediation between being and not being, most clearly experienced in the cult; and late antiquity's desperate religious need for just such mediation drafted the notion for heavy metaphysical duty. The gap between pure timeless deity and sheer temporality was to be bridged by entities that as images *of* deity are neither quite timeless nor merely temporal, that are neither being itself nor mere nonbeing but precisely the temporal visibility of the timeless.[5]

Origen constructed the first and paradigmatic Christian system fully to exploit the concept of mediation by image.[6] He envisaged a chain of mediations: the *Logos* is the Image of the Father; other spiritual beings, including human souls and including salvifically the soul of Jesus, are images of the Image;[7] and finally even bodies can be images of souls.[8] The chain of images carries being and revelation downward from God and enables returning knowledge of and love for God.

Origen's vision is splendid, and it can be transposed from the metaphysics of timeless being within which it was conceived, but appropriation to it of the Genesis passage has tended to distort understanding of that passage itself: that we are created "in the image of God" has been presumed to mean that we *resemble* God, in a way analogous to the aesthetic relation between image and archetype.[9] The question about humanity's specific creatureliness then becomes: Wherein do we resemble God that other creatures do not? What characteristics do we share—of course analogously—with God that other creatures do not share with us and that so make up a differentiating resemblance to God?

To this question, the tradition has answered, "We resemble God by being personal subjects as he is." And if that is to be the question, this must surely be the general answer, whatever the passage in Genesis may have meant. So Thomas Aquinas: "Such resemblance to God as can be called an image is found only in rational creatures. . . . That in which rational creatures surpass others is intellect or mind."[10] And indeed we will devote an entire chapter to the remarkable fact that God and we are both personal.

Nevertheless, this is a skewed way of putting the question about human uniqueness. The skew is signaled by a dilemma the traditional answer presents. Subjectivity's indissoluble mutuality of potentiality and actuality compels us to ask: Do we resemble God by the sheer fact of subjectivity or by the qualities in

5. The foundation of this metaphysics is in Plato, *Republic,* 505–604; *Timaeus,* 28–29C; *Cratylus,* 430E–431D. To the development within philosophy, Hans Willms, ΕΙΚΩΝ: *Eine Begriffsgeschichtliche Untersuchung zum Platonismus,* reprinted in *Philo of Alexandria: Four Studies* (New York: Garland, 1987).

6. To the following, Robert W. Jenson, *The Knowledge of Things Hoped For* (New York: Oxford University Press, 1969), 29–37. With detailed reference to the texts.

7. E.g., *Commentary on John,* ii.2–3.

8. E.g., *Commentary on Matthew,* xvi.20.

9. So Thomas Aquinas, *Summa theologiae,* i.93.1: "There is a certain resemblance to God found in the human person, that derives from God as from its exemplar."

10. Ibid., i.93.6.

which subjectivity is fulfilled? That is, do we resemble God by intelligence or by knowledge and wisdom? By the possession of will or by virtues? By the capacity to judge or by right judgments? And neither answer proves fully satisfactory.

Catholic theology has tended to the former answer, Reformation theology to the latter.[11] Gerhard describes the difference: "Many of the older theologians . . . refer 'the image of God . . .' to certain essential faculties of soul, as mind, will, memory, etc.,"[12] whereas he and his fellows hold that "the image of God in the first human was realized justice and sanctity."[13] The issue is certainly undecidable. If we give the Catholic answer, it appears that the very devils must be in God's image;[14] if we give the Reformation answer, it appears that fallen humanity, having lost perfect righteousness, must now be at best partially human[15]—note the past tense in the citation from Gerhard. Nor have combinations and qualifications truly resolved the dilemma.

The problem is not imposed by Scripture's teaching of creation. There, God has indeed made humans "a little lower than gods,[16] and crowned them with glory and honor."[17] But nowhere is it suggested that such rank and glory consist in superiorities either of capacity or of achievement. On the contrary, the psalmist just quoted is a moralizing naturalist who has been contemplating creation as a whole and has wondered: "What are humans that you are mindful of them?" Accordingly, humanity's coronation to "dominion over the works of your hands" appears in the psalm as a gift not predictable from a survey of humanity's characteristics.[18]

11. This disjunction in fact describes the general situation quite well. It may be doubted, however, that sophisticated thinkers on either side would be satisfied with it as a description of their precise positions. Thus Thomas Aquinas taught, *Summa theologiae*, i–ii.85.1, that the way in which human nature was originally "good" had three aspects. First, the inherent properties constituting human nature are good. Second, the human person "has from nature an inclination to virtue." Third, there was the gift of "original righteousness, that was in the first human conjoined with integral human nature." The fall left the first aspect unaffected and obliterated the third. The second, however, is weakened but not undone. That is, there is a longing for the good which is connatural with *both* the sheer capacities of human nature as it subsists in the actual creature and the virtue in which those capacities should be fulfilled. Discussion of this whole complex follows.

12. Gerhard, *Loci*, ii.8.16.

13. Ibid., ii.8.36.

14. Martin Luther, *Ennaratio in Genesis*, 46: "If it is simply these capacities that are the image of God, it must follow that Satan was created in the image of God."

15. Luther's own formulation, *Ennaratio in Genesis*, 47, is certainly liable to this charge: "I understand the image of God so: that Adam then posessed his nature in such a way, that not only did he know God and understand that God is good, but that he lived a truly divine life, that is, that he was without the fear of death or other perils, content with the grace of God." There is surely no item of this description that well suits fallen humanity.

Indeed, in a most ironic reversal, identification of the image of God as actual righteousness exerted strong pressure on Reformation scholastic theologians toward a real semi-Pelagianism. If they were not to say that the image and so our specific humanity is simply gone, then they had to posit a continuing actual righteousness in fallen humans also prior to justification.

16. Here the variously evasive translations must surely be corrected.

17. Psalm 8:5.

18. Psalm 8:5.

II

Evidently we must partly rework the question of humanity's peculiarity among the creatures. But we dare not abandon it, nor even its historical link with Greek reflection—at least not within cultures descended from that reflection.

The Greeks' theology received one of its guiding themes when Socrates began to ponder not the world but himself, impelled by worry whether he was "a monster more nondescript . . . than Typhon, or a living being of more coherent character, sharing by nature in a divine . . . destiny."[19] The human person, thought Socrates, is either somehow devised for eternity or, if a purely temporal being, then one singularly ill-begotten for the situation, a bad ontological joke.

It perhaps was the glimpse of such negative possibilities that more than anything else drew the gospel and Greek reflection together. For also Israel had looked into the abyss of anthropological nihilism: "Who knows whether the human spirit goes upward and the spirit of animals goes downward?"[20]

In Israel, such questioning arose from contemplating the possible negative answer to Ezekiel's question. If human life is otherwise as Israel understood it but no resurrection is foreseen, then eventually it must be acknowledged that "all is vanity," since the dead "have no more reward, and even the memory of them is lost," and this "same fate comes to all, to the righteous and the wicked." An entire book of Israel's Scripture is devoted to probing this nihilism, which it does with a depth and relish that make modern and postmodern efforts seem pusillanimous;[21] the final advice is to enjoy yourself while you live and not fret yourself with aspirations, for "Better a live dog than a dead lion."[22] This author of Ecclesiastes resigns himself. Job instead goes over to the attack on God: "As the cloud fades and vanishes, so those who go down to Sheol do not come up. . . . What [then] are human beings, that you make so much of them? . . . Will you not . . . let me alone? . . . If I sin, how does that hurt you, you watcher of humanity?"[23]

Is there a difference between humans and other animals, that has ontological status? That is, are there grounds in reality for having different hopes for one another than we do for the beasts of the field? And so for treating one another by different standards? On earth, ours seems to be the only species of featherless bipeds[24] and seems also to have certain neurological capacities not found otherwise, though this is not so certain. Are distinctions of that sort the only ones that obtain?

It is of course sometimes urged, in both late antiquity and late modernity, that we need and indeed ought not have different standards for dealing with one another than we do for dealing with other animals. But to treat other animals like

---

19. Plato, *Phaedrus*, 203A.
20. *Ecclesiastes* 3:21.
21. With one footnote to Ecclesiastes, Nietzsche could have spared us a great deal of his rhetoric.
22. Ibid. 9:1–5.
23. Job 7:9–21, translation slightly altered.
24. Bertrand Russell's notorious crack, which I have not tracked down.

humans is also to treat humans like other animals, and in this century we have seen how that actually works out. Anthropological nihilism, which can seem relatively harmless in such jejune manifestations as the "animal rights" movement, has been tested in frightful adult practice.

Germany's National Socialists thought it scientifically established that the Jewish strain degraded the European genetic pool. Setting out to cull their human herd of these threats to its genetic future was only what any responsible farmer would do on such information. They were, indeed, quite explicit in describing the human gene pool as a herd to be genetically improved; moreover, the holocaust of Jews was organized on the basis of an antecedently established program of positive and negative eugenics that in its negative mode had been directed against defectives of indubitably Aryan ethnicity. We should remember also that the sort of science that obtained these results was practiced also in England, Scandinavia, Italy, and the United States, resulting, for example, in the American Planned Parenthood organization and in Scandinavian state-mandated eugenic sterilization programs.

The Nazis' genetic estimates were bizarrely mistaken. But suppose they had not been, suppose it were established with the sort of certainty appropriate to relevant science that Jews—or Norwegians or Bantus or the inhabitants of some one island—*are* on average inferior in intellectual and cultural capability, as any relatively self-contained strain of *homo sapiens* of course might very well be, would the Nazi program then be justified? Perhaps if it were less cruelly managed than by the Nazis? Perhaps if the undesirable strain were simply prevented from reproducing?

Nor can we suppose that the Nazis' anthropological nihilism has become exceptional. Western universities and popular forums have recently been dominated by theoretical nihilisms that are historical and conceptual siblings to Nazi ideology.[25] As for our practice toward one another, Europe and North America have only substituted individualist sentimentality for the Nazis' rationalist husbandry—or perhaps more likely have hidden the latter under the former, for it is noteworthy how often the results of terminations justified sentimentally are the same as those that would result from the ethnic or class prejudices of the terminators.

Abortion on demand is already established in America and parts of Europe— and indeed in postcivilized China there is mandatory abortion—and euthanasia and infanticide on demand apparently soon will be. These terminations serve the individual purposes of the terminators[26]—the individualism is most remarkable when these are simultaneously the terminated—and they are justified by senti-

25. Martin Heidegger is the great forebear of all the French-American deconstructionist and similar movements; his embrace of National Socialism was in no way extrinsic to his philosophy. To all these see now John Milbank, *Theology and Social Theory: Beyond Secular Reason* (Oxford: Blackwell, 1990), 259–325.

26. Except of course as advocated by population-control ideologists; with these we are back with the Nazis.

ment about the inferior life predictable for the terminated or about the superior rights of the terminators. As we destroy crippled horses, so we kill born and unborn children whose mothers for whatever reasons do not think they should raise them, or elders who have lost hope and burden the system or their families, or trauma victims in disheartening coma, or persons simply in pain they do not wish to endure or we do not wish to see them enduring. And there is no reason why we should not, if there is no ontological difference between humans and other animals.[27]

Greece had found a uniquely human dignity in the freedom from natural determinisms possible for citizens in the polity—thereby, of course, excluding those whose place was instead in the economy, at that period women, servants, and children, who could thus acceptably be aborted or exposed at will.[28] But already in Socrates' time the free polities of Greece were disintegrating. The awful question loomed: May we then all be intrinsically no more special than are women and children? Many welcomed the new gospel for just this reason; its proclamation of resurrection, which had answered Israel's version of anthropological despair, created a new community in which also Greece's hope for freedom could be reborn, not least by including the previously excluded.[29] Against the threat of anthropological nihilism, the disillusioned heirs of Athens could find new hope in Jerusalem.

III

The traditional teaching of God's image, whether in Catholic or Protestant modification, is right in seeing the uniqueness of humanity strictly in relation to God; and no other assertion of human uniqueness is likely to be sustainable in the long term. Its difficulties arise from not conceiving humanity's specific relation to God as *itself* our uniqueness, but instead seeking a complex of qualities, supposedly possessed by us and not by other creatures, that are claimed to resemble something in God and so to establish the relation.

In Genesis, the specific relation to God is *as such* the peculiarity attributed to humanity. If we are to seek in the human creature some feature to be called the image of God, this can only be our location in this relation. As the relation is the occurrence of a personal address, our location in it must be the fact of our reply.

That is: our specificity in comparison with the other animals is that we are the ones addressed by God's moral word and so enabled to respond—that we are

27. It is noteworthy that precisely those Western societies at the moment most thoroughly secularized, the Netherlands and the Northwest of the United States, lead in making euthanasia, assisted suicide, etc. acceptable—as also in drug abuse and prostitution.

28. Again, see now Milbank, *Theology*, 326–379.

29. The baptismal formula reported in Galatians 3:28.

called to *pray*. If we will, the odd creature of the sixth day can after all be classified: we are the praying animals.[30] That we have the dispositional property of being apt to hear and speak is of course required for the occurrence of this converse but should not be regarded as itself the human specificity—and indeed, who knows how many sorts of things possess it?

To forestall the objections that will crowd to mind, it should be noted that blasphemies, deliberately stopped ears, mindless oaths, decisions to eschew prayer, and so on are all in their perverse ways prayers, together with the multitudinous prayers of religions that misidentify the addressee. It should further be noted that no responding word is instantaneous with the address to which it responds; if the response of some comes only at the Last Judgment and then is "Curse you, God," just so they are human.

Moreover and most important, on this conception the image of God is not an individual possession. For the actual address by which God takes up his conversation with us begins materially with the foundation of human community in heterosexual desire and reproduction[31] and with the establishment of fundamental human polity;[32] these will be the burdens of the next chapter. The word that creates us human itself establishes our connectedness, and therefore we can respond only *together*; prayer is foundationally corporate.

Who then were Adam and Eve? They were the first hominid group that in whatever form of religion or language used some expression that we might translate "God," as a vocative. Theology need not share the anxious effort to stipulate morphological marks that distinguish prehumans from humans in the evolutionary succession. If there is no ontological difference between us and our hominid progenitors, the effort is pointless; if there is, the division may not coincide with the establishment of our species.

We also must not be misled by a habit of referring to prayer as if it were merely linguistic. We respond to God's address not only in language but with a wide repertoire of gestures and objects. Augustine analyzed ritual action with a formula that became decisive for Western theology: "The word comes to a ritual object, and so there is, . . . as it were, a visible word."[33] In this dictum, Augustine directly instanced only "sacrament," God's ritual word to us, but his analysis must apply equally to "sacrifice," our ritual word to God. The life of humanity before God is an antiphony of God's word to us and our word to God; and the whole antiphony is both audible and "visible."

---

30. For a development of this notion in the specific context of the question about human evolution, see Robert W. Jenson, "The Praying Animal," now in *Essays in Theology of Culture* (Grand Rapids: Eerdmans, 1995), 117–131.

31. Genesis 1:28.

32. With the "tree of the knowledge of good and evil," according to Martin Luther, *Ennaratio in Genesis*, 79: "The church was instituted first [of social structures] that God might thus show . . . that man was concreated for another goal than other creatures." To this, and the only apparently bizarre exegesis, see the next chapter.

33. *In Johannem*, 80.3.

In the usage of this work—which here may not entirely coincide with Augustine's and which we will take this occasion to stipulate—"audible" words are sentences in a language, signs constructed by known or knowable syntactic and semantic rules. In the immediate context, the point about these signs is that they are replaceable following the language's rules: "Jones is wise" can be replaced without loss by "Jones q," if we simply stipulate 'q = ^{df} is wise.' Thus the *body* of the sign, the sheer mark or sound that it is, is not essential and can be eliminated by translation, also within the same natural language. It is convenient to call linguistic signs audible, whatever other sorts of tokens are sometimes used, since our ability to generate sounds with great freedom of modulation[34] makes them the artifacts most immediately available for this use.

There are, however, many and powerful signs that are not items of a language, that are not so rule-governed as to be disposable by translation: processions, handshakes, loving-cups, the blood of slaughtered beasts, images, sexual caresses, and so on. They are seen, felt, tasted, smelled, and indeed also heard. Their common feature is their sheer givenness, their irreplaceability as objects in their own right, and that is to say, their otherness over against us, their *spatiality* as we have just discussed it. Thus at baptism, the verbalized blessings enter the consciousness of participants without remainder; the body of water cannot so accommodate itself and persists in externality. It is natural to call such signs, whatever senses they affect, visible, since sight is our chief sense for space.[35]

Therefore it is by its "visibility" that our converse with one another is *embodied*, that in it each of us presents him or herself to others as an object. The body, we saw in earlier connections, is the person insofar as he or she is available to others. It is by its "visible" aspects that our converse makes us available to one another. We may even say that my body simply is the ensemble visibility of my self-presentation to others. And that is why prayer cannot but be extravagantly embodied, for here we speak to the Creator, whose identity can be acknowledged only by utter availability to him. The associations around the word "sacrifice" are not fortuitous: sacrifice is embodied prayer, and just so sacrifice is self-surrender to another.[36]

Who were Adam and Eve? They were the first hominid group who by ritual action were embodied before God, made personally available to him. Theology need not join debates about whether, for example, the cave paintings were attempts to control the hunt or were thanksgivings for the hunt, were "magic" or "religion." The painters were human, as we may know simply from the fact of

34. This is of course an evolutionary contingency; therefore no theological weight should be placed on the notion of sound as such.

35. The embodiment of discourse here adduced is very probably the same phenomenon as what poststructuralist theory calls text. If that is the case, then the poststructuralist attribution of priority to "text" is a drastic attribution of priority to space over against time. And if that is the case, poststructuralism is the perfect antithesis to Christianity.

36. We should be very cautious about monolithic theories of what sacrifice does, or of how it originated, such as the founders of positivist sociology developed or as René Girard has recently developed.

their ritual. And so they were presumably fallen, and therefore with their rites did indeed try to bind the contingency of the future, to do magic. But by the very act of giving visibility to wishes directed beyond themselves, they nevertheless in fact gave up control and worshipped.

IV

It is time to clarify, insofar as possible, the necessary claim that God initiates humanity by speaking *to* a group of creatures, to make them a community. How are we to conceive this speech?

Once the conversation of God with humanity is under way, his speech to us is not another event than our speech for him to one another. Insofar as God's speech to us is the gospel, this assertion is unproblematic. It is the risen human Jesus whose actuality among us is God's self-introduction to us; and it is the story of his human life from Mary's womb to the Ascension that is the narrative content of that introduction.[37] Just so, God's word in and by the church is not an event other than the continuing antiphony of the church's own narrative in proclamation and prayer. The address by which God summons the humanity of believers is his *torah* itself. And therefore it is not a paranormal phenomenon, though it may of course sometimes include such phenomena: "The Word is near you, on your lips and in your heart, that is, the word of faith that we proclaim."[38]

Nor is this hypostatic oneness of God's word and the community's word new in the post-Resurrection church. On the contrary, that the church's word is God's word is simply an instance of the Resurrection's general concentration of Israel's privileges in Jesus, and its extension of privileges within Israel to the whole body of Christ. It is the gift of prophecy that is here fundamental.

As we have seen, the word that "comes" to the prophet is a word to the prophet him or herself just insofar as it is a word spoken by the prophet to the community, and vice versa. Thus the "servant of the Lord" of II Isaiah is a prophet and just so can be an individual servant in Israel or Israel as servant to the world or eschatologically both at once. Moreover, the claim that the prophet's word comes to the prophet in each case directly from the Lord is simultaneous with the apparently contrary phenomenon of prophetic tradition, such that earlier prophecy becomes the stock of later prophecy, such indeed that a prophet can rework his own prophecy from one occasion to fit a new one.[39] What the prophet hears within his or her community can be the very word she or he is to speak to the community from God; and in the church it is always so.

Those who believe are human precisely by the Lord's word in the church, a word that is on the community's lips and mouth and so on their own. But of course these same persons did not first become human when they believed, and most of humanity has not believed at all. We nevertheless say that all humanity is created

---

37. For somewhat fuller development of this point, pp. 1:133–138.
38. Romans 10:8.
39. E.g., Jeremiah 3:31.

by God's speech. We have therefore to describe a word by which God calls forth humanity outside the boundaries of Israel and the church. Here too we must discern a sort of prophecy and a mutuality of speech in and for and to the community. This work, for reasons that follow, will use the label "mandate" for this word.

To discern this mode of prophecy, we will appropriate, somewhat speculatively, the Reformation's distinction between "gospel" and "law" as modes of God's speech to us, as already described in other context. It was a fundamental contention of Reformation theology and one that provoked little controversy: one "use" of "the law," one purpose and outcome of God's speech to us in the mode of command, is to maintain the world's human community.[40] This "use" is often identified with a natural law "written in the hearts" of all humans.[41] And for Martin Luther himself, whose drastic use of this concept is a chief incitement of the following, to live in the world and to be "under the law" are the same thing; God's rule by the gospel in the church and his rule by the law in the world are then God's two "regimes,"[42] his two ways of establishing his will *ad extra*.[43]

"Law," as we earlier analyzed its distinction from the gospel or other promises, is any address that so opens a future as to lay on the hearer, and so remove from the speaker, some of the conditions of that future's advent. Therefore if we humans address one another at all we speak law. For, as we have seen, every address somehow opens a future, and only rarely and unreliably can address be promise. Since we are finite we can take on ourselves only a tiny part of the conditions for the futures we hold out to others, and not even so reliably; for those we address there can be no firm barrier between, for example, the promise, "I will find you some food," and the law, "Sorry, friend. I did my best. But you know, you really should pull yourself together." As the finitude of someone who says the former more and more intrudes, its actual import must approximate more and more to that of the latter.

Thus all our speech to one another finally somehow obligates; "law" is the necessary discourse of all community. The next obvious question: Whence derives the force of this obligation? "Interrupt your progress at stop signs," you tell me. But if I ask, "Who says so?" is your only response "I say so?" Western social theory since the Renaissance has been a single long effort to find a response that does not involve your saying, "God says so." It must now be accepted that the attempt fails.[44] The West is relearning by bitter experience what every field anthropologist has known all along, that the appearance and perdurance of community depend finally

---

40. So the *Konkordienformel*, vi.1.

41. E.g., ibid., vi.5.

42. *Regimente*.

43. E.g. *Von weltlicher Obrigkeit* (WA xi.250–280), 251.

44. I may now refer to the comprehensive and convincing epistemological demolition of Western social theory in all its branches and successive moments by John Milbank, *Theology*, 9–205. It is most telling that sociologists, political scientists, and "critical theorists" have with one accord responded to this powerful book with silence.

upon the community's religion. Our living together depends upon the presence among us of, as the Chinese used to call it, "the mandate of heaven."[45]

We have seen that all moral action relies on some eternity and that religion is the cultivation of eternity; therefore this result should not be surprising. What must now be said is that insofar as a group *is* drawn to be a civil community, insofar as it does cohere by mutually obligating discourse, it is in fact the one true God who speaks therein, by whatever religion and theology this may be understood,[46] and so through whatever religion and theology the speech may be mediated. We will shortly face the reality of false religion, of idolatry and unbelief; but also the errors and perversion of religion cannot prevent God's creative act by any community's religious discourse.

And so a last point in this section. The question of the relation between initial and "continuing" creation replicates itself: How does our discourse ever get started? Speech presupposes language, but language supposes speech;[47] seemingly there must be a first Speaker, in whose address the distinction of speech and language does not obtain. Were an argument for the existence of God attempted within the framework of thought here represented, it would be on such lines.

We have argued that the speech of God by which he creates us human and our morally obligating mutual speech are the same event. There must indeed have been a first address of God by which he initiated our discourse, but we need not necessarily think of a voice from heaven intruding at some point in the hominid descent. We may think rather of an unpredictable event of initial linguistic community, of the initial exchange of "law," of obligating address, a discourse that was cultic, that like all contingent events occurred by and in the freedom of the Spirit, and that was of the sort that, like the Creation or the Resurrection, can only be understood within the narrative harmony of "the whole series of [God's] acts and designs from eternity to eternity."

The first specifically human event was an initial and—in the sense earlier analyzed—miraculous occurrence of mandate-inspiration. Who, once again, were Adam and Eve? They were the first community of those thus inspired, for whom the word they had for others—if only for each other—was the word that "came" to them, by whatever experience it may have come.

V

If we exist because we are addressed by God and if we have our specific identity as those who respond to God, then we do not possess ourselves. If I exist as I participate in a conversation, then to be myself I must hearken to and respond to

---

45. By thus appropriating a nice phrase, I do not, of course, intend to appropriate the particular political theory that used it.

46. The position taken here seems to me congruent with the teaching of the second Vatican Council on non-Christian religions; see Miikka Ruokanen, *The Catholic Doctrine of Non-Christian Religions according to the Second Vatican Council* (Leiden: E. J. Brill, 1992).

47. The debate between French and German theorists about whether "text" or discourse is prior itself makes the point by its inconclusiveness.

an other than myself. If to be in the image of God is to be embodied before God, then to be specifically human is be available to an other. In the jargons of this century's philosophical and theological anthropology,[48] the human person is "self-transcendent," "a question" directed to her or himself, an "eccentric" entity that can receive itself only as what it is not, a "future-open" entity that now is itself only as it projects what it is not yet.

Such anthropology depends historically on the gospel and the Scriptures; it is Christian or ex-Christian. As Henri de Lubac, the twentieth-century Catholic theological reformer with whom we will very shortly converse at some length, put the contrast: "For the ancient Greeks—and one may say almost the same of all thinkers other than those whose thinking flows from revelation—every nature must find in itself, or in the rest of the cosmos of which it is an integral part, all that it needs for its completion."[49] Just this is what the gospel denies to human nature.

I am *called* to be myself, and am myself in that I respond; but what God can declare, I must ask. I am in that I am detached from what in myself I would have been, to anticipate what I will be; but my future is exactly what I do not possess. Insofar as I speak in this exchange, it is only as a questioner that I can move from what I grasp to what I do not; thus to be human is constituted, from the creature's side, in asking: What is it to be human?

Consider the situation when that question, "What is it to be human?" is asked. There is a subject, an asker. There is that about which the subject asks, some of the subject's objects. And in the case of this question, the subject himself appears among the objects. In asking this question, we somehow take up a vantage outside ourselves to make ourselves our own objects, get beyond ourselves to look back at ourselves. Moreover, this questioning self-transcendence is ineluctable: when we note about ourselves that we transcend ourselves—or when we deny that we do—this act is itself an event of the transcendence we note or deny. We may build as many layers of this dialectic as we like.

If there is a *mystery* in created humanity that is counterpart to the mystery of God, it is such self-transcendence, it is that I am subject of the object I am and object of the subject I am.[50] When the image of God has been understood as a resemblance of the human person to divine personhood, the profounder thinkers have necessarily looked for ways in which individual human personhood

---

48. Wolfhart Pannenberg, *Anthropologie in theologischer Perspektive* (Göttingen: Vandenhoeck & Ruprecht, 1983), provides an exhaustive report and theologically powerful critique and appropriation of this tradition. Pannenberg's work is unlikely to be surpassed soon, and this chapter's general dependence on it is here acknowledged.

49. Henri de Lubac, *The Mystery of the Supernatural*, tr. R. Sheed (New York: Herder & Herder, 1967), 155.

50. In speaking of the reality here called self-transcendence, I use and through the work will use the languages of "subject" and "object," of "self" and what is not "self," of what is "inside" the person and what is "outside" of him or her. These languages are themselves historical products, which constitute a particular family of human self-understandings, which we may identify as modern. To these points and the history, see now Charles Taylor, *Sources of the Self: The Making of the Modern Identity* (Cambridge: Harvard University Press, 1989), 111–198.

resembles God's triunity, for *vestigia trinitatis*, "traces of the Trinity."[51] The one real candidate for the role is self-transcendence.

With all other objects of the subject that I am, my relation to them runs and must run on two distinguishable tracks.[52] I *know* them: I describe, analyze, interpret, and perhaps even explain them away. And I *will* them: I draw, repel and plan for them. The authenticity of either act generally depends on its separation from the other: that I do not claim that to be the case which I only will to be the case, or will only what I know to be anyway so. But when I know and will myself, the two tracks cannot be kept so separate. The person about whom I observe that he is, for example, lazy, is here none other than the one making and abhorring the observation.

Because we are created by a word addressed to us, our knowledge of ourselves and our decisions about ourselves are not separable. My understanding of myself and my choice of myself are not two acts. The line between, in the language of modernity, the "facts" about me and the "values" I exemplify shifts, depending on with which we begin.

Thus we *transcend* ourselves, toward God and each other. In this chapter it is humanity's essential self-transcendence toward God that is our concern. Even when we say that the image of God is nothing but our location in the God-relation itself, we may still inquire how this relation and the other relations of our daily life, including our religious life, are themselves related.

The question has been agitated under various rubrics. But in modernity it has perhaps been most directly and fatefully[53] argued between schools of Roman Catholic theology, as the question about the relation between "nature" and "supernature." We will in the following take this debate as our track.[54]

Augustine's confession, "You have made us for yourself, and our hearts are restless till they find their rest in you,"[55] has been a motto throughout subsequent theological history. Thus Thomas Aquinas taught, in thoroughly Augustinian fashion: "The soul . . . cannot be happy unless it beholds God directly."[56] But he

---

As the occurrence of "self" at the end of the last sentence shows, that we know we speak of ourselves in a certain way, and know something of the history by which we come to do so, does not mean we can decide to speak in some other way. What would that be? There is no transhistorical language, and postmodernity has no language of its own. To be sure, this work, like all serious theology, is metaphysically revisionary: it twists old language and invents new. But one does such things precisely with the language one already has from history; in Neurath's famous image, revisionary metaphysics is always a matter of repairing or remodeling a ship while sailing in her.

51. Foundationally, Augustine in *De trinitate*; e.g., xv.1. See Alfred Schindler, *Wort und Analogie in Augustin's Trinitätslehre* (Tübingen: J. C. B. Mohr, 1956).

52. The following of course depends on the analyses of German transcendetal thinkers, in too general a fashion for specific citations to be useful.

53. One party to the debate set the theological terms for the second Vatican Council, arguably the most important event of church history since the Reformation.

54. In so doing, I follow the lead of the remarkable book by R. R. Reno, *The Ordinary Transformed: An Inquiry into the Christian Vision of Transcendence* (Grand Rapids: Eerdmans, 1995).

55. Augustine, *Confessions*, i.1.

56. *Quodlibitates*, 10–17.

also taught: this "ultimate goal of a rational creature exceeds the capacity of its own nature."[57] Both maxims are surely true. The question is, how are we to join them conceptually and in religious practice?

The Catholic scholasticism of the seventeenth through the nineteenth centuries labored to establish the "gratuity" of the "supernatural," that is, of all that God's grace provides beyond what we can accomplish by "nature," by capacities constitutive of humanity. It wanted to make clear that if God leads us to the supernatural gift of inclusion in his life, to the "vision of God," this is neither owed to nor enabled by anything we are or do as the creatures we are, that is, "naturally." At least in part, the purpose was to meet the Reformation's criticism of late-medieval and Jesuit semi-Pelagianism, of a practical erosion of the formally always accepted doctrine that we are saved by grace alone.

The gratuity of supernatural gifts was to be established, in Henri de Lubac's retrospective account of this theology, "by dissociating the two orders" of nature and supernature. The conceptual effort was to posit "the existence of a natural order that could be . . . self-sufficient," so that if God gives us more than is provided in it, this is not in the train of any teleology established in that order itself. Thus there was supposed to be a merely natural human life, leading to penultimate but in themselves integral fulfillments.[58] And there was also supposed to be a supernatural human life leading to a further gratuitous fulfillment, the "vision of God." The first of these could have been, it was taught, complete in itself without the second.[59] This construction was long an established framework of standard Catholic theology, and was the chiefly accepted assurance that Catholic theology was not semi-Pelagian, as Protestants continued to charge.

A series of French Catholics through the first two-thirds of this century, from Maurice Blondel[60] just before its beginning to de Lubac in the decades before the second Vatican Council, judged that this theology had led to something nearly opposite to its intention. As de Lubac analyzed it, the attempt to describe a purely natural human life with its own natural fulfillment had to make this natural order a double of the supernatural order, complete with a religious aspect. And then, since it is the natural order in which we first find ourselves, the supernatural order becomes in practice "a kind of shadow of that supposed natural order." In our daily life we are to exercise our own powers in pursuit of attainable goals; and this interpretation covers also daily religion.[61] Thus in the daily practice of religion Pelagius ironically triumphs: we are to go about our lives as if we were saved

---

57. *Compendium theologiae*, 144: "Ultimus finis creaturae rationalis facultatem naturae ipsius excedit."

58. *Mystery*, 46.

59. Ibid., 69–70: "It is said that a universe might have existed in which man, though without necessarily excluding any other desire, would have his rational ambitions limited to some lower, purely human beatitude."

60. Maurice Blondel, *Action: Essay on a Critique of Life and a Science of Practice* (1893), tr. O. Blanchette (Notre Dame: University of Notre Dame Press, 1984).

61. *Mystery*, e.g., 46–48.

by our own efforts, even as we know there is another order in which grace is responsible for a mysterious final salvation.

De Lubac does not deny "that a universe might have existed in which man . . . would have his rational ambitions limited to some . . . purely human beatitude." But he insists that this concept of a "pure nature" is meaningful only as a contrary-to-fact abstraction.[62] "In our world as it is, this is not the case. . . . In me, a real and personal human being, in my concrete nature, . . . the 'desire to see God' cannot be permanently frustrated without an essential suffering. . . . My finality . . . expressed by this desire, is inscribed upon my . . . being as it has been put into this universe by God. And by God's will, I now have no other . . . end really assigned to my nature."[63]

It is the chief proposal of this *nouvelle theologie*, as it was called: human nature "as it actually exists, is . . . open to . . . [a] supernatural end." This does not mean that the granting of that end, the attaining of the vision of God, is in any way owed to or promoted by anything I naturally am or do.[64] In the exercise of my natural powers and opportunities I can in no way earn or require that I attain my supernatural end; nevertheless I have no other.[65] The older theology was right in saying that the supernatural is not "owed to nature," but only because the reverse is the case: "Nature . . . owes itself to the supernatural if that supernatural is offered to it. . . . The supernatural . . . is (not) explained by nature; . . . nature . . . is explained . . . by the supernatural" as the latter's dependent presupposition.[66]

Within its limits, we should simply appropriate this teaching. Yet an ambiguity remains, of the very sort over which Western theology of grace has so often come to grief. De Lubac is compelled to say, "The idea of the possible gift presupposes . . . the idea of a certain fundamental and interior aptitude for receiving that gift;"[67] representatives of the Catholic theology he attacked, or of the Reformation, could easily argue that the old hemi-demi-semi-Pelagian temptations are thereby reinstated. Moreover, to deal with the fundamental relation of nature and supernature, de Lubac finally takes refuge in "paradox,"[68] always a danger sign.

The root of these afflictions, and of Western theology's general problem with "grace," can be discerned in a certain presumption de Lubac makes. He must make his own distinction between nature and supernature, and he does so by positing that the "initiative" of God's grace is "double." Then he uses very different lan-

62. One wonders if de Lubac ever realized how close his positions are to those of much Reformation theology, notably those of Karl Barth. To the latter on this point, Robert W. Jenson, *Alpha and Omega* (New York: Thomas Nelson, 1963), 112–140.

63. *Mystery*, 69–70.

64. Ibid., 41.

65. Ibid., 95.

66. Ibid., 123–124.

67. Ibid., 169.

68. Ibid., 217–241.

guage for the two initiatives of grace: the one "brings [man] into being;" the other "calls him."[69]

De Lubac, with most theology Protestant or Catholic, thus presumes that creation is itself effected not by a divine call but by a prior divine act of other sort. God's personal call to us, when it happens, deals with an ontological situation otherwise originated. So long as this presumption is maintained, the problem about nature and grace is insoluble. If we suppose with de Lubac that a human nature itself uncalled is antecedently apt for the call of grace, we will eventually be brought to one or another "semi-Pelagianism." If we suppose, with those de Lubac rebuked, that a nature itself uncalled is antecedently neutral to the call of grace, we will, as de Lubac showed, still be brought to a kind of "semi-Pelagianism," only by a more circuitous route.

We have seen: it is not only our salvation that is accomplished by God's address, but our being as such. Such insight as that of the *nouvelle theologie* will be freed of ambiguity only when this is acknowledged conceptually. We may begin by noting that de Lubac's prime contention, that we are by nature "open " to grace, is one thing and assertion of a natural "aptitude " for grace something else. It is quite possible to assert the first without the second, if both nature and grace are aspects of one conversation conducted by God with us.

"Let there be . . ." and "Christ is risen" are but two utterances of God within one dramatically coherent discourse. A creature who exists by hearing the first is indeed open to the second, in a straightforward way that requires no dithering about "aptitudes." De Lubac wrote: God's "sovereign liberty encloses, surpasses and causes all the bonds of intelligibility that we discover between the creature and its destiny."[70] That is the precise and compendious truth, *if* God's liberty here evoked is that of a speaker conducting a conversation with other persons, a conversation that he conducts coherently and that is in fact from his side coherent.

Thus the openness of nature to grace is *dramatic* openness, the openness of one utterance to another in the dialogue of a story that satisfies the criterion of successful narrative, that its events occur "unpredictably but on account of each other." We are indeed prepared in our very nature for the deifying address of God, because we have a nature only in that we have already been caught up by the dialogue in which this concluding address occurs.

VI

From all the foregoing, we may conclude: *faith* is the true life of humanity, at least short of the Kingdom. Or we may say: if the image of God consists in the action of prayer, it is faith that performs this action.

In such a formulation, we use "faith" in a more relaxed way than often in theological polemics. Both Catholic and Reformation theologians have sometimes

69. Ibid., 106.
70. Ibid., 129.

insisted that faith is sharply to be distinguished from love or hope, though with opposite intent;[71] we here draw no such sharp divisions and propose indeed that in most contexts none should be drawn.[72] Here we use "faith" as the word is used in the ordinary way of the church's proclamation and worship: for the creature's fundamental dependence on the Creator, in the mode of that relation proper to personal creatures. Martin Luther's catechetical explanation of the first commandment provides a classic statement: "To have a God is nothing other than to trust and believe him from the heart. . . . The two are inseparable,[73] faith and God. So whatever you hang your heart on . . . is actually your God."[74]

We should note, to the side of the present argument, that something announces itself in Luther's aphorisms: the possibility that we may hang our hearts on something that cannot bear the weight. What is "actually" *my* God may nevertheless be no God. Faith, as the personal relation of a creature to the Creator, has its whole import from the side of its object; thus the faith in which my humanity terminates may, if it misidentifies its object, undermine itself and my humanity. We will of course return to this negative image of human fulfillment, which in Scripture and the church is called unbelief and idolatry, the primary mode of sin.

We have already seen how in Israel and the church faith came to be understood as the true relation to God. There remains in this chapter only to register the New Testament's identification of faith in God as faith in Christ. John's Gospel is much the most powerful witness.[75] This Gospel is most explicitly of the four written to display how things are because of the Resurrection; thus it both reckons conceptually with Jesus' identity as one of the three in God and most directly of any New Testament document displays the positive outcome of the Ezekiel-question.

As we have noted before, the prototypical event of faith was when "the word of the Lord came to Abraham." In the central account, the Word confronted

---

71. The Reformation has insisted: faith justifies without love, even though love is the necessary outcome of faith. Catholicism has insisted: faith without love does not justify, even though faith is necessary for there to be love. The conceptual possibility of the "without" is assumed by both.

72. Ecumenically, this is of great importance. Thus the Orthodox-Lutheran dialogue in Finland was able to say, *Dialogue between Neighbors*, ed. Honnu T. Kamppuri (Helsinki: Luther-Agricola Society, 1986), 86: "In referring to man's relation to God and salvation, Lutherans tend to stress faith and the life of faith, whereas the Orthodox prefer to stress love. The words 'love' and 'faith' have many different meanings both in the Scriptures and in general usage. Therefore, whenever faith and love are discussed, it is absolutely necessary to note the precise meaning these words carry in the biblical context where they occur. The theological conversations now held in Turku have proved conclusively that the doctrines of both churches on faith and love in salvation are essentially similar."

73. *Gehören zuhaufe.*

74. *Grosser Katechismus*, 2–3.

75. The life-achievement of Rudolf Bultmann, *Das Evangelium des Johannes* (Kritisch-exegetischer Kommentar über das Neue Testament, beg. Heinrich Meyer, 10. Auflage) (Göttingen: Vandenhoeck & Ruprecht, 1941), remains the most powerful modern commentary on such Johannine matters and should be consulted on all passages and matters cited in the following.

Abraham personally. Equivalently as "the Lord" or as "the word of the Lord," he then spoke the promise by which Abraham was to live.[76] And Abraham, it is said, "believed the Lord, and the Lord reckoned it to him as righteousness."[77] Precisely in the line of the history thus begun, in John's Gospel Jesus the Word comes calling for faith, most directly with a straightforward invitation to believe what he says.[78] And those who do so thereby fulfill "the work of God,"[79] and "the will of (the) Father,"[80] that is, what the Old Testament and Paul call righteousness and what John most often calls life.[81]

There is a passage in which almost all parts and connections of John's understanding of faith come together: "Do you not believe that I am in the Father and the Father is in me? . . . Believe me that I am in the Father and the Father in me; but if you do not, then believe me because of the works themselves. Very truly, I tell you, the one who believes in me will also do the works that I do."[82] We will consider John's interpretation of faith in the sequence of this passage.

First comes a statement of *what* faith believes. It is one of a set of statements in John that stipulate propositions as the direct object of "believe": we are to believe "that . . ."[83] These propositions amount to the christological segment of a Nicene doctrine of Trinity: we are to believe that Jesus and the Father are "in" one another, so that what the Son does and says the Father does and says;[84] that Jesus is the Son or "Holy One" or Christ *of* the Father and the Father the one who suits this preposition;[85] that the Father has sent the Son and the Son has come from the Father, and that both are identified by this;[86] that what the Son says is what the Father says;[87] and perhaps most pregnantly, always in the first person, that "I am he."[88]

Therefore faith in the Son is not in John a relation to the Son in abstraction; faith's referent is rather the *homoousia* of the Father and the Son. Often the specified object of faith is thus precisely *the one who sends* the Son.[89] Or again, someone who believes in the Son just so does *not* believe in the Son but in "him who sent" him.[90] Astonishingly: "Believe in God, believe in me."[91]

76. Genesis 15:1–5.

77. Ibid. 15:6.

78. So simply "believe me": 4:21; 5:38; 5:46; 6:30; 8:45–46; 10:37–38; 14:11. Or equivalently we are to believe his "words": 2:22; 4:41; 4:50; 5:47.

79. 6:29.

80. 6:40.

81. E.g., 3:15–16; 6:47; 11:25–26.

82. 14:10–12.

83. *Hoti.*

84. 14:10–11.

85. 1:49; 6:69; 10:37; 11:27.

86. 11:40; 16:27; 17:8.

87. 5:24; nagatively, 5:38.

88. 8:24; 13:19.

89. 4:53.

90. 12:44.

91. 14:1.

Our paradigm passage next stipulates the ground of such belief. Primally, this is that we believe what the incarnate Word says: "Believe me . . ." or "Believe my words . . ."[92] But there are also "the works";[93] these are done as "signs" by which his "glory" is revealed,[94] and they too evoke faith.

Faith with the latter basis is often, as here, presented as somehow a lesser mode of faith: those are more blessed "who have not seen and yet have come to believe,"[95] and it is a test of faith not to demand "signs and wonders."[96] Yet the signs are in fact performed and do evoke faith.[97] This is due to the trinitarian relation, for the glory revealed in the signs is the glory the Son has with the Father eternally.[98]

The summarizing characterization of someone who believes that the Father and the Son are one, whether because of the Son's words or because of his works, is that such a person believes "in" the Son. The prepositional phrase is John's most common use of "believe."[99] It is interchangeable with "believe in his name."[100] And such belief is a decidedly *personal* relation to the Son: to believe in the Son and to "come to" the Son are the same thing.[101]

Finally on the path of our paradigm passage, the signs of divine glory will be done also by those who believe. Faith as faith "in" Christ, as coming to him, is just so a unitive and therein transforming relation: those who "believe in the light . . . become children of light."[102] The culminating statement of John's understanding of faith does not happen to use the word "faith": "The glory that you have given me I have given them, so that they may be one, as we are one. I in them and you in me, that they may become completely one, so that the world may know that you have sent me and have loved them even as you have loved me."[103]

We come to the last point here to be noted, the only one that does not directly appear in our paradigm passage: this personally unifying relation to the Son, belief "in" the Son or "in his name," is identical with belief taken absolutely.[104] To believe in the way that constitutes a right relation to God is to believe that the Son is in the Father and the Father in him, and therein to be in the Son and the Father as the Father and the Son are in one another.

---

92. E.g., 4:21; 5:38; 8:45–46; 10:37–38; 14:11.
93. 10:37–38; 14:12.
94. 2:11; 2:23.
95. 20:29.
96. 4:48.
97. 2:11.
98. 17:5.
99. E.g., 7:5; 7:31; 3:36; 9:35–37; 11:25–26; 12:ll.
100. E.g., 1:12.
101. 6:35.
102. 11:36.
103. 17:22–23.
104. Bultmann, *Johannes*, 31, n. 3: "*Pisteuein* used absolutely is in John consistently equivalent with *pisteuein eis to onoma autou* (1:12 etc.), *eis auton* (2:11 etc.), *eis ton houion* (3:36 etc.)." For proof of these equivalencies Bultmann cites 3:18; 4:39–41; 11:40–42; 12:37–39; 16:30–31. For instances of "believe" absolutely yet clearly christologically, 10:25–26; 11:15; 11:40.

And that is the final achievement of "the image of God." We are counterparts of God as we believe in the Resurrection, and so in the *homoousia* of Jesus and his Father. We are counterparts of the Father as we find ourselves in the Son in whom the Father finds himself; as de Lubac said, human creatures have no other "finality" than this, no other purpose or fulfillment. Obviously, it is an equivalent proposition: the final specification of "the image of God" is *love*. As Jesus said, "the greatest and first commandment" is to "love the Lord your God with all your heart, and with all your soul and with all your mind."[105]

---

105. Matthew 22:34–40parr.

NINETEEN

Politics and Sex

I

Human being is self-transcendence from and to God and from and to one another. How does the latter occur?

The decisive point was developed with unprecedented power by Karl Barth[1]—if with some unreliable concepts.[2] God's address to us is the Son, who is the human person Jesus of Nazareth. To receive myself from God and be directed toward him is therefore to receive myself from and be directed toward a fellow human. And it is to receive myself from and be directed toward a human person who precisely to be himself brings others with him. For Jesus as the Son is the man whose whole existence is his life for others: "What concerns him, and that totally and exclusively, is the . . . other person precisely as such. . . . For this other is . . . the object of the saving work in the doing of which he himself exists."[3]

We may simply adopt Karl Barth's conclusion: "The humanity of every person consists in the determination of his or her being as being-together with the fellow-human."[4] To view human being "without the fellow-human" is to miss it altogether,[5] for "a human without the fellow-human . . . would *eo ipso* be alien to the man Jesus." and so be precisely inhuman.[6]

---

1. *Kirchliche Dogmatik*, (Zollikon-Zürich: Evangelischer Verlag, 1932–1968), III/2:242–344.

2. Barth himself calls attention to the way in which his thinking in this matter is dominated by his concepts of image-reflection-analogy; Ibid., 384–385. Barth's general reliance on this uncontrollable language may be surrogate for an undeveloped doctrine of the Spirit; to the latter Robert W. Jenson, "You Wonder Where the Spirit Went," *Pro Ecclesia* 2 (1993):296–304. Since Barth's eschatology is strictly a matter of the revelation of what is already real, what is in fact anticipated in the Spirit is understood as instead reflected from its protological givenness.

3. Ibid., 249.

4. Ibid., 290.

5. Ibid., 270.

6. Ibid., 271.

Or we may put it so, more in the language of the previous chapter: the person as whom God is there for us, to evoke and be the object of our self-transcendence, is the crucified and risen Jesus of Nazareth. Therefore in that we make a community with God, we make a human community as those for whom this Jesus died and for whom he now lives. If I depend upon the address of God, and am human in that I respond, just so I depend upon a communal human address and am human in that I respond.

There is of course the alternative account Barth rejects: the posit that human persons are self-transcendent by themselves. This account would hardly seem at all plausible except as we fear the account just given, except as we do not want our freedom to depend on God and each other. It turns the relational event into an occult entity and claims self-transcendence as the private possession of the individual: I myself in myself possess a "power"—whatever that means—to go beyond myself. Modernity is constituted by boldness in making this claim[7] and postmodernity by despairing of it while still living according to it. But modernity did not create the claim itself from nothing; in the line of history here mostly considered, it began when Socrates identified his direction to eternity with his essential self, the "soul."[8]

We may perhaps indulge in some phenomenological recapitulation of the relations just posited. You out there, some of my objects, are yourselves—objectively!—subjects. As such, you in turn have me, quite straightforwardly, for your object. The same address and response by which we are thus subjects for each other establishes a shared world, a reality between us as the total referent of our discourse, to be an objective space in which we meet. I come to share your objects, one of which I am—as of course you come to share mine, one of which you are.

My self-transcendence, my location outside and ahead of myself, is thus simply the fact that I share your exteriority to me and the possibilities this otherness poses to me. If I can see myself, it is because I see also from your focus of regard; if I can reform myself, it is because I am not captive to my judgments alone; if I can interpret myself, it is because I share your and others' relation to myself. The structure of our mutuality is constitutive of my personhood.

Modernity's claim to reified self-transcendence must of course deny the epistemic relations just asserted. So John Locke: "We may as rationally hope to see with other Mens Eyes, as to know by other Mens Understandings. So much as we our selves consider and comprehend of Truth and Reason, so much we possess of real and true knowledge."[9] The Enlightenment's empty individualism of freedom must be an individualism of knowledge as well. Here is another place where modernity has undercut itself, for on the basis of such "empiricism" anything like self-*knowledge* must become impossible, and self-transcendence must

---

7. Immanuel Kant is surely the great spokesman of modernity also in this connection.
8. Most interestingly, from my point of view, in the *Symposium*.
9. *An Essay concerning Human Understanding*, 1.4.23.

become empty self-questioning and arbitrary self-assertion, that is, what post-modernity supposes it to be.

How, next, is the person as object identical with the person as subject, to be recognized by the subject as him or herself? Only in that you, insofar as you have me as an object, know this object as a subject, so that you address me as identically subject and object. As you then share with me your response to me, as you answer my address, I have my self as *my* self, as the object identical with myself that does this.

But that means that *death* is the key. For while I live I cannot see my life whole, and so also cannot see the whole that would be constituted in the full coincidence of the subject I am with the object I see I am. I cannot do this because only when I had died could I look back at my life as a whole, but "where death is I am not." There is the story of my life, in which it is decided who I am that has this life, only when the moving finger has written a last line; but then I am no longer there to read it. My life as such is there for me only in memory, and the moment of my death cannot be an item of my memory.

Only for others will I be a shaped and finished whole, when I have died. Therefore I have possible shape and wholeness for myself only insofar as others already now take me for their object, thereby anticipating my completed objectivity, and as they then communicate with me in this reflection. Only in conversation do I occupy a position from which to interpret my life as a coherent whole, a position from which as a living subject I can anticipate the dead object I will be, and so from which I can grasp the identity of the I that does this with the life I remember.

Again a negative possibility shows itself. I am dependent on others for the communication in which I can interpret my life as a possibly coherent whole, in which indeed I can grasp my subjective identity with my objectively remembered life. As things stand, this dependence must inevitably by experienced as a threat, the very threat that makes us flee to the individualist account of human self-transcendence.

For others may so address me as to bind me to their anticipation of my completed self, the object I will be when I am dead, and so close my freedom. Our discourse will then be the deadly chatter of a mass society. Or others may lie to me about myself and so "free" me to arbitrary self-invention. Our discourse will then be the mutual cosetting of moral atoms. Within late modernity and postmodernity these two catastrophes coincide; we call the coincidence fascism.

I fear manipulation and lies from others because I suspect that others are themselves manipulated and lied to, depersonalized and adrift. I suspect this precisely because I have been manipulating and lying to them. How this circle of alienated collectivity began to turn is the mystery of "original sin."[10] We can give no reason why human discourse should have begun so. But once the circle is turning it clearly cannot stop, unless something intervenes.

10. Pp. 148–152.

II

It is time to return to concrete positions already won and begin again from them. We are the praying animals; just so we are essentially communal animals. Because the very call that creates us summons us toward the God who calls, our hearts are indeed, as Augustine said, ontologically *restless*: we can each of us never find him or herself in the self she or he already is—though we can of course try, which is yet a mode of sin.

If I am created by a word from beyond me, I must hearken to what is beyond me, and then I hear not only God but you. Or rather, appropriating results of the previous chapter, I hear you *in* hearing God: in the church I hear God's gospel from the mouth of his witnesses; and in the world I hear God's law from the mouth even of those of his counterparts who do not rightly identify him. If I pray, and pray with ritual embodiment, I just thereby become publicly available and so available to you, even should my prayer itself be misaddressed. We will develop resultant political theory in conversation with the chief work of Christian politics to date, the *De civitate Dei* of St. Augustine.[11]

Augustine's theory posits a great division: there is the "heavenly polity"[12] and there are "earthly" polities. The heavenly polity, whose interim earthly reality is the church, is the original polity, and earthly polities are stopgaps in view of sin.[13] "In the first man . . . the foundations were laid, with respect to the human race, of two societies or polities," the one by Adam's creation, the other in view of his fall.[14] Indeed, the true polity was created before humanity, with angels for its citizens, and was thus antecedently waiting to receive us.[15] The principle of the earthly polity is violence, the necessary but self-contradictory securing of peace by war,[16] yet this earthly polity also is God's instrument.[17]

An eminent Augustinian, Martin Luther, varied Augustine's theory in illuminating fashion. According to his exegesis of Genesis, the community of the church is coeval with and indeed constitutive of humanity. The church was founded, according to Luther's fancy, in Paradise[18] when God arbitrarily picked

---

11. A good summary of post–World War II interpretation of Augustine's theology of politics is provided by Miikka Ruokanen, "Augustin und Luther über die Theologie der Politik," *Kerygma und Dogma* 34 (1988):22–41. Ruokanen's presentation is, in my judgment, marred in one respect: after noting that the *civitas Dei* is not identical with the church, he thereafter tacitly assumes that it simply is not the church. This gives his illuminating insistence that the contrast of *civitas Dei* and *civitas terrena* is eschatologically based a somewhat more transcendental flavor than seems to me quite right.

12. Augustine of course writes of the *civitas*, which is conventionally translated "city," as in the usual title for translations of *De civitate Dei*. But *civitas* is here the equivalent of the Greek *polis*, and for political-theoretical contexts English has anglicized the Greek rather than the Latin.

13. E.g., *De civitate Dei*, xiv.1.

14. Ibid., xii.27.

15. The initial citizens of the heavenly city are the angels, created on the first day; ibid., xi.9.

16. E.g., ibid., xv.4.

17. Ibid., v.33: "God is the author and giver of (the earthly polity's) felicity; . . . he himself grants earthly rule, whether to the good or to the bad."

18. *Ennaratio in Genesis* (WA 42), 79.

a tree[19] as "the temple and altar" by relation to which humanity would have opportunity to hear, obey, and give thanks for God's word—or not.[20] "The economy" appears only later when there are two to divide labor.[21] Thus Luther sets the church within what would be the classic pairing of polity and economy and makes the church occupy the place of an original polity. Polities other than the church, in which God rules by "law" and associated compulsion, appear only in the situation of sin.

Returning to Augustine himself, the ultimate good, insofar as it is not simply the person of God, is *peace*.[22] Augustine provides a general definition of peace as "the tranquility of order:"[23] unforced mutual service between beings ordered to each other by their differences, whether between Creator and creature, between spiritual creatures and corporeal, or between those differently gifted or placed within the community of spiritual creatures. The authentic peace of a human polity is then "the ordered concord of citizens, constituted in leading and obeying,"[24] a leading and obeying that are precisely not "dominion" or "servitude."[25] And the peace of the original and final polity, which in its earthly journey and struggle is the church, is "the perfectly ordered and concorded society constituted in enjoying God and one another in God."[26]

Thus the two actual polities are ordered by differing objects of love: "Two loves make the two polities, love of self the earthly polity . . . love of God the heavenly."[27] Communal love of God is actual as right worship, in which the true polity "adheres" to God, whether now by faith or eternally by sight.[28] Love of self has communal form as "lust for dominion" (*libido dominandi*):" for a *society* to love itself first is to seek to turn other societies to its own service. Just so such a society is determined also in its own life by this passion: "Since what it desires is to rule . . . it is itself ruled by this lust for rule."[29] In the heavenly polity, citizens mutually serve in love; the earthly polity is necessarily dominated by its "princes," those in whom the constitutive *libido dominandi* is most powerful.[30]

If what unites citizens is love of the one God of all, they are just so bound together in love; they "enjoy . . . one another in God." If they have no such

19. According to Luther, the name "tree of the knowledge of good and evil" was given by Moses only after the fact, "on account of the . . . outcome"; ibid., 72.

20. Ibid.

21. Ibid., 79.

22. *De civitate Dei*, xix.11: "Fines bonorum nostrorum . . . pacem."

23. *Tranquillitas ordinis*, a lovely phrase.

24. Ibid., xix.13: "Pax civitatis, ordinata imperandi atque obediende concordia civium."

25. Ibid., xix.15: God intended humans to have dominion over the "beasts, not one another."

26. Ibid., xix.13: "Pax coelestis Civitatis, ordinatissima et concordissima societas fruendi Deo et invicem in Deo. Pax omnium rerum, tranquillitas ordinis."

27. Ibid., xiv.28.

28. Ibid., xix.27.

29. Ibid., Praefatio.

30. Ibid., xiv.28: "Illa in principibus eius . . . dominandi libido dominatur; in hac serviunt invicem in caritate."

encompassing love, there is no such transcendent basis for community;[31] self-loving persons can only be a "multitude . . . associated by rational consent" jointly to pursue particular goods,[32] the universal good not being available. If we are isolated in self-love, we can together be a polity—or a sort of polity—only by contract, as modern theory will name Augustine's "rational consent"; and in a state that understands itself so, those whose own self-love is strongest will inevitably dominate.[33] The earthly polity, it seems, is a sort of substitute for the true polity; it is the best that can be provided without common worship of the one God.

Augustine adopts a definition cited by Cicero from Scipio, thus co-opting great Roman authorities, that for a collectivity to be an authentic polity, a *res publica* (our "republic"), it must be a *res populi*.[34] It is always hard to translate *res* in a given context. "Thing" is the first and usually misleading dictionary entry, but the current idiom that speaks of an individual or group "doing its thing" in fact suggests itself here. We may translate Scipio's requirement: a true "public thing" must be "a *people's* thing," its own defining project and passion.

Scipio next defines "a people:" it is a "fellowship of . . . persons associated by consent in law." And finally, Scipio sets a limiting condition for "consent in law": this cannot occur except where there is antecedent "justice." It is justice that makes social contract a consent "in law," and justice is therefore not itself constituted by the procedure of contract or by the positive law established in contract.[35] For social consent to constitute a true polity, the consent must already be itself righteous in its content, a consent in and to *antecedently* practiced justice.

Rome, says Augustine, was therefore by its own strict definition never a true polity, because its state was never the project of a "people" so defined, of an intrinsically just community.[36] Only on the less stringent definition, which allows a "people" to be constituted not in justice but merely by contract jointly to pursue certain common interests, was there ever a Roman people and so a Roman republic.[37]

If we follow Augustine we will understand politics as the joint moral deliberation of a community, the process of its consenting in justice or at second best to a formal simulacrum of justice. There are ethical reasonings and choices to be made not only by individuals but antecedently by communities. Thus we will,

---

31. Ibid., xix.23; "Ubi ergo non est ista iustitia, profecto non est coetus hominum iuris consensu."

32. Ibid., xix.24: "Coetus multitudinis rationalis, rerum quas diligit concordi communione sociatus."

33. All the efforts of "liberal" theory, in current discussion most notably John Rawls, *A Theory of Justice* (Cambridge: Belknap Press, 1971), fail to repress this insight.

34. Ibid., ii.21; xix.21.

35. Ibid., xix.21: "Populum enim esse devinivit coetum multitudinis, iuris consensu et utilitatis communione sociatum. Quid autem dicat iuris consensum, disputando explicat; per hoc ostendens geri sine iustitia non posse rempublicam: ubi ergo iustitia vera non est, nec ius potest esse."

36. Ibid., xix.21. That the Roman people were never united by virtue, is the detailed, not to say wearisome, burden of the works first several books.

37. Ibid., xix.23–24.

for example, shortly urge that sexuality must be socialized as monogamy. But if monogamy is universally mandatory, it is far from universally inevitable; in an actual society its desirability may have to be argued and its establishment agreed and enforced. The effort, moreover, may fail. Politics are the process of such deliberation.

The substance of communal morality is a specific discourse, in which the agreements and disagreements are between those who assert and those who deny propositions of the form "Our community should in future . . ." Politics, in the original and only useful acceptation of the word, is a community's argument with itself about what to teach in schools, about the proper division of wealth, about what punishment fits what crime, about when if ever to use force with other communities and what force to allow ourselves, and so on. The polity is the forum in which such discourse can occur and terminate in decision, whether this is a meeting of all citizens, a monarch's bed, a representative assembly, a club of optimates, or whatever.

That is to say, politics are the process of that mutual moral address by which, as we saw earlier, God speaks to us to initiate and sustain humanity. The polity is nothing less than the public space in which God calls us to be human in that we call each other to come together in justice. To be sure, if we are to say so glorious a thing of "politics," we must indeed use the word strictly in the "original acceptation." It is itself a chief symptom of late and postmodern societies' debility, and of the distortion of humanity within them, that we are likely to use the word very differently.

There can be a collective of persons and a state apparatus with little real politics. An absolute ruler may repress deliberation of what *ought* to be done, even with himself, follow precedent, whim, ideology or pure interest, and manage affairs for a time and after a fashion—recent evidence that it can only be for a time and after a fashion is provided by the collapse of the Stalinist empire.[38] An isolated tribal community may live with little awareness that it reasons morally until an outer world poses questions that its customs do not master. A ruling class, united by premoral interest, may live as innocently as any tribe, again until upset from outside itself.

Indeed, the specifically modern societies that began in hope for the greatest possible expansion of politics, that is, for democracy, seem now driven to a sort of neotribal existence.[39] The present near extinction of politics in America, the most structurally modern of nations, is often noted: the multifarious and empowered citizen assemblies of the time before its Civil War, and the citizen-amateur representatives and higher officials for which its federal and state constitutions were designed, are scarcely a memory. What Americans are likely now to call politics is in fact the functioning of an almost entirely depoliticized col-

---

38. Machiavelli will always prove right in the short term and wrong in the long term.

39. Alisdair MacIntyre, *After Virtue* (Notre Dame: University of Notre Dame Press, 1984), 245: "The barbarians are not waiting beyond the frontiers; they have already been governing us for quite some time."

lectivity and state: the manipulation of a mass of petitioners and their interests by professional managers of affairs. If there is now a functioning American polity, it is the very tight oligarchy of the federal judges.[40]

Also in a collective whose communal moral discourse is rare or repressed, the managers will of course need to weigh the various *interests* of the multitude; even pure dictatorships cannot long function at clear cross-purposes with dominant mass wants. In a modern nation it is, for example, in the interest of investors that inflation be suppressed and of borrowers that it have some latitude, and those who have power in such a nation must weigh these opposing interests. But it is only in that somewhere in the community such interests are *argued* as possible *goods*, and not merely weighed as interests, that there is a functioning polity.[41]

The proposition that politics are the process of moral discourse by which community is created and sustained is true generally and not just of the church. We have already investigated how God's creating address occurs in the various "public things" amid which the church finds herself. We therefore say with Augustine that it finally is God who establishes and rules also earthly polities. Is there anything more discriminating to say?

Augustine is not here so helpful as we might wish. He says that since earthly polities are established by contract to seek particular goods, their worth will be determined by what goods these are;[42] thus some earthly polities will be superior to others. A people that does not worship the true God "nevertheless loves the peace proper to it, and this peace is not to be denigrated."[43] Moreover, believers must serve earthly polities when they can, for the sake of "human society," which they are not allowed to "desert."[44] Apparently the heavenly polity and earthly polities are not in Augustine's understanding quite so antithetically related as he sometimes seems to say.

Indeed, Augustine even says that the old Roman virtues were gifts of God for the good of his creation.[45] The *libido dominandi* itself can be a substitute for justice: to preserve the Roman Empire from the ills that destroyed its predecessors, and so to benefit his creation, God gave Rome individuals who served the glory of Rome because they identified their own glory with Rome's, and so "for

40. It seems actually to be the case that politics, in the proper acceptation of the word, are now legally *forbidden* to representative assemblies or elected officials, for cumulative decisions of the supreme and appellate courts have in advance defined as "unconstitutional" all legislation or regulation with moral content; Russell Hittinger, "A Crisis of Legitimacy," *First Things*, no. 67 (November, 1996):25–29.

41. Thus in the countries of Eastern Europe under the Soviet system, politics had in fact emigrated from the state to various locations that current discussion denotes together as "civil society." This "civil society" was in fact the polity, and has since been unveiled as such.

42. Ibid., xix.24.

43. Ibid., xix.26.

44. Ibid., xix.6.

45. E.g., ibid., xv.4.

this one vice, the love of honor," eschewed economic greed and other socially more destructive vices.[46]

We may in general say that Augustine identifies the political problem as the problem of the center, of some common object of "love." A people must be gathered by something, if there is to be any sort of "consent." The question is: By what? A sort of hierarchy of polities appears, ranked by what is at their center.

III

In Augustine's analysis, the only polity fully satisfying the earthly polity's own definition of authenticity is that "republic whose founder and governor is Christ," which in this age is the church.[47] Contrary, however, to what modern prejudice may lead us to expect, Augustine does not then describe the church as a theocracy, a polity ruled by priests or shamans. Indeed, it seems to be Augustine's understanding that because the true polity's center is God in Christ, it otherwise needs no "dominating" figures at all. Its politics, insofar as Augustine here describes them, are a mutuality of service in which rankings and differentiations rest upon and further mutual justice and are simply "enjoyed" in "tranquility."

If we try to characterize Augustine's true polity in more modern terms, the language cannot be avoided: it is an organic democracy. In it moral discourse is sustained mutually by persons enjoying varying gifts and offices, between whom what elsewhere would be dominion and servitude has no such tone. It is clear what text Augustine has always in mind: "Among the gentiles those whom they recognize as their rulers lord it over them. . . . But it is not so among you; but whoever wishes to become great among you must be your servant."[48]

In the heavenly polity, Jeremiah's prophecy has been fulfilled from before the creation: "No longer shall they . . . say to each other, 'Know the Lord,' for they all know me, from the least of them to the greatest."[49] The heavenly polity is the community prophesied by Joel, in which all are prophets,[50] as that community preexists in the apocalyptic seers' heaven and as it is temporally anticipated in Israel and the church. The baptized have, in the vision of Hebrews, already come "to the city of the living God, the heavenly Jerusalem."[51]

Democracy as actual organically structured sovereignty of the people would be the most political of communities and the most communal of polities. For apart from public moral deliberation no *demos* exists to be sovereign. "The people" as such do not exist as a personal agent except insofar as they are joined in mutual ascertainment of the good, for the people as such have no common interest and

46. Ibid., v.13.
47. Ibid., ii.21.
48. Mark 10:42–43parr.
49. Jeremiah 31:34.
50. Joel 2:28–29.
51. Hebrews 12:22–23.

so *can* be joined only by a common good. It is only as deliberation transforms interests into convictions and commitments that an eventual general consensus or vote can manifest one sovereign will of the people.

Such free deliberation is not dangerous to the position of Christ within his church but is always very dangerous to representatives and officials. Would-be democracies, including the temporally struggling church, are therefore always tempted to avoid the more vital and so more upsetting sorts of public moral discourse by, with Rousseau,[52] positing a premoral "will of the people" that obtains prior to discourse and needs only to be uncovered, whether by a divinatory leader gifted to know and enforce it or by a mechanistic counting device. Late modern history has sufficiently demonstrated the disastrous character of such totalitarian democracy. It may of course be doubted that the temptation can be resisted, that an actual democracy "can long endure" on this earth.

We have leaped from the best to the worst of polities, both now called democracy. Subsequent to the true polity in Augustine's own interpretation is the republic constituted by contract to pursue particular goods and just so ruled by one sort or another of dominant persons. The religion and structure of such a polity are paired. As the objects of such a polity's passion are creatures, so it is permanently tempted to idolatry.[53] As its love is foundationally for itself, so it is tempted to recruit divine help for earthly dominion, reversing the true order: "The good use the world in order to enjoy God; evil persons on the contrary try to use God in order to enjoy the world."[54] And as it pursues earthly goods that are plural, so it is led to the formal structure of idolatry, that is, polytheism.[55]

Nevertheless, despite this theologically baleful assessment, Augustine, as we have seen, does not think all earthly polities are equally distant from justice or true religion. Beyond an obvious admiration for the ancient virtues of his own republic, he does not, however, provide much by which to measure the distances. The next few paragraphs state a theory that cannot be fathered on Augustine.[56] The most powerful antecedent to these paragraphs, and their closest parallel, are analyses provided by Paul Tillich in early essays, written in the turmoil of the Weimar Republic, here acknowledged once for all and not cited in detail.[57]

It follows from the positions developed in this and previous chapters: a polity is the context of divine mandate. It is the forum of that word by which the community's humanity and that of its members is created. The goodness of a polity, we may suggest, is its openness to this analogue of prophecy.

A polity, we have said, is the arena in which a community's ethics are done, in which the question is posed, with possibility of effective decision: What *ought*

52. Esp. Jean Jacques Rousseau, *Du contrat social*, ed. Ronald Grimsley (Oxford: Clarendon Press, 1972).

53. Ibid., xiv.28.

54. Ibid., xv.7.

55. Ibid., iv.

56. As of course much of the foregoing may be illegitimately fathered on him.

57. *Political Expectation*, tr. and ed. James Luther Adams, and Victor Nuovo (New York: Harper and Row, 1971).

our community do about . . . ? For long stretches of a community's life, its life may be wholly guided by established maxims and its moral reflection therefore not apparently prophetic. But the facts of temporality and other peoples make it certain that new moral knowledge and understanding will some day be needed— as when medical technology continuously reduces the term of fetal viability, demanding of liberal America that it face facts which could once be suppressed and with which it seems unable now to deal. Then the community will spin in a moral void unless it hearkens to the mandating bite of its own moral discourse, to the address of God that is the spring and content of its own moral deliberation.

There are what may be called prepolitical questions, consensus in which is presupposed by the very decision-procedures that constitute a polity, alike whether these are elaborate republican legal procedures or the arbitration of a chieftain between combatants. Such questions demand decision about who in fact is a member of the polity, as does, for example, the question of involuntary or problematically voluntary "euthanasia." And they therefore cannot themselves be politically adjudicated; they require a word of mandate.

A polity is good insofar as it provides for the speaking of such mandates, for it to be said among the people, "This is the will of heaven." A society's religion marks the spot where this happens. This is by no means a general approbation of religion. Nearly all religions are straightforwardly fictitious—there is, thank the true God, no Moloch or Great Goddess—and all religion, Jewish and Christian included, is used by its devotees to evade and drown out the word from God by which it is called. As already promised, we will return to these points. But even those who cry, "Lord Moloch . . ." cannot evade thereby confronting the Lord. They risk hearing, "You called? I am the Lord. But my name is not Moloch and I do not savor the smoke of your children." The Lord's word in such an evil society includes condemnation; but even in that case, so long as the society lives it will be from this word that it lives.

If we are to rank polities, therefore, we will say that the better polity is the one that, first, is gathered by a less wicked religion; and that, second, more cultivates its community's religion while less recruiting it to the *libido dominandi*. A good polity is one that institutionalizes space for divine mandates' challenge precisely to its own established consensus.

The evaluative principle here offered thus turns out[58] to be a generalization of a traditional Western catholic teaching about the relation of "church and state." But by being made applicable to all polities, simply as they are polities, the doctrine ceases to be interpretable merely as a proposition about polities that happen to have the church in their midst and is revealed as a claim about what makes a collective a polity in the first place. The generalization is sustained by the sort of argument just practiced, that locates polity in the conversation between the triune God and his counterpart creatures, a conversation always in progress whether acknowledged or not.

58. To my surprise.

Finally, in Augustine's language a possibility shows itself more horrid than any he himself could envision. He speaks of earthly polity as constituted in *coetus rationalis*, which might be translated "rational contract." The word "contract" is of course the fateful word of modern social theory; it signals among other things the notion of a polity with some *thing* rather than some *one* at its center, constituted sheerly in impersonal procedures of consent. We have arrived yet again at the great modern antagonist of the doctrine of creation, mechanism.

The United States was in position to make the experiment. James Madison and his fellow political engineers believed that "the great improvements" that "the science of politics . . . has received"[59] enabled construction of a state machinery that would produce the blessings of justice and liberty[60] independently of the justice and devotion to freedom of those who are the polity's cogs and levers. By principles analogous to the Newtonian laws of action and reaction, they set out to balance interest against interest and center of power against center of power[61] in a system that should be an analogy of the cosmos supposedly described by Newton. They were not such mechanists as to think that the polity-machine would run indefinitely without virtue in the people; something very like Augustine's "justice" was presupposed. But they sought to depersonalize the state itself.[62]

Only the most perspicacious analysts[63] then suspected what would come of this: the closing of the polity to the moral discourse that is its own proper matter and basis. But that was the inevitable outcome, for only persons speaking not for interests but for their own moral judgment can conduct authentic moral discourse; "representatives" of other persons who are not there and functionaries in office can only conduct a weighing of interests. Thus the American people's moral discourse was first exiled to a sort of surrogate polity, an alternative public sphere of reform movements and educational and charitable enterprises created by evangelical Protestantism,[64] and then starved also in that exile, as the state in the twentieth century has steadily attacked the legitimacy and power of the civil society.

Here is the place where we must notice the modern consort of the polity, the separately describable economy. Persons are economic agents insofar as their mutual agency is *not* guided by decision about what should be done but rather by an indeed quasi-Newtonian balancing of interests. Let us suppose, for example, that a municipality has in one way or another come to political decision about reducing the level of pollution in a river running through it. Then industries, workers, and taxpayers in their premoral reflections, and indeed a politically untrackable congeries of effected groups or individuals, will—necessarily and

---

59. *The Federalist*, 39.

60. Ibid., 103, 104, 241.

61. Ibid., 39, 43–45, 258, 241.

62. Further to this, and to the following from a different viewpoint, Robert W. Jenson, "The Kingdom of America's God," now in *Essays in Theology of Culture* (Grand Rapids: Eerdmans, 1995), 50–66.

63. To Alexis de Tocqueville, Allan Bloom, *The Closing of the American Mind* (New York: Simon & Schuster, 1987).

64. Jenson, "Kingdom."

quite without room for moral decision—weigh in with their interests; and a balance of taxes, imposts, regulations, wage levels, and so on, will eventually emerge.

Thus the economy is the human collectivity insofar as it is a sphere of natural necessity like the solar system or the ecosystem. "Economics" or, as it is better named, "political economy"[65] is an attempted analogue of the natural sciences, and a much closer analogue than the alleged "science of politics" that the American founders invoked. The economy, we may say, is the community insofar as it accepts the short-term, seemingly mechanistic, continuities of history as binding also for it.[66] The economy is the human community insofar as it does not take up its freedom. Short of the Kingdom, the community will have this character also.

Just so we are returned to Augustine's central contention: the political problem is solved only in a polity whose "founder and governor" is God. Its permanent solution can therefore only be eschatological; no polity of this age can be more than a temporary, because inwardly self-subverting, arrangement.

No earthly polity can be established that can itself resolve its own prepolitical questions, such as the contemporary American conflict about death. Modernity's "liberal" polities, for example, embody areligious principles of equality and procedure, devised precisely to adjudicate between the prepolitical convictions of contending religions; and they have fulfilled this mission well. But just so they cannot adjudicate between religion and secularism, since they are themselves among the principles of secularism.[67]

Finally, the eschatological solution will have a specificity that Augustine did not quite give it. It is precisely because God is *triune* that we can be one in him: this specific God and he alone can be both a personal center for his creatures and a system of relations in which they can be directly related to each other; this God can even be understood as a system of "checks and balances." Centered on him, we are both centered on a person and centered on no individual: we are rescued alike from depersonalization and domination.

IV

One question remains on this line: What is the *content* of the "justice" that according to Augustine plays so decisive a role? Augustine says little material to the matter, apparently presuming that not only his Christian but his old-Roman read-

---

65. To these paragraphs, see now the splendid analysis by John Milbank, *Theology and Social Theory* (Oxford: Blackwell, 1990), 27–48.

66. Milbank argues convincingly that the more ideological versions of political economy, which advocate capital*ism* or commun*ism*, are created by identification between traceable or postulated mechanisms—my short-term continuities—and the universal teleology rule of God; *Theology and Social Theory*, 37: "For the 'theodocist' version . . . the economic heterogenesis of ends, or 'the hidden hand' of the marketplace, holds the initiative throughout history. God, or 'providence' or 'nature,' is the Machiavellian sovereign who weaves . . . benefits out of . . . interests and individual discomfitures."

67. This was made clear to me by remarks of Professor Robert George of Princeton.

ers would sufficiently understand. We can now make no such presumption. We turn to the "Ten Commandments."

These commandments explicitly present themselves as a description of the justice proper to God's polity: they state the moral content of the Lord's intention to create Israel as a distinct nation.[68] The "first table" of commandments thus directly enjoins the communal adherence to the one God which for Augustine is the heart of true justice: exclusive devotion to JHWH is first stipulated, then the essential marks of his proper cult, which are worship without his putative image, care instead for his name, and observance of the Sabbath.

Then follow the commandments of "the second table," which are to constitute the justice of Israel's mutual life. Here a decisive duality of function appears. These commandments are mostly negative in their explicit formulation, defining sorts of crime. But communities of course do not flourish merely by avoiding crimes; they cohere by positive virtues shaped in and to the course of their histories.[69] Thus the history of Israel and the church fills the commandments of the second table with positive meaning which is not apparent in their text, if they are taken out of the narrative in which they are reported and so read as sheer prohibitions.[70]

In their bare negative formulation, on the other hand, the commandments of the second table apply to all polities, including those that do not belong to the narrative in which the commandments appear and that must therefore substitute joint pursuit of self-interest for love of God. In this role the commandments state minimum conditions: no society can subsist in which the generations turn against each other; in which vendetta has not been replaced by public organs of judgment and punishment; in which the forms by which sexuality is socialized, whatever these may be, are flouted; in which property, however defined, is not defended; in which false testimony is allowed to pervert judgment; or in which greed is an accepted motive of action. Indeed, even the commandments of the first table have a kind of negative and so general application: no society can long subsist that violates its own religion.

Whether or not we wish to call the commandments in this negative abstraction natural law is perhaps mostly a matter of conceptual taste. The commandments are explicitly given by God to Israel and the church, but any people must know them in their negative mode if it is indeed to be a people even by less stringent definition. And existing peoples show that they do know them.

We must adduce at least one actual instance of the way in which the commandments specify minimal justice; and at the present moment of Western history there is little choice about what this must be. A society in which an unborn

68. Exodus 20:2.

69. Stanley Hauerwas's relentless clarification of this point would be an essential contribution had he made no other. His thinking is perhaps most compendiously presented in an early work, *The Peaceable Kingdom: A Primer in Christian Ethics* (Notre Dame: University of Notre Dame Press, 1983).

70. Hauerwas must again be acknowledged.

child can legally be killed on the sole decision of the pregnant person cannot be "a people" even by the least rigorous of Augustine's definitions; it can only be a horde.

As a universally forceful negative command, "You shall not kill" specifies the decisive break between precivil and civilized society: the replacement of vendetta by courts and their officers. The decision that someone rightly must die is no longer to be made by interested parties and is instead to be made by maximally disinterested communal organs. The "someone" in question is of course a member of the human community in question, who is within the scope of its law. If unborn children are members of the human community, then allowing abortions to be performed on decision of the most interested party is a relapse to pure barbarism.

The only question then is, *Are* unborn children members of the human community? The unanswerable argument is provided by Roe v. Wade itself, the decision that undid American public morality. The justices of the American Supreme Court had it right at the beginning of their decision: there is no plausible way to draw a line across the development of the unborn child before which it is not a human person and after which it is. But what follows is quite obviously the opposite of the law the justices laid down.[71] Unless interfered with, the child *will* at some time be a human person; and if at any given point in its development we cannot know that she or he is not yet that, what we do not at that point possess is any justification for treating the child as other than a member of the community, embraced in society's protection from private decisions to kill.

The argument just conducted is an argument in "natural law" if ever there was one. It should be comprehensible and convincing to any rational person. But in late modern societies it is not.[72]

When abortion is the subject, few outside the remaining orthodox Christian congregations and conservative or orthodox synagogues are capable of reason. The result of American polling is uniform: most Americans believe both that abortion for other than exceptional reasons is the unjust taking of a human life and that women should have the right to procure abortion for any reason that compels them. That is, the American people have in this matter abdicated moral coherence.

---

71. Actually reading the celebrated case is a terrifying exercise. It brings home as few experiences do the way in which unreason rules our public life. To those accustomed to sermons and churchly documents, the decision also offers a hilarious parallel to the worst of these, in the incoherence between its doctrine and its application.

72. Late modernity's inability to reason morally is perhaps chiefly caused by its conversion of natural *law* theory into natural *rights* theory. The conversion pivots on eliminating the notion that action has natural ends. When no ordained ends of action are acknowledged, what is left is one or another sort of utilitarianism. But it turns out that anything at all can be justified on utilitarian grounds. At this point, the discourse of "rights" is used to set limits to such justifications and ward off utter nihilism. Thus whereas rights-discourse was once an alternative to ends-discourse, it is now used to limit the evil results of its first use. But—and this is the key point in this context—these limitations are inevitably arbitrary; rational argument about proper action is not possible, only enforcement of negotiated agreements.

The commandments are given to the church and synagogue. The world's "public things" neither survive without these same commandments nor reliably endure them in the rational rigor even of their merely negative import. Therefore, again, of no polity other than synagogue or church can it be said that the gates of hell will not prevail against it.

V

In themselves, most commandments of the second table are generally accepted; however their application may at key points be burked: it is still widely granted that a society will not flourish in which property is regularly at risk, or in which the killing of human persons is anyone's prerogative but the community's, or in which justice is perverted, or in which greed is unrestrained. But can we say this of "You shall not commit adultery?" Does the polity indeed have a vital interest in what, as it is now said, "consenting adults" do "in the privacy of their bedrooms?" We come to the second topic of this chapter.

Earlier ethical systems regularly made sexual ethics the longest chapter. It has more recently become fashionable, also in churchly circles, to think that surely there are weightier matters of the law, to which attention should instead be given. But the older tradition had the better insight, not because chastity is more intrinsic to righteousness than is, for example, economic fairness, but because other modes of justice are not achievable in a generally unchaste society. It is for this reason that this chapter pairs the matters named in its title.

To repeat positions earlier won: it is only in that I am there for you as an object, as a body, that I can also be a subject for you, that is, that human freedom occurs. Human being in its self-transcendence is posited in community, and community depends upon bodily givenness, in my reality for you and for myself as this particular something available to your intention.

We must now note a point not earlier made much of: prior to the resurrection, my embodiment is of course not separable from a biological organism—or is only exceptionally. Even the "spiritual body" of which Paul speaks,[73] insofar as it is anticipated in baptism, is not now separable from an "organic body," as indeed appears repeatedly in Paul's constructions.

This organism, which under modern conditions I am likely misleadingly to call "my body" without qualification, is appropriately to its role a marvelous thing. Its chief marvel is its sexuality. For present purposes sexuality may be said to have two components.

The one is *sensuality*, the common denominator of perception, of the subject's awareness of an other and captivation by that awareness. Sensuality, we may say, is the sheer fact that the subject is drawn to an object; it is captivation by touching and seeing and hearing and smelling and tasting.

73. I Corinthians 15:42–49.

The other is humanity's provision with bisexual reproductive apparatus. A presupposition of the history in which human nature is enacted is the provision of new humans in succession. The Creator has arranged—surely his most humorous idea—that this provision shall take place in consequence of an act performed between humans of two bodily kinds. These kinds are objectively distinguished from and directed to one another by sheer plumbing: inescapably, the vagina and the penis are made for each other.

Sexuality is the coincidence of sensuality and objective male-female differentiation. It is the location of the most intense sensuality of which we are capable in the plumbing by which humanity is divided into two mutually fitted kinds. This union brings it about, on the one hand, that the apparatus of reproduction does not work impersonally, but that I live in the event as a captivated subject, of that objective other whose different body presents him or her to me. And the union brings it about, on the other hand, that the subject's captivation by an object does not float freely to alight where it may, but is directed to a determinate other, picked out by an objective difference from the object-self of the subject.

Sexuality is therefore the way in which our directedness to each other, the intrinsic commonality of human being, is built into the very objects as which we are there for one another. It is sexuality that rescues the communal character of human being from being a mere ideal or demand laid upon us and makes it a *fact* about us. Karl Barth was the pioneer in this insight: the human person "has no choice whether to be co-human or something else. Human being just has this basic form. And this is made inescapable by the circumstance that we cannot say 'human' without saying 'man' or 'woman,' as also 'man *and* woman.'"[74] It is for this reason that "humanity is not an ideal and not a virtue."[75] It is for this reason and this reason only that politics and the political mandate of justice are givens of human existence and not mere options or ideals.

We may simply adopt Barth's theologoumena: "The woman is for the man the eminent . . . co-human, and the man is this for the woman."[76] "In and with existence as human and as this specific human, each one is man or woman. . . . This distinction and relation is of all human distinctions . . . the decisive one . . . for only it is structural."[77]

Because we are female and male, we are directed as subjects to each other by the very objects that we are for each other, and we are so directed by objective differences between those objects. Sexuality is the *factuality* of that intention of one another as objects which is our reality as subjects. For my femaleness or maleness is constituted not in malleable or contingent psychology or social construction but in the shape of the body I am, which can be hated and even mutilated but cannot actually be given the shape of its counterpart, not even by the

---

74. *Kirchliche Dogmatik*, III/2, 344.
75. Ibid., 349.
76. Ibid., 347.
77. Ibid., 345.

most sophisticated technology. Thus sexuality is the fact of that identity of subject and object that is the peculiar structure of humanity.

In Genesis' first creation story, when God created "man" he created "them male and female."[78] "Man" as a singular is equivalent to "them, male and female" as a plural. This lapidary identification is a compressed version of the extended Jahwistic narrative that follows. In the longer story God says, "It is not good that the man should be alone; I will make him a helper as his partner."[79] The word here translated "good" is the one that appears in the first account's judgments that ". . . it was good." Thus the ordination of humanity to its purpose, without which no creature is yet itself, is not accomplished in "the man" so long as he is "alone." "The man" is "good"—and were he not good he would not exist—only when there is the sexual other. The creation narratives contemplate no such thing as a humanity that is not female humanity or male humanity, each in relation to the other.

That we find and make many difficulties with our maleness or femaleness does not alter the fact of them. As the sort of fact it is, a fact that enables communal subjectivity, our maleness or femaleness is also a task and opportunity, and one which we rarely conduct well. Our femaleness or maleness does not therefore lapse; this is both our rescue from final disaster and a rock on which we often stumble.

VI

We move to certain consequences of sexuality's role in human being. A first is to ground a platitude: the family is the essential institution of any community. More precisely, the family is necessary to the existence of the polity; it is what saves the famous political imperative "Come, let us reason together"[80] from being a mere and then certainly vain exhortation. The institutionalization of sexuality is the foundation of all communal institutionalization.

The laws that regulate sexuality, that stipulate what constitutes a family and enforce its integrity, are therefore a condition of all other law-making: as the community establishes and grasps itself by "consent in law," legislation about sex is the necessary first step. Only very determined thoughtlessness could believe what is now common opinion: "What someone does in bed is not the law's business, so long as no one is hurt." On the contrary, what I do in bed is the area of my action in which the community has the must urgent interest, the area for which it must legislate if it is to legislate at all.

It is not meant that if the late modern West's dissolution of sexual law were carried to the end, there would not still be libraries of constitutions and statutes.

---

78. Barth's attempt to exegete Genesis' "image of God" directly by "male and female," ibid., III/1:205–233, would obviously be congenial to this work, but unfortunately the text of Genesis will not bear it.

79. Genesis 2:18. The passage is remarkably exegeted by Karl Barth, ibid., III/2:351–353.

80. Stolen, of course, from a very different context: Isaiah 1:8.

What is being lost is the law's *legitimacy*, its purchase in Augustine's "justice," or indeed in Scipio's second-best "contract." A community establishes the *right* of its law by its willingness to legislate for itself at that point where its own being is at stake.

We may get at the matter so: sexuality is the reality test of law. Every discourse tends to its own sort of dreaming arbitrariness, and must be checked by encounter with an appropriate sort of stubborn fact. Willingness and ability to regulate sexuality is law-making's test of this sort. There is a motto of conventional nihilism, "Mastery, not truth makes law"; where law avoids sexuality, the motto states the lamentable fact. Where law fails its reality test, it is indeed but a product of dominance. And law that can claim no other justification than the decision of its makers can be maintained only by essentially arbitrary power; a totalitarian state is one in which a major part of law is in this condition.

When we first notice these connections between sexuality and politics, moderns are likely to be much bewildered. Let the offense be at least well directed: we should deprecate the recent "sexual revolution" not so much for the behavior released, pitiful though most of it is, as for its consequences as a political choice. A sexually anarchic society cannot be a free society. For no society can endure mere shapelessness; when the objective foundation of community is systematically violated the society must and will hold itself together by arbitrary force. Nor is this analysis an exercise in theoretical reasoning; it merely points out what is visibly happening in late-twentieth-century Western societies.[81]

To derive a second consequence of sexuality's humanizing role, we must note a particular connection between terms now established in our discourse: "promise" and "visibility." A wholly disembodied word—were such a thing possible—could still be "law" but could not be "promise." Visible words are speech with the body, with the object-self; and my objective self is what binds me to the conditions that impede my commitments. When, to retrieve the earlier example, I say to my child, "I will send you to college," my actually doing so is conditioned by a vast web of circumstance; my bondage to these is my body, my availability and so vulnerability to the world out there. If my statement is a promise, what makes it so is that I brave some of those conditions. Making a promise is therefore always an overcoming of the promiser's mere circumstantial objectivity.

We may say: making a promise is always somehow a jolt to the body, a specific mobilization of this in itself communally immobile thing. An act of communication that says, "I will take care of it for you," inwardly includes a movement of the body to the one addressed, an overcoming of distance. Since the body is from this point of view the sum of the impediments to promise-keeping, promises are made binding by their embodiment, by their actuality as visible and not merely audible words. We make promises with a handshake, a kiss, a signature,

81. Thus the simultaneity of the lack of sexual regulation in young males of American cities' *Lumpenproletariat* and their criminality is regularly taken as coincidence. It is nothing of the sort; the first causes the second.

or a seal. God promises his Kingdom with a toast, his life with an invigorating wash.

Intercourse is the ultimate creaturely gesture of this sort, the movement of my body to the other that cannot be surpassed without harmful consequences. For here the one body actually engulfs the other and that body enters the first, only in this active abolition of distance to be mutually the bodies they are. Therefore if intercourse is a gesture and not a mere technique of sensation or reproduction, it can be the embodiment of an ultimate promise: the promise of myself if it kills me, of shared life "until death do us part."

I can promise no particular thing unconditionally, for I possess no particular thing certainly; without reservation I can promise only myself. Yet nor do I possess myself until I am dead, and then the promised self is withdrawn. Therefore "I give myself to you, until death parts us," is the closest approach to unconditional promise in the power of a creature. I may, to be sure, fail to keep also this promise. But if I do, this is mere failure; nothing can prevent me, for death is the last sanction and death is already accepted by the promise made. Just so it is the promise that only the final gesture of intercourse can embody.

Clearly I cannot make this promise a second time without thereby breaking the first, for I have only one death to give. So also this promise includes in itself the promise not so to address another. That is, if intercourse says what it alone can say, it says *faithfulness.* Therewith we have named the chief Jewish and Christian virtue in this realm.

We can of course stipulate together that intercourse shall be the sign of a lesser address. We can make it be the gestural embodiment of "I am yours forever, maybe," or "I am yours for this pleasant weekend." But then we have no gesture left for final commitment, and so become incapable of it. A society in which this was a widespread condition could not long cohere.

We can even arrange that intercourse shall promise nothing at all, that it be a sheer technique. This arrangement makes the sexual structure of fascism. Utterly to silence intercourse is to drive the objective basis of community below the level of communal consciousness. A society in this condition can be held together only by arbitrary leadership and force. Totalitarian politics and "sexual liberation" are but two sides of one phenomenon.

A third and in this chapter last consequence of humanity's sexuality is already in fact established: a just society will encourage and insofar as possible enforce heterosexual monogamy as the paradigmatic socialization of sexuality. The precautions built into that proposition should be noted. It is not here asserted that polygamous societies cannot function, or that love cannot flourish in other forms of marriage, or that monogamous polities can enforce monogamy with equal rigor under all circumstances, or how the sensual impulses of those who identify themselves as "homosexual" should be socialized—or that any socialization of sexuality or sensuality guarantees happiness or its own success.

It is not accidental that most openly polygamous societies are traditional tribal societies. In a community in which behavior is determined by rules supposed to have descended unchangeably from the beginning, the objective base of society can remain below the level of communal consciousness and law. In that situation, sexuality may be socialized apolitically; most often this will then be done obediently to herd biology and so polygynously. In cases where historical polity is achieved without altering these arrangements, women will be excluded from the polity.

Short of the Kingdom, even monogamous communities will doubtless be compelled to admit divorce in some instances, and so a modicum of serial polygamy; even in the biblical canon the absolute prohibition remembered from Jesus was amended.[82] But a measure of a community's humanity will be its effort to restrict divorce, and a measure of other evils in the community will be the need to ease the restriction and let the pressure escape here. Divorce for adultery is the obvious first concession, since with an unrepentant adulterer one cannot live monogamously. Moreover it must be recognized that staying with the spouse may indeed kill and that society cannot require martyrdom—not even the church can *require* it. It must even be recognized that the death to be avoided may be moral or spiritual, though here casuistry must proceed slowly and cautiously. But only humanity's trivializers will fail to mourn the ontological loss inflicted by even these concessions.

Finally, the inclusion of "heterosexual" in the rule is a—perhaps now necessary—redundancy. For homoeroticism is of course not a mode of sexuality at all, but an escape from it. Homoeroticism is a group of sensual techniques, devised to abstract sexuality's pleasure without commitment to its function; doubtless these are sometimes used also as visible words of affection. There could not be a monogamy—or polygamy—other than heterosexual; talk of "same-sex marriage" is a mere triumph of Humpty Dumpty.

We need not here resolve the question of whether there are such things as sensual "orientations" and if so how they are acquired. What must anyway be clear is that "homosexuality," if it exists and whatever it is, cannot be attributed to creation; those who practice forms of homoerotic sensuality and attribute this to "homosexuality" cannot refer to the characteristic as "the way God created me," if "create" has anything like its biblical sense. No more in this context than in any other do we discover God's creative intent by examining the empirical situation; as we have seen, I may indeed have to *blame* God for that empirically present in me that contradicts his known intent, but this is an occasion for unbelief, not a believer's justification of the evil.

Abstention from sexuality is not in itself an evil. Indeed, one of the blessings enabled by the church's anticipation of the Kingdom is that celibacy can be a specific vocation within her. Nor is deprivation of sexuality a sin. Abstention or deprivation is not, however, the same as defection.

VII

The tone would contradict the matter, were we so to end our discussion of sexuality. We may recoup with another piece of Luther's beguiling exegesis of Genesis: "It was very different . . . then, before sin, when Adam and Eve . . . were

---

82. Mark 10:11par.

absorbed in God's goodness and justice. There was then between the two of them a marvelous conjunction of spirit and will. Nothing in the whole world was sweeter or more charming for Adam than his Eve."[83] Had they remained so captivated by God and each other, the "intimate relation between man and wife would have been purely delightful. The act of procreation particularly would have been sacred and highly esteemed . . . accompanied by lofty delight" and done "without hiding."[84]

And we may summarize the entire chapter with a proposition parallel to that which ended the previous chapter. As love is the fulfillment of our self-transcendence toward God, so it is also the fulfillment of our self-transcendence toward one another. Jesus said, "'You shall love the Lord your God. . . .' This is the . . . first commandment. And a second is like it: 'You shall love your neighbor as yourself.' On these two commandments hang all the law and the prophets."[85]

Yet Jesus does not say of our love for each other what he says of our love for God, that it may be with "all" our "heart . . . and soul . . . and mind"; he mandates only such love for each other as we have for ourselves. Therefore in our transcendence toward one another the equivalence between love and faith does not hold as it does in our transcendence toward God. We can have saving faith neither in one another nor in ourselves. Precisely with that negation, this chapter must end.

83. *Ennaratio in Genesis* (WA 42), 50.
84. *Ennaratio in Genesis* (WA 42), 89.
85. Matthew 22:34–40parr.

TWENTY

Human Personhood

I

Humanity's uniqueness is the specific relation God takes up with us. This relation is not itself a resemblance. The "image of God," if we are to use this phrase comprehensively for humanity's distinctiveness, is simply that we are related to God as his conversational counterpart.

With these propositions in place, however, we are free to recognize what may indeed be called a human resemblance to God, and at the very place where the tradition located it. Because God speaks with us, we know he is personal. As we answer him, we too are personal.

It is often and convincingly claimed that personhood first became a metaphysically deep concept within the Christian doctrine of God, and especially within the thinking of the Eastern fathers and their Byzantine appropriators; this was important from a different angle in the first volume of this work.[1] Pagan antiquity of course knew that some entities were personal and some were not but understood being a human person as simply one characteristic of being a human being and being a divine person as one characteristic of being a divine being. For pagan antiquity's theology, being is the embracing category, and personhood is secondary.

Christian theology was compelled to drastic revision: in the Cappadocian and Neo-Chalcedonian doctrine of Trinity, personhood is not an aspect of God's being but is rather correlated to the three *who live* deity, also when we speak of the Trinity himself as personal. That the three are God is a characteristic of the specific per-

---

1. And I will again adduce the argument of the Orthodox metropolitan John Zizioulas, *Being as Communion* (Crestwood: St. Vladimir's Seminary Press, 1985), for its typicality and its unique ecumenical influence. He moreover provides more than a sufficiency of patristic and other citations.

sonalities they are;[2] it is divine personhood, not divine being, that is metaphysically primary.[3]

The contest between the concepts of personhood and being would of course be moot if the first volume's revision of the latter concept were followed. In order to recognize Orthodoxy's point without constant circumlocution, the preceding and following few paragraphs prescind from that proposal.

It is a chief truth of Eastern insistence on the Father's "monarchy": it is not God's divinity—not his being—that is the origin of the triune life but the Father as person. God is not first divine and thereupon triune. He is first triune and thereupon divine. The Father's love, an exclusively personal reality, is the origin of the Son, and the Father's personal intent to be free in order to love is the origin of the Spirit.[4] It is, moreover, the Father with the Son in the Spirit who are the one God. "If God exists, he exists because the Father exists."[5]

Since with God personhood is prior to being, it must be so absolutely. Within thinking enabled by the Cappadocian achievement, it is the fact of personhood that "enables entities to be entities" and not vice versa.[6] Also things that are themselves impersonal belong to a creation that results from the Creator as a personal freedom beyond it; this contradicts all pagan antiquity's theology, for which even divine personhood and freedom, if affirmed at all, are phenomena within the itself impersonal whole.

But *are* there other persons than the divine three? Can there be created persons? If the ground of God's personhood and freedom were his divinity, if personhood were a predicate of beings of a certain sort, then such freedom would surely be an exclusive predicate of divine beings. But since it is the other way around, since God's free personhood is the ground of his nature, the triune communion is not bound even to the purity of its own deity and can open to others than the three if God so wills it; and then as respondents in that communion these others will also be personal. We have arrived again at a central position of this work, and one to which we have come from several starting points.

It will be the task of this chapter to analyze human personhood as it is created by God's triune personal life. A decisive caution must stand at the beginning: we must not be guided by any general principle of likeness, so as to trace the structure of human personhood from that of divine personhood. We could thereby easily violate Thomas Aquinas's principle, which we have regularly in-

2. Zizioulas, *Being*, 17–18, can even say that the Father being a person is the "cause" of there being God.

3. It must be acknowledged that much recent Orthodox theology undoes this insight. Building upon the more unfortunate possibilties of the Palamite doctrines of divine being and the "energies," those that can lead to what the first volume of this work identified as an ironically appearing Orthodox modalism (I:153), it effectively subordinates the persons to both the divine being and the divine work. To this, Dorothea Wendebourg, "Person und Hypostase," *Vernunft des Glaubens*, ed. Jan Rohls and Gunther Wenz (Göttingen: Vandenhoeck & Ruprecht, 1990), 502–524.

4. This last of course is a point where volume 1 of this work went beyond the patristic teaching.

5. Zizioulas, *Being*, 41.

6. Ibid., 39.

voked: that essence and existence are distinguished in creatures and not distinguished in God. We have described a triune person as an existent with no other reason than his own existence and that of other persons who are the same being he is; we must not so describe created personhood.

In the first volume, we analyzed personhood around three poles: transcendental unity of apperception, Ego, and freedom. The previous paragraphs suggest continuing in these terms; it is not thereby proposed that they provide the only terms in which the analysis might be conducted. This is also the place to warn that discourse about the "I" or Ego is easily misunderstood, since throughout the modern period the word has been used for different things in different theories. This chapter will speak of the Ego in a relatively commonsensical way: it is the entity we denote with the subject term of such first-person descriptive or hortatory sentences as "I painted that house" or "I ought to be more energetic."

II

The phenomenon Immanuel Kant called "the transcendental unity of apperception" surely obtains. We would not call an entity personal that was not conscious, that did not in Kant's peculiar language "apperceive"; nor would we call a consciousness personal that was not focused at a viewpoint. A personal consciousness is precisely "transcendental," that is, a perspectival focus that is not itself within the field there focused.

It is perhaps just possible to conceive a consciousness that was from no viewpoint. The modern sciences in their first flowering drew a picture of the universe that if perfected would have been "a view from nowhere." And Aristotle conceived a consciousness whose whole content might be such a picture: his God is a universal consciousness without perspective, the consciousness perhaps of an omniscient and passionless classical physicist.

But Aristotle's God is not, and therefore the metaphysical situation his reality would establish not only does not obtain but could not have obtained. God is Father, Son, and Spirit. Each is other than the other two, and each is a person; and since a divine person *is* a subsisting relation to the other divine persons, each of Father, Son, and Spirit is precisely a perspective. Moreover, since there are created persons only as enabled within the triune community of persons, the proposition is universal: all consciousness is perspectival. It will be seen that these arguments reproduce arguments of the first volume, the other way around.

Thus Kant's phenomenological observation is not theologically neutral, whatever Kant may have supposed. Indeed, however far Kant may have departed from specific Christianity, the insight he followed was enabled only within the history of Christian theology. The pioneer of "the first-person standpoint" as an epistemic attitude seems to have been Augustine himself.[7]

7. Charles Taylor, *Sources of the Self: The Making of the Modern Identity* (Cambridge: Harvard University Press, 1989), 133. Taylor traces the development from Plato through Locke, 115–176.

Augustine's reflexive identification with his own subjectivity was undoubtedly shaped by his Neoplatonism, with its cosmological and psychological pyramid stemming from "the One" through "Mind." But he would hardly have come to it had he not also been a worshiper of the Christian God. The Creator was the supreme goal of Augustine's consciousness, and unlike Greek deity the Creator is too intimate to his creatures to appear in our knowing only as something we know, however encompassing and dominant; he must be apprehended as "the . . . underlying principle of our knowing activity" itself.[8] Just in this reflection Augustine drew attention to our consciousness in its own depth, and made "us aware of this in a first-person perspective."[9]

God's consciousness is focused and so is ours; and of both facts we can give some account. As Augustine perhaps did not quite say, divine consciousness is focused because each of the persons God is has *dramatic location* in and by community with the others. And human consciousness is focused by its accommodation in this same mutuality.

Thus transcendental unity of apperception, wherever it occurs, is enabled by the triune life. And the unity of consciousness is therefore always a *narrative* unity. It has the integrity of a location within a story and is unitary because the story is coherent. Just so it occurs in and by virtue of *community*, foundationally by virtue of the triune community.

Here an error is to be avoided. The Kantian notion of a transcendental unity of apperception is individualistic as he uses it. The rest of the world provides raw data, which are then pulled together into an experienced world from the inalienably private focus of my consciousness. The intent of this chapter would be radically perverted were its appropriation of Kant's notion to carry this supposition with it. There *are* no raw data of experience; the world that I receive and unify in my experience is always already the world interpreted in the discourse of a community, first the community of the Trinity and then the human communities I thereupon inhabit.[10] And I experience reality from a perspectival point precisely because I am located in those same communities.

The triune narrative and the triune community are in contingent fact God's history with a human community actual in that history. We humans belong to the triune history and community only by virtue of this contingency; none of us nor all of us together are one of the Trinity. We belong as those whom the Son brings with himself, whose whole life and intention are the others to whom he is sent and for whom he died. Thus we created persons have each our perspectival integrity as we are simultaneously located within divine history and community and within human history and the human community. This is true both of the human person Jesus and of the rest of us, but differently.

---

8. Ibid., 129.

9. Ibid., 136.

10. That the experienced world is always the interpreted world is a currently fashionable doctrine. Where the triune community is not reckoned with, the doctrine is of course nihilistic.

According to our christological conclusions,[11] the identity of the eternal Son is the human person Jesus. Thus the viewpoint from which this man grasps reality is identically that of *the one whose* place in the human narrative and community is that of a Palestinian Jew, Mary's child, an unordained rabbi, one of Rome's victims, and so on, and that of *the one whose* place in the triune narrative and community is that of the Son of the Father and the defining beneficiary of the Spirit.

With each of the rest of us the viewpoint from which consciousness stems is that of one of those *for whom* this Jew and prophet and victim lived and died, and who is some *particular one* of them as, for example, a lay deacon, a professor of physics, Susannah's child, and so on. Just and only so it is also that of one of those who appear with the Son before the Father in the Spirit. It is apparent that those who do not acknowledge the Son must be in constant danger of mislocating the viewpoint from which they are conscious, and so of losing perspective on their world: they do in fact grasp the world only from a position within the christological story but do not know that they do this.

What brings my experience, in Kant's sense, together to be *my* experience is nothing I am by myself, Kant and his successors to the contrary. It is the coherence of the narrative in which I belong and it is the justice of the community of that narrative. Or we may say it is the grammar of the language of that community, in which it tells its narrative. Both as I narrate my life and as I live in community, I must be competent in a language I do not invent: the givenness of a specific language and my induction into it are, in Kant's proper sense, a transcendental condition of unified consciousness.[12]

The transcendental viewpoint of those whose community is finally the church and only in the meantime other "public things" and that of those whose community is the latter only have the same abstract structure. To avoid God, modernity and its precursors posited a focus of consciousness that was itself this abstraction, the same for all by virtue of its pure formality. No such thing subsists.[13] My life has originating focus either within the community of the church and the communities of the *libido dominandi* or within the latter communities only.

I can, to be sure, pretend I am self-existent, the condition of my own hypostasis. And I can try actually to live by that pretense, in violation of the conditions by which I subsist to pretend things. Sin, which is always itself the same old thing, has many faces; one is acting as if my essence and existence were not distinct. Augustine was led to the transcendental unity of his own consciousness by his passion for God. Within the reflection he inaugurated, to seek only myself at the focus of my consciousness is to mistake myself for God. A great deal of Western epistemology is simply Eve's and Adam's error.[14]

11. 1: 134–138.

12. Taylor, *Sources*, 35: "There is no way we could be inducted into personhood except by being initiated into a language. We first learn our languages of moral and spiritual discernment by being brought into an ongoing conversation by those who bring us up."

13. This point the whole of subsequent Western thought has learned from Schleiermacher.

14. Taylor, *Sources*, 157: "The Cartesian proof is no longer a search for an encounter with God within. . . . Rather what I now meet is myself."

III

In the foregoing, a step was elided. The transcendental unity of a hypothetical human consciousness was described as "that of one of those *for whom* this Jew and child and prophet and victim lived and died, and who is some *particular one* of them as, for example," an American, a professor of physics, and so on. But this use of identifying descriptions anticipated its justification. A focus of consciousness simply in and of itself, even if that focus is a place in a community and narrative, would not be that of a describable someone. And so it would not be personal.

That I from the focus of my consciousness identify that of which I am conscious as included in *my* experience, in such fashion that "my" has descriptive content, depends on my identifying myself as, continuing the hypothetical case, one of those for whom Jesus died and among them as an American, a professor of physics, and so on. It depends, that is, on finding myself as a describable object. The "I" in "That so-and-so is I" remains to be discussed.

The "I" in "I did that" seems on face value to have the same function as "John" in "John did that." The point of my saying to you, for example, "I painted the house" is to point out an entity within the experience of us both that is claimed to be the agent of the house's new appearance; the claim moreover is arguable between us.[15]

If this face value is accepted, my Ego is something within the field of my consciousness, there *for* me as it is for you, and in the presently relevant respects there for me just as John or Mary is there for me. At face value, it belongs to my personhood that I recognize myself in a figure presented *to* my consciousness by the narrative and community in which I am located, so that this Ego is not itself located at the perspectival point from which I recognize it. It belongs to the face value of our self-referential language that there is a structure of deferral[16] built into personhood, that the two personal pronouns in "I recognize that I did that" do not initially point in the same direction, but must catch up with each other.

At the turn of the nineteenth and twentieth centuries, Maurice Blondel, earlier mentioned, built a specifically Christian theory of personhood[17] on the observation of such deferral[18]—though not under that label—that was profoundly subversive of established modern social and psychological theory. He traced an intrinsic dynamic of human life by which we are kept from premature identity with ourselves: the will is driven from its occupation in immediate experience, through explicit willed action and through unmediated exterior expansion, into

15. The obviously privileged epistemic position of such first-person sentences is variously interpreted, and not directly relevant to the narrow claim made here.

16. The word is of course deliberately chosen, to relocate Derrida's pun where it belongs.

17. Blondel is the only social theorist after Augustine who is not all too faintly praised by John Milbank; for Milbank explicitly on Blondel, *Theology and Social Theory: Beyond Secular Reason* (Oxford: Blackwell, 1990), 210–219.

18. *Action* (1893): *Essay on a Critique of Life and a Science of Practice*, tr. Oliva Blanchette (Notre Dame: Notre Dame University Press, 1984).

communally mediated action. Each step is precipitated by the same contradiction: "the willed end" is not "equal to the . . . principle" of the will itself.[19] We can neither refrain from moral action nor be content in what any action makes of us: "It is . . . impossible to find ourselves as we will to be . . . impossible to stop, to go back, or to go forward by ourselves. In my action there is something I have not yet been able to understand and equal."[20]

It is, said Blondel, the antecedent if unrecognized presence to each human will of the infinitely different will of God that creates this self-contradiction within human action: "Man does not equal the fullness of his spontaneous aspiration through his deliberate intention except on the condition of annihilating his self-will by installing in himself a contrary and mortifying will."[21]

> This conflict . . . explains the forced presence of a new affirmation in consciousness; and . . . the reality of this necessary presence . . . makes possible in us the consciousness of this very conflict. There is a "one thing necessary." The entire movement . . . brings us to this term, for it is from this term that the determinism itself begins, the whole meaning of which is to bring us back to it.[22]

It has been a defining character of modernity to deny the face value of our experience, with its inner deferral, and insist that the Ego I can know and describe is somehow itself the transcendental unity from which I grasp it. That is, it has been a defining character of modernity to deny the Augustinian restlessness, to insist that I am antecedently identical with myself. The denial is carried out in practice by what has been called "exigent introspection:[23] the great endeavor of modernist human self-understanding in all fields has been to turn consciousness instantaneously back on itself, in hope of catching a glimpse of the "I" that I know and will as myself, at work as itself the gathering focus of that knowing and willing.

We may take William James's *Principles of Psychology* as a classic statement of the modern effort[24] and also as a paradigm and typical victim of it.[25] The vast work states its contention and its method plainly enough: "Introspective Observation is what we have to rely on first and foremost and always."[26]

---

19. Ibid., 374.

20. E.g., 314.

21. Ibid., 353.

22. Ibid., 314.

23. Louis A. Sass, *Madness and Modernism: Insanity in the Light of Modern Art, Literature and Thought* (New York: Basic Books, 1992), 221.

24. If asked, "Why James?" I could only reply that it seemed an interesting idea to do so.

25. As statement and paradigm, we might have adduced the remarkably similar and earlier analyses of Jonathan Edwards; see Robert W. Jenson, *America's Theologian: A Recommendation of Jonathan Edwards* (New York: Oxford University Press, 1988), 29–34. But Edwards would not have done as victim, and the present work's dose of Edwards is heavy.

26. William James, *Principles of Psychology, The Works of William James*, ed. Frederick H. Burkhardt (Cambridge: Harvard University Press, 1981), 1:185.

The "first fact" such introspection discovers is "that thinking . . . goes on." The second is that a thought is never just "this thought or that thought, but my thought. . . . The universal conscious fact is not 'feelings and thoughts exist,' but 'I think' and 'I feel.'"[27] Thus the flow of consciousness includes consciousness of its own continuity. The next step of introspection must be to spy out this continuity, that we call " *myself, I* or *me*."[28] We are looking for the "I" in "I think/feel/ will such-and-such."

Looking for this entity, James first finds the complex of "material" things— starting with the body and including family and friends!—that we identify with ourselves and that expands and contracts with circumstance.[29] Next appears "the social self"; this is the "recognition" that we get from one another. According to James, "a man has as many social selves as there are individuals who recognize him."[30]

But these various material and social selves are too adventitious to one another, temporary, and miscellaneous to account for there being one self to have them. We must turn our attention to our consciousness *of* them "and the identification of ourselves with" that consciousness.[31] Now we seem to discern, somehow in the stream of consciousness, an "innermost centre," compared with which material and social selves "seem transient external possessions, each of which in turn can be disowned, whilst that which disowns them remains." Can we catch a glimpse of "this self of all the other selves?"[32]

James initially seems to succeed. He discerns a "spiritual something" that "seems to go out to meet" the other contents of consciousness's stream, that is "what welcomes or rejects" otherwise floating thoughts and feelings as *my* thoughts and feelings, that "is the source of effort and attention, and the place from which appear to emanate the fiats of the will."[33] An *agent* of the self's unity thus appears, and seems indeed to appear to "direct sensible acquaintance."[34]

This introspection, however, is still insufficiently exigent for James, too content with such abstractions as "something."[35] We must try to be more concrete, to catch "one of these manifestations of spontaneity in the act."[36]

But so soon as this final attempt is made, the center does not hold: "Whenever my introspective glance succeeds in turning round quickly enough" to catch the subject immediately in the act, "all it can ever feel distinctly is some bodily process."[37] Introspecting with maximum exigency, we discover no subject of

27. Ibid., 220–221.
28. Ibid., 232.
29. Ibid., 280–281.
30. Iibd., 281.
31. Ibid., 284.
32. Ibid., 284–285.
33. Ibid., 285.
34. Ibid., 286.
35. Ibid., 286–287.
36. Ibid., 287.
37. Ibid.

experience at all but only "a collection" of "objective" phenomena, at the level of the "material"—not even the "social"!—"selves."[38] Exigent introspection's quest for its own principle of identity in fact dissolves it.

But perhaps one possibility remains. James had so far tried to discover the "I" that is the focus of consciousness in the "I" of which I am conscious. This attempt having undone itself, his final resource is to reverse the direction of internal viewing and try to discover the latter in the former. James turns to investigate, in his terms, "the pure Ego": introspection must whip round more quickly yet, to catch the transcendental unity of consciousness functioning as itself the identifiable person.

This too fails. The focus point of consciousness remains a mere postulate. All that can be "verified" introspectively is the occurrence of one "pulse" of consciousness after another, each recognizing prior pulses as parts of the—otherwise wholly unspecifiable—"same self as me." The pulses hang together by various "phenomenal relations," and that contingent fact is as far as our quest reaches.[39]

Where are we left? We are in fact back with what we called the face value position, only now as the result of failure. There is the transcendental unity of consciousness, necessarily posited but not describable as anything I can find in myself. There is the miscellany of objective material and social candidates to be the Ego, by which consciousness must make shift to identify itself. And there are successive "pulses" of this self-identifying. We are left where we must either cease to insist that the focus of consciousness and the Ego must be antecedently identical and develop the resultant face value position or persist and thereby disintegrate what we seek.

It can be argued that late modernity and postmodernity are one long demonstration of such persistence and disintegration, perhaps most apparently in the arts and in our personality disorders—by this pairing it is not suggested that the modernist arts are devoid of great achievement.[40] The present work is not the place to carry out the argument.[41] Two brief observations only are offered.

We may adduce the defining penchant of modernist[42] visual art: the disintegration of personal narrative. Why is the woman in the paradigmatic work of modernist painting, Edouard Manet's *Dejeuner sur l'Herbe*, so singularly naked? Why does no one notice? And what is she thinking about so smugly? Since she no more attends to her companions than they do to her? The whole deliberation of the painting is to provoke such narrative questions and prevent all answers.

---

38. Ibid., 290–292.

39. Ibid., 322.

40. On the contrary, modernism's art, by its perch on the edge of chaos, has produced a body of marvels comparable only to those of early Renaissance Italy.

41. And I am probably not the one to do it.

42. It should be noted that "modernist" in literary and artistic criticism is the equivalent of "postmodern" in other discourses. Much confusion has been generated by not noticing this.

The naked lady is in fact dropped in from another painting altogether; the act of the painting is sabotage of the painting's own suggestions of narrative.[43]

And if we ask what the consciousness evoked by James's introspective pressure would be like if actually lived by an individual, the answer is fairly obvious: it would be the specifically modern kind of madness. Schizophrenia, apparently undocumented before the late eighteenth century, was at first—and in itself tellingly, about the diagnosticians—interpreted as resulting from an undeveloped sense of self; it is surely the opposite, the havoc wrought in a consciousness lived, for whatever reason, in all too exigent awareness of itself.[44]

It was all very well for James, in his society, to rest content with this outcome. But if all we grasp about the unity of the person is that successive pulses of consciousness do happen at the phenomenal level to refer to other such pulses as predecessors, and that this sequence of events does contingently string together offerings from the miscellany of material and social selves, we lack any assurance that this must continue to happen, that is, that I actually exist as a moral subject. But exactly such assurance is the one thing needful for life to go on in less sheltered historical conditions.

Christian theology has no need for such despair or acrobatics. It knows that something *outside* the individual focus of consciousness grants and guarantees its precision and steadiness, the coherence of God's life and the person's relation to it, and is therefore not surprised that introspection fails to discover the person's coherence. It knows also that there is not a sheer plurality of social identities presented to my consciousness, because not individuals but the one human community, constituted a unity by Jesus' life and death for all, presents me with my identification. And it knows that the "material" identity, the body, and this social identity are not really different things.

The man Jesus identifies himself as a Palestinian Jew, Mary's child, who died for his sisters and brothers, and as Son of the Father and resting place of the Spirit. Each of the rest of us may identify her- or himself as one of those for whom this one lived and died and lives, and who is particular within this community as the self seen and offered by this community and by others that "recognize" him or her.

Thus the structures of the communities within which individuals have their transcendental focus and from which they receive their Egos shape the structure of their personhood. There is a personhood proper to a representative democracy and a different personhood proper to a popular tyranny and so on. Moreover, the voices of others are constitutive within the individual's life: I am who and what I am precisely in conversation with those who offer me my self.

43. Thus the circumstance that the pioneers of abstract art all believed themselves to be carrying out the insights either of popularized Buddhism or of dialectical materialism, that is, believed themselves to be abolishing history, is far from the coincidence it is sometimes taken for.

44. The astonishing book earlier cited, Sass, *Madness*, argues this interpretation of schizophrenia with immense clinical detail, simultaneously arguing, with equal erudition, the identity of standpoint between schizophrenia and specifically modernist art.

The soteriological significance of these last points can hardly be overestimated. So long as it is supposed that the individual human person inhabits a sort of shell from within which he or she deals with others outside the shell, the key soteriological propositions of Scripture are unintelligible. For example, "It is not I who live but Christ who lives in me" can at most be taken as overheated rhetoric.

Finally, because theology knows these things it can rest content with the one thing with which modernity could not be content, deferral of the subject's identification between itself as transcendental viewpoint and itself as Ego. Indeed, it calls this deferral freedom and regards the freedom of the supposed autonomously self-contained individual as the most barren of slaveries. I am not bound within my own self-equivalence; it is not so that I intractably am what I am what I am what . . .

IV

The interpretation of created freedom is perennially controverted in the Western church—and this is surely one point where aloofness from such broils has not been for the good of the Eastern churches. There are several notable places where we could join the argument; Martin Luther's reply to Erasmus, *On the Bondage of the Will*, commends itself by unique willingness to state and argue the issues without shielding equivocation.

The phrase "the free will" has generated many cross-purposes. Those who affirm "free will" often affirm different things, usually without noticing; and those who deny "free will" often deny different things, regularly mistaking the opponent against whom they direct the denial.

Thus Augustine explicitly teaches that the existence of human free will, *liberum arbitrium* in his fateful phrase, is an essential truth of Scripture and reason.[45] Yet in modernity his doctrine of predestination[46] is customarily cited as the paradigmatic denial of free will; as is his reiterated more general teaching that all human wills "are so absolutely in God's power that he makes them incline to whatever he wills whenever he wills it."[47] Vice versa, in the course of Luther's savage assault on "free will," he offhandedly affirms anthropological features that some would say are all they ever meant by the phrase.

We will not here try to straighten out the historical confusions of language and analysis. We will simply follow Luther's treatise, noting the phenomena adduced in it and following the arguments he attaches to them; perhaps we may avoid some ambiguities by thus following the track of one interlocutor.

45. E.g., *De gratia et libero arbitrio*, ii-iii.
46. E.g., *De praedestination sanctorum*, vii.15: "Thus when the gospel is preached some believe and some do not believe. Those who believe when the preacher speaks outwardly hear and learn inwardly from the Father; those who do not believe, hear outwardly but neither hear nor learn inwardly. That is: to the believers it is given to believe and to the others it is not."
47. *De gratia*, xx.41.

Luther agrees with his opponents that human creatures have a dispositional property[48] of being apt for willing action. We may put it so: the question "Was Jones willing to go to Chicago or was he coerced?" is a meaningful question, whereas the question "Was that rock willing to fall or was it coerced?" is not. Indeed, Luther considers human possession of the property a triviality too obvious for discussion.[49]

Moreover, when someone possessed of this aptitude makes a choice and is permitted by the circumstances to do what he or she has chosen, Luther says the action is done "freely." Such action displays *voluntas faciendi,* or "willingness," the contingent unity of choosing and doing.[50]

But if the great denier of free will affirms all the foregoing, what then is it he thinks we do not have? All Luther's arguments are directed against forms of the same supposition: that our wills are antecedent to themselves, that we not only choose but choose what to choose. This supposition, Luther argues, is absurd.

It is, to begin, absurd to claim a power to alter the choices by which all our powers are marshalled in the first place.[51] If contingent circumstances permit us to act upon courses we have chosen, our action is willing and free; and that is all that can or need be said.

The claim that we can choose what to choose supposes that there occurs in us "a sort of absolute willing,"[52] a will that does not yet will anything.[53] This, Luther argues in very modern fashion,[54] is a "dialectician's figment" that results from "ignoring realities and attending to words," from the metaphysician's besetting fallacy of supposing that because we need a word for certain purposes, in this case the word "will" to speak of our determinate choices, the word must therefore denote something merely by itself. Whether a word denotes by itself is settled only by experience; and if in this case we consult the facts of experience we will find only our determinate choices and the circumstances that do or do not allow us to act on them.[55]

But why is Luther so urgent that we not make this claim, however foolish it may be analytically? The concern is soteriological. The claim supposes that the dispositional property of being apt for willing action is itself a sort of occult power actually so to act, is itself the sufficient condition of its own actualization. On the contrary, says Luther, if I am actually to act with *voluntas faciendi,* I must be "seized" (or "rapt")[56] into willingness by *another* than myself; and moreover such rapture is

48. "[D]ispositivam qualitatem et passivam aptitudinem."

49. *De servo arbitrio* (WA 18), 636–637.

50. Ibid., 634.

51. Ibid., 634.

52. Ibid., 669: "inter haec duo, posse velle bonum, non posse velle bonum, dari medium, quod sit absolutum Velle."

53. Ibid.: "purum et merum velle."

54. Or of course in very "nominalist" fashion.

55. Ibid., 669–670.

56. Luther's verb is *rapi.* No English translation at once provides an active-voice verb and an equivalent of "rapture." The translation strategy here chosen is to alternate between two English verbs; readers are begged to remember that the original has only one.

always determinate . Willing action, the making and carrying out of personal choices, is enabled only in community, only by the provocation of an antecedent and determinate other will; it is not enabled within me as a closed system.

There are, moreover, only two by whom we are or can be thus seized:[57] God and Satan. We are in fact seized by Satan, and so are unfree for God; this is the occasion of God's saving action. God's act is to seize us for himself and so make us unfree for Satan. *Within* either rapture we often act "willingly":[58] the usual choices of human life, to marry or not, to obey some civil law or not, to order steak instead of fish, and so on, are made and sometimes can terminate in action.

Luther has withheld the great word *libertas* both from the dispositional property and from "willing" action simply as such; he withholds it also and vehemently from the rapture worked by Satan.[59] But then Luther does finally let the word fall, for the rapture by God. Indeed he crowns it as "royal freedom," *regia libertas:* God "seizes us for his booty, by his Spirit he makes us his slaves and captives— which is not bondage but royal freedom—that we willingly may choose and do what he chooses."[60] It is *God's* appearance to seize us which qualifies resultant "willingness" of action as—at last—freedom.

We may ask why it must be God who seizes us for freedom. Why cannot your promises or importunities seize me for freedom; or for that matter why is not Satan's rapture freedom? The answer is plain, though not explicit in any one set of texts: rapture to freedom is not causative but participatory. Were you to be the ground of my freedom it would have to be because you *shared* freedom with me, which you cannot do because you no more have freedom in yourself than do I. As for Satan, he is an empty parody of freedom, a sort of personification of his own bondage, so that although he can indeed seize me into a *voluntas faciendi,* this can only be that of those who consent to share his slavery. *Liberum arbitrium* belongs to God and to those with whom he shares it.

But if, as Luther has argued, it is *absurd* to say that any will is antecedent to itself, how is it then meaningful to say it of God's will? How does a "dialectical figment" suddenly become a deep truth when it is predicated of God? And how is it now meaningful to speak of our sharing in this capacity? The clue is in the last feature to be noted from Luther's teaching: when God is on the scene to snatch us into freedom, it is always "by his Spirit."

It is not absurd to say that the *triune* God freely chooses his own determinate choices, for the Spirit is God and is precisely the freedom of the Father over against the Son, as whom the Father has what he chooses and in whom the Father knows what he chooses. Of a *monadic* will it is indeed absurd to assert that it chooses what to choose, but such a will is precisely what God is not.

It would also be absurd to say that human persons as individuals have or can share God's triune free will. But as members of the community whose uniting

---

57. *Rapi.*

58. Ibid., 634–636.

59. E.g., ibid., 670.

60. Ibid., 635: "Nos rapiat in solium suum, rursus per spiritum eius servi et captivi sumus (quae tamen regia libertas est) ut velimus et faciamus lubentes, quae ipse velit."

and animating spirit is God the Spirit and who therefore stand with the Son before the Father, we share the liberation that the Spirit brings the Father and the Son. True human freedom—or anyway the sort that Luther is willing to dignify with the name—is an ecclesial reality.

All this is true of the man Jesus and of his sisters and brothers in the church, only differently. The risen Jesus, as present to and in the church, is at once *liberated by* the Spirit and *giver of* the liberating Spirit, so that it can even be said, "the Lord *is* the Spirit." And "where the Spirit of the Lord is, there is freedom."[61] It cannot be said of us, individually or together, that we are the Spirit or that where we are there is freedom. But *with* the risen Jesus, as the *totus Christus*, we other members of the church are free as he is. Individually, we are *being* freed, as we live into the free community.

As for those who do not yet belong to the church, they act "willingly" within the communities whose uniting principle is the *libido dominandi*. They are creatures of the triune God and do not escape God's choice that their human choices occur freely; nor is the Spirit who evokes all created spontaneity other than the Spirit who enlivens the church. There is of course an inherent contradiction: that Satan's rapture is a sphere of the Creator Spirit's presence. It is the same contradiction we have encountered whenever the word "sin" has fallen.

V

So far, this work has used the word "soul" only to quote Socrates; this may be surprising, since the word has traditionally provided the overall rubric of theological anthropology. Do we, a la Socrates, "have souls"? It depends on what one means by "soul." For it might be said that these three chapters have all along discussed nothing else than the fact and nature of the human soul.

In the Hebrew Old Testament, the word translated "soul," *nephesh*, is a word for the human person as such, insofar as he or she is living and active and effective within community.[62] A key passage of the second creation-narrative, so far omitted from our account, tells that God, having "formed the man from the dust of the ground," then "breathed into his nostrils the breath of life" so that "the man became a living soul ."[63] It is not soul itself that is breathed into the not-yet-living man; and what comes of God's breathing is not that the man *acquires* a soul but that he *becomes* one. Implicitly, our whole discussion of human personhood has had this passage as its guide.

The Greek of the New Testament displays no similarly consistent anthropological terminology. Comparing with the Old Testament, we may note that

---

61. II Corinthians 3:17.
62. Johannes Pedersen, *Israel: Its Life and Culture,* tr. Aslaug Møller (London: Oxford University Press, 1926), 1–2:99–181.
63. *Nephesh hayah.* The translation offered by the New Revised Standard Version is unreliable throughout this passage.

the word sometimes translated "soul," *psyche*, shows a certain shift away from denoting the living person to denoting the life *of* the living person. Thus in Jesus' saying, "Those who want to save their life will lose it, and those who lose their life for my sake . . . will save it,"[64] the word translated "life" is *psyche*. When *psyche* then appears paired with "body" (*soma*), the difference is between life and that which might not live or no longer lives; thus "the destroyer" can kill the body but not "the life" itself.[65] Here it may appear that "soul" and body can be independently dealt with; it is by way of such language that a different sense of "soul" will enter Christian thinking.

"Soul" as mostly encountered in Scripture is what anthropologists have called body-soul, a representation of the difference between the living person and the corpse. Socrates' "soul," very differently, is what has been called an escape-soul, a representation of the person's seemingly possible liberation from his or her own body, as in dreams or shamanistic practice. It is "soul" of this second sort of which Socrates could say that death is "nothing other than the release of the soul from the body,"[66] and that the good person practices and longs for just this separation, in which human personhood first achieves its true nature.[67] This is the "soul" that Platonism located decisively on the upward side of a metaphysical distinction between "spirit" and "matter." And this is the "soul" that became ambiguously fateful for Christian thinking.

Christianity adopted the Socratic notion of the soul not so much for its anthropologically interpretive power, which is in fact nil or close to it,[68] as for its apparent eschatological service. What of the dead who have died in the Lord? Their bodies are in the earth; is that where *they* are? They are to rise in the body; but what of the meantime? Thus the one New Testament appearance of "souls" actually separated from their bodies is in the Revelation: "I saw under the altar the souls of those who had been slaughtered for the Word of God," where they are waiting for the final redemption.[69]

The very thing that makes the Socratic notion of soul seem useful for eschatology is what creates the difficulty in our present context. Christianity attributes to embodiment a worth Socrates did not: the body is constitutive for the identity of the person. For Socrates, the soul that departs its body is the person perfected; whereas the Christian creeds locate the perfecting of the person not in the survival of the soul but in the resurrection of the body.

64. Mark 8:35parr.

65. Matthew 6:25par; 10:28par.

66. Plato, *Phaedo*, 64C: "ten tes psyches apo tou somatos apallagen."

67. Ibid., 64–67.

68. This is, it may be interesting to note, one point on which Jonathan Edwards and William James agree. The posit of an *entity*, "the soul," as what "has" and "does" the person's defining behaviors, is no more necessary than is the posit of a "material substance" as what "has" mass, inertia, etc. Or if "the soul" is so described as genuinely to guarantee the person's self-identity, it is described as divine and so unacceptably for Christian theology. In James, *Principles*, 1:325–329; to Edwards, Jenson, *America's Theologian*, 29–34.

69. Revelation 6:9–10.

Thus the adopted Socratic notion of soul has through theological history been a fruitful source of puzzlement. In the Aristotelian language which Western scholasticism adapted to state the difficulties, the Socratic soul is a "substance," that is, it does not require any other created reality to exist. But the human embodied person is also a substance. Given their creation, the soul and the besouled body both subsist in themselves. The question then has been: How are these two substances related? It was understood that they could not be regarded as two substances who merely happen for a time to be associated; theology was never quite so alienated from Scripture as to suppose such a thing.

After centuries of convoluted discussion, Thomas Aquinas devised a solution that is satisfactory if one accepts certain other scholastic positions. The soul, according to Thomas, is the "form" of the body, that is, the principle of that liveliness that distinguishes a body from a corpse—in this relation, we may say, Thomas's soul is a body-soul. Nevertheless, the soul must also be a substance other than the body, for its defining activity, consciousness, is in principle independent of bodily mediation, even though contingently it is in this life so mediated—in this relation, Thomas's soul is an escape-soul. Finally, this independent substantiality of the soul can be conceived because, although the soul is not matter instantiated by form, being itself the form of the body, it is nevertheless form instantiated by the act of existence.[70]

Only one—but of course one is fatal—of the propositions on which Thomas relies is unacceptable within this work: that our creaturely consciousness is in principle a disembodied act. Sheer cognition may just possibly be conceivable as such an act, by abstracting the notion of "sight" as did the chief Greek thinkers. But our actual created consciousness is not so pure; it is compound of hearing and seeing as sensuous acts, and of smelling, tasting, and feeling as well, all apprehensions of external reality not readily attributable to a disembodied spirit.

This is a convenient place to make explicit what has been assumed through this volume: the personal body, as the person's availability to others and thereupon to him or herself, is just so constituted first in those modes of presence that resist dissolution into subjectivity. William James should not have been so disappointed to find "only" objective and "material" phenomena by which to constitute his Ego.[71] One might even say that "my body" is a way of referring to the logical product of "I see," "I taste," "I smell," "I touch," and so on.[72] The discourse of systematic theology—as that of "philosophy"—too easily elides the sensuousness of human being. Let this paragraph at least recognize the temptation.

Nor has theology generally, popular or scholarly, been up to the subtlety of Thomas's solution. It may safely be said that nearly all Christians, once habituated to think of themselves as "having" a soul, have tended to revert to Socrates' pagan simplicity and conceive the soul as the real person hidden somehow "in" the body, until we "die and our souls go to heaven." But such devaluation of

---

70. *Summa theologiae,* i.75–76.
71. For all James' "pragmatism" he remained in fact a thorough idealist.
72. I am indebted for this realization to an unpublished lecture by Susan Ashbrook-Harvey.

embodiment cannot cohere with the gospel, and must be repudiated no matter how embedded in piety.

If we must speak of souls, it will perhaps be best to discipline ourselves to the sense that predominates in Scripture: the soul is simply the person in his or her liveliness and communal uniqueness. And the person—the soul, if we will—does not have the body as something else than itself; the body is the very same person insofar as he or she is available to others and so to him or herself. We will have to deal with the eschatological problems without much help from Socrates.

TWENTY-ONE

The Other Creatures

I

It is time to turn our attention from ourselves. What are we to think of all those creatures that are not marked by the human peculiarity? Galaxy clusters and gravity waves and aardvarks are as exactly creatures of God as are we. Has theology nothing more specific to say about them? Scripture speaks much of angels. What are we to think of them? And what of the devil?

Our attention cannot, to be sure, turn abruptly. The transition must be made by two propositions that are still about humanity, that is, about humanity's relation to the other creatures.

The first of these is that galaxies and angels and aardvarks—and the devil, in whatever sense he may be said to exist—are indeed only creatures and not gods or almost-gods: we are not to put our faith in them. That is, the church eschews humankind's ordinary way of relating to the world.

That we are dependent on both the regularities and the apparent whims of surrounding reality is a primal human experience. So also is awe before the world's beauty and majesty. It is then a primal mode of our sin, that we enact this awe and dependence religiously. Thus pious Romans sacrificed to nation and sexuality and fire and water, and tribal peoples ask the collective of the animals they hunt to bless the hunting, and so we could continue through all cultures. Judaism and Christianity are given no leeway in judging such worship: throughout Scripture it is humanity's great fall that we have "worshipped . . . the creature rather than the Creator."[1] The bluntness of the distinction may offend those who

---

1. Romans 1:25.

do not know the Creator in his personal identity, that is, whose faith is not in the Son; but neither Israel nor the church dare mitigate it.[2]

Most profoundly and universally, humanity has found itself under the heavens, and looking up has perceived itself at once sheltered and tyrannized by a panoply that appears identically as a divine society and as the most calculable aspect of the universe; in archaic civilizations celestial calendars are at once sacred scripture and basic technology. The sun is not originally a symbol or manifestation of the sun-god; the great light *is* the god. He daily pours out his blessings or his curses and yearly withdraws himself and returns; and all our flourishing depends on him. Nor are the other lights, each with his or her power, some easily predictable and some less so, less than full members of the pantheon.

Humanity has *worshipped* this "host of heaven," rather than simply calculating its influences, because in its cycles we have found our primal defense against the threat of the future, the most secure instance of the eternity of perdurance: the heavens present an apparently immutable repetition of movements and conjunctions, whose rule of the agricultural seasons controls an equally immutable wheel of life and death. But Israel and the church want no defense against the future, which they hear as promise rather than as threat; what is coming is the "new thing" the Lord will do, indeed it is resurrection. Therefore Israel and the church do not seek security in the cosmic cycles' determinism; instead they proclaim our true habitation in history, constituted by open possibilities.[3]

It has been a major contention of much twentieth-century theology, perhaps most powerfully represented by the thought of Friedrich Gogarten:[4] where the teaching of creation comes, even sometimes when it is not quite or no longer believed, it frees us from "enclosure by the world,"[5] from interpreting human life as regimented within divine cosmic process. Science alone does not break the spell. It is quite possible to know all about astronomy and geology and the underlying sciences and be as idolatrous of the world-process as any shaman; the great and profound case is Benedict Spinoza, while the religious speculations of famous scientists have throughout modernity displayed a repertoire of lesser superstitions.

In the language of Gogarten's and allied theology, the gospel "secularizes" the world for cultures it invades; that is, it strips the world of the presumption of

---

2. Recent waves of "creation spirituality" are simply apostasy to paganism. And it is precisely such unguarded, even unargued, judgment that is required of the church.

3. The classic and enormously influential exploration of this great divide between the religions is Mircea Eliade, *Cosmos and History; The Myth of the Eternal Return*, tr. W. R. Trask (New York: Harper, 1959). Eliade finally chose the eternal cycles.

4. The great monument of this whole movement, in my judgment, is Gogarten's *Der Mensch zwischen Gott und Welt* (Stuttgart: Friedrich Vorwerk, 1956). Gogarten's naive flirtation with National Socialism permanently alienated him from Karl Barth, to whom he had been the closest of all those briefly united as "dialectical theologians"; but as Barth once said to a student, "Perhaps non-Germans can allow themselves to read a little of his work."

5. "Umschlossenheit von der Welt"; e.g., ibid., 139.

divinity. To see how this happens, we need look no further than, again, the first chapter of Genesis: on the fourth day "God said, 'Let there be lights in the dome of the sky to separate the day from the night; and let them be for signs and for seasons and for days and years, and . . . to give light upon the earth.'"[6] In our already secularized situation, we will not at first feel the offense of these sentences. We must think of a priestly thinker somewhere in the warrens of the second temple, who with them deliberately blasphemed the universal religion of human-kind: "Gods nothing! Those are lamps, clocks, and calendars the Lord put up there for the general convenience." The priestly account does not even set the heavenly bodies' appearance at the beginning where the birth of gods would be; the initial burst of energy, the first general sorting-out of the universe, and even the beginnings of created life precede it.[7]

Israel was commanded: "When you look up to the heavens and see the sun, the moon, and the stars, all the host of heaven, do not be led astray and bow down to them and serve them."[8] The Deuteronomistic history stereotypically identifies the act by which Israel's kings broke the covenant as making "offerings . . . to the sun, the moon, the constellations, and all the host of the heavens."[9] And according to an exegesis reported in Acts, when the Lord "turned away" from the people of Israel in the desert and so for a time left them to be like the other peoples, what this meant materially was that he "handed them over to worship the host of heaven."[10]

If we are not to worship the world, what *are* we to do about it? Genesis stipulates our role with respect to part of it: we are to "have dominion over" all creatures within the sphere of our action.[11] Two problems immediately appear.

First, this mandate indeed covers only part of creation; precisely the religiously most tempting part cannot be included. As the Lord said to Job: can humans "bind the chains of the Pleiades, or loose the cords of Orion?"[12] How then are we to regard the Pleiades or Orion? We will return centrally to this question.

Second: What is the nature of human dominion? Recent ecological ideology has often blamed the Bible or Christianity for the West's destructively exploitive relation to the Earth.[13] In the simplistic way the charge has been made it is, to be sure, mostly a case of late-modern secularists' general historical and religious

6. Genesis 1:14–15.

7. Thus the science is not bad, except perhaps for the last item. And even it may turn out to be right, if life originated before the organization of our solar system.

8. Deuteronomy 4:19.

9. E.g., II Kings 23:5.

10. Acts 7:42. Whether Luke has the ancient gods or the angels here in mind makes no difference to our present point.

11. Genesis 1:28–30.

12. Job 38:31–33.

13. The terms of discussion were determined, perversely, by Lynn White, "The Historical Roots of Our Ecological Crisis," *The Environmental Handbook*, prepared for the first national environmental teach-in (New York: Ballantine, 1970).

ignorance.[14] Genesis' second creation story makes it more than plain what the dominion is that the Lord intends for humanity: we are *gardeners* of someone else's garden. We are to *tend* our area of creation on behalf of the Creator to whom it continues to belong, taking our own subsistence from his generosity; the ecclesially much abused word "stewardship" here perfectly fits the case. Nothing could be more opposed to exploitive modernity's understanding of the world as a conglomerate of "natural resources" available for our use as we feel a need and technology enables.

Yet there is a connection to be registered. The gospel's secularizing of the world was a historical condition for the venture of Western technology; one does not shoot rockets at the moon if one takes it for a goddess.[15] And the consequences of Western technology, particularly when it has been colonized on the territory of tribal or archaic peoples, have undoubtedly been ambiguous.[16]

If the doctrine of creation has liberated us from worshiping the encompassing world, but we have not believed in the Creator himself or have ceased to believe in him, the liberation is dangerous,[17] for fallen humanity may then find in it license without stewardship; the gospel is also in this way a two-edged sword. In the hands of Western or Westernized culture that does not honor the gospel that enabled it, powerful technology must be always on the verge of rampage. "Since the natural world . . . remains God's creation, self-aggrandizing exercise of divinely commissioned dominion must recoil on humanity itself. . . . The ecological crisis at the end of self-emancipating modernity may be understood as a reminder that the God of the Bible remains lord of his Creation."[18]

The second transitional proposition, already in place: as it in fact is, humanity is the reason for the rest of creation. The Son for whom God creates is one of us, and neither an angel nor a virus nor an instance of whatever other creatures may inhabit the cosmos; the creation is stage and players for our story with him.

It does not follow, when galaxy clusters and angels and aardvarks are once there, that they do not have their own meaning for the Creator. One possible move

---

14. I once heard the holder of a named chair at a famous university, a great authority and guru in the "deep ecology" movement, make it the chief premise of a lengthy attack on Christianity, in a public lecture, that Genesis 1 wickedly sets aside a whole day for the exclusive creation of humanity.

Wolfhart Pannenberg, *Systematische Theologie* (Göttingen: Vandenhoeck & Ruprecht, 1991), 2:234, has the central point: "Modern secularism cannot simultaneously boast of its emancipation from religious constraints and unload responsibility for the consequences of its absolutizing of earthly cravings on the religious origins from whose restrictions it has freed itself."

15. Better than any scholarly analysis is the action in Tom Stoppard's play *Jumpers*: a torch singer abandons her work and takes to her bed when men walk on the moon.

16. "Ambiguous" is the strongest word truth allows; mass hunting and slash-and-burn agriculture are, after all, ecologically benign only so long as infant mortality and institutionalized petty warfare keep down the human population. Few "native" decriers of technology's debits volunteer to do altogether without its benefits.

17. This too is a theme of Gogarten; e.g., *Der Mensch*, 161–167.

18. Pannenberg, *Systematische Theologie*, 2:235.

at this point is to affirm such meaning but say we cannot know what it is. So Karl Barth: to praise humanity's unique role involves "no derogatory judgment about any of our fellow creatures—which is none of our business anyway. We do not know what relation God has reserved for himself with respect to them, or what then their necessary uniqueness within the whole cosmos may be."[19] But although caution here is surely good advice, perhaps we need not be quite so agnostic.

Late modernity has of course denounced the claim itself. The idea that the universe is there to be the scene of our fellowship with God is seen as a piece of naive presumption. Who are we, creeping about on a speck in a minor eddy of the universe, to make such a claim? Perhaps it was plausible when the universe seemed smaller, but not now when we know something of its vastness. To this three rejoinders may be made.

The first is the simple phenomenological observation that all experienced universes are exactly the same size, that is, immense, since the experienced universe provides the standard of immensity. Israel's—or Greece's or the Bantus'— experienced universe was no whit cozier than is that of a modern cosmologist.

The second is that it currently seems possible to account for the specific complexity and immensity of the actual universe in terms of what is necessary for something like humanity to exist. It is indeed a nagging question for believers as for others: Whatever is such weird abundance for? Could not a universe without black holes and variously flavored quarks and free-floating bits of genetic information and other such extravagances have worked out just as well? And why should the world's distances be measurable only by such preposterous units as light-years? But *given* the existence of humanity, it has recently been argued that this universe is the very one appropriate to humanity's accommodation.

We need not here decide whether the so-called anthropic principle,[20] if it obtains, provides an argument for design in the universe. We will not evaluate the version of the principle which adds that for there to be a universe at all it must be a universe so ordered as eventually to contain intelligent life. Nor in general should we put much theological weight on considerations such as these momentarily before us.

But given that humanity does exist and that the universe is as it is, the observations are indeed interesting. The measured size of the universe is the exact correlate of a cosmic expansion with the rate and of the length that could enable carbon-based life at this point in the expansion. And for there to be a universe hospitable to intelligence, the initial conditions of the universe had to fall within a vanishingly narrow cut of the open possibilities, precisely the cut that would produce the otherwise implausible universe we find. Perhaps such observations do at least suffice to counter the notion that modern knowledge of the universe confounds all claims for human centrality.

---

19. *Kirchliche Dogmatik* (Zollikon-Zürich: Evangelizcher Verlag, 1932–1968), III/2:90.

20. To which see John D. Barrow and Frank J. Tipler, *The Anthropic Cosmological Principle* (New York: Oxford University Press, 1986).

It is, however, a third consideration that is theologically decisive: What has size or complexity to do with the matter? If there is such a God as the gospel presents, he is invested in historical particularity. In the present tense, that is, in space, this means he will be invested in *some* speck or other in some cosmic eddy or other, as in the history of that speck he is identified with the Jews among the nations and with Mary among the Jews. We will be impressed by relative sizes only if we have antecedently affirmed some other god than the Lord, of a more normal, ahistorical sort or at least of less surprising historical judgments.

II

We will not begin with galaxies and the like; if creation includes angels and heaven as their habitation, these are yet more remarkable and deserve the priority the tradition has given them. Moreover, we will find that when we have finished discussing them, we have said much of what must be said about the rest of creation.

The first point to be made is that, again, whatever else the angels in their heaven may be, they and it are creatures like us. The risen man Jesus is even "far above" them,[21] and so therefore will we be.

We may let John of Damascus represent the general tradition. Angels are "intelligent beings." Their "nature is graced with immortality." They are "bodiless and immaterial but only relatively to us . . . for only the divine is properly so." Despite immortality, they are "changeable, and can remain and grow in the good or turn to evil." Despite disembodiment, "when they are in heaven they are not on earth." When they arrive on God's errands, "they do not appear . . . as they are, but in forms appropriate to their beholders." And they "aid us and supervise our affairs."[22]

Throughout the religions of humankind, "spirits" more or less so specifiable play a great role. Not quite gods but nor quite like us—so, for example, they are "bodiless and immaterial but only relatively" or although immortal are changeable—they often play a more central role in daily cult than do the proper gods.[23] They are in fact the everyday version of that ambiguous realm of mediation between deity and time which we have heretofore encountered in less representational forms.[24]

Also Israel and the church have reckoned with spirits, but in paradoxically restricted roles: either they are God's immediate and wholly dependent servants,

---

21. Ephesians 1:21.

22. John of Damascus, *The Orthodox Faith*, iii, 45–50.

23. A good summary is A. Schimmel, "Geister, Dämonen, Engel: I," *Die Religion in Geschichte und Gegenwart*, ed. Kurt Galling (Tübingen: J. C. B. Mohr, 1958), 2:1298–1301.

24. That Pseudo-Dionysius should in the sixth century have installed the church's angels in the place of earlier heirarchies of mediation, saying of them exactly what, e.g., Origen had said of his ranks of images, was thus both a sort of remythologizing of the angels and in its way immensely perceptive. Remarkably, Karl Barth provides a clear and sympathetic explication of Dionysius's doctrine; *Kirchliche Dogmatik*, III/3:445–452.

that is, "angels,"[25] or they are merely evil.[26] And our relation to them is entirely secularized: in the Old Testament a religious relation to spirits appears only as prohibited sorcery[27] and in the New Testament only as cultural temptation.[28] In effect, religion's spirits are evicted from their generic religious functions and given new ones.

The particular Old Testament spirits who entered Judaism's and the church's imagination as "the angels" are beings who elsewhere would be gods or very close to gods themselves,[29] but in Israel are made to be created servants of the one God. The scene in the prologue to Job[30] presents them: the Lord holds audience in heaven, and those who come are "sons-of-god,"[31] that is, beings who belong to God rather than to earth, just as "daughters-of-Zion" are women who belong to Jerusalem. The historical tension in the phrase appears in the contrast between an appearance in Deuteronomy, where it denotes actual gods to whom JHWH allows rule of other nations than Israel,[32] and the Septuagint rendering of the present passage simply with "God's messengers."[33]

In the scene in Job these personages are court functionaries. The office of one of them is stated: with the title "the Accuser"[34] he is investigating and prosecuting attorney for earthly affairs. In other contexts the same group can appear as a liturgical chorus[35] or as a feudal council.[36] And of course there are the spectacular winged cherubim and seraphim[37] and in apocalyptic vision great personalities with names.[38]

In the New Testament, the Old Testament figures are presumed furniture of reality. But they play actual roles in three narrowly delineable contexts: at very particular points in the Gospels' narrative, as enablers of the earliest history of the church, and in apocalyptic. Around Jesus' birth there is a positive eruption of angels;[39] angels minister to Jesus following the temptation[40] and in Gethese-

25. Hebrew *malakh* and Greek *aggelos* both translate "messenger."

26. Genesis 32:22–32.

27. Leviticus 17:7; Deuteronomy 18:10–11.

28. Colossians 2:16–19.

29. E.g., Friedrich Horst, *Hiob* (Biblischer Kommentar Altest Testament, vol. 16) (Neukirchen Kreis Moers: Buchhandlung des Erziehungsvereins, 1960), 1:12–13.

30. Job 1:6–12. We may think also of Micaiah's vision, I Kings 22:19–23.

31. *Benai ha-elohim*. Somewhat prematurely translated "heavenly beings" by the New Revised Standard Version.

32. Deuteronomy 32:8–9; here the Septuagint surely has a better text.

33. We may also note Micaiah's vision, I Kings 22:19–23: "I saw the Lord sitting on his throne, with all the host of heaven standing beside him to the right and to the left of him," from whom the Lord asks volunteers for earthly service.

34. "The Satan," who is not here seen as himself wicked.

35. Psalm 29:1; Job 38:7.

36. Psalm 89:6–7.

37. Psalm 18:9; Isaiah 6.

38. Gabriel's initial appearance is in Daniel 8:15–16; 9:21; Michael's in Daniel 10:13, 21.

39. Matthew 1:20–24; 2:13–19; Luke 1:11–19; 26–38; 2:9–15.

40. Mark 1:12–13parr.

mane;[41] the angels are specifically absent from the Crucifixion lest their presence prevent it;[42] and angels are the initiating witnesses of the Resurrection.[43] As the apostolic mission begins, prisons and other impasses are opened by angels.[44] And it is "with his angels" that the Son of Man will come "from heaven" to judge the earth,[45] while the heaven to which a door opens in Revelation is populated with them in all their hierarchies and roles.

What are we to make of these representations? That the figures who appear in Scripture and churchly tradition are indeed "representations"[46] in Hegel's sense, that is, images whose literal descriptions should not be taken for concepts, can hardly be denied. The question then is, how can the angels be located conceptually?[47] If anywhere?

Theology has never affirmed the angels without in fact demythologizing them a bit, whether this was acknowledged or not. Thus, for example, although a chief feature of the biblical depictions is the angels' spectacular embodiment and another is their spatial coming and going, the main tradition has conceptualized them as disembodied subjectivities whose "locations are purely mental."[48]

A first key to the angels' mode of being is their identification with heaven. They are, as in the birth narrative, precisely "the heavenly host."[49] And of heaven the fundamental doctrine is: "The heavens are the Lord's heavens, but the earth he has given to human beings."[50] Among angelologists, it is Karl Barth's clear recognition of these relations[51] that makes him our necessary interlocutor in the following.

The second key is the angels' appearance in the Gospels and Acts at just the, so to speak, ontologically perilous junctures. They show up at the conception and birth of the human who will be identified as the Son, at the Resurrection when this identification is established, and in between at the points where, in our earlier phrase, deity might have broken. And they then appear at similarly dangerous junctures in the life of the church.

41. According, anyway, to whoever wrote the present Luke 22:43–44.

42. Matthew 26:53.

43. Mark 16:5–8; Matthew 28:2–5; John 20:12.

44. Acts 5:19; 8:26; 10:3–7; 12: 7–11, 23; 27:23.

45. Matthew 16:27; 25:31; see also 13:41, 49; 24:31; Mark 13:27; John 1:51.

46. *Vorstellungen.*

47. The most sustained—and in itself magnificent—effort to answer this question is undoubtedly that of Thomas Aquinas; *Summa theologiae*, i.50–63. Angels are beings "in whom their existence is other than their essence, even though their essence is without matter," *De ente et essentia*, v.44–48. We will not, however, go further into his doctrine. Karl Barth's critique, *Kirchliche Dogmatik*, III/3:452–466, is decidedly *in malam partem*, but the central gravamen is plainly right: Thomas's posit of "separate" intelligences fills a necessary place in Thomas's metaphysics; but it is quite beside the point of elucidating the figures who appear in Scripture.

48. John of Damascus, *The Orthodox Faith*, iii.45,49.

49. Luke 2:13–14.

50. Psalm 115:16.

51. Barth, *Kirchliche Dogmatik*, III:429–430.

III

According to Barth, heaven is created with the earth[52] as earth's boundary by mystery:[53] it "is the heart of that in creation which is unfathomable, distant, and uncanny for . . . earthly creatures."[54] Thus heaven is not a space related to earth as to another space; we cannot by travelling within creation move from being in the one to being in the other. We must say: so far so good.

It does not follow that heaven is in no way locatable, that we cannot point to where it is. And we can follow Barth a certain distance in what he says to this matter also.

According to Barth, both heaven and earth have their being "in the course" of God's movement to solidarity with us,[55] which in fact encompasses all his action *ad extra*. This movement is in itself a movement of God *to* creation, but since a particular creature *within* creation, humanity, "is the goal and object of this movement" it must also be a movement "within the created world."[56] And as God is himself the starting point of his movement to us, so insofar as the movement occurs within creation it has a created starting point identified with him; and that is "heaven." Heaven is defined as "the place in the world from which" God's action, insofar as it is an innerworldly action, originates.[57]

There must, according to Barth, be such a distinction between origin and goal of God's movement, also within creation, to establish a "distance between him and humanity," without which there could be "no dealings or intercourse" between us.[58] God, I noted earlier, must have his own place within creation if he is not simply to absorb the creature within himself.

But we do have to ask: *Where* is this place within creation from which God comes to the rest of it? And now it will not do to say with Barth that heaven as a "realm" is merely "unknown and incomprehensible."[59] According to Barth, we know that the creation subject to our knowledge or action, "the earth," is at all points bounded by mystery and that God comes to us from that boundary, and that is all we know. Barth has thus forgotten an essential point about the biblical heaven, that it *opens* to earthly apprehension. So Ezekiel: "As I was among the exiles by the river Chebar, the heavens were opened, and I saw visions of God."[60] And so the Revelation: "And after this I looked, and there in heaven a door stood open! And [a] voice . . . said, 'Come up here, and I will show you what must take place after this.'"[61] Heaven is indeed the earth's bounding by mystery, but the

---

52. Ibid., III/3: 468.
53. Ibid., 493.
54. Ibid., 494.
55. Ibid., 479.
56. Ibid., 501.
57. Ibid., 503.
58. Ibid., 503.
59. Ibid., 515.
60. 1:1.
61. 4:1.

boundary is drawn by the mystery's speaking to us and opening to our view; just so it locates itself.

In the paradigm passage from Revelation the mystery revealed is the future—and noting that, we are set on a path very different from Barth's. As we discussed earlier, heaven is finally defined within apocalyptic metaphysics, where it is the created future's presence—*as* future!—with God.[62] There is future in God, but not so as to transcend God: God *anticipates* his future and so possesses it, and so there is a present tense of creation's future with God, and therefore there is also its place with God. Just so heaven is, as earlier described, the created space God takes, from which to be present to his other creatures.

Since there is this space, God can if he chooses open a door to what is in it. To be sure, the future is present and knowable in heaven only as what is not yet, and so, at least for us, only in the form of ambiguous icons of itself; as I noted earlier, if creation's future were within creation present in its own character, it would not be the future. But as riddles and ambiguous pictures, there the future is, also for us if God chooses.

Let us attempt a formulation, influenced by the style of Barth's teaching but nevertheless diverging from anything he could have said: heaven is the origin of the call of God's coming Kingdom, insofar as that call is a created force beckoning within the creation. The creation is liberated to its End and Fulfillment by God the Spirit; heaven is the telos of this dynamism insofar as it as a teleology within creation itself.

But now we are very close to falling back into the very aspect of Barth's position that we rejected. We are close to saying that heaven is a sheer dynamic of all earthly events—in our doctrine, the dynamic of their pull by God's future—and is therefore located everywhere and nowhere. We can agree with Barth: heaven is wherever within creation God's coming originates. But in Scripture believers can very well *point* to such "wherever"s. Jacob said of the location of his dream and the monument he erected to mark it, "How awesome is this place. This is none other than the house of God and this is the gate of heaven."[63]

In Jacob's dream, heaven appears as a space separated vertically from earth. But when he wakes, the earthly location of the dream, with the stone that Jacob erects to mark it, is itself a "house" of God,[64] a temple where he may be found. As such, it is a "gate of heaven," a conjunction of heaven and earth. And it was the marked-out place itself from which for centuries the Lord's initiatives then moved Israel's history.[65]

In the Old Testament, the stereotypical usages at first seem, so to speak, topographically clear: the Lord "looks down" from "heaven, his holy habitation"; from there he examines humankind and judges or blesses them;[66] and when the

---

62. I:196–198.
63. Genesis 28:17.
64. Ibid., 22.
65. So above all in the great composition I Samuel.
66. E.g., Deuteronomy 26:15; Psalm 2:4; 80:14.

Lord or the Angel of the Lord calls or answers us he does so "from heaven."[67] The writers plainly are thinking of a boundary somewhere *up* there and of God as located just beyond it. But these relations can suddenly be confused; so, for example, the holy mountain can itself be the place from which the Lord comes, and the spatial heaven and earth together the *goal* of his coming.[68]

Again, at Sinai the fire and storm were on and around the mountain and were themselves "where the Lord was" to speak to Israel. Moses thereupon drew near to the darkness, and the Lord said he should tell Israel, "You have seen for yourselves that I spoke with you from heaven."[69] Deuteronomy's version makes the identification-in-difference in parallel construction: "From heaven he made you hear his voice. . . . On earth he showed you his great fire, while you heard his words coming out of the fire."[70]

It is the Temple that fully confounds spatial simplicities. As the Chronicler summarizes Solomon's dedicatory prayer, it begins straightforwardly: "Will God indeed reside with mortals on earth? Even heaven and the highest heaven cannot contain you, how much less this house that I have built." But then the prayer for the Temple is: "May your eyes be open . . . toward this house, this place where you promised to set your name, and may you heed the prayer that your servants pray *toward* [emphasis added] this place."[71] So there can be the astonishing parallel construction: "The Lord is in his holy temple; the Lord's throne is in heaven."[72]

At the heart of the Temple, where the normal religion of antiquity would have put the image, there is instead an empty throne formed by the wings of the "cherubim." It is in fact something like an attribute of the Lord, that he "is enthroned on the cherubim." Most directly these are the statues on the ark,[73] but the throne "upon the cherubim" can also take the place of heaven in the classic pairing of "heaven and earth."[74]

In fact the cherubim are *at once* the throne in the Temple and the storm-wings upon which "God . . . rides through the heavens."[75] The magnificent psalm paints the full picture, in which heaven above and the winds of heaven and the throne in the Temple and the firestorm on Mount Sinai are all one: "He bowed the heavens and came down; thick darkness was under his feet. He rode on a cherub and flew; he came swiftly upon the wings of the wind. . . . Out of the brightness before him there broke through his clouds hailstones and coals of fire."[76]

---

67. E.g., Genesis 21:17; 22:11.
68. Habakkuk 3:3.
69. Exodus 20:18–22.
70. 4:36.
71. II Chronicles 6:18–21. The longer version in I Kings 8 has the same structure.
72. Psalm 11:2.
73. E.g., I Samuel 4:4; II Samuel 6:2.
74. Psalm 99:1.
75. Psalm 18:9; Deuteronomy 33:26. Almost certainly, of course, the latter vision was the model for the throne.
76. Psalm 18:9–10.

It is clearly time to adduce the concept of sacrament. Sacraments, in the classic formulation, "*contain* [emphasis added] the grace they signify":[77] the event of a sacrament defines a place, and at that place *is* the divine reality that the sacrament communicates to the world. Precisely so, the place from which God comes is throughout Scripture a sacramental reality: it is neither a delineable region of created space, related spatially to another such region, earth, nor is it therefore unlocatable by earthlings.

Scripture knows many sacramental places and events, many gates of heaven. God takes location from which to act in his creation by taking on created body: by riding the cherubim-storm, by filling the Tabernacle and then the Temple, by walking about Palestine, by suffering in the flesh, by taking bread and cup as body and blood. Also in this respect the Resurrection merely concentrates and extends Israel's privileges christologically. Israel's service around the cherubim-throne or the congregation gathered round the bread and cup, or Israel and the church in a hundred less vital ways, locate heaven by surrounding and so defining its gate.[78]

In ontological finality, the space that is heaven is the space defined by the risen Son's location at the right of the Father. Space, we have seen, is the distention in God that accommodates a present tense of creatures. Those created by accommodation in the triune life do not thereby become persons of God; God's act of creation posits space as the formal possibility of their otherness. When now we speak specifically of heaven as God's own space we are speaking of the space between the man Jesus and the Father, insofar as this space is *at once* the space between a creature and God and the inner-triune difference between the Son and the Father. The latter difference is the possibility of space and creatures in it; its identity with the former is the possibility of God's spatial location over against them.[79]

Much of the previous two paragraphs is made from usual propositions of classical sacramentology. What is not usual is these propositions' use to say that the heaven from which God draws earth to its future is locatable by earthlings, that on earth we can point to it at the sacramental places of Israel and the church. What is not usual is refusal to posit heaven as located "elsewhere" than, for central instance, the place of the Eucharistic congregation around bread and cup: what is not usual is denial of a distance between heaven and the altar. Any picture of God ruling the hearts of his believers from the church's table, font, and pulpit, and ruling the rest of creation from someplace *else* called heaven is, it is here claimed, radically inappropriate.

---

77. Council of Trent, Session VII, First Decree, Canon 6.

78. To cite also in this volume the Jewish thinker Michael Wyschogrod, "Incarnation," *Pro Ecclesia*, 2 (1993), 210: "There is no place in which God is not present. But this truth must be combined with the insistence that God also has an address. . . . He dwells in Number One Har Habayit Street [Jerusalem]."

79. All this is very much against Barth, who makes the heaven-earth relation a *mirror* of the God-creature relation; e.g., *Kirchliche Dogmatik*, III/3:490.

The caution with which the previous paragraph is formulated should be noted. It is not said that earthly volumes delineated and occupied by the bread and cup or its congregation, or by Israel's or the church's other locations of heaven's gate, *delimit* a spatial realm that is heaven.[80] Using language of late scholasticism and the Reformation, it is not said that sacramental spaces locate heaven "circumscriptively," that is, that their "length, breadth, and depth" make a volumetric of heaven.[81] Circumscriptively, heaven is no place at all; and were circumscriptive location the only sort, heaven would indeed be earth's boundedness by mystery everywhere in general and no place in particular. God is not somehow housed inside sacramental locations: he does not rule the world by causal chains that originate, for example, from inside the space occupied by the loaf and cup.

But these demurrers issued, it is indeed asserted: we can point to the "holy habitation" from which the Lord watches earth, from which he judges or blesses us, from which he calls to us and answers our appeals, which he "rends" to come to us. We can tell ourselves and others where to direct our intention when we invoke the Lord's coming; and to do this we must point to those gates of heaven that orient and gather his earthly congregation.[82] God moves the world by the will as which he is present amid his people.

It is time to return to the angels, for whose sake all this speculation was initially launched. Barth noticed something ontologically decisive about the biblical angels: they are not stable individual identities interacting in an alternative world called heaven. As God's will is "done . . . in heaven," "the obedience, that God finds in this heavenly event, is that of a subject," but this subjectivity can be understood equivalently as one or as many.[83] Moreover, angels "exist only in that they *come* and *go* in [their] service"; they "are exhausted . . . in their function."[84]

So far, yet again, so good. But what is this function? According to Barth, what the angels do is the only thing any creature can according to his system do, *witness*.[85] The angels' difference from other creatures is that their witness is "pure,"[86] since they are wholly disinterested and immediately in God's presence.[87] But this specification is both too narrow and too uncontrollable to clarify the biblical phenomena we are trying to interpret.[88] We will begin instead from what we called the second key to the nature of angels.

---

80. It will be seen that the concern of Johannes Brenz, addressed in the first volume, is here taken up again.

81. Martin Luther, *Vom Abendmahl Christ, Bekenntnis* (1528), WA 26:395.

82. In the foregoing, Martin Luther's exegesis of Jacob's monument is reproduced, only the other way around. *Ennaratio in Genesis* (WA 42), 43:599: "Go to the place where the word is spoken and the sacraments are ministered, and there set up the title 'The Gate of heaven.'"

83. *Kirchliche Dogmatik*, III/3:522.

84. Ibid., 428–429.

85. Ibid., 538.

86. Ibid., 566.

87. E.g., ibid., 577, 584.

88. Barth's conception of the role of angelic witness seems to betray a disaster in his Christology also. Many passages in his discussion seem to put the angels where the humanity of Christ should

In the Gospels, the angels appear at precisely those points where conflict threatens between the course of events as predictable by extrapolation from the past—in modernity, the course of events as mechanistic interpretation can abstract it—and God's total direction of events to an eschatological transformation. In the predictable courses of events, virgins indeed do not have babies nor is anyone in swaddling cloths the Lord, nor do humans fully vanquish temptation or the fear of death, nor do they rise from the dead—and the ancient world knew these things quite as well as do we. In Acts, the first years of the church required the apostles to seize possibilities that, in any "realistic" view, were not there to be seized; so angels opened them. And at the end, all the continuities of nature and history must, if the gospel is verified, be wrenched into a fulfillment utterly beyond their own energies; thus the Revelation is one long display of angels.

We may say with Barth that the angels' function is "witness" if we give the concept an eschatological and so ontological weight Barth does not. We do this by reminding ourselves that God creates and sustains all things by speaking. What the angels' speech witnesses *to* is itself again speech, God's speech, and so the angelic witness belongs to the action to which it testifies. Thus the angels' witness participates in bringing to pass the content of the witness.

As directed to us, the angels' witness counters our unbelief. In our subjectivities, there is indeed conflict between earth's various and, when isolated, purposeless regularities and creation's eschatological plot. We do indeed direct our lives by extrapolating from the past, and we are irresistibly tempted to that doleful sort of interpretation that under the conditions of modernity becomes mechanism. The angels tell us we need not do this, need not live by the past, for "to you is born this day . . . a Savior . . . the Messiah, the Lord."[89] They tell us not to adapt to "Babylon the great" for she is "Fallen, fallen!"[90] As to where we hear the angels speak so, the first answer is straightforward: in Scripture.

But the angels do not witness only to *us*. They do not merely tell of Babylon's overthrow; Michael and his troops march with the Lamb to accomplish it. That the world's various partial determinisms are bound together with the eschatological dynamism of total history, and so with each other, is the actuality of the angels. That a Virgin conceives is not merely what Gabriel talks *about* but is the very reality of Gabriel. Again, that the Lord is risen is not merely a contingent content of the angelic witness; the only describable earthly events of the Resurrection, as we earlier noted, were the appearances and the angelic witness.

The angelic witness is God's creative Word itself, insofar as it is a moving impulse *within* created nature. There is a moment of truth in analyses that identify the angels with "powers of nature that otherwise considered are also the objects

---

be. E.g., ibid., 580: "God is present on earth also without the angels. . . . But where his presence becomes event, experience, and decision for the earthly creature, there is it the doing of the angels, in which this becomes true."

89. Luke 2:10–11.
90. Revelation 18:2.

of scientific description."[91] But the powers of nature have their place in an eschatological plot which the sciences do not describe; they are themselves just as they are
linked in a total created teleology to which modernity's sciences have eschewed
reference. It is as the powers of nature are summoned to their place and brought to
themselves that there are angels. Angels are precisely the messengers between the
Eschaton and the world's partial regularities, and so also between those partial regularities themselves insofar as they are united by the common call of their future.

Heaven is the presence in creation of earth's final future; it is the only "realized" eschatology and is just so the call of that future on earth's internal regularities. The angels are the various aspects of this eschatological teleology. Their peculiar unity of personality with impersonality also results from this position. As
mediation between the Eschaton and what would otherwise be the mere mechanisms of creation, they mediate also the otherwise impersonal universe with the
world of persons, divine and created, that is beyond and within it. For the Eschaton
will be the triumph of community, and time as leading to the Eschaton is the history of free personal actions. As for the described forms of particular angels and
sorts of angels, these are of course apocalyptic images like the heavenly landscapes
they inhabit.

The angels are not the Holy Spirit; they are creatures. The angels are the
eschatological teleology of creation *insofar* as this teleology is itself creaturely. The
Spirit is God's own inner dynamism, which from beyond creation liberates creation to transcend itself, and so gives creation its angelic energy.

If the Eucharist should open not only to hearing but to seeing, perhaps at
the elevation of the consecrated bread and cup with the words "Through him and
in him and with him," what we would see is described by an English hymn mod-
elled on the Liturgy of St. James: "Christ our God to earth descending, comes
our homage to demand. . . . Rank on rank the host of heaven spreads its vanguard
on the way; as the Light of light, descending from the realms of endless day, comes
the pow'rs of hell to vanquish, as the darkness clears away. At his feet the six-
winged seraph, cherubim with sleepless eye, veil their faces to the presence . . ."
We would find ourselves in John the Seer's picture, joined in both the angels'
presentation of creation to God and their mission from God to earth. This must
not happen before the End, or at least not commonly, for we would see not only
the angels but the Light of light, the Presence from whom even the seraphim and
cherubim must veil their faces, and though all the baptized are indeed prophets
we are mostly not seers appointed to bear this sight even in apocalyptic representation, nor yet devotees so perfected in prayer as perhaps indeed even now sometimes to bear it.[92]

---

91. Pannenberg, *Systematische Theologie*, 2:129.

92. We have no call to dispute in principle the claim made, e.g., for the hesychast monks, though
we may perhaps be skeptical about some of its circumstances. Gregory Palamas is of course the theologian of the hesychast experience; so e.g., *Triads*, iii.1.6, "The grace of adoption, the deifying gift of
the Spirit, [is] a light of glory which the saints behold, a glory beyond ineffability, a light hypostatic
and uncreated, eternal being from eternal being, appearing to those who are worthy partially now . . .
and in the age to come more fully, which shows God to them through God himself."

The language of this discussion has oscillated between concepts in which I have attempted to interpret the reality of the host of heaven and the iconic language that imposes itself in the angels' own presence. The oscillation is proper: we must both *explain* that the angels are aspects of creation's deep teleology and *sing* at Eucharist, "Therefore with angels and archangels and with all the host of heaven." And it is with the latter sort of discourse that we must end. Our demythologizing concepts, necessary as they may be, cannot replace the iconic language of Scripture and worship. When we hear, for example, that "war broke out in heaven: Michael and his angels fought against the dragon,"[93] the depiction and name of the great warrior and the invocation of his army are words that we, to whose sight the gate of heaven mercifully does not open, nevertheless overhear through it; and we may trust them as we dare not trust our conceptual explanations.[94]

As to when the angels now appear, the matter is not so puzzling as is sometimes supposed. Christ's birth, death, and Resurrection are not repeated; the angels' word for them now speaks in Scripture. In the life of the church, the angels do continue to appear when the opportunities and threats are like those of the church of Acts. And at the End, they will join our chorus. That is, the three New Testament occasions of angelic visitation remain as actual as ever.

IV

Most of what must be said about the creatures who are neither human nor angelic has already been said. They with us constitute "earth"; despite all their fascination and frequent spectacular oddity they are not the mystery of creation but that which is bounded *by* mystery, that which can *be* mysterious because there is heaven. They exist in that God wills there to be a stage for the story of the Son; and their coherences and regularities are partial orders established and unified in a teleology constituted by their bending to this eschatological plot. Thus arises the teleology that creation has also within itself.

The last point requires further comment. The modern sciences were established by, among other choices, the decision to abstain from teleological explanations. The fruitfulness of this decision doubtless justifies it pragmatically, but in itself the policy is extremely odd. For the world resolutely presents itself as purposefully designed; nor is the creation's comprehensive teleological self-presentation one of the particular appearances critique of which is vital to rationality. Especially the biological world is one great gallery of things all of which give every appearance of being designed for a purpose, as a leading exponent of strict neo-Darwinian mechanism has with exasperation described the matter of his discipline.[95] If the world's teleological appearance is false it is difficult indeed to account for it.

93. Revelation 12:7.

94. The question that destroyed the unity of Hegel's epigones was whether when conceptual truth, *Begriff*, comes, representational truth, *Vorstellung*, simply retires. We are here with the "right-wing" Hegelians.

95. Richard Dawkins, *The Blind Watchmaker* (Harlow: Longman Scientific & Technical, 1986).

If we insist that the eye, for example, is not evolved to enable seeing, or indeed that each organic cell is not elaborately designed for its unique purpose, the insistence has in fact no other basis than ideological determination that the world *shall* not manifest design.[96] No mechanism has ever been found or even specifically imagined that can have energized and directed the move from unsighted organisms to sighted organisms, or from animals without such organs as fins or limbs to animals with them, or so on; Darwinian ideology has only insisted there *must* be such mechanisms.[97] Nor has any mechanism been found or imagined that can have either deterministically or at random compiled the genetic information encoded in even the most primitive viable cell.[98] It is of course not here suggested that the *narrative* of generationally successive life forms and structures is false, or that life forms do not generationally adapt to changing environments, or that a narrative could not be constructed of the progress from prebiotic soup to cells with their DNA, only that there are no grounds but ideology for denying that these narratives are teleological as they insistently appear to be.[99]

Denial of teleology is perhaps not quite so implausible in the case of inorganic creatures. If we do not confess the Creator, we may even feel the teleology of living creatures while denying that of their environment; this leads to the common modern position that humans, themselves "looking for meaning" and so demanding a teleology in their own case, bewail a "meaningless" and therefore alien universe in which they find themselves exiled—thereby in part repristinating the experience of late Mediterranean antiquity. Yet theology must affirm the teleological character also of the cosmic history from "big bang"[100] onward; and also here theology has perhaps a less counterintuitive task than does the ideology that excludes it.

Theology need not demand that the sciences reopen themselves to teleological explanations—though for all anyone knows this too might prove beneficial. But even if the particular sciences must continue to bracket teleology, it is integral to any plausible general interpretation of the world. The exchange "What big teeth you have, Grandma!" "The better to eat you with, my dear!" is indispensable in the story and therefore far closer to reality than any nonteleological reduction can be.

---

96. The current state of actual knowledge of evolution is presented with concision and maximum optimism by Christof K. Briebricher, "Evolutionary Research," *Interpreting the Universe as Creation*, ed. Vincent Brümmer (Kampen: Kok Pharos, 1991), 90–99.

97. "Survival of the fittest" can only select *after* the new structure is there, and in fully viable form. It would precisely deselect the supposed intermediate forms.

98. The point is made with great concision by Nancy R. Pearcey, "DNA: The Message in the Message," *First Things* 64 (June/July 1996):13–14.

99. For an elegant parallel argument to this and the following, against the adequacy or indeed coherence of any comprehensive nonteleological account of evolution, cosmic and biological, Keith Ward, *God, Chance and Necessity* (Oxford: One World, 1996). Ward's book is vitiated only by his implausible assumption, apparently ineradicable from Anglican theology, that there are such things as "theists," who jointly present an alternative explanation.

100. If that phrase is indeed appropriate to the beginning of the cosmic story.

There now remains only to imagine the teleology that creation might still have were it *not* the stage for Jesus' story. We are posed a by now familiar sort of question: Might God have made a world, otherwise like ours, that did not include Jesus? And nor then us? And we must first answer in a familiar way: he could have, but we must be very reluctant to specify this contrafactual reality. Yet perhaps, since we have here to do with God's work precisely as *other* than God, we may pry a very little further. Perhaps we can discover some strictly formal characters of the world's actual story that would obtain in any world God might have created.

We may from this viewpoint summarize previous teaching: the world is what Father, Son, and Spirit command in order to ordain a community that can include others with themselves. This, we may suppose, would be true of any world the real God would create. Moreover, any world could exist only as a referent of the triune conversation, and any world would therefore be as flexible to that conversation as is the actual one. That is, any world would be some counterpart of the divine perichoresis, merely in its character as mutual movement.

Jonathan Edwards rhetorically inquired, "What other act can be thought of in God from eternity, but delighting in himself?"[101] Now our ventured suggestion: the world precisely in its sheer formality is a contingent demonstration of the coherence and beauty of the triune life, and therefore any possible world would have at least this meaning for God, that he would *enjoy* it. Expressly leaving humans and the devil out, Martin Luther could write: "No creature lives for itself or serves itself . . . the sun, for example, does not shine for its own illumination. . . . Every creature serves the law of love."[102] It is this play of love, counterpart to that which is his own life, that would belong to God's purpose for any possible creation.

Also the immensity and complication of the world belong to this play, and so to the world's beauty. The world is finite, but it is the project of an infinite ingenuity which delights in itself and so in what it can devise. Therefore were we to investigate creation through all eternity, we would never come to a core or outer limit, though God does set them. The molecules revealed the atoms, and these the "particles," and these new and yet more wondrous kinds of inner complexity; and we may be sure that such revelations will continue—for creatures—*indefinitely.* The firmament pulled back to reveal the solar system, and this to reveal the galaxies, and these to reveal the fabulous history of mass and energy, and of what that history will uncover we can know only that we can never come to an end of uncoverings. A unified theory of everything will *not* be verified.[103]

The world is indefinitely complicated because it is counterpart to the internal perichoresis of the infinite God. Why are there mosquitoes? Divine amusement can only answer: Why not? As Augustine taught, if we abstract from other creatures' bane or blessing for *us*, we will see that when they "flourish in their

---

101. *Miscellanies,* 94.
102. *Operationes in Psalmos,* WA 5.38:14–20.
103. Or if it is, it will be of such empty generality as to be of interest only to pure mathematicians.

own places and natures, they are disposed in beauty and order; they bring each its measure of grace to their mutual polity."[104]

We too may enjoy the world in this purely aesthetic fashion. We may do so because to be human is to participate in the triune conversation that is finally pure music and so pure delight, and because all creatures are the matter of this conversation. Unbelieving "ecological" reflection always seems to end with one of two dour possibilities: other creatures are to be valued because of their possible usefulness to us, or we are nihilistically to value other creatures as we value ourselves. But when we acknowledge our place in God, we may perceive a better way: we may after all expand the second "great commandment" to include not only our human neighbors but all our fellow creatures, if only we modulate to the aesthetic mode: "You shall delight in each creature as in yourself."

What we may do about Pleiades and Orion is have fun with them, even from our distance. This delight can take many forms, from the writing of sonnets to lying on the grass staring at them to probing their chemistry and physics. All such delights are great gifts of the Creator to us.

V

The devil and his sort can appear only as an addendum to the creation, but just so they must appear. It must not "after Auschwitz" be debated whether irreducible created evil is actual; the very offer to argue the matter would be itself a new evil. The only question is about evil's ontological status: Is it merely an abstract defect or perhaps the cumulative result of human wrong choices and their necessary retribution? Or is there someone out there laughing at us?

The doctrine of creation teaches that all things are grounded in and embraced by God's moral intention, so that they are good. But in Scripture and believing experience we also see all things disrupted and retarded by moral determinisms and sins and amoral accidents. If the determinisms of creation are indeed eventually bent to a final free purpose, they do require to be bent, and sometimes the angel of that teleology must be Michael the warrior. If faith is appropriate to the world in which we find ourselves, confusion and cowardice are somehow also appropriate to it. The parallels do seem compelling: as *God values* the creation, so there seems to be an active and somehow powerful *subjectivity that despises* it, that hates all being.

The New Testament employs the representation "the devil" more specifically than does the Old. The devil appears as a definite personality in the story of Jesus;[105] in the primal church he "prowls around, looking for someone to devour";[106] and

---

104. *De civitate Dei,* xi.22: "in suis locis naturisque vigeant, pulchroque ordine disponantur; quantumque universitati rerum pro suis protionibus decoris tanquam in communem rempublicam conferant."
105. Matthew 4:1–11par.
106. I Peter 5:8.

under several guises he is indispensable to the drama of Revelation. We must ask in this case also: How is this representation to be conceptually interpreted?

The parallel to the angels is unmistakable, and indeed the ontological antithesis cannot be between God and the devil but only between God's angels and the devil. Barth has again the right starting point: the devil and his spirits appear with the angels under the title "God's Messengers and Their Adversaries."[107] And from this starting point, he rightly leads into the problem of the devil's origin, though again on a path we cannot follow.

The tradition, which Barth rejects, has almost unanimously conceived the devil and his spirits as "fallen angels."[108] This is not so much because of the few biblical passages that show that their authors had some such opinion[109] as because no other account seems possible. Everything that is not the Creator is created by him. He creates all things "good." Therefore if there are bad creatures, they must have *become* bad; as it is with humans so it must be with spirits. But if the devils were once good spirits, what can they then have been but angels?

Barth has so conceptualized the angels that their fall is excluded.[110] He therefore, with his usual implacable logic, concludes that the devils cannot be creatures at all. But the notion of actualities that are neither God nor his creatures is surely unacceptable by Christian theology. Barth says they are the subjectivity of "nothingness," as the angels are of heaven.[111] But that there should be *personalities* resident within the "nothingness" that God does not will surely stretches the notion beyond tenability.[112]

The fall of angels is indeed inconceivable, but so is evil as such; nevertheless evil occurs. Given Eve's and Adam's creation, their sin is a surd to reason. Given their fall, grace is a surd to reason. Surely the same must be said of evil spirits; and having said that, we have probably already said rather more than we should.

Barth's derivation of the devil and his spirits from "nothingness" does, however, rejoin the tradition insofar as all agree these entities can only be described negatively. The ontological question about the devil can only be, What *ails* him? Within this work, it is convenient to analyze this person—if such it can be called—in the terms we have used before.

God is in himself the one as whom and among whom he finds himself; in himself he is the community that presents him with his Ego. Creatures are not triune; therefore God and our fellow humans must present us with ourselves. What ails the devil is that he wants to do it God's way and of course cannot.

---

107. *Kirchliche Dogmatik*, III/3:608–623.

108. For a classic account, that shows also its difficulties, Thomas Aquinas, *Summa theologiae*, I.63.

109. Most plausibly, Jude 6: "And the angels who did not keep their own position, but left their proper dwelling."

110. *Kirchliche Dogmatik* III/3:622–623.

111. Ibid., 613: "They are not godly, but ungodly and antigodly. But neither has God created them; and so they are also not creaturely."

112. Indeed, it is precisely at this point that Barth's dialectic of *das Nichtige*, brilliant and sometimes illuminating as it is, reveals its systematic inadequacy.

The devil will not give himself over to be anyone else's object. He will not allow himself to be defined by anyone else's gaze; no one is permitted to have their own view of him. He wants to be triune like God, to be in himself the object as which he finds himself; but as a creature he is not, and so he ends with *no* object in which to find himself and is in fact no self. The devil is what we would be could our sin finally and wholly triumph.

God is embodied for himself and for us, as Jesus. Just so he can give himself over to us, and just so his omnipotent rule is not a tyranny. A purely disembodied consciousness, a consciousness that was always looking at us and never letting us look back, that always fixed us in its gaze and never let us see what it looked like, would be a universal tyrant—except of course that such a thing could not be a truly free agent at all. A subjectivity that refused all embodiment would be a pure and utterly compulsive hatred, and nothing else at all.

The difference between the angels and the devil is that the angels are willing to *inhabit* creation; indeed this willingness is their being. The devil is a negative angel because he is unwilling to inhabit anything; this unwillingness is his being, such as it is. And so enough of the devil, whom notoriously "one little word" can overthrow.

TWENTY-TWO

Sin

I

Sin is a fact of humanity's history with God as Scripture narrates it. It is sometimes supposed that the reality of sin is a fact also of general experience, but the supposition must be qualified. Our large or small moral disasters ought indeed to appear as sin to any who notice them, but this is because we ought all to be conducting our lives toward humanity's only actual goal in God and experiencing our lives and those of others within that narrative.[1] As it is, we are protean in our ability to obfuscate reality, to interpret our sin as "mistake" or "failure" or within decadent Western modernity as the result of "illness"; and this skill itself belongs to one aspect of sin, the last to be considered in the following discussion.

The only possible *definition* of sin is that it is what God does not want done.[2] Thus if we do not reckon with God, we will not be able to handle the concept; without acknowledging God, we can—though perhaps not for long—speak meaningfully of fault and even of crime but not of sin. Moreover, nothing in the following should be construed as attempting any further definition of sin; all that is intended is some display of the fact of sin in a few of its aspects. Even in that, we will sometimes proceed impressionistically or curtly, since we will merely be showing negations of human characters analyzed in preceding chapters;[3] history's entire tedious smorgasbord of sins presents only various ways of *not* being one thing, righteous.

---

1. Though of course if we were doing that there would be no *sin*, strictly speaking, to notice.

2. This simple definition is at the heart of all the dialectics Karl Barth spins around the matter; *Kirchliche Dogmatik* (Zollikon-Zürich: Evangelischer Verlag, 1955), IV/2:449.

3. This chapter might even have been omitted, since all its matter appears elsewhere in the work. But I do not wish to be accused, as sometimes I rightly have been, of sharing the modern aversion to the whole subject.

It also follows from this definition that we cannot and must not try to understand how sin is possible, since what God does not want is *not* possible—except of course that in this case it nevertheless happens.[4] On the other hand, once sin is there it is only too understandable. The aphorism again holds: starting from righteousness, sin is inexplicable; starting from sin, righteousness is inexplicable. As for the terrible question posed by God's actual permission of sin, this work has done what it can with that and will not here return to the struggle.

Theology has expended some energy in asking which kind of sin is most basic. Very little depends on answering this question. Even the unavoidable attempt to distinguish kinds of sin, in order to have headings under which to organize discussion, cannot escape a certain air of arbitrariness.[5] We have to begin someplace; and one aspect of sin does seem to claim the honor—or rather the infamy: we will consider sin primally as idolatry or unbelief. Then we will consider it as lust and injustice and finally as despair.

II

The Old Testament judges Israel first, last, and foremost for idolatry; and when Paul specifies the occasion of God's wrath against the gentiles, he adduces only one thing, that they have "served the creature rather than the Creator."[6] "You shall have no other gods besides me" is the first of the commandments and jealousy the first of the Lord's attributes. One can serve the Lord, or one can plunge into the religious world's welter of possibilities and quests, but one cannot do both at once.

Within the Western church and the culture shaped by her the possibility and nature of false religion have been probed more deeply than ever before or elsewhere. What must be called the *critique of religion* has become an enterprise with its own history, the thread of which has been lost only in the very last decades. We will pick up that history at its modern stage, from which we have just named it.

"Critique" is a key word of modernity generally. As we have noted in other connections, the eighteenth-century Enlightenment consisted in drawing lessons from the experience of the previous century. The most creative lesson was the power of the new science; and the culturally decisive component of the new science's epistemic policy was the "critique of appearances." It certainly appears that the sun goes round the earth; the archetype of new science was persistence in asking, with a quixotically open mind, "But does it really? Let us look again and more closely." "Enlightenment" was the determination to apply this policy

4. Even the subtlest and deepest of such attempts, by Søren Kierkegaard, must be rejected in advance; *Begrebet Angest*, ed. Villy Sorensen. (Copenhagen: Gyldendal, 1993).

5. Genesis 3 will not help us in this matter. It is doubtless legitimate to read it in light of the churchly doctrine of a fall, motivated by the desire to "be as God." But in *Genesis'* own context, Eve's and Adam's sin is simply disobedience to a direct divine command specific to their situation, for which they are then punished. See Claus Westermann, *Biblischer Kommentar Altes Testament* (Neukirchen: Erziehungsverein, 1970), 2:322–368.

6. Romans 1:18–25.

universally and so not only in the external creation but also to the hitherto intractable problems of human life.

When critical thinkers then undertook the critique of *human* appearances, the inevitable first and primary object of suspicion was Christian religion, in its European-American role as established religious opinion and practice. It was handed-on wisdom which new science had discredited as mere bondage to appearances; generalizing this pattern, the Enlightenment applied a hermeneutic of suspicion to all established tradition.

In the case of religion, there might have been some difficulty in finding a standard of judgment. But Christian theology itself seemed to point to one, in the "natural" theology it had recognized as its partner and sometimes as its foundation. For if there is indeed a theology given with our nature, it must itself be immune to contest by us. This left more specifically Christian doctrine to fill the role of questionable appearances.

The Enlightenment's suspicion-driven critique of distinctively Christian teachings was begun in English-speaking nations and exported. Already Herbert of Cherbury, in the early seventeenth century, had come to what would be the Enlightenment's classical results.[7] Cherbury renounced revelation just because it occurs within and creates particular tradition. "Reason" must strip away the narratives and rites introduced in history to reveal a faith whose tenets are natural to humankind universally: there is a personal Supreme Being; virtue is his appropriate service; failure of virtue requires repentance; in this and a future life God will reward virtue and repentance. From John Locke's followers in Britain to the "broad and catholick" party in New England to the *Neologen* of Germany, the critique will be much the same throughout the eighteenth century, and the resultant catechisms similar, though not always so bracing.

After a respite initiated by Schleiermacher, the critique of religion recurred and intensified at the mid–nineteenth century, in the thinking of Ludwig Feuerbach.[8] Feuerbach's advance on the original Enlightenment was that he adopted Schleiermacher's conception of religion as a unitary human propensity and so eliminated "natural" religion's immunity to critique: *all* our concepts and pictures of God are interpreted as human projections of human values—and so as what Judaism and Christianity mean by "idols."[9] The storm of critique on this principle then broke with Karl Marx, Friedrich Nietzsche, and Sigmund Freud. Since also "natural theology" was now suspect, the norms of this assault were unclear, if not indeed deliberately camouflaged.

Finally Christian theology took the critique of religion back into itself and just so perfected it, with the book that made the young Karl Barth famous and

7. Authoritatively to Cherbury, Emanuel Hirsch, *Geschichte der neuern evangelischen Theologie* (Gütersloh: G. Bvertelsmann, 1919, 1:244–252).

8. See now Van A. Harvey, *Feuerbach and the Interpretation of Religion* (Cambridge: Cambridge University Press, 1995).

9. Feuerbach of course did not make this last observation, being himself too thorough and unconscious an idolater.

marks the division between modern and postmodern theology, his *Commentary on Romans* of 1922.[10] The achievement of this book is a critique both more honest and more radical than that even of Feuerbach and his epigones: it could acknowledge its norm, and it could be total and uninhibited not from unacknowledged religiosity[11] but because its norm lies outside the religious enterprise.

The message of Jesus' death and resurrection appears as an event adventitious to the human religiosity amid which it occurs, or so Barth's Romans and this work claim. The gospel is news of a historical contingency, and so claims to be and if true is in fact a word that does not emerge from the mechanisms of our religious projections. When the gospel occurs, it therefore confronts the human religious impulse whole and judges its hearers' religion by standards not provided by religion itself, whether "natural" or "revealed."

Trying to state Romans' position is a treacherous undertaking, for the book is a Socratic assault upon all positions. But Barth did write in the foreword to one reissue, "If I have a system, it consists in what Kierkegaard called 'the infinite qualitative difference' between time and eternity."[12] Of the many images with which Barth evokes this relation of difference, one is perhaps the most illuminating: time is touched by eternity as a cylinder is touched by a tangent plane.[13] There is indeed a line of tangency, yet there is no part of the cylinder that is also on the plane or part of the plane also on the cylinder.[14] Beings whose home and dimensions were constrained by the cylinder, whose life proceeded around the surface of the cylinder, and who did not extend beyond it would be stopped when they came to the line of tangency but could not grasp the impediment itself.

Religion is our attempt nevertheless to get some purchase on this "line of death" across our temporal history, to find a stretch of our time that is after all a bit of eternity, which we can enter to negotiate. Religion thus consists in blurring the "fundamental, sharp, and corrosive" difference between God and creature.[15] Religion, Barth agrees with Schleiermacher, is the highest possibility of humanity, our quest for that beyond ourselves in which alone we can be fulfilled. But just so it is our attempt to use what is beyond us for our own purposes and so betrays what it invokes. "Our self-respect demands, on top of everything else, . . . access to a superworld. Our deeds want deeper foundations, transcendent recognition and reward. Our lust for life covets also pious moments and prolongation into eternity."[16]

---

10. *Der Römerbrief,* 2nd ed. (Munich: Chr. Kaiser, 1922).

11. Or indeed in Feuerbach's own case, from religiosity acknowledged in a certain way. Feuerbach's claim to be a sympathetic interpreter of religion was surely deluded at its root but had considerable surface plausibility. Harvey, *Feuerbach,* presents the claim in the best possible light.

12. Ibid., xiii.

13. Barth wrote "circle" and "line," but the point is clearer this way. He had not perhaps been reading popular expositions of relativity.

14. Ibid., 5–6.

15. Ibid., 25.

16. Ibid., 20.

In the overlap we thus posit between time and eternity, "there appears the religious fog . . . in which by the most various tricks and methods of confusion and mixture . . . sometimes human or animal doings are elevated to be experiences of God and sometimes the being and deed of God is experienced as human or animal."[17] There "Not-God" is born,[18] the divinity useful for mediation precisely because it is not pure;[19] and "the setting-up of Not-God is punished in that it *succeeds*: the divinized powers of nature and the soul are now indeed gods, and rule us."[20]

This analysis both pursues idolatry to its root and reveals its full extension. Idolatry is not an accident, as if some of us just happened to hit on wrong candidates for deity. Nor is it restricted to actions that give divine honor to straightforwardly inappropriate objects—though at present also such relatively crude manifestations again flourish.[21] Idolatry is our persistent and ingenious and even noble attempt to use deity for our own ends; in this attempt we necessarily posit a middle realm in which to meet and negotiate with deity, and "idols" are whatever then emerges to conduct the negotiation.

But of course we would not entertain images or concepts of the divine at all if they did not serve some role in our communal and individual projects—if there were no advantage at all in positing them, that is, if they provided no opportunity for negotiation. Therefore *every* actual image or concept of divinity is in Barth's sense an idol, just because we entertain it, however materially Christian or biblical it may be.

If this critique is right, there can be no exit from idolatry except perfect nihilistic irreligion, were it possible, or the contingent event of God's word and of faith in it, when and as this occurs. Idolatry and unbelief are thus discovered to be the same thing. For if we leave impossible pure nihilism out, there are just two possibilities: faith in the word of God or "turning away" from it to whatever else. Eve and Adam, that is, humanity, did the second when they disobeyed God's explicit command, positing a less arbitrary God than the real one.[22]

The writing or sympathetic reading of this book, filled as it is with ideas and images of God, can therefore only be an act of idolatry, except insofar as the Spirit

---

17. Ibid., 25.

18. Ibid., 25.

19. Archetypically within Christianity, the Arian *Logos*.

20. Ibid., 26.

21. G. K. Chesterton, *in persona* Father Brown speaking to a group of late moderns, in *The Incredulity of Father Brown* (1928) (reprint, London: Penguin Books, 1958), 70–71: "It's drowning all your old rationalism and skepticism, it's coming in like a sea; and the name of it is superstition, . . . calling all the menagerie of polytheism, . . . Dog Anubis and great green-eyed Pasht and all the holy howling bulls of Bashan; reeling back to the bestial gods of the beginning; . . . and all because you are frightened of four words: 'He was made Man.'"

To see from what deadly nonsense the gospel once delivered Western culture, and to which the repaganizing of that culture is returning us, one need only view an episode or two of such a television series as *Ancient Mysteries*.

22. Genesis 3:2–6.

appropriates our writing and reading to the church and her sacramental and verbal speaking of the gospel. With mention of church and sacraments, however, we move in a way Barth did not. For the rescue from idolatry remains enigmatic within Romans, nor will we now seek it quite where Barth later did.[23]

Martin Luther's[24] well-known description of sin as the "incurvature" of the soul upon itself is initially an account of idolatry, and very like Barth's. Luther's primal spiritual and theological problem was a radical version of the traditional Augustinian problem of distinguishing true from false worship.[25] Sin, for Luther, is first of all that we seek to use deity for our own purposes and so must invent gods that can be used. The reforming polemic against "works-righteousness" is simply an inner-churchly version of this: we will not let God be what he really is, the absolute Giver who brooks none of our contributions and who just so cannot be manipulated, and thus we craft a false God even from biblical and Christian materials.

Luther's first solution was the "theology of the cross," which held that the real God manifests himself so exclusively in suffering that no one could possibly seek him in self-serving fashion. This solution is congruent with Barth's Romans. But Luther's mature solution[26] was that idolatry is broken rather by the true God's objective intrusion as the church's audible and visible word. It will be seen that Luther's later insight has been all along a warrant of the system here offered.

God puts himself as an unavoidable object in our way, and so makes moot the question of our meaning in seeking him. We may say that God makes himself the ineluctable object of some of our images and concepts, those provoked by his intrusion, and so makes them true despite the idolatrous character they have as images and concepts we have crafted.

All these subtleties said, we can return to a simplicity: there is a difference between believers in the true God and idolaters. For believers are indeed objectively confronted with the true God and captivated in that confrontation, however perverse their reasons for enduring the captivation and however idolatrous the images and concepts by which they do it. Jews and Christians would be idolaters if they could, but in fact are not in position to succeed—and we cannot be sure there are no others in the same situation.

Sin is idolatry. We are sinners in that we revolve in our own self-reference and do so piously.

23. For brief description of Barth's move, in itself to be affirmed, Robert W. Jenson, "Karl Barth," *The Modern Theologians*, ed. David F. Ford (Oxford: Blackwell, 1989), 1:31–34.

24. For the following I now spare myself passage-hunting by referring to David S. Yeago's pathbreaking article, "The Catholic Luther," The Catholicity of the Reformation, ed. Carl Braaten, Robert Jenson (Grand Rapids: Eerdmans, 1996), 13–34. This article states the thesis of a book that may have appeared by the time this work is in print.

25. Luther's initiating and underlying problem, it now appears, was *not* an unsuccessful effort to "find a gracious God," as is still generally assumed.

26. First arrived at in 1518; see Yeago, "Catholic Luther," 24–26.

III

Luther's "incurvature" of the soul on itself is not a *kind* of sin, basic or otherwise; it is rather a formal structure common to all the possibilities. Thus it fits sin also in the aspect we next instance, as lust.

There can be no doubt who should guide us in this matter: Augustine by his *Confessions.* Augustine's description of his own career of lust remains unmatched. The principal passage is deservedly one of the most renowned in literature: "To Carthage then I came, and a welter of corrupted loves assaulted me from all sides. I was not yet in love; I was in love with being in love. With secret yearning I despised myself for not yearning enough. I searched for an object of love, loving to love."[27]

The essence of Augustine's situation was that his love had first and foremost itself, and just so its own absence, for its object. He was "in love with being in love," he was "loving to love."[28] As idolatry is worship hiddenly turned from God to the would-be worshiper, so lust is love hiddenly turned from the creaturely beloved to the would-be lover. One could translate Barth's analysis of idolatry into an analysis of lust simply by substituting "the neighbor" for "God."

Our histories in this posture of incurvature are of course superficially various; every penitent or continuing voluptuary will have a different story to tell. But a striking feature of sin, especially as lust, is its unoriginality; Augustine's own course is immediately recognizable, in its dismal typicality through the ages.

He made friends, but "fouled the stream of friendship[29] with sordid desire."[30] Friendship was for Roman antiquity the great social virtue, a chief component of the antecedent justice that enabled human society. The infiltration of friendship with cravings, of whatever sort, was thus a primal communal evil.

He at last attained to a proper heterosexual affair, only to be "beaten with the fiery rods of jealousy and suspicion and worries and angers and quarrels."[31] It perhaps does not need Augustine to teach us: if sexual union has any meaning at all for those who achieve it, a more than momentary sexual relation inevitably becomes an occasion of fear and anger if either lover must suspect interchangeability in the role. Nor is it accidental that Augustine connects the assault of lust with going away to school; the reflection of love into lust is something intrinsically juvenile, even if it lasts a lifetime.

---

27. *Confessiones*, iii.1: "Veni Carthaginem, et circumstrepebat me undique sartago flagitiosorum amorum. nondum amabam, et amare amabam, et secretiore indigentia oderam me minus indigentem. quaerebam quid amarem, amans amare."

28. Augustine's conception of lust thus is identical with modernity's conception of freedom. Stanley Hauerwas, *The Peaceable Kingdom* (Notre Dame: Notre Dame University Press, 1983), 8: "The modern conception has made freedom the content of the moral life itself. It matters not what we desire, but that we desire. Our task is to become free, not through the acquisition of virtue, but by preventing ourselves from being determined, so that we can always keep our 'options open.' We have thus become the bureacrats of our own history."

29. *Amicitia.*

30. *Confessiones*, iii.1.

31. Ibid.

Augustine has also an explanation for the incurvation of love, which is parallel to his explanation of the earthly city's subjection to the *libido dominandi*. "There was a hunger hidden in me for the food that nourishes the soul, for you yourself, my God; yet in that hunger I did not seek the indicated food."[32] If the soul does not love God, neither will it finally love anything but itself or rather its own consequent vacuity. God is the one object of love who can only be loved for his own sake or not at all; when we love him we are kept from total incurvation and so are free to love friend or spouse or child or enemy also—or, for that matter, good food and drink or elegant mathematics or the amazing structure of the universe or athletic endeavor or beauties of art and literature, though with such things we are going beyond what Augustine would have mentioned.

Finally in Augustine's account it appears that lust, once alive, can fasten on all sorts of occasions. He moved from sexual lust into general lustfulness. Impersonal objects of pleasure have "no soul"; just so they present themselves in analogy with the sexual partner who appears as a mere occasion of satisfaction. Augustine's own soul, when once it thoroughly itched with lust, "protruded itself, avid to be scratched by the touch of sensible things" generally.[33]

So Augustine became "elegant and urbane." He became a fan of the theater, where, as he understood it, spectators are invited to love characters not in fact there to be loved, so that the soul can without hindrance love itself in their empty simulacra.[34] And he took to the study of law, as a vehicle of ambition without intrinsic content—"the more fraudulent the more praised."[35]

We must note next, here perhaps not following Augustine, that the distinction between love and lust does not lie in the lover's sentiments but in the communal situation within which the lovers have their personhood. Decayed romanticism's notion that "real" romantic love is somehow distinct from spousal roles—indeed first to be liberated by a deliciously illicit passion—is precisely backward from the truth, as is daily demonstrated in the courts and mass media. The Lord has told us what he does not want in his created community, by giving his Commandments. In the present connection, he has said: "You shall not commit adultery. . . . You shall not covet." The prohibited crimes are communally disastrous acts, not private motivations.

The crimes of desire forbidden by the commandments are immediate instances of lust: I *cannot*, for paradigmatic example, sexually love my neighbor's spouse, I can only lust after him or her. For, as we have seen, he or she is a person in and by a communal situation, and this situation includes being this particular spouse. To take my neighbor's spouse as my love, I must detach the person from that spousehood, that is, I must insofar depersonalize her or him, and just so create an object of lust. The point is not psychological: I can of course

---

32. Ibid.
33. Ibid.
34. Ibid., iii.2. The romanticism of Augustine's understanding of theater, and of literature generally, is unmistakable.
35. Ibid., iii.3.

sincerely long for and cherish my neighbor's spouse, also sexually, as can she or he me. What I cannot do is *love* her or him in the sense of the second "great commandment."

The same obtains, in a sort of reverse, for fornication. Marriage includes the public and legal declaration of faithfulness. Sexual union without marriage is sexual union without this declaration; therefore those who indulge in it merely thereby treat each other as replaceable and so impersonal occasions, whatever their subjective resolve. Faithfulness is a public reality or it is nothing.

Here is doubtless the place where some judgment must be made about homoerotic practice also. It follows stringently from the earlier chapter's analysis of sexuality and its role in human being: homoerotic acts, however occasioned or motivated, constitute desertion in the face of the threatening other sort of human, defection from the burden of co-humanity. Therefore homoeroticism is, in the present terms, always lust, and powerful attraction to it is a grievous affliction. That Scripture, on the rare occasions when the matter is mentioned, treats homoerotic acts as self-evidently sin, disaster, or both,[36] is not an accident of Scripture's historical conditioning but follows directly from its whole understanding of human being.

Finally, love for the beautiful cosmos or for lobster or for theater can—perhaps at certain points contra Augustine—truly be called love when two conditions are fulfilled; it is when these conditions are not fulfilled that our desire for such things is mere lust. We love Pleiades or Orion or a good wine when we, first, sheerly delight in them as does God, and when we, second, integrate our delight into communal love, when we freely publish our research into Orion or pour the wine out for friends or invite others to share our music—which last, of course, the musicians themselves necessarily do. Augustine described for all time the introversion also of such love into lust: my soul "scratches" itself on what *I* crave for *myself*—on food that will make me obese, or on knowledge cultivated for ambition's sake, or on beautiful things cherished in solitary passion. "I love lobster" is ambiguous: it may describe a very tiny virtue or betray a considerable moral disaster.

Sin is lust. We are sinners in that we refuse to grow up toward love.

IV

Next on our roster, sin is injustice, closely linked to idolatry and lust. The classic denunciation of perverse religion is from the prophet Amos: "I hate, I despise

---

36. The same few passages—Genesis 19:5; Leviticus 18:22; 20:13; Romans 1:26–27; I Corinthians 6:9–10; I Timothy 1:9–10—are laboriously exegeted on both sides of the "culture wars," but their sense is in fact perfectly obvious. That these passages do not work with the "modern understanding" of homosexuality as an "orientation" is both obvious and beside the point; it is not an orientation but an activity that was in question then *and* is theologically and ethically in question now—the question of whether there are "orientations" and of how they occur if there are such is an empirical question, from the solution of which nothing whatever follows ethically or theologically.

your festivals, and I take no delight in your solemn assemblies. . . . Take away from me the noise of your songs." The Lord speaking by Amos then demands, as the alternative to rejected worship, not cultic or theological reform but: "Let justice roll down like waters, and righteousness like an ever-flowing stream."[37] And those who need the rebuke and the exhortation are the lustful "who drink wine from bowls, and anoint themselves with the finest oils, but are not grieved over the ruin of Joseph."[38]

Amos leaves no doubt what injustice is, which fulfills lust and empties worship. The unjust are those who "trample the head of the poor"[39] and "push aside the needy in the gate."[40] They pant for the opening of the business day, in which as untroubled denizens of the market they will take whatever profit the market will sustain.[41] To include a telling item from Amos's follower Isaiah, they "add field to field, until there is room for no one but" themselves.[42] And in such pursuits they necessarily hate the scrupulous judge "who reproves in the gate" and indeed those "who speak the truth" generally.[43] Injustice is the straightforward negation of "righteousness"; that is, injustice is the action of those who do not take their roles in community as opportunities of love.

The connection between idolatry and the endemic injustice of this world was, we may remind ourselves, seen clearly by Augustine: false religion is *the* thing that makes earthly polities merely earthly, that is, founded in mere simulacra of justice. Moreover, Augustine's critique of religion anticipated Barth's: what ails false religion is its posit of a realm of intermediary beings, in whom time and eternity are mixed.[44] The problem with such divinities is that they cannot finally keep us from devouring one another; that can be done only by the command and mercy of the one God we cannot turn to our advantage.

The previous sentence has a somewhat Hobbesian ring, in its expectation that, in Thomas Hobbes's own language, a "war of every man against every man" can be averted only by "a common power set over them."[45] But Augustine and this system have in mind God as the power of love, antecedent to violence; whereas Hobbes has in mind a coercive human sovereignty, consequent to an original state of war. The great cofounder[46] of modern political theory described with precision the birth from violence of Augustine's *unjust* society.[47] But Hobbes intended

---

37. Isaiah 5:21–24.
38. 6:6.
39. 2:7.
40. 5:12.
41. 8:5.
42. Isaiah 5:8.
43. Amos 5:10.
44. *De civitate Dei*, ix–x.
45. Thomas Hobbes, *Leviathan*, xiv.
46. With Machiavelli.
47. I am in the following much indebted to John Milbank, *Theology and Social Theory* (Oxford: Blackwell, 1990), 9–48.

his description positively, as an analysis of the origin of the only "justice" he could imagine and as the theoretical basis of the modern political regime.[48]

The first notable feature of Hobbes's analysis is the entire absence of God as an agent.[49] And the second is a correlated inflation of the notion of human "dominion." What Augustine deplored as the *libido dominandi*, and what in ancient political theory was only dialectically related to right and law,[50] becomes for Hobbes the fundamental right and the foundation of justice and law. In our original condition,[51] "the augmentation of dominion over men" is according to Hobbes the primal right of each individual, since it is necessary to the individual's self-preservation against all others, each of whom is in turn identically situated and compelled.[52]

For Hobbes, society and polity must be products of human making,[53] there being no one else to do it. Nor then can human action have any intrinsic moral teleology or transcendent guidance; there is no "highest good." That is, there is no antecedent justice, such as the Romans and Augustine posited, to be the prior foundation of community and law. Therefore "to this war of every man against every man, this also is consequent: *that nothing can be unjust.*"[54]

Human action is, according to Hobbes, in itself sheer empty desire, and just so insatiable.[55] That is, lust is the first principle: in the original condition "every

---

48. It will have been noted that this work makes no positive use of the "social sciences" that have followed upon Hobbes. This is because of their almost complete intellectual vacancy. The great success of "scientific method" depends on the interaction of three epistemic policies: (1) determination to test all hypotheses by renewed and suspicious observation; (2) reformulation of all hypotheses until they consist only of algebraically manipulable expressions; and (3) "analysis," that is, replacement of the givens of actual experience in the variables of these hypotheses by components designed to fit, e.g., mass, energy, etc. When the method is extended to humanity, the third component necessarily drops out, which empties the enterprise. In the "social sciences" the equivalents of masses and the like have to be the same old persons and communities everyday thinking has always dealt with. In moving from tables to atoms, we keep our hold on the everyday objects we finally seek to know, in that our predictions still cash out for the everyday objects; but if we were to move from persons and societies to, e.g., organic molecules, it would not be so. To predict the behaviors of persons and communities, we have to stick with persons and communities as the values of our hypotheses' variables. But this leaves us with policies 1 and 2 by themselves, that is, with slightly disciplined versions of policies thought has always followed. Thus the familiar phenomenon that the only truths the social sciences ever actually propound are things everybody already knew. In psychology of a certain kind one can maintain a pretense by positing psychic "masses" in the style of Locke or Freud, but the fictitious character of these entities sabotages thought at policy 1.

49. I will not enter the hopeless argument about what Hobbes "really" thought about God or intended by his occasional pious references.

50. See Milbank, *Theology*, 10–13.

51. Hobbes is like so many parasitic on the faith he renounces: his posited state of nature, which may or may not be supposed ever to have obtained, is clearly a hangover from the notion of pure creation.

52. *Leviathan*, xiii.

53. Ibid., introduction.

54. Ibid., xiii.

55. Ibid., xi.

man has a right to everything, even to . . . another's body."[56] Or, equivalently, the primal "right" is self-defense.[57] There is a circle in which each human individual is a mortal threat to every other: I must defend myself against you, and that is the reason you must defend yourself against me, and that is the reason I must defend myself against you, and so on. "In such condition," in Hobbes's famous saying, humanity's life must indeed be "solitary, poor, nasty, brutish, and short."[58]

It is then but a further piece of self-defense, now against the miseries of this description, that I transfer my right of self-defense to some "common power set over" us and that so do you.[59] It is this "mutual transferring of right" that is the "contract" by which community and justice and law first are founded.[60] Consequent on this "law of nature" that to survive I must transfer some of my right to a common power is another such law, that I must—still strictly for my own self-preservation—stick to the contract. And this second "law of nature" is the sole "fountain and original of justice."[61]

Finally, the sovereign power, whatever may be its constitution, is absolute once in place.[62] It is subject to no review and no inherent right of reform. Any limitations are either fictitious, with the fictions themselves belonging to the apparatus of power, or destructive of the state.

What Hobbes has described as the proper human polity is in fact the sheer absence of community, a polity in which empty individualism and collective tyranny each perfect the other, with nothing in between.[63] Because there is God, such a condition cannot in this world be fully attained by any human group; Hobbes has in fact described the political aspect of eternal damnation. But in the measure to which the mandate of heaven is unheard in a society, in that measure the society will approximate to this condition.

Therefore any actual polity short of the Kingdom will fall somewhere between Hobbes's hellish polity and Augustine's heavenly one. The evil symbiosis of collective tyranny and insatiable individualism will be somewhere at work in it, ready to destroy both the community and its members; it and we in it will more or less fit Amos's description of the unjust and be more or less at risk for Amos's condemnation. Western modernity's liberal regime has recently been much diagnosed in these terms,[64] often as if it were something new; and indeed it is the only regime to date whose ideology has taken the symbiosis of tyranny and lust for a good thing. But Western modernity only shows blatantly what under one or another disguise infects every community.

56. Ibid., xiv.
57. Ibid., xiii.
58. Ibid.
59. Ibid., xiv.
60. Ibid.
61. Ibid., xv.
62. Ibid., xviii.
63. The great analysis of this situation is Hannah Arendt, *The Origins of Totalitarianism* (New York: Harcourt Brace, 1966).
64. Within theology, most strikingly by the many writings of Stanley Hauerwas.

Description of this baleful dialectic is not despair—the next aspect of sin to be delineated. Since God in fact rules, there can if he grants it be relatively good polities, and these can be made better, and truly reprehensible polities can be survived and even overthrown. In this age, we can neither live exclusively in the polity of God nor quite attain to damnation, no matter how hard we strive for the latter; and it makes a great deal of difference at what point in the intermediate spectrum we find ourselves. It makes a difference simply because Christians must wish their neighbors well.

Sin is injustice. We are sinners in that we oppress and subserve one another, in that we parry the demands of community.

V

I am not self-existent, the condition of my own hypostasis, but I can pretend to be. My essence and my existence are distinct, but I can pretend they are not. And I can and do try to live out that pretense, in violation of the conditions by which I exist to pretend anything. Noting this possibility, we come to despair.

Sin as despair is the effort to suppress Augustine's restlessness that draws our hearts to God. Sin as despair is acting as if I were not delivered over to the future, as if in what I already am I were my proper self. If we were to allow ourselves a second *definition* of sin, it would be a description of despair that would provide it.

Jesus told the parable: "The land of a rich man produced abundantly. . . . Then he said, 'I will . . . pull down my barns and build larger ones, and there I will store all my grain and my goods. And I will say to my soul, Soul, you have ample goods laid up for many years; relax, eat, drink, and by merry.' "[65] We are threatened by the onrush of the future: by the possibility of future crop failure or of too-consuming love or of God's forgiveness or of a falling brick. Sin as despair is that we set out to guarantee ourselves against such threats. Like the man in the parable, we store up the past, last year's harvest and last year's deeds of love and plans already formulated, pretending the store will last forever. But of course it hardly needs a specific voice in the night to say, "You fool." By every word of moral sense that God gets through our defenses, he makes us know that some night our life will be demanded of us, and that we cannot control what night that will be. Then whose will it be, all this stored-up self of mine?[66]

Thus what we usually call optimism is a contrary of hope and is a mode of despair. Optimism is the conviction that all we have with which to invoke a better self and a better community and a better world is what we are in ourselves and the insistence that this must be enough. What we more usually call despair is the same conviction and the knowledge that it is not enough.

Despair is a more psychological aspect of sin than others we have considered. We will not delay long with its possibilities; they are too multifarious. Re-

65. Luke 12:16–20.
66. Luke 12:16–20.

fusal of the future is self-destruction, and it therefore creates and sets free within us impulses and voices that counsel death: "What if coke kills? Who cares?" "Curse God and die." "You know the word that will finally destroy your spouse's affection and end your happiness. Say it." Exploration of this deadly inwardness is beyond the bounds of this work. We observe only: the line between such sin and what we have been taught to call mental illness is indefinite and porous, if indeed it obtains at all.[67]

If warehouses do not prove an adequate fortress, if indeed all earthly treasuries are places where "moth and rust consume and . . . thieves break in and steal,"[68] and if seeing this we flirt with more overt despair, we have one final refuge from the future: we can become religious. We can pretend to heed the rebuke "You fool" and try to recruit its speaker to the further improvement of our barns. We are returned again to idolatry.

We have several times glanced at this feature of religion but must now note it explicitly: human religion as such is refusal of the future. Perhaps there are only two possible deities: the gods whose transcendence is the fixity of the past and the security we seek in it and the God whose transcendence is the unmanageability of his futurity. The first deity is Barth's "Not-God"; the second is the God of the gospel. The first deity is the divinity of the religions, including the Christian religion insofar as we use also that religion for our defense against the future. The second is the God against whose futurity we try to barricade ourselves.

The coincidence of despair and religion strives toward a *summum malum*, which in its forms within Mediterranean antiquity and descendent civilization is often labeled gnosticism.[69] This is the identification of divinity with the posited but in fact nonexistent unity of the human subject with itself at its transcendental point of origin. James's description of exigent introspection's quest, if cast in overtly religious language, would be a classical exposition of gnostic despair.

Since despair would be the essence of sin if it had one, a panoply of despair's aspects could again open before us, leading beyond the limits of this work. We will limit ourselves to one—that may not commonly be so identified.

VI

Rationality is not a capacity, it is rather a virtue; and irrationality is not an incapacity but a sin, of despair. Rationality is epistemic openness to God's future: it is obedience to the command, "Be prepared to change your mind. Test your

67. I do not of course suppose that the "mentally ill" are especially sinful, or are not to be cherished and assisted in their affliction. We of course all sin one way or another; and sin is always also an affliction.

68. Matthew 6:19.

69. The most illuminating description of ancient gnosticism, despite now disputed historical reconstructions, remains Hans Jonas, *Gnosis und spätantiker Geist* (Göttingen: Vandenhoeck & Ruprecht, 1954). It has recently been argued that a demotic version of gnosticism is the native religion of America; Harold Bloom, *The American Religion: The Emergence of the Post-Christian Nation* (New York: Simon & Schuster, 1992).

opinions, by whatever are in any instance the appropriate warrants." Sin as irrationality is disobedience to this command.

Rationality as a virtue is, like other virtues, variously shaped in the histories of particular human communities; it is differently displayed in the glories of Confucian wisdom and of Western science and of Persian poetry and in all such achievements. The universally identical command to be rational, on the other hand, is like all fundamental commands negative, the prohibition of a crime.

And irrationality is indeed a crime. When I maintain my opinions merely because I already hold them, I shut myself against the future and so against the new possibilities others represent to me. And so I violate community. I violate community even or especially when I hold my opinions simply because my community itself already maintains them.

Thus the command of rationality is in itself obvious. Yet obedience to it is rare and partial. The usual policy of humankind has been to take myth as the paradigm of truth and so to take the untestedness of an opinion as the standard of its viability. It is a chief mark of the break from tribal or archaic society that we acknowledge the mandate to test opinions, that we admit that knowing is a task and its success a promised good. The most sophisticated defenses against the mandate of rationality, however, are those thrown up by seemingly radical obedience to it.

Late modernity has been much given to such gambits. Every proper cognitive effort includes its own submission to relevant testing and therefore is a wager we might lose, often a serious wager. I put my opinion on the table, risking whatever of my life is invested in that opinion. But there is a way of so adducing this openness of the venture as to excuse myself from risking anything.

Late modern intelligence can endlessly generate new sides to every question. In and of itself this is of course a blessing. But the vice paired with it is a refusal of commitment that empties the wager—is use of the future's seemingly endless fecundity of options as an excuse now to make no bets. So, for classic example, we reflect that there may be God or there may not be God; and we rehearse the considerations on both sides, decide to wait and see, and praise "agnosticism" as heroic virtue. While this appears to be radical openness to the future, it is actually perfectly reactionary, since it allows everything in my life to remain exactly as it was; while it appears to be heroism it is in fact avoidance.

Also in cognition, the one who refuses to risk his or her life will lose it. Only the one willing to say, "This is true," and just so open a serious possibility of being wrong, will save his or her reason.

Finally to this matter, religiosity is the final recourse of irrationality also.[70] The founding thinkers of postmodern epistemic nihilism—of the doctrine that no serious conflict of opinion can be adjudicated except by covert or overt violence—have one and all been evangelists of a post-Christian religion. From Nietzsche through Heidegger to the latest French *poseur* or American camp fol-

---

70. For the following, I may with gratitude spare myself the proof-texting and refer to the omniverous study in Milbank, *Theology*, 259–325.

lower, their project, whether acknowledged or not, has been "the invention of an anti-Christianity":[71] violence, which according to them is always what really happens in human discourse, is interpreted as an ontological ultimate. We may be confident of the failure of this religious founding; utter damnation begins, if at all, only beyond this world. But that sin must finally fail is, in this connection too, no excuse for yielding to it.

Sin is despair. We are sinners in that we take no risks.

VII

In each of its aspects as described, sin shows itself as inescapable, underivable, and encompassing. The tradition, particularly in the West, has dealt with these phenomena under the rubric of "original sin."

The Council of Trent taught:

> If anyone does not confess, that the first man Adam, when he transgressed the command of God in Paradise, immediately lost the holiness and righteousness in which he had been created, and incurred . . . the wrath of God . . . and captivity under the devil . . . , let him be anathema. If anyone teaches that Adam's sin injured only him and not his progeny . . . let him be anathema. If anyone teaches that this sin of Adam, which by origin and propagation is but one, . . . is removed by natural human powers or by any other remedy than the merit of the one Mediator . . . let him be anathema.[72]

The Augsburg Confession taught: "Consequent to Adam's fall, all humans, in that they are born according to nature, are conceived and born in sin. That is, from their mother's womb on they are filled with lust and by their natural power can have no true fear of God or faith in him; moreover, this infection or inherited sin is truly sin."[73]

The dogmatic status of "original sin" would thus seem ecumenically assured, at least for the West. There has of course been controversy in the matter between Tridentine Catholicism and Reformation theologians; the opportunity for disagreement can be seen in Trent's reference to the absence of righteousness where Augsburg has the presence of lust. But it is the much greater agreement we here want to register.

Thomas Aquinas's exposition can be paradigmatic. He states the fundamental teaching as he understands it: sin has been "handed on by origin from the first parent to his progeny."[74] He then continues:

71. Milbank, *Theology*, 280.

72. Sessio V: Decretum super peccato originali.

73. Art. ii: Von der Erbsünde.

74. *Quaestiones disputate de malo*, iv.1: "Pelagiani negaverunt aliquod peccatum per originem esse traduci. Sed hoc ex magna parte excludi necessitatem redemptionis facte per Christum, que maxime videtur necessaria fuisse ad abolendum infectionis peccati quod a primo parente in totam

To understand how this may be, we must consider that each human individual may be taken in two ways: in one way as a particular person, in the other way as a member of one or another community. Actions may be predicated of the person according to either mode: an action that the person does as such and by his or her own choice pertains to the person individually, but insofar as the person belongs to a group an action may belong to him or her . . . that is done by the group or by the majority of the group or by a principal member of the group. . . . The gift of original justice . . . was given to the first human in his creation; and this gift was not given to him as a single person only but as the initiating instance of human nature as a whole, from whom human nature was to be derived to his posterity. . . . And so the defect is handed on to his posterity in the same way in which human nature is handed on.[75]

Sin is thus "original" in two ways. First, none of us has an origin prior to it, from which to transcend and so perhaps deal with it; each of us is a sinner "from the mother's womb." Friedrich Schleiermacher's formula is precise, in his language: for the human creature there can be "no moment, in which consciousness of sin as something present and active would not be an ineluctable part of his self-awareness."[76]

Second, this is so because humanity as a whole somehow sins as one. In some way, we are all one agent of sin, who sin with our initiating instance, "Adam." Again we may hear Schleiermacher: "Original sin . . . is best understood as the encompassing deed and encompassing guilt of the human race."[77]

It is of course the second originality that demands explanation. The classical attempt is that "human nature" is given to each of us by our biological generation, which hands on a deprived and infected version of that nature. This proposal is at best difficult. Schleiermacher is again surely right, that "the representation of an alteration of human nature . . . by the first sin of the first human" is not a theologically sufficient explanation.[78] An Augustinian counterpoint must be maintained: "In principle, Augustine believed, it is possible to live without sinning. In practice, no one succeeds in doing so. And why . . . do not people do what they are capable of doing? Because they do not want to."[79]

The difficulty with the classical proposal is its use of the notion of "human nature":[80] this in itself suggests an impersonal something that makes humans

---

eius posteritatem derivatum est. . . . Et ideo simpliciter dicendum est quod peccatum traducitur per originem a primo parente in posteros."

75. Ibid.

76. *Der Christliche Glaube* (1830), cited by 7th ed. (Berlin: Walter de Gruyter, 1960), 1:370.

77. Ibid., 374.

78. Ibid., 390.

79. Colin Gunton, *Theology through the Theologians* (Edinburgh: T. & T. Clark, 1996), 213.

80. Not, it should be noted, with an alleged understanding of sexual activity as intrinsically bad.

human and the alteration of which would imply an alteration in the definition of humanity. We have in fact conducted our discussion of humanity almost entirely without using the notion. If it were to be introduced, it would be with the interpretation given in the first volume: for each of us to "have human nature" is to play a part in the coherent history of humanity, which is made one and coherent by the one determinate call of God to be his partner.[81]

Within the metaphysics that this work has bit by bit proposed, on the other hand, there is no difficulty in seeing how idolatry, lust, injustice, and despair are both my acts and acts of all of us historically together, and how they are the one precisely in that they are the other. I am one with myself by and in the communities that present me with myself; and vice versa these communities are what they are by the actions of the persons bestowed on them. Humanity is finally one diachronically extended community, and that community and we in it are idolatrous, lustful, unjust, and despairing.[82]

Moreover, we just so are compelled to posit a "fall" of humankind, occurring within created time. Hominids who do not yet invoke God cannot sin. But so soon as members of the human community are on the scene, they in fact do; this is the lamentable puzzle of the matter. The story told in the third chapter of Genesis is not a myth; it does not describe what always and never happens. It describes the historical first happening of what thereafter always happens; moreover, had it not happened with the first humans it could not have happened at all, since then the first humans would have been omitted from an "encompassing deed of the human race."

We may one last time pose the question: Who were Adam and Eve? And in this context the answer must be: the first community of our biological ancestors who disobeyed God's command.

VIII

Finally, we must note a sort of analogy to human and angelic sin in the rest of creation. The famous Pauline passage is hard but cannot be ignored: "The creation was subjected to futility, not of its own will but by the will of the one who subjected it, in hope that the creation itself will be set free from its bondage to ruin[83] and will obtain the freedom of the glory of the children of God. We know that the whole creation has been groaning in labor pains until now . . . while we wait for adoption, the redemption of our bodies."[84]

---

81. 1:133–138.

82. Schleiermacher is the pioneer of this way of understanding the matter. To this, Gunton, *Theology*, 216.

83. "Decay" in the New Revised Standard Version is surely a somewhat misleading translation of *phora*.

84. Romans 8:20–23.

The diction of the passage comes from the tradition of apocalyptic.[85] In it "creation" refers to the human and other than human creation together as one subject of suffering and striving. This whole is here taken insofar as it is determined not by human guilt but by the innocence of the other creatures; creation as a whole has not itself willed its condition. In the narrative of the passage, creation is poised in the moment just before its great deliverance, when its teleology will be fulfilled in the glorification of the *totus Christus*. But until the labor of this birth is over, the creation is "subjected" to pointlessness[86] and to endings that are merely endings.[87]

The world that tempts us to take it as a pointless and declining cosmos is a world whose true teleology has somehow been agonizingly suspended. Just at this point, we may think of the devil *and his fallen angels*. For if the angels are the inner-creaturely reality of creation's direction to God, then demons must be precisely gaps in created teleology, junctures where creation's dynamism can skid out of control.

This subjection is, according to Paul, decreed by God, and precisely as a hopeful act. How the act can be hopeful is not explicitly stated. But the presumption must be that a creation that simply continued on the way of its own teleology while humanity went on the way of sin could not suffer the birth pangs of that humanity's redemption, while an adoption of human children into glory that occurred independently of the rest of creation would not be a "redemption of our bodies."

We must, surely, halt here. The mystery of evil that is not sin or caused by sin, of arbitrary disaster to the garden we are given to tend and of undeserved— for often it is—disaster to us from that garden, can hardly be plumbed very far. What little the present structure of thought can offer to that point has already been offered. Jesus said, "Those eighteen who were killed when the tower of Siloam fell on them—do you think that they were worse offenders than all the others living in Jerusalem?"[88] And if we were not to qualify some of Paul's language, as indeed we have just been doing, we would seem to deny that the actual creation is the one God made with the teleology with which he made it.

But the connections Paul presumes must somehow obtain. If the whole creation has a goal, and if that goal is the adoption into God of the *totus Christus*, of Jesus with his sisters and brothers, then sin and the Crucifixion must be the crises of *all* creation's teleology, as this is actually worked out within God's will. It is vital to remember that the creation's teleology is a *dramatic* teleology, so that such crises cannot be strange to it.

85. To this and the following see most helpfully Otto Michel, *Der Brief an die Römer* (*Kritisch-exegetischer Kommentar über das Neue Testament*) (Göttingen: Vandenhoeck & Ruprecht, 1955), 52–62.

86. *Mataiotetos.*

87. To *phthora*, which is not easy to translate into English. German *Untergang* is perfect.

88. Luke 13:4.

On account of sin, there is, says Paul, a sort of despair in the cosmos itself, a curse of pointlessness in which all events seem to lead into empty infinity. As we deny our end in God, so does the world, which was made to enable this end, lose its meaning. The very course of cosmic events, insofar as it evidently tends toward either pointless infinite continuance or toward collapse back into nothingness, is other than it might have been. Our world's redemption from the curse of humanity's sin must be much of the matter of this work's last reflections.

TWENTY-THREE

God's Speech In Creation

I

The first Vatican Council taught: "God, the source and goal of all things, can be certainly known from created things, by the light of natural human reason."[1] If we abstract from systematic connections perhaps made by conciliar fathers themselves and strictly consider the text they produced, the council's teaching is simply traditional. So Thomas Aquinas: "All things made by God are by nature such as . . . hiddenly to proclaim to us the divine reasons by which they have come to be."[2]

The council, following the tradition, presented its teaching as an exegesis of Paul's argument in the first chapter of Romans, explicitly citing verse 1:20: "For from the creation of the world the unseen things [of God] have nevertheless been seen, through having become known in the creatures."[3] We too may therefore appropriately begin our reflections with this passage. But for systematic purposes we need to have Paul's argument more fully before us, particularly the previous verse: "For what is known of God is manifest among them, for God has made it manifest to them."

We must note at the beginning that the knowledge from creation of which Paul here speaks is the knowledge that specifically the gentiles have, or rather repress, and that its counterpart in the passage is the knowledge given to Jews as *torah*—which according to Paul they also violate, though differently.[4] Thus the

---

1. Dogmatic Constitution, caput ii.
2. *Quaestiones ad Thallasium*, xiii.
3. This verse and the next cited are my translation; the published versions are misleading, as any translation is likely to be that is not willing to use rather strange English.
4. 1:16; 2:1–24.

passage offers no immediate occasion or basis for constructing any *layered* scheme of "natural and supernatural" or "natural and revealed" knowledge. The only question to which the council in its dependence on Romans dogmatically directs us is that of a cognitive relation to God mediated by the creation to those outside the covenant with Israel, in a way *parallel* to that established with Israel at Sinai. Since those within the covenant presumably have both kinds of knowledge, they must for the redeemed stand in some relation, but Paul does not reflect on that.

We must likewise be clear from the start that there is no question in Paul of a knowledge of God that human agents derive by intellectual operations on observed phenomena. That is, Paul has nothing to say for or against what modernity usually means by "natural theology" or about what fathers of the council may have conceived under some such label. If God is manifest among the gentiles, this is because God has *made* himself manifest, just as the knowledge of God in Israel is the result of what he did at Sinai and by his prophets. And if then God has become known "in the creatures" this is because in this case God uses the creatures in general to accomplish his revelation. We must be careful in reading Paul not to be led astray from his point by "intellectual trends of our era [that] have replaced a concept of revelation with a concept of truth as something lying within the control of the human rational agent."[5] We must speak first of God's self-revelation by way of creation and only thereupon of a theology therein enabled.[6]

Finally among these initial observations, we must note Paul's verbs and their mutual relations: the "unseen" things of God are nevertheless "seen" in that they "have come to be thought" through creatures. The language of the independent clause is that of apocalyptic: by way of the creatures God opens his unseen things to view, just as he opens a door to heaven for John in the Revelation.[7] The dependent clause then specifies that the door in this instance requires no paranormal inspiration but is opened in usual ways of creaturely experience; though we must remember that this distinction is modern and not one Paul would have made.

II

Neither the conciliar declaration nor the points just made say *how* God gives us knowledge of himself by way of creation; they do not, that is, answer the question Western theology has traditionally had about the Romans passage. To join the text with this question, in a way surely not alien to the council, we may appropriately turn to Thomas Aquinas's commentary on the text.[8]

In appropriating Thomas's exegesis of Paul, we will be guided by the contemporary construal of Thomas's theological epistemology, which does not start

5. Colin E. Gunton, *A Brief Theology of Revelation* (Edinburgh: T. & T. Clark, 1995), 21.
6. Ibid., entire.
7. 4:1.
8. *Super epistolam Sancti Pauli ad Romanos lectura*, §§102–116.

with his argumentative "paths to God" (*viae in Deum*)—his "proofs," as we are likely to call them.[9] Insofar as the *Summa theologiae* provides guidance for Thomas's commentary on the Romans passage, this is done not by the mere fact that its second *quaestio* contains cosmological argument for God but by Thomas's antecedent and founding stipulation, in the first *quaestio*, that *all* knowledge of God is dependent on divine initiative.[10] That the arguments which Thomas does then adduce do not within themselves call on the gospel or Scripture does not by itself tell us how Thomas thought creation's mediation of knowledge of God works; particularly it does not say he thought it worked as moderns are likely to think it must.

Indeed, Paul, according to Thomas in his commentary,[11] does not attribute to gentiles without faith an authentic knowledge of God. All competent knowledge forms the soul in some virtue, and competent knowledge of God forms the soul in love of God, which is precisely what Paul says the manifestation of God to the gentiles has not done; convicting them of this is Paul's purpose in bringing up the matter. The cognition actually present in the gentiles is, according to Paul according to Thomas, a cognition that is "emptied"[12] and "captive."[13] Thomas can characterize this incompetent knowledge from several viewpoints:[14] sometimes he regards it as operationally equivalent to ignorance, though it can be called knowledge because it is culpable; sometimes as a potentiality waiting upon faith to become actual, so that he can gloss "known" in verse 1:19 of Paul's text as "knowable";[15] and sometimes as idolatry.

Thomas indeed supposes a continuity between what creation provides the minds of unbelieving gentiles and the true knowledge that will subsist in faith if they come to it, so that he can call also the first "real knowledge of God, *in a certain respect* [emphasis added]."[16] But whatever this respect is, whatever the epistemic quality of the knowledge which revelation in creation gives the gentiles, their knowledge so gained is nothing they could use as a foundation for the knowledge of faith.[17]

---

9. Certainly they are not so intended in the *Summa theologiae*, whatever may have been intended in the less mature *Summa contra gentiles*. To Thomas's understanding of our knowledge generally, Robert W. Jenson, *The Knowledge of Things Hoped For: The Sense of Theological Discourse* (New York: Oxford University Press, 1969), 58–85; there also more bibliography.

10. *Summa theologiae*, i.i, esp. art. 1–3.

11. The following is much indebted to Eugene F. Rogers, *Thomas Aquinas and Karl Barth: Sacred Doctrine and the Natural Knowledge of God* (Notre Dame: Notre Dame University Press, 1995); this is the now published version of the dissertation cited I:6. Indeed, I will at key points cite the conclusions he draws from his minute reading of the relevant passages rather than redoing that labor.

12. Romans 1:21 is the reference.

13. Rogers, *Thomas Aquinas*, e.g., 146–149.

14. Ibid., 124–135.

15. As does, to less theologically clear purpose, the New Revised Standard Version.

16. "Quantum ad aliquid"; see Rogers, *Thomas Aquinas*, 135.

17. I am not as certain as Rogers seems to be about the exegesis of "in a certain respect" here and for present purposes do not need to be.

All this established, it is now safe to ask *how* Thomas thinks God gives us knowledge of himself by means of creatures. That is, we may now consider Thomas's "proofs" for God, more accurately described by his own rubric for them as the mind's "paths" to God.[18] In the commentary on Romans, he groups reflective paths to God under three headings.

There is the *via* by "causality." Creatures come and go in time. Just so they make us think of something faithful over time, on which they depend, since only by contrast with this thought do we apprehend their coming and going. If our thoughts follow this track, we think God's existence, the sheer fact of a first principle, that is, of a principle that is not one of the principles within created time.

There is the *via* by "excellence." The creatures show themselves jointly dependent on and so inferior to this first principle. Just so they make us think of this principle in its excellence. Reflecting on these lines, we think God's deity.

And there is the *via* by "negation." If we once have the thought of a supremely excellent principle and of his existence, the creatures show that they are not to be compared with him. Along this way, we think the various aspects in which God is incomparable; that is, we think his "attributes."

The "ways" do not start with a nature or world grasped from a position neutral to faith. Thomas, at least when commenting on Paul, presumes no such reality.[19] Thinking along the *viae* does not lead to God by recruiting him to the further explanation of a world initially grasped apart from him. Rather, it leads to God by recruiting the world to God's service in making himself known.[20] It engages all creatures as possibilities of revelation: of their own reality as creatures and of God as Creator.[21]

It thus seems that the most natural way of reading Thomas's exposition of Paul on revelation "in the creatures" would be as a description of God's self-*communication* to us by them. And if we were to set Thomas's teaching within this category, it would be precisely congruent with that taken throughout this work. For Thomas as in our earlier chapters, also idolatry and unbelief would be construed as perverse responses to God's in itself authentic address, an address that occurs also outside Israel and the church and that calls all humanity to a goal that is in itself the same as that which faith grasps.

Yet Thomas himself does not put it quite so, and we may again suppose we know why: the traditional interpretation of the *Logos* inhibits discourse about God's actual speech. The creation informed by the *Logos* remains for Thomas as for most of the tradition primally an object of seeing rather than of hearing and so an object to be worked up by our agency rather than an intrusion to which we

18. *In Romanum*, §115. See Rogers, *Thomas Aquinas*, 141.
19. Rogers, *Aquinas*, e.g., 113.
20. Ibid., 123: "Paul [thinks Thomas] will not let a secular view of the world go forward, one that leaves God in God's heaven and abandons human life to a terrestrial intelligibility internal to this world."
21. Ibid., 140: "In cosmological proofs within sacred doctrine Thomas upholds the world of *revelabilia*."

must hearken. We have no need to share this inhibition; and for our encouragement Scripture contains an entire literature centered on divine speech heard in creation.

III

It is often said that old Israel had no talent for metaphysics. This patent error results from two prejudices. Dominant German scholarship, in the shadow of Kant, has often supposed that only positions materially consistent with those of the Greeks are "metaphysical," so that, for example, a poem about *hearing* creation cannot be serious ontology; that it is not may then of course be regarded as a virtue.[22] And modern biblical scholarship has typically slighted the so-called wisdom literature.

We will be guided by exegete-systematician Gerhard von Rad's remarkable meditation on some of the metaphysical wisdom poems.[23] Primary among these poems is Proverbs 8, which we must brutally excerpt: "Does not wisdom call, and does not understanding raise her voice? . . . The Lord created me at the beginning of his work. . . . Ages ago I was set, at the first before the beginning of the earth. . . . When he established the heavens . . . when he assigned to the sea its limits . . . when he marked out the foundations of the earth, then I was beside him, like a master worker, and I was daily his delight."[24]

The "wisdom" who here speaks is initially the practical, ethical, and occasionally religious wisdom that Israel's teachers—rather than her prophets or priests—cultivated, as have those of all humanity.[25] This wisdom is experiential knowledge of how things go in the world, whether in the earth and heavens or in human life. It is the wisdom by which "kings reign, and rulers decree what is just,"[26] just as it is the wisdom by which the young may attain maturity.[27]

In this passage, however, wisdom suddenly appears in a seemingly very different role: she is a personal voice somehow speaking from the creation and proclaiming herself as the wisdom by which God orders it. In the dramatic language of the poem, she presents herself as the architect at the Builder's side.

Experience of the world's ways thus turns out to expose us to the call of someone who addresses us with God's own wisdom. What we encounter by sober involvement with creation reveals itself as God's personal intent in creating it. Knowledge of such wisdom would indeed be "more to be desired" than silver,

---

22. For exposure of a notable and ecumenically significant case in which this prejudice has distorted scholarship, Risto Saarinen, *Gotttes Wirken auf Uns: Die transzendentale Deutung des Gegenwart-Christi-Motivs in der Lutherforschung* (Stuttgart: Institut für Europäische Geschichte, 1989).

23. *Weisheit in Israel* (Neukirchen: Keukirchener Verlag, 1970), 189–228.

24. Proverbs 8:1–30.

25. To this, von Rad, *Weisheit*, 151–188.

26. Proverbs 8:15.

27. E.g., ibid. 4:1–27.

gold, or jewels:[28] the one who ordered his or her life by it would track the very purposes God has built into the world in which we must live.

The world's ordering wisdom is not, to be sure, available on the surface of things. It is in the creation and just so *hidden* in it. Another wisdom poem laments—or celebrates—wisdom's hiddenness: humans with their observation and technology can probe many secrets of creation, "but where shall wisdom be found? . . . Mortals do not know the way to it. . . . It is hidden from the eyes of all the living." Only "God understands the way to it."[29]

Parallels to Greek *Logos*-speculations are obvious, and theology has sometimes exploited them. Yet the difference is profound. The meaning of the world is not, in these wisdom poems, available in the world to be worked out by us; we do not know the way to it. It is precisely a voice calling *to* us. As we observe this difference we confront a question.

The experience of the world's ways by which we may acquire wisdom is not, in Job and Proverbs, an experience mortals have at their disposal;[30] and indeed wisdom's speeches are cast in the exact style of divine self-revelation. Yet the voice that speaks from the experienced world is nevertheless not God's voice[31] and assuredly not that of a mediating entity between divinity and nondivinity. The speaker is explicitly one *creature* among the rest[32] but one who must be there for the others to make sense. Wisdom is the "mysterious addition by which the world orders itself and just so turns to address itself to the life of humanity."[33]

And of course the most astonishing thing—to us epigones of the Greeks—is precisely that the created world-order *speaks*, that it "turns to humanity appealing and commanding, in direct address, as a personality."[34] In their occupation with the wise order of the world, Israel's teachers encountered a *someone*, who spoke to them of virtue and of God. The poems and von Rad's meditation on them leave us with the question: Who is this speaker? Who is the creature who is the ordering instance of other creatures, who speaks from creation to us, and who just so speaks for God although she is not God?

If previous positions taken in this work are correct, the speaker must somehow be a preexistence of the incarnate *Logos*. His preexistence, as we analyzed it,[35] is in one mode a narrative pattern of Israel's previous story. Thus this mode of Jesus' preexistence is just what we are looking for: a specific created reality within creation, which is the Word by which God creates. Yet this answer will have to be

---

28. Ibid. 10–11.
29. Job 28:1–28.
30. Ibid. 200.
31. Von Rad, *Weisheit*, 211: "In these texts . . . it is not JHWH who speaks.
32. Ibid., 210: "The texts do not speak of . . . a principle or a universal rationality, but of a created something, which has its specific reality as do other created things."
33. Ibid., 204.
34. Ibid., 204.
35. 1:138–144.

refined, for while the incarnate *Logos* is a creature, as is the world-wisdom, he is also God, which the world-wisdom is not.

A first refinement might be to move one christological step to the side and say: the creature who speaks in the creatures for God is the *Logos*'s human nature, insofar as the incarnate *Logos*'s preexistence within Israel's history posits his human nature as a determinate teleology within Israel's created history and so as a determinate teleology of creation as a whole. This would seem to be even more precisely what we are looking for. Yet again there are difficulties; the idea of the *Logos*'s human nature speaking on its own has a rather too Antiochene ring, nor can it be entirely without significance that throughout the poems wisdom is obtrusively and consistently "she."

Finally, surely, we must say: it is the preexistent reality of the *totus Christus* that is the creature among the creatures who makes sense of the rest of them and whom Israel's teachers heard when the creation made sense to them. That is, *Israel herself*, as within creation the determinate possibility of the Incarnation, spoke to her teachers. And following what we concluded in the previous chapter, we must say that Israel spoke to them from heaven, spoke to them from that created presence of the End within which she was already in full possession of her destiny.

Heaven does not fall silent so long as the End is not yet. However we are to construe the relation of Israel and the church,[36] theology must appropriate in the present tense the experience of Israel's teachers. The body of the *totus Christus* is a creature, that creature that makes sense of the rest. This body is in the created heaven a self-possessed conscious creature. And this creature speaks through the phenomena Thomas observed, of creatures' dependence, inferiority, and comparability to—something. It is thus that God reveals himself through our experience of creatures.

IV

But now it is time to ask: How does it *happen*, that in dealing cognitively with creation we hear a *voice*, however the voice is to be identified? To this question Israel's teachers provide no answer; they have heard the voice, report what she says, and in their situation have no further questions.

According to Martin Luther, "Sun, moon, heaven, earth, Peter, Paul, I, you, etc., are all words of God, or perhaps rather syllables or letters in context of the whole creation. . . . In this way the words of God are embodied realities (*res*) and not mere language."[37] What God has to say becomes actual and not merely possible utterance, in that there are creatures. And Luther's choice of language to

---

36. Pp. 190–195, 335–336.
37. *Ennaratio in Genesis*, 17: "Sic Sol, Luna, Coelem, terra, Petrus, paulus, Ego, tu, etc. sumus vocabula Dei, imo uno syllaba vel litera comparatione totius creaturae. . . . Sic verba Dei res est, non nuda vocabular."

evoke this event is intentionally suggestive; for the chief context in which *res* was a technical term for him was the doctrine of sacraments.

In Augustinian sacramentology, as we have adduced it in other contexts, words in a language "come" to ritual objects, "elements," and so there are sacraments. We may now note that this meeting does something for both the words and the elements: the elements become "visible words" and the words achieve embodied actuality. Thus if God wishes to speak to persons beyond himself, creatures are necessary for him, and not only in that there would otherwise be no auditors but also in that otherwise such speech would be disembodied and demonic. And then we may think of the other side of the meeting also and think of "sun, moon" and the rest as "elements" that may become visible words as interpreting words "come" to them.

As for the word that comes to creation, to let the creatures be signs, we already know of it. This word is at once the word of the gospel that sounds in the church and the word of the law that sounds also outside the church. That is, when the creatures come to speak, it is as "elements" within the continuing moral and religious discourse through which God speaks to humanity and by which he makes us specifically human. Apart from this actual speech, the creatures would indeed remain dumb.

Having asserted that last proposition, we must immediately mark it as contrary to even possible fact, for the discourse referred to is the word of God that creates all things in the first place; therefore there could in fact be no dumb creature. The being of creatures is precisely response to God's command; that is, it is *answer*. The creatures, we said in the previous volume, have their being not as *phenomena*, things appearing, but as *legomena*, things told of.

The creation is not a cosmos that once it exists has a history; what God creates *is* a history. Within this understanding, the Bultmann school's central notion comes into its own, and loses the ad hoc appearance we noted earlier.[38] All events and all words are "word-events"; there is no event that does not speak and no meaning that does not occur. "That is real which has a future";[39] and the future is there only in utterance that presents it.[40]

The creatures are "elements" in the event that the spoken word of law and gospel brings them to visible speech. In the churchly sacraments we see how the creatures offer themselves to become signs of God: water can be the sign of repentance and new birth because of its daily role to threaten and sustain and cleanse life, and bread and cup can be the sign of incorporation into Christ because of the place of eating and drinking in all community and because of their incorporation into us. How do the creatures as such offer themselves to be signs of God? We return to Thomas's *viae*.

In their sheer contingency, the creatures *betray*, in both senses of the term, God's command that calls them forth. We have learned from Thomas some of

38. 1:166.
39. Gerhard Ebeling, *Das Wesen des christlichen Glaubens* (Tübingen: J. C. B. Mohr, 1959), 255.
40. Ibid.

the detail of this betrayal. The creatures are enduring and splendid and marvelously various. But simultaneously they provide ample opportunity to think of ephemerality, of imperfection, and of comparability. Just in this simultaneity, they provide opportunity to think eternity, perfection, and incomparability. And within the discourse that God sustains with humanity the opportunity is always taken up, even if as the opportunity to "capture" and "empty" the thought it provokes, even if as the thought of Barth's not-God.

V

No more than in the first volume dare we claim the knowledge of God without observing his hiddenness. And here again it is vital to avoid the great contemporary denial of Nicea: the supposition that God's hiddenness is quantitative, constituted in metaphysical distance from us, through which we may perhaps catch "glimpses of the Divine."[41] God is not hidden because we can see only some of him through the metaphysical distances. He is hidden because his very presence is such as at once altogether to reveal and altogether to hide him.

We may return yet again to Thomas. He teaches both that God as Being itself is supremely knowable and even in this life is in fact known to us, and that in this life we can know nothing at all about God.[42] For to know *about* something is to say such things as "It is intelligent" or "It is a cathedral" or "It is heavy"; it is to put the thing into a class of some sort. But God is in no class. He is the cause of the class of all things and just so belongs to none of them.[43] If God belonged to a class, it would be the class of beings; but this gets us no further, for beings of course do not make a class of beings.[44]

But what knowledge do the *viae* then bring us?[45] Thomas's answer: because all things are God's "effects, dependent on him as their cause and reason, we can learn of God from [the creatures] *that* he is [emphasis added],"[46] that is, simply that there is a first principle. All the attributes that Thomas then attributes to God merely—as we would now say—unpack the sheer assertion of his existence.[47] To pick up the citation: "we can learn of God . . . that he is, and to know what must necessarily pertain to him if he is to be the cause of all things while transcending all his effects."

In their deep logic, the propositions that we can in this life assert of God are therefore negative: "Of God, we cannot know what he is but only what he is not."[48]

---

41. *Guidelines for Inclusive Use of the English Language,* Evangelical Lutheran Church in America (Chicago: 1989), 14.

42. To the following, Jenson, *Knowledge,* 69–87.

43. E.g., *Summa theologiae,* I.13.1.

44. Ibid., i.3.5.

45. Or, for that matter, the biblical revelation, which is not our immediate concern?

46. Ibid., I.13.1.

47. Jenson, *Knowledge,* 70–71.

48. Thomas, *Summa theologiae,* i.3.prol.

All such propositions, according to Thomas, work in the following fashion. "There is God" implies "There is a first cause." If then there is a character F such that "There is a first cause" and some statement true of creatures, as for example "Creatures are composite," together entail that "F is instantiated," we can go on to that proposition, in the present case "Perfect simplicity is instantiated," which is the same as "God is simple." Thus "God is simple" adds to "There is God" only a *denial* of one aspect of creatureliness.[49]

Yet the combination of such denial with the affirmation of God's being constitutes a very specific kind of negation. We have arrived again at the doctrine of analogy, now from the other side. We do actually know that God is simple, even if in knowing this we know nothing *about* him. We do truly predicate the word "simple" of God, "analogously." Yet what it is in God that we thereby denote, remains—we come to the word—hidden.

To appropriate Thomas's teaching we must translate it in the same way as earlier. God both presents himself to us by the creatures and is hidden behind them. In the dominant tradition this is grasped by thinking of creatures as *images* of God, which both resemble him and do not resemble him. We need not altogether reject this thought, but by itself it is vulnerable to the antique and late modern interpretation of God's hiddenness as dimness caused by metaphysical distance.

We will subordinate the dominant position to another also found in the tradition: creatures, said Luther at the center of his theology, are *masks* of God, behind which he hides but through which he speaks.[50] A mask is not supposed to resemble the one it masks, yet it is the medium through which the one masked addresses us. Just so are the creatures to God.

God is not hidden from us by his absence but by the fullness and character of his presence. He is the Creator, who fully presents himself to us in every event of his creation. What hides God are the sins and evils with which that creation is filled. As we saw in the first volume, it is God's moral intentions that are "not as our ways" that are incomprehensible to us and hide his goodness from us. True natural theology, actual knowledge of God in the creation, therefore lives only in the great "Nevertheless" of faith in the Creator.

VI

But now: have we described a knowledge of God "by natural human reason" that answers to the teaching of the council? That depends, at two junctures.

We certainly have not described a knowledge of God achieved by a human cognitive activity within a realm of "nature" independent of "grace." There is no

---

49. Jenson, *Knowledge*, 71–72.

50. To this briefly but compendiously, Gerhard Ebeling, *Luther: Einführung in sein Denken* (Tübingen: J. C. B. Mohr, 1964), 220–233.

such realm. We have not attributed knowledge of God to a rational capacity with an integral "natural" goal other than "supernatural" enjoyment of God, or with warrants of argument derived from such a goal. There is no such actual human goal. If the teaching of Vatican I requires the supposition of such a rationality and such a knowledge, either the council or fundamental positions taken in this work are wrong. But Henri de Lubac, by whom we were instructed to disbelieve in an ungraced nature, did not consider himself in conflict with the teaching of this council.

The council's reference to "natural human reason" is at least in part reference to reason as it functions also where the gospel is not heard. We have not here affirmed a knowledge of God possessed outside the church that is not idolatrous—though nor have we denied the possibility of its occurrence. But also idolatrous religion, we earlier maintained, is response to the true God's speech and makes humanity vulnerable to him. What has here been affirmed doubtless would not satisfy some—or perhaps any—members of the council. But it need not for that reason fail to agree with what the council actually recorded as its teaching.

Finally we must return briefly to a matter raised in the very first chapter of this work. "Natural theology" appears often in the tradition as a branch of "philosophy." Thus the relation of Israel's and the church's knowledge of God to natural theology is, in this construal of the latter, the same as the relation of theology to philosophy. But what is philosophy?

Perhaps we may allow ourselves the conceit: philosophy is what disciples of Socrates do. In the earlier discussion we said that philosophy is the theology of Olympian-Parmenidean religion. The Christian theology deriving from the gospel's penetration of Mediterranean antiquity is permanently constituted in the conversation, at once appreciative and polemic, of the gospel-claim with this religion. And now we must further note that Western civilization is the creature of that conversation.

Within the branch of Christian history most—perhaps all—readers of this work inhabit, there will always be a polarity between two traditions of reflection, locked in permanent attraction and rejection. If we wish, we may distinguish these traditions as "philosophy" and "theology." But we must be clear that this is *not* a distinction of genre.

The relation is not symmetrical. Since the gospel is intrinsically a missionary message, and since Mediterranean antiquity was there before it was invaded by the gospel, Christianity is the intruder even in the civilization it co-created. Within the West, it is therefore possible to be a disciple of Socrates and not of the prophets or apostles, though it is not possible to be unaffected by them. So there will be "philosophers" who are not Christian theologians. But within Western civilization, and so within the theological enterprise located there, it is not possible to be a disciple of the apostles and not a disciple also of Socrates. Therefore the labels "philosophy" and "theology" cannot mark a real distinction for those most likely to read this book.

VII

"Petition and praise are response to challenge and blessing. These then are what all occasions say to us. By every actual occasion, the risen Lord says: 'There are possibilities. Ask,' and 'There are marvels. Praise.' That believers are able to hear these addresses, that we are able so to interpret natural spontaneity, depends on . . . our knowledge of the risen Christ."[51] That is surely the concluding thing to be said about creation.

51. Robert W. Jenson, "The Holy Spirit," *Christian Dogmatics,* ed. Carl Braaten, Robert Jenson (Philadelphia: Fortress, 1984), 2:173.

PART VI

THE CHURCH

TWENTY-FOUR

The Church's Founding

I

It could be argued that in the system here presented, also ecclesiology belongs in the first volume. There is a difference between the matter of this part and that of other parts of this volume, between the church's place in the gospel and that of the creation as such or even the creation taken finally into God. Christ is personally the second identity of God, and the *totus Christus* is Christ with the church; therefore the church is not in the same way an *opus ad extra* as is the creation, even when it is perfected in God.

We believe in God the Creator, but of the world only that it is created. We believe in God the Eschatos, but of the Eschaton only that it is creation's translation into him. That is, we do not place our faith in the world, not even looking forward to its transformation in God. But we do place our faith in the church. Or so this section will maintain; thereby this work takes the Catholic side of what in ecumenical dialogue has sometimes been identified as the "basic difference" between Catholic and Protestant understandings.[1]

Nevertheless it has seemed less misleading to locate the church, with the creation and the Kingdom, among God's works *ad extra*. For though we rely on the church as on the presence of God, we do so just in that the church within herself directs us to a presence of God that is not identical with herself. In a formula we

---

1. So, from the Protestant side, the important work of André Birmelé, *Le Salut en Jésus Christ dans les Dialogues Oecuméniques* (Paris: Cerf, 1966), whose entire analysis of the dialogues circles around this identification. And so from the Catholic side J. M. R. Tillard, "We Are Different," *Mid-Stream* 25 (1986):283. According to Tillard, Catholics must teach and Protestants cannot that the "Church on earth is at the same time . . . the fruit but nevertheless also the instrument of Salvation." For my direct argument on the point, see *Unbaptized God: The Basic Flaw in Ecumenical Theology* (Minneapolis: Fortress, 1992), 90–103.

have already used and will often return to, the church *is* the body of Christ for the world and for her members, in that she is constituted a community by the verbal and "visible" presence *to* her of that same body of Christ. The body of Christ is at once his sacramental presence within the church's assembly, to make that assembly a community, and is the church-community herself for the world and her members.[2]

Related to this decision is another. In this work's doctrine of creation, every step was determined by the teaching of the priestly creation account, of psalms and prophets, and of John's prologue, that the world is created by God's uttered Word. It might then have been expected that its ecclesiology would follow the same line, with the Reformation emphasis that the church is in a special sense "the creature of the gospel." Instead, this part begins with a traditional question about the founding of the church and builds its central chapters around certain concepts of the church. That is, it presumes the actual historical existence of the church and inquires into its origin and nature.

It may be recalled that at the very beginning of this book's first volume, it was said: "Whether we are to say that God uses the gospel to gather the church for himself, or that God provides the church to carry the gospel to the world, depends entirely on the direction of thought in a context."[3] This and the following chapters will follow the first direction and consider the church in its own proper entity, in which it is in God's intention antecedent to the gospel.

The chief reason for this choice is what seems a historical mandate to follow the lines of recent ecumenical discussion. As has often been observed, it is only in this century and most decisively in its ecumenical efforts that the church has come to see herself as a theological question. Through most of the church's history, she has understood herself as a presupposition of theology rather than as a problem within it;[4] and until the second Vatican Council no great council had supposed it necessary to promulgate doctrine about the church simply as such.[5] Ecclesiology became a direct object of theological concern when the threat appeared that the communal presupposition of theology might not be in place. It was as the division of the church came to be seen in a new light that the church herself became a theological problem.

---

2. 1:204–206.

3. 1:5.

4. So Georges Florovsky, "Le corps du Christ vivant," *La Sainte Église Universelle*, G. Florovsky, F.-J. Leenhardt, R. Prenter, A. Richardson, C. Spicq (Paris: Delachaux et Niestlé, 1948), 9–10: "We cannot begin with an exact definition of the church . . . for in fact there is none that can claim . . . recognized doctrinal authority. . . . And nevertheless the reality of the church is always the indispensable foundation of the whole dogmatic structure. . . . The church is more a reality that one lives than an object that one analyzes."

5. Yves M.-J. Congar, *Die Lehre von der Kirche: Vom Abendländischen Schisma bis zur Gegenwart*, Handbuch der Dogmengeschichte, ed. M. Schmaus, A. Grillmeier, L. Scheffczyk, Bd 3, Fasz. 3d (Freiburg: Herder, 1971), 123: "For the first time in her hundreds of years of history the church defined herself (or anyway did so in a formal decree): in the 'dogmatic constitution' *Lumen gentium* . . . with other constitutions, decrees and declarations."

Thus the decisive interlocutors throughout this part will be the second Vatican Council and the subsequent ecumenical dialogues with their theological enablers and commentators. Other thinking about the church will be recruited on a more ad hoc basis.

The broken fellowship between East and West had been seen, at least from the Western side, as a lapse, which was to be sure scandalous but which did not call the church as such into question, even when it endured for centuries. Nor, in an opposite way, did the division created by the Reformation within the West seem to threaten theology's churchly presupposition, so long as theologians of each communion could think that the other communion was not "really" church, and so could with good conscience do their work for their own communion only. Reformation and Tridentine systems indeed came to include discussions *de ecclesia*, but these were heavily polemical and chiefly devoted to particular features of the church, especially those thought lacking in the opposed party. Thus Catholics could sometimes make it seem that the hierarchy is all there is to the church and Protestants suggest the same about the priesthood of all believers.

But contemporary dialogues between East and West have discovered an alienation seemingly as intractable, even amid elaborate protestations of sisterhood, as the more clarified divisions within the West.[6] And, conversely, between separated churches of the West, the very fact of a dialogue in which renewed churchly fellowship is recognized as the goal—however distant—constitutes recognition that somehow there is church on both sides of the dialogue. If one party were not church, why would the other party or parties want to be reunited with it? But if, for the key inner-Western instance, the Catholic Church and the Lutheran Church are both church, and yet are not in fellowship, where then is the one church of the creeds? The church that does theology?[7]

If there is a group that regards itself as church and there is another group that it regards as also church, and yet these two cannot celebrate the Eucharist together, the claim about both groups is compromised. Were strict logic applicable here—which thank God it is not[8]—we would have to say that at least one and possibly both were simply not the church, for there is and can be only one

6. For a glimpse of this, from the Orthodox side, Thomas Hopko, "Tasks Facing the Orthodox in the 'Reception' of BEM," *Orthodox Perspectives in Baptism, Eucharist and Ministry*, ed. G. Limouris, N. M. Vaporis (Brookline: Holy Cross Orthodox Press, 1985).

7. E.g., André Birmele, "Ökumenische Überlegungen zu Pneumatologie und Ekklesiologie," *Der Heilige Geist: Ökumenische und reformatorische Untersuchungen*, ed. Joachim Heubach (Erlangen: Martin-Luther Verlag, 1996), 180: "The challenge that is at the basis of the ecumenical movement is ecclesiological: the question of the oneness of Christ's church. . . . Thus the theme 'ecclesiology' shapes the entire ecumenical work."

8. The defiance of such logic is a major achievement of the second Vatican Council, with its teaching, in *Lumen gentium* 8, that the one church "a society established and organized in this world, subsists in (*subsistit in*) the catholic church governed by the successor of Peter." All attempts fail, so to read "subsists in" as to establish *either* an identification of the Roman Catholic Church with the one church *or* a simple inclusion in the one church of groups outside the Roman Catholic Church.

church, actual as such in the one Eucharist.[9] How then is either to proceed with a fully satisfied conscience to think for the church? That is, to do the work of theology? It is self-doubt about theology's own communal possibility—often, to be sure, subliminal—that has driven it finally to consider the church simply as such.

II

We turn to the particular matter of this chapter: the triune God's act to institute the church. Bluntly stated, God institutes the church by *not* letting Jesus' Resurrection be itself the End, by appointing "the delay of the Parousia." The "modernist" Catholic Alfred Loisy's notorious *mot* states the exact truth: "Jesus announced the Kingdom, but it was the church that came."[10] In its own context, Loisy's saying carried several layers of irony;[11] we may appropriate it more simply.

We need not uncritically adopt Luke's scheme of saving history[12] to observe that of all New Testament writers he thought most about the peculiar historical situation of the church; and in his view the church, in remarkable agreement with Loisy, is what came when the Kingdom was to be expected. At the Resurrection-appearance that Luke dramatically places last, "the Ascension,"[13] Luke has the disciples ask, "Lord, is this the time when you restore the kingdom to Israel?" Jesus avoids the question; in place of an answer he promises the gift of the Spirit, as the power to conduct a mission to Jews and gentiles. Then a time is marked out for this mission by Jesus' departure from among them and by the angelic promise of his return.

As we argued in the first volume, Jesus' Resurrection "first," so that there is a time when he is risen while his people continue to die and be born in their generations, resolves an antinomy at the heart of Israel's hope. One aspect of this concerns Israel's historical mission. Israel's calling was to be a blessing to all nations; and the prophets interpreted the fulfillment of that calling as the gathering of the nations to fellowship with her in worship of the true God.[14] But when it is eventually seen that Israel's destiny can be fulfilled only in a new creation beyond this age, no space seems to remain for such a gathering in this age. Yet this aspect of Israel's mission must surely be understood as at least in part a *preparation* for

---

9. The basic argument here, of course, is Paul's in I Corinthians 10–11, which I will instance many times in the following.

10. *L'Evangile et l'Église* (Paris: 1902), 153: "Jésus annonçait le Royaume, et c'est l'Église qui est venue."

11. For some of these, Michael J. Hollerich, "Retrieving a Neglected Critique of Church, Theology and Secularization in Weimar Germany," *Pro Ecclesia* 2 (1993):305–332.

12. The classical exposition is of course Oscar Cullmann, *Christ and Time; The Primitive Christian Conception of Time and History*, tr. F. V. Filson (Philadelphia: Westminster, 1950).

13. Luke 1:6–11.

14. 1:69–70.

the End: when God's people is wholly taken into God and Israel's hopes are thereby fulfilled, that people must already be the Israel to which the gentiles have come.[15] Had Jesus' Resurrection been immediately the End, Israel's mission would have been aborted.

The church is nothing other than an appropriate if beforehand unpredictable sidestep in the fulfillment of the Lord's promises to Israel. The church is, just as Loisy insinuated, an eschatological *detour*[16] of Christ's coming; but, as the author of II Peter wrote, to those worried about the Lord's delay, "The Lord is not slow about his promise . . . but is patient"[17] precisely for the sake of Israel's mission. Nor indeed are detours uncharacteristic of the whole plot of JHWH's story with his people—we will have yet another to consider.

Thus the church is neither a realization of the new age nor an item of the old age. She is precisely an event *within the event* of the new age's advent. We must be very careful about our language here; loose rhetoric can have disastrous spiritual consequences. Protestants have sometimes proclaimed with satisfaction or even glee, "In the Kingdom there will be no church," thereby in fact blaspheming. Catholics and Protestant social activists have sometimes oppositely talked of the church as a sort of overlap of the Kingdom onto the old age, thereby in fact depicting her as a space available for idolatry, as Karl Barth explored the phenomenon. The previous generation's great interpreter of Orthodoxy to the West, Georges Florovsky, made the point precisely, in language then current: "One may say that the church is 'anticipated eschatology.'[18] But not that she is 'realized eschatology.'"[19]

When Jesus enforced the immediate claim of the Kingdom and enacted that claim visibly in healings and exorcisms, God's rule was established over those who heard, saw and believed. When and where God's rule is established, the Kingdom occurs.[20] Yet the Kingdom did not thereby cease to be future. And when the risen Christ in the audible and visible words of the church enforces the rule of God, the Kingdom occurs. But the church which both carries this sacramental presence and is established by it is nevertheless not yet the Kingdom herself.

Under all three of the rubrics we will adopt in the following chapters, the foundation of the church's being is the same: the church exists in and by *anticipation*. God's one "people" cannot gather in this world before the last day; there-

---

15. Ernst Käsemann, "Die Anfänge christlicher Theologie," *Zeitschrift für Theologie und Kirche* 57 (1960):166–168, describes the great theological division in the very earliest church as being between those who thought of the coming of the gentiles as *ensuing* on Christ's return, and so fought against the mission to gentiles, and those who took the position just described.

16. Exegetes of Romans 11:13–24 have sometimes commented on Paul's seeming ignorance of horticulture: species twigs grafted into varietal stock will not produce varietal fruit. It may however be that Paul is quite aware of the anomaly and that it is part of his point.

17. II Peter 3:9

18. The agent who anticipates is of course God.

19. "Le corps du Christ vivant," 30–31.

20. Luke 11:20.

fore the church can now be the people of God only in anticipation of that gathering as the community that lives by what God will eschatologically make of it. The church is the "body" of that Christ whose bodily departure to God's right hand his disciples once witnessed and whose return in such fashion we must still await.[21] The church is the "Temple" of that Spirit whose very reality among us is "foretaste" or "down payment."[22]

Just so the church now truly *is* the people of God and the body of Christ and the temple of the Spirit. For it is what creatures may anticipate from God that is their being. Just so also, the church is grounded in God himself, the *Eschatos*. All God's creatures are moved by God to their fulfillment in him; the church is doubly so moved, as one among God's creatures and as the creature that embodies that movement for others.

Language used earlier is both most accurate and most evocative. We may cite Martin Luther for many others: "This definition gets at the essence of the matter: the church is the place or people where God dwells to bring us to enter the kingdom of heaven, for it is the gate of heaven."[23] The church is a moment in the coming of the Kingdom, and just so is the gate of the Kingdom's present tense with God, that is, of heaven.

Whether we say that the sacramental presence of heaven within the church is the gate of heaven or with Luther that the church herself is the sacramental gate of heaven depends again on the momentary direction of our thought. The distinction may conveniently be made by a famous sociological distinction already several times invoked. If we think of the church as a *community*, we may call the church herself the gate of heaven. If we think of the church as an *association*, the audible and visible word of the Kingdom that occurs within her is the gate of heaven, located by her gathering around it.

But having again used this piece of social theory, this is the appropriate place to warn about such borrowings. The church is not simply heaven, describable in this age only in the imagery of apocalyptic; but neither is she simply a phenomenon of this age, patient of the concepts and hypotheses of secular social theory. Therefore, *at least*[24] with respect to the church herself, "theology . . . will have to provide its own account of the final causes at work in human history."[25] Borrowings from secular theory may sometimes be convenient but must be done strictly ad hoc and with great circumspection and usually, as just preceding, with considerable bending of the recruited concepts.

---

21. Acts 1:9–11.

22. II Corinthians 1:22; 5:5; Ephesians 1:14.

23. *Ennaratio in Genesis*, WA 43:601.

24. It may be doubted that *any* actual community can be well described by modernity's secularized social theories. Within the limits of a systematic theology, we should not try to decide whether John Milbank is correct that the successive modes of Western social theory are a succession of Christian heresies and so necessarily distort reality; though for my part I am persuaded; *Theology and Social Theory: Beyond Secular Reason* (Oxford: Blackwell, 1990).

25. Milbank, *Theology*, 380.

Readers will not be surprised when it is now said that the needed social theory is and can only be the doctrine of Trinity itself. The insight is, at least *in nuce*, a stock item of the dialogues' ecclesiology. So the principal dialogue between East and West: "The church finds its model, its origin and its end in the mystery of the one God in three persons."[26] We will proceed as we have several times before, discussing the church's triune institution according to each identity's role within it.

We may set a rule at the beginning, summarizing much of this work's first volume. Given the Incarnation, so that the human person Jesus is in fact the Son who lives with the Father in the Spirit, the distinction between the immanent Trinity and the economic Trinity holds only in the same way as does the distinction between two natures in Christ. Therefore the Father's role as unoriginated Originator of deity is concretely not other than his role as the One who sends the Son and the Spirit on their ecclesial missions; the Son's role as the one in whom the Father finds himself is concretely not other than his role as the head of the church that in him finds the Father; the Spirit's role as the one who frees the Father and the Son is concretely his role as the one who frees the Christian community.

III

The Father, just as the singular identity so named, is the "pre-" of all being. He is this as the one who speaks the Word that grants purpose and so being to others than himself; using language leading to our point here, as he determines their destiny. That to which he directs all things is the *totus Christus*. Thus an act role-specific to the Father mandates the church: specifically as the Father he *predestines* the church and all things for the church. The unmediated and wholly antecedent will that is the Father dictates that there be the church, as something other than the world or the Kingdom, and that this church be exactly the one that exists.

That there is the church because the Father predestines it is Augustine's foundational teaching: of his "two polities," the specific character of the one, which encompasses its true justice, is that it "is predestined to rule eternally with God."[27] It is in this context, of the existence of two polities, one of which is eternally determined to share God's life and so is "heavenly" in its entity, that Augustine most directly states his famous doctrine: the two polities "come from the same mass, which is initially a mass of damnation; but God like a potter . . . makes from that mass one pot for honor and the other for ignominy."[28]

It may be that the occasion of Augustine's doctrine of predestination was as much the Donatist controversy, fought with inheritors of the old "North African

---

26. Joint Roman Catholic-Orthodox Commission, *The Mystery of the Church and the Eucharist in the Light of the Mystery of the Holy Trinity* (Munich report, 1982), ii.2.

27. *De civitate Dei*, xv.1: "civitates duas, hoc est duas societates hominum, quarum est una quae praedestinata est in aeternum regnare cum Deo."

28. Ibid.

tradition's vivid sense for the boundary" between church and nonchurch,[29] as it was the fight with Pelagius. Before and during the persecutions, the North African tradition had come to draw the line between church and world by moral and religious criteria that were all too malleable to the *libido dominandi* of the insiders. Augustine shared his tradition's apprehension of an inviolable line between the community of saints and the polities of this world but had seen the destruction done in the church by human attempts to draw it. He "transferred that boundary to a terrain in which it is no longer under human control. . . . Neither the mysterious inner dispositions of the heart nor the ultimate riddle of divine election can be . . . claimed by one social group to the exclusion of another. . . . The Augustinian doctrine of grace . . . is . . . the anti-Donatist form" of the old North African countercultural understanding of the church.[30]

We may note that Augustine's teaching that the true members of the church are the predestined, who cannot now be enumerated, is the origin of the idea that the true church is "invisible," though this proposition itself should not be fathered on Augustine. The concept of the invisible church has occasioned little but trouble through theological history, and no use will be made of it in this work. The church is not an invisible entity; she is the, if anything, all too visible gathering of sinners around the loaf and cup. What is invisible is that this visible entity is in fact what she claims to be, the people of God.

There are of course other places in this work at which the explicit discussion of predestination could have been located, and indeed in substance the doctrine has already been present at several and will appear at others. John Calvin, with whose name the doctrine is so much associated, located it differently in each edition of the *Institutes*: as an interpretation of the proclamation's power to create faith, as a pair to the doctrine of providence, and finally within soteriology. Karl Barth, perhaps the greatest of all teachers of predestination, made the doctrine the systematic pivot of his doctrine of God.[31] I have followed both Philip Melanchthon's more modest location of the doctrine and his Augustinian reason for it: amid the "ruins of nations, we know from God's own testimonies that the church of God will remain. To grasp this comfort, we need to know . . . about predestination."[32]

But if the doctrine of predestination is to be the "comfort" for which Melanchthon invokes it, if it is to enable confident faith about and within the church, it cannot make election and reprobation equal partners. It cannot pose them as equal possibilities and leave the balance in doubt.[33] The church is predestined to abide, finally in God; the world's polities are predestined to perish.

29. William S. Babcock, "Roman North Africa," *Schools of Thought in the Christian Tradition*, ed. Patrick Henry (Philadelphia: Fortress, 1984), 46. See Babcock for this paragraph.

30. Ibid., 46–47.

31. Robert W. Jenson, *Alpha and Omega: A Study in the Theology of Karl Barth* (New York: Thomas Nelson, 1963); G. C. Berkouwer, *The Triumph of Grace in the Theology of Karl Barth* (Grand Rapids: Eerdmans, 1956), 76–108.

32. *Loci communes* (1559), 913.

33. John Updike, *In the Beauty of the Lilies* (New York: Ballantine, 1996), 38–49, provides a brilliant fictional display of resulting dialectics.

Barth has the required and pathbreaking insight.[34] Actually to carry the affirmative meaning that all the great teachers of predestination have insisted the doctrine must have, it must first and comprehensively be a doctrine about "the election of Jesus Christ." Standard developments of the doctrine have tended to treat the choice of Jesus to be the Christ as one thing and our election into the church and the Kingdom as another.[35] This despite such New Testament theologoumena as "He was destined before the foundation of the world, but was revealed at the end of the ages for your sake. *Through him* you have come to trust in God"[36] or "For those whom he foreknew he also predestined to be conformed to the image of his Son, *in order* that he might be the first born within a large family"[37] or again, "He chose *us in Christ* before the foundation of the world."[38]

Thus much theology has made it possible to think of the God who predestines us in abstraction from Christ and so in nontrinitarian fashion; and then of the chosen or reprobated humans as correspondingly monadic individuals. The picture of God in solitary eternity arbitrarily sorting future persons into two heaps is rejected by all serious teachers of predestination but is nevertheless irresistibly suggested by much of their teaching. To overcome it, we must lay it down from the start: the one sole object of eternal election is Jesus with his people, the *totus Christus*.

Augustine

Augustine taught, with his elegant precision: "Just as this One is predestined, to be our head, so we many are predestined, to be his members."[39] What must be clearer than it is even in Augustine's aphorism is that these two choosings are only one event in God.

Jesus, precisely as the head of his actual church, is in eternal fact the Son, the second identity of God. But it might have been otherwise. We have insisted we cannot probe that "otherwise"; nevertheless, the contingency remains. And the contingency there is in the biblical God is the contingency of freedom, that is, of election. That it is the man Jesus who is the Son is an event of decision in God;[40] and that the church, with the very individuals who belong to the church, is the body of this person is the *same* event of decision.[41] This event is the only act of election or predestination that occurs: "In the beginning with God was this one, Jesus Christ. And just that is the predestination."[42]

---

34. For the following, *Kirchliche Dogmatik* (Zürich: Zollikon, 1948), II/2:37–66. To the entire matter, Jenson, *Alpha and Omega*.

35. See Barth's biting polemic, *Kirchliche Dogmatik*, II/2:128.

36. I Peter 1:20–21.

37. Romans 8:30.

38. Ephesians 1:4.

39. *De praedestinatione sanctorum*, xv.32.

40. Note Colossians 1:19–20: "For in him all the fullness of God was *pleased* to dwell, and through him God was *pleased* to reconcile to himself all things [emphases added]."

41. Barth endlessly and from every possible direction comes back to this point. E.g., *Kirchliche Dogmatik*, II/2:125: "This lifts him out of the succession of all other elect persons and precisely this . . . joins him again with them: that he as elect man is in his own humanity the God himself who elects them."

42. Barth, *Kirchliche Dogmatik*, II/2:157.

It is eternally decided in God that the Son is the man Jesus, specific in his actual life and death, and so it is decided that the Son is for us. The Father, exactly in his identity as the Father, is the sole antecedent chooser and sender in this decision.

This must first mean that the Father chooses Jesus to be the Messiah of Israel and Israel to be his people. In the New Testament this is more assumed than asserted, it being at the very basis of the gospel. Thus when Peter, in the sermon reported as the first, said that Jesus was raised to be "Messiah,"[43] this was in order to assert the Resurrection rather than to say what a resurrection would mean, which latter he presumes his hearers will know. Matthew does not need to explain further, when he puts Jesus' whole mission under the passage from Isaiah: "Here is my servant, whom I have chosen, my beloved, with whom my soul is well pleased. I will put my Spirit upon him, and he will proclaim justice to the Gentiles."[44] At the beginning of Jesus' ministry, all three synoptic Gospels expect readers to understand when the Father's voice at Jesus' baptism adopts this same passage for its own word of ordination. And at the end, the crowds at the Crucifixion know what is at stake: whether or not this victim "is the Messiah of God, his chosen one."[45]

This firmly in place, we may then appropriate another of Barth's pathfinding moves: his christological construal of the relation between election and reprobation. The decision made in the existence of Jesus as the Son must indeed be "double" predestination, must include both election and reprobation; as a recent fictional exponent of demotic Calvinism put it, double predestination "makes good sense. . . . How can you be saved if you can't be damned?"[46] But whereas this *Grübler* concluded, within his abstract dialectics, that he would just have to wait and see which was determined for him, election and reprobation are not parallel in the gospel and are not primally to be divided between different human individuals. Rather, according to Barth, "In the election of Jesus Christ . . . God has appointed the first, election, blessedness, and life, for humanity and the second, rejection, damnation, and death, for himself."[47]

According to Barth's insight, the dialectic of election and rejection is first to be construed not between human individuals, and so abstractly, but as the inner dialectic of the one person's, Jesus Christ's, story. As man he is elect, as God self-reprobate; but just so, within a proper Christology, he is reprobate and elect also as the man he is. Thus the dialectic of election and rejection is historical and so has *direction*: rejection is there always and only for the sake of election.[48] Indeed, in that God in Christ takes our rejection on himself, it can no longer be our

---

43. Acts 2:26.
44. Matthew 12:18.
45. Luke 23:35.
46. Updike, Lilies, 41.
47. Barth, *Kirchliche Dogmatik*, II/1:177.
48. E.g., ibid., 190.

rejection, only Christ's.[49] Christ is the accepted rejected one, and we who would have been rejected will be accepted in him.

Now we can consider the election of the community as such. And now and not later we must consider it. For we are not permitted to leap directly from the election of Christ to the question of individuals' election to salvation. The chief predestinarian book of the New Testament, the Gospel of John, knows election only as the creation of the church. The Johannine Jesus says, "I am the good shepherd. I know my own and my own know me. . . . I have other sheep that do not belong to this fold. I must bring them also, and they will listen to my voice. So there will be one flock, one shepherd."[50] And then he tells why certain sheep rather than others follow him to make the church: the Father has given them to him. Moreover, what his Father has given him, "no one can snatch . . . out of the Father's hand"; and "The Father and I are one."[51] "The flock" of the Son is the community chosen in the triune perichoresis. Nor is this understanding peculiar to John; in the passages earlier cited from Pauline and other epistles, the "we" or "you" is always and directly the church.

Only now may we come to God's drawing of the *boundary* between the polity of God and the world's polities, that is, to the predestination of individuals. The decisive consideration follows from all the preceding: the "pre-" in "predestination" must be the same "pre" as in "preexistence of Christ." It was established in the first volume: this "pre" is primally the priority of God's futurity to all being and only so is the priority of his anteriority to being; and just so it is the reconciliation of both, the priority within created time of the death and resurrection of Christ and of his audible and visible word in the church.

Therefore it is not that God has *already* decided whether I am or am not of his community. He *will* decide and *so* has decided; and *has* decided and so *will* decide; and so *decides* also within created time. Where usual doctrines of individual predestination go astray is that they construe a person's predestination by God as one event, in eternity "before " the events of his or her life, and the speaking of the gospel to that person and her or his baptism as other consequent events. But we have seen how such notions of before and after cannot accommodate the gospel's evocation of preexistence.

The eternal "pre-" of Christ's existence, which is identical with the "pre-" of predestination, occurs also within time, as the Resurrection and as the contingency and divine agency of Israel's and the church's proclamation and prayer, visible and audible. Thus—to put it in the most strenuous possible context—to the penitent's question, "But how do I know I am among the elect?" the confessor's right answer must be, "You know because I am about to absolve you, and my doing that *is* God's eternal act of decision about you."

49. Ibid., 181.
50. John 10:14–16.
51. John 10:29–30.

If I am in God's polity rather than out of it, if I am on the "heavenly" side of Augustine's great divide, the decision that this is so is God's alone and so a *pre*destination. But since the God in question is the biblical God, this does not mean that the event of divine decision is an event lurking somehow behind or above the event of Christ's coming to me. Barth was again insofar right: the old-Calvinist doctrine that Jesus Christ is merely the "*mirror*" of God's otherwise established predestining is grossly inadequate, and so is the old-Lutheran doctrine that God in Christ lovingly wills all to be saved but that some by their own decision are not—that is, that predestination is not really predestination.[52] A right doctrine of individual predestination is precisely a doctrine about what happens to and for individuals when they encounter Christ in his gospel: that the judgment they then hear is nothing less than God's eternal act of decision.[53] Baptism *is* the Father's giving of sheep to the Son's fold.

God's history with us is one integral act of sovereignty, comprehended as his decision to reconcile us with himself in Christ Jesus.[54] The existence and specific membership of the community are predestined in this decision, with the "pre-" appropriate to the biblical God.

We cannot, to be sure, quite leave it there. A form of the old worry, "Is soand-so—am I—among the predestined?" obviously still remains. Most of humankind have not been brought into the church before death; that is to say, they have not completed the history from reprobation to election. Therefore that reprobation is always for the sake of election does not in itself mean that none will remain outside the people of God. Nor, to be sure, does it mean that any will. The question must be kept for the final part of the work: Will the eschatological place of reprobation be populated?

IV

Had the Father determined that the saints of canonical Israel should rise together with Jesus, so that Jesus' resurrection was the End, his and their resurrection would still have been in the power of the Holy Spirit,[55] but there would have been no church of Jews and gentiles and so no final revelation of the Spirit's "face."[56] Had God raised Jesus without yet raising Israel's saints *and* let Jesus' disciples also simply wait until the End, the Spirit would, so to speak, have ascended with Jesus. It is in the situation posed by these two—after the fact inconceivable and indeed nonsensical—possibilities that the Spirit's intervention at Pentecost has its dramatic necessity within God's history. Pentecost is the Spirit's particular personal initiative to delay the Parousia: when the Spirit descends

---

52. *Kirchliche Dogmatik*, II/1:64–83.

53. Barth, of course, would not tolerate this consequence; just at this point, his version of the fatal definition of time and eternity by mutual exclusion intrudes.

54. E.g., ibid., II/2:97.

55. Romans 1:3.

56. 1:86.

eschatologically yet without raising all the dead and ending this age, the time for the church is opened.

Ecumenical ecclesiology increasingly recognizes the Spirit's specific role in founding the church;[57] this is in large part the result of Orthodox initiatives. Contemporary Orthodoxy has developed a consistent critique of Western ecclesiology and ecclesial practice:[58] the West has failed to acknowledge that Pentecost is an "intervention of the Holy Trinity" that is "new" over against the Resurrection and "issues from the third Person of the Trinity" in his own identity;[59] thus it has developed an ecclesiology that "provides no place . . . for a plotted work[60] of the Spirit as such—that is, of freedom—a work not separate from that of Christ but nevertheless distinct and of equal weight. The fullness of the church, as a synergy of the ministry and the people in their wholeness, cannot come to expression."[61] The West has forgotten that "the life of the church is founded in *two* correlated mysteries: the mystery of the holy Supper *and* the mystery of Pentecost [emphases added]."[62] We saw in the first volume that and why such critique can be justified.

On "the day of Pentecost," as Luke describes the event, the regrouped disciples "were filled with the Holy Spirit." The strange linguistic phenomena that ensued[63] were interpreted by Peter as the fulfillment of a concluding prophecy of the Old Testament: "In the last days it will be . . . that I will pour out my Spirit upon all flesh." In the new community all, old and young, male and female, bond and free, shall prophesy.[64] Then follows the first proclamation of the Resurrection and the first conversions to this gospel.

Orthodoxy exhorts the West to recognize in this event a specific church-instituting act of the Spirit, which emerges just from his identity as Spirit. We may summarily describe it: the Spirit *frees* an actual human community from merely historical determinisms, to be apt to be united with the Son and thus to be the gateway of creation's translation into God. It is the heart of Orthodoxy's contention: "Insofar as anything is merely historically given, it is the vehicle of

57. So the reports of World Council of Churches assemblies at Uppsala (1968), *The Holy Spirit and the Catholicity of the Church*, 14–16; and Nairobi (1975), *Confessing Christ Today*, 33, 40.

58. The emergence of this unified critique depends very much on the influence of Vladimir Lossky; see above all *A l'image et à la ressemblance de Dieu* (Paris: Aubres-Montaigne, 1967). A concise—and utterly unsympathetic—description of the movement is provided by André de Halleux, "Pour un accord œcuménique sur la procession de l'Esprit Saint et l'addition du Filioque au Symbole," *Le theologie du Saint Esprit dans le dialogue entre l'Orient et l'Occident*, ed. Lukas Vischer (Paris: le Centurion, 1981), 81–82.

59. Nikos Nissiotis, *Die Theologie der Ostkirche im ökumenischen Dialog* (Stuttgart: Evangelisches Verlagswerk, 1968), 74–75.

60. "Economy."

61. Olivier Clément, "Quelques remarques d'un orthodox sur la Constitution De écclesia," *Oecumenica: Annales de Recherche Oecuménique 1966*, ed. F. W. Kantzenbach, V. Vajta (Neuchâtel: Delachaux et Niestlé, 1966), 109.

62. Florovsky, "Le Corps du Christ vivant," 19.

63. Their character can hardly now be reliably reconstructed.

64. Acts 2:1–41.

'nature'[65] and so inimical to freedom. . . . Even Jesus has to be liberated from past history. To achieve that liberation is the work of the Spirit."[66]

Orthodox critique has discovered the lamentable fruits of the Western church's pneumatological deficit in an unstable ecclesial oscillation between institutionalism and spiritualism.[67] Institutions constitute a community's diachronic identity and simply in their own power as institutions establish a purely inner-historical continuity through time. The historical ground of the church's institutions is the events told in the Gospels. And however peculiar a historical event one of these events, the Resurrection, was, the relation of the community thus founded to its historical ground obeys the usual regularities: when one knows the circumstances of the church's historical origin one can predict what general sort of institutions the church must have—and indeed we did something rather like that in the first volume, in discussing the institutions of Scripture, creed, and teaching office.[68]

Thus Orthodox critique observes that "the institutional elements of the church . . . belong strictly speaking to Christology";[69] that is, that their existence and character can be accounted for by analysis that does not include the Father or the Spirit among its terms. Institutions appear historically, as the diachronic self-identity of historically initiated communities. If the church understands herself as founded in events prior to Pentecost and not also in the event of Pentecost *as* a divine initiative commensurate to the Resurrection, she will be tempted to seek her self-identity through time in a sanctified but still worldly institutionalism, in a "hierarchical sacramentalism."[70] So, for instance, the episcopal college will come to be seen less as "the expression of the local churches in communion . . . than as a sort of appellate senate."[71]

65. The usage of "historically" and "nature" here differs from that now common in the West, but that need not here distract us.

66. This summary of John Zizioulas's position, more compendious than Zizioulas himself has achieved, is provided by Colin Gunton, *The Transcendent Lord: The Spirit and the Church in Calvinist and Cappadocian Theology* (London: The Congregational Memorial Hall Trust, 1988), 12–13.

67. Nissiotis, *Die Theologie der Ostkirche*, 77: "The pneumatological understanding of the church's being presupposes a basic recognition of the sanctifying work of the Spirit. This sanctifying is often understood either as sacralizing or consecration or as . . . a subjective appropriation of the redemptive work of Christ. But sanctifying means rather a founding structural work of the Spirit." Note that the point is by no means made only by the East. So the Western dialogue, Arbeitsgruppe der deutschen Bischofskonferenz und der Kirchenleitung der Vereinigten Evangelisch-lutherischen Kirche Deutschlands, *Kirchengemeinschaft im Wort und Sakrament* (Paderborn: Bonifatius-Drueckerei, 1984), 12: "So ist die Kirche vorgegebene Stiftung und kraft des Geistes immer neues Geschehen. Beides ist zusammen zu sehen. Nur jeweils die eine dieser Grundbestimmungen zu betonen, konnte ein institutionalistisches oder ein schwämerisches Missverständnis fordern; beide Gefahren sind in der Geschichte der Kirchen immer wieder aufgetaucht."

68. 1:22–41.

69. John D. Zizioulas, "Die pneumatologische Dimension der Kirche," *Internationale katholische Zeitschrift*, 2:139–140.

70. Clément, "Quelques remarques," 109.

71. Ibid., 115.

The terms once set so, the unease the church will feel within so alien a self-understanding will likely find release in a reaction of free-floating spiritualism,[72] the other pole of the West's unstable ecclesial history. If Christ and the Spirit are not experienced in the *mutuality* of their ecclesially founding roles, neither will the church's institutions and her charismatic reality be seen in their proper congruence.[73] It is the East's chief gravamen against the West: "In Western thought there is often a tendency to separate 'charism' and 'office' from one another."[74]

"Even Jesus has to be liberated from history." This liberation is of course primally the Resurrection.[75] But had there been no Pentecost, had Jesus risen into the eschatological future while we were simply left behind, had he no present-tense actuality within the church's moment, he would still be for us an item of mere memory, imprisoned in history. That it is not so is the church-founding work of the Spirit, who "unites the Head with the Body of Christ."[76] The liberation of Jesus is accomplished not only by the Resurrection but also by the Spirit's liberation of a community to receive and be his actuality within the present time of this age.

Every individual person has and is a spirit: this is his or her personal liveliness, as a "wind" that stirs that to which he or she directs personal energies. But also every community has a spirit, which is not a mere aggregate of members' spirits. So an athletic team can be composed of superior athletes and still regularly lose, if it lacks "team spirit," if it has not become a community. A community's spirit is the liveliness that blows through it, the freedom in which it is more than the sum of its parts because each member moves in the liberating impetus from all the others.[77] The relation between a community's spirit and that of some one or more individual persons varies from situation to situation. It is the church's founding miracle that her communal spirit is identically the Spirit that the personal God is and has.

At Pentecost the prophetic Spirit was "poured out" to make not individual prophets but a prophetic community.[78] The Spirit of life and freedom vivifies and frees precisely "those who are *in* [emphasis added] Christ Jesus."[79] "There are varieties of gifts, but the same Spirit. . . . For just as the body is one and has many members . . . so it is with Christ. For in the one Spirit we were all baptized into one body."[80] "Now the Lord is the Spirit, and where the Spirit of the Lord is, there is freedom. And all of us . . . are being transformed."[81]

---

72. Thus the "enthusiastic" movements at the time of the Reformation had long been present underground, precisely during the time of the Western patriarchate's most open self-presentation as a wordly power and bureaucracy, waiting for opportunity to emerge.

73. Zizioulas, "Die pneumatologische Dimension der Kirche," 139–140.

74. Johannes Mabey, "Das Charisma des apostolischen Amtes in Denken und Beten der Ostkirchen," *Catholica*, 27:263–279.

75. Romans 1:1.

76. Nissiotis, *Theologie der Ostkirche*, 71.

77. I: 86–94.

78. Acts 2:14–36.

79. Romans 8:1–11.

80. I Corinthians 12:4–13.

81. II Corinthians 3:17–18.

The *truth* of such propositions as "The church is the body of Christ" or "The church is the bride of Christ" resides, we noted before and will develop again, merely in the risen Christ's self-understanding that it is so; for he is the *Logos* itself. But it is not every creature of which such propositions *could* be true, so long as the risen Christ is the one he is. Christ could not know himself in a polity alien to Israel without ceasing to be Christ. Indeed, he could not know himself in any community of this age simply as it is. The miracle by which the community of Jesus' disciples and their converts *can* be the body or bride of the risen one is that the spirit of this particular community is identically the Spirit of God. The Spirit founds the church by giving himself to be her spirit and so freeing a community within this age to be appropriate for union with a person risen into the eschatological future.

Nor may "can be" and "is" here be abstractly distinguished. That the Spirit makes the church a community that "can" be united with the risen one and that the Spirit actually unites the church with him are one act, for it is the risen Christ who himself bestows the Spirit.[82] And since the church is a community within created time, the qualification of the church to be united with the risen Christ must be a qualification of the institutions by which she perdures in time. We return to Orthodox mandates: the work of the Spirit to unite the Head with the body of Christ is a "foundational *structural* [emphasis added] work,"[83] a qualification indeed of her "hierarchical" order,[84] that is, of the structures by which the church exists as a community and not as a mere collective of pious individuals.

In the structures peculiar to the church, institution and charism therefore fall together.[85] Or, to use language native to Western theology, the necessary institutions of the church are sacramental.[86] For a central instance, bishops, who administer organizations often not very unlike this world's organizations, do so—where the church's polity is legitimately structured—through their sacramental roles: their chief presidency of the Eucharist, their power to ordain, their collegial care for the church's unity, and their calling to teach.

Finally, in this section also we must remind ourselves that the church is an event within Israel. The Spirit did not first begin to liberate a human community when he intervened at Pentecost; indeed, the description of the Spirit's being and work[87] here presupposed was derived in the first volume mostly from the Old

---

82. Acts 1:33 again.

83. Nissiotis, *Theologie der Ostkirche*, 77.

84. Mabey, "Das Charisma des apostolischen Amtes," 263.

85. Ibid, 265: "Office is charism, because the Spirit, that lives and gives life, is the source of office in the church."

86. E.g., with respect to the ministry, "Reflexions de théologiens orthodoxes et catholiques sur les Ministéres" (report of an ad hoc group meeting at Chambesy, 1977), *Episkepsis* 183 (1978):8, "Since Christ is never present except by the Spirit . . . the church's ministry is by its nature charismatic. . . . This vision of the sacramentality of the ministry roots in the fact that Christ is at once the one whom the Spirit makes present for the community and the one who gives the Spirit to the community."

87. 1:146–161.

Testament. It is the Spirit who made prophets who makes the prophetic community; the Spirit who raised up "judges" to free the tribes from historical impasse who frees the church from history's intrinsic impasse; the Spirit promised as new life for Israel's dry bones who is eschatological life's "down payment" in the church. Perhaps we may formulate so: the Spirit makes the common dynamism of Israel and the church, impelling Israel to become the church and liberating the church for the fulfilling of Israel.

V

There is of course a plain sense in which the church was indeed founded by the acts of the Son narrated in the Gospels. We need not, however, join the attempt to decide between them: whether Christ founded the church by being baptized, or by choosing the apostles, or by celebrating the last supper, or by, as the risen one, breathing the Spirit on his disciples or mandating the mission. Nor in systematic theology need we join the debate about whether Jesus subjectively intended to found the church. For it is the Son's whole life, from his conception by the Holy Spirit to his Ascension, that in fact founds the church.

In the whole of what he did, said, and suffered, he is the person he is, and that person is not one to be bereft of a community of those for whom he was sent; nor as the risen Lord can he be denied. Moreover, the friend of publicans and sinners, and the refugee in gentile Phoenicia who acclaimed the faith of a local woman,[88] cannot have as his community anything short of a community of Jews *and* gentiles. Christ, we may say, delayed the Parousia by living the story he did and so by being the human person he is, who if he rose to be Lord could not lack just such community as is the church.

This much laid down, we may then recognize that of course some events in the Gospels' narrative more determine the fact and character of the risen Jesus' community than do others. If he had not, for example, told the parable of the mustard seed, we should be the poorer but the church would not be very different. Most notably the call of special disciples, the teaching of the "Our Father," and the events by which the Eucharist and baptism were initiated make the church the community she is. We will conclude this chapter by discussing these "institutions" in order.

The exact relations between the broad movement of Jesus-followers in Galilee and Judea, his calling of more specific disciples,[89] his appointing and sending of "the Twelve,"[90] the later identification of the Twelve with "the" Apostles, and the situation depicted in Acts,[91] where the Twelve are a kind of ruling council of the nascent church, will probably remain historically uncertain. But so much is

---

88. Matthew 15:28.

89. John 1:35–51; Mark 1:16–30par.

90. Mark 3:13–19par; Matthew 10:1–16. Should it be that these accounts are retrojected from an initial post-Pentecost situation of the church, nothing changes for our concern.

91. Acts 1:21–26.

clear: the community of Jesus' disciples was never structurally homogeneous but was instead "hierarchical"; that is, it displayed concentric circles of differing responsibility. When his followers regrouped after the Resurrection, this structure remained. And when the Spirit freed this community to be the church, it was "Peter, standing with the eleven" who then "raised his voice" to begin the mission.[92] The church's hierarchy, that is, her character as an organic rather than an abstractly egalitarian polity, is thus founded in Jesus' mission as told in the Gospels.

It was then a representative of the disciples who asked Jesus to teach them a model of prayer.[93] The model Jesus provided[94] specified petitions none of which were foreign to Jewish prayer.[95] In two ways only was it distinctive.

Jesus' prayer, like its close Jewish parallel, the *Prayer of Eighteen Benedictions*, falls into two clear strophes, both by poetic form and by content. Each prayer has a strophe of petitions for temporal needs and a strophe of petitions for the fulfilling of the Lord's eschatological promises. But the order of the strophes is reversed: whereas the more typical prayer in commonsensical order tends first to daily need and then moves to the time of Messiah, Jesus' prayer immediately locates its petitioners before the Kingdom and almost as an afterthought attends to the penultimate.[96] When a disciple of Jesus prays this prayer, the "we" with whom he or she identifies is precisely the "we" of those who surround the gate of heaven. That the church is "anticipated eschatology" is historically founded in Jesus' and his disciples' practice of prayer.

Second, Jesus instructs his disciples to begin with a peculiar personal address to God: "Father" or "Our Father."[97] In the Gospels, address to God as "Father," or yet more shockingly as "my Father," is unique to Jesus; and, as has often been observed, "Father" was not in Judaism generally a regular form of second-person address to God. It was, indeed, by addressing God as specifically his Father that Jesus made himself out to be specifically the Son,[98] for which implicit claim he was crucified. Jesus invited his disciples to enter and share his relation to the Father, to address the one he called "my Father" as their communal Father, to, as it were, piggy-back their prayers on his.

Prayer is the actuality of faith; therefore the pattern of this address to God is a defining structure of the specific faith of Jesus' disciples: we approach God as maturing children approach a loving and just father, daring to do so because we

---

92. Acts 2:14.

93. Luke 1:1–2.

94. Matthew 6:9–11par.

95. For individual comparisons with the Prayer of Eighteen Benedictions, Karl Georg Kuhn, *Achtzengebet und Vaterunser und der Reim* (Tübingen: J. C. B. Mohr, 1950), 25–46.

96. Ibid., 40–41.

97. To this and the following, see now Donald Juel, "The Lord's Prayer in the Gospels of Matthew and Luke," *Princeton Seminary Bulletin*, Supplementary Issue, *The Lord's Prayer*, 2 (1992): 56–70.

98. For subtle and persuasive examination of the synoptic Gospels and *Acts*, abstracting from the more overt presentation of John, see ibid., 59–63.

come together with one who is native to such sonship. The church is the community that, because the Father has raised Jesus to confirm his sonship, accepts Jesus' invitation as she finds it in the Gospels to pray to the Father with the Son—and just so in their Spirit—and indeed shapes all her life to that pattern.[99] That the church "finds its model, its origin and its end in the mystery of the one God in three persons" is historically founded in Jesus' affiliation of his disciples with his personal address to God.

At the heart of Jesus' fellowship with his disciples was their fellowship at meals.[100] All meals are intrinsically religious occasions, indeed sacrifices, and were so understood especially in Israel. For all life belongs intimately to God, so that the killing involved in eating—which we do not at all avoid by eating vegetables—is an intrusion into his domain. Therefore food can be taken only with thanksgiving to God for the privilege, and the food must itself be offered back to him, as the visible word of the thanksgiving.

Sharing a meal is therefore always a communal act of worship and establishes fellowship precisely before the Lord. Jesus' meal-fellowship with his disciples was for them an embodiment of his message: it opened to the fellowship of the Kingdom[101] and it included "publicans and sinners," a chief occasion of the Pharisees' offense.[102]

The disciples' meal-fellowship with their Lord was broken by the Crucifixion. It was renewed by the Resurrection, and the appearances of the risen Lord were disproportionately appearances to share a meal.[103] After Pentecost the renewed meal-fellowship was the distinctive act of the community;[104] and the leaders among the initial evangelists had to come from those "who ate and drank with him after he rose from the dead."[105]

A formal meal in Israel begins and ends with the offering of thanksgiving[106] and with offered and shared bread and cup as the embodiment thereof.[107] The

---

99. I have said it in the first volume, but must in present circumstance repeat it: those who cannot or will not shape their prayer and other religious discourse to this pattern are, quite transparently, outside Christian faith. For the church to bend her discourse to the demands of such persons, in any degree at all, is simple apostasy.

100. Ernst Lohmeyer, "Das Abendmahl in der Urgemeinde," *Journal of Biblical Literature* 56:217–252; Joachim Jeremias, *The Eucharistic Words of Jesus*, tr. Norman Perrin (Philadelphia: Fortress, 1977).

101. Luke 12:8.

102. Mark 2:15par; Matthew 11:19par; Luke 15:1.

103. Oscar Cullmann, *Early Christian Worship*, tr. S. Todd, J. B. Torrance (London: SCM, 1953), 14–18.

104. Acts 2:46–47.

105. Acts 10:41.

106. Many of the extant texts are collected in part one of *Prex Eucharistica*, ed. Anton Haenggi, Irmgad Phal (Freibourg: Editions Universitaires, 1968). See Louis Bouyer, *Eucharist: Theology and Spirituality of the Eucharistic Prayer*, tr. C.U. Quinn (Notre Dame: University of Notre Dame Press, 1968).

107. Jeremias, *Eucharistic Words*, 35, 108–110, 173–178, 232–233; Ferdinand Hahn, "Die altestamentlichen Motive in der urchrirstlichen Abendmahlsüberlieferung," *Evangelische Theologie*, 27:337–374.

material content of the verbal thanksgiving varies but includes thanksgiving for the food and some remembrance of the Lord's saving actions in history, past or indeed future. Whether or not Jesus' last meal with his disciples was a Passover meal, there must have been a last communal meal of some sort, and Paul and the synoptic Gospels depict it as complete with such formal thanksgivings.

In Paul's and the synoptic Gospels' accounts,[108] at the start of this meal Jesus took bread, offered the opening thanksgiving, broke the loaf, and distributed it to be eaten, as the disciples' embodied participation in the prayer. After the meal, he took a loving-cup of wine, offered the concluding thanksgiving, and passed the cup around, to be shared as embodied participation in this concluding sacrifice of thanksgiving. The accounts evidently functioned as liturgical rubrics before their incorporation into the Gospels' narrative context; this shows in all the accounts but is most explicit in the oldest, provided by Paul,[109] where each thanksgiving and distribution is followed by the formal rubric "Do this."

The canonical texts present a quite deliberate institution: Jesus' disciples are told "Do this" in a narrative context where only the church's post-Resurrection actions can obey the command. What is "this"? If we suppose that the rubrics were formulated in the primal church, "this" must embrace the entire narrated action. If we suppose that Jesus spoke them at his last supper, they must refer to the thanksgiving he has just performed. The practical outcome is the same, since the sharing of bread and common cup belongs anyway to the thanksgiving.

There is a further mandate: "When you do this, do it for my remembrance." Meal-thanksgiving has always some narrative remembrance of God's acts for Israel as its content; Jesus here tells his disciples to include him among them. And there is one further element in the texts: "This is my body . . ." and "This is the cup of the new covenant in my blood" or "This is my blood of the covenant." Interpretation of these mysteries must be postponed. The ritual mandate then is: offer meal-thanksgiving, including Jesus among the things for which you give thanks and embodying your joint participation in the thanksgiving by sharing bread and passing round a loving-cup of wine.

That the church's distinctive action is a sacrifice of praise and thanksgiving embodied as elements of a meal and that the verbal reality of this self-definition has specific narrative content, of God's history with Israel and conclusively of Jesus, is thus historically founded in Jesus' life with his disciples, in their meal-fellowship generally and in the specific meal of the "night in which he was betrayed." As founded by Jesus' actions, the church is not an all-purpose religious community; it exists, as many liturgies have it, to remember *Jesus'* death, to proclaim *his* resurrection, and to await *his* coming.

---

108. To the following, Robert W. Jenson, *Visible Words: The Interpretation and Practice of Christian Sacraments* (Philadelphia: Fortress, 1978), 67–77.

109. I Corinthians 11:23–26.

Finally, the church is a missionary community and just so a distinctive, even "countercultural" community. It is her practice of baptism that makes and marks her so.[110]

A rite of washing entered the lives of Jesus and his disciples with John the Baptizer's rite of repentance. People came to John to be washed of their old habits of life and so renewed for the Kingdom: they were "converted."[111] Jesus came to John for baptism, as some of his disciples also must have done, but the life he thus entered was more radically new than in the case of others. The Gospels depict Jesus' baptism as the call to be a prophet;[112] and the voice of the Father names *this* new prophet Messiah and Son. Jesus' baptism was conversion to his calling.

When after the Resurrection the mission was launched, baptism in the style of John thus lay near at hand to the missionary community's need for an initiation rite.[113] May we say that Jesus' baptism was Christian baptism's institution?[114] Within the New Testament itself there are parallels between the two, which are undoubtedly significant for our understanding of baptism, but there is no actual claim that Christians should baptize because Jesus was baptized; in the second- and third-century fathers, on the other hand, Jesus' baptism is regularly regarded as Christian baptism's foundation. Perhaps Thomas Aquinas's judicious division is appropriate: baptism's power to "confer grace" was established when Jesus was baptized, but a mandate actually to baptize could only occur after his resurrection.[115]

In any case of these relations, the actual canonical mandate to baptize is the record of a resurrection-appearance whose content was an explicit command to "make disciples" by washing "in the name Father, Son, and Holy Spirit" and teaching the observances of the Christian community.[116] The mandate of baptism is thus two-sided: the church is to practice it as did John, as a washing of *repentance*; and she is to use this rite to *initiate* into herself and her trinitarian worship those whom her mission brings to faith.

Baptism's character as a drastic transition is then perfectly enacted by the developed rite itself, as we see it in the liturgically ordered but still persecuted church of the third and early fourth centuries.[117] Many texts and ceremonies varied, but the plot was uniform throughout most of the church, or anyway of the

110. To the following, Jenson, *Words*, 126–135.

111. Mark 1:4–5parr.

112. E.g., Werner Kümmel, *The Theology of the New Testament*, tr. J. E. Steely (New York: Abingdon, 1973), 123–124.

113. To this and the immediately following in greater detail, Robert W. Jenson, "Baptism," *Christian Dogmatics*, ed. Carl Braaten, Robert Jenson (Philadelphia: Fortress, 1984), 2:315–318.

114. My attention was called to the following circumstances by Robert L. Wilken.

115. *Summa theologiae*, iii.66.2.

116. Matthew 28:19–20.

117. To this and the following, Aidan Kavanaugh, *The Shape of Baptism* (New York: Pueblo, 1978); Hugh M. Riley, *Christian Initiation* (Washington, D.C.: Catholic University Press, 1974); Georg Kretschmar, "Die Geschichte des Taufgottesdienstes in der alten Kirche," *Leiturgia*, ed. K. F. Mueller, W. Blankenberg (Kassel: Stauda, 1954), 4:81–86.

church whose rites survived and determined history.[118] The drama spanned several acts. And it lasted for months or years, since its first act was the catechumenate.

The catechumenate was a period of rigorous training for the new life to come, by instruction, prayer, ritual blessings, purifications, and exorcism. These rituals continued directly into those of baptism's second act, preferably on Easter night.

When the time for the bath had come, the Spirit was invoked on the water, the candidates were stripped, they faced west to renounce Satan and their old life, they were exorcized, and they confessed the new faith. Then came the bath itself, with invocation and confession of the triune name. On emerging from the water, the neophytes were anointed, clothed in new white garments, and led to the third act of the event.

This took place in the congregation, which had paused in its Eucharist to await the neophytes. The bishop conducted the rite of the Spirit: laying on of hands or marking with oil, or both, and prayer.[119]

A very early text of such prayer is preserved: "Lord God, who have made them worthy to obtain the remission of sins by the bath of new birth, make them worthy to be filled with the Holy Spirit. . . ."[120] Then the neophytes, of whatever age, received the bread and cup for the first time.

It is this lengthy and severe rite that determines the place of the church in the world, or does when it is not curtailed beyond recognition. The church is one community or polity among others, for it is possible to move from them into her. But unlike the move between, for example, the general business community and the Chamber of Commerce, initiation into the church is repentance, a renunciation of previous attachments. Therefore one cannot go back from the church into the world; one can leave the church only into final judgment.

---

118. In the farthest East, there probably were significant deviations from the order sketched in the following; e.g., Gabriele Winkler, "The Original Meaning of the Prebaptismal Annointing and Its Implications," *Worship* 52 (1978):24–25.

119. To the historical complexities of this matter, Burkhard Neuenhauser, "Taufe und Firmung," *Handbuch der Dogmengeschichte*, ed. Michael Schmaus, Josef Geiselmann, Aloys Grillmeier (Freiburg: Herder, 1967) IV/2:103–106.

120. Hippolytus, *The Apostolic Tradition*, 21.

TWENTY-FIVE

The Polity of God

I

In ecumenical ecclesiology it has become customary to discuss the church's reality under three headings drawn from the New Testament: the church is the people of God, the temple of the Spirit, and the Body of Christ. The trinitarian echoes of the pattern are obvious, as must be its attractiveness to this enterprise.

But much twentieth-century theology has succumbed here also to an endemic strategy of evasion:[1] "people," "temple," and "body" have been treated as unconnected "images" or "metaphors"[2] of the church, which at most need to be balanced or variously emphasized,[3] that is, which need not be taken seriously as con-

---

1. This error was foreshadowed in the development of Catholic ecclesiology in the late nineteenth and early twentieth centuries. See Yves M.-J. Congar, *Die Lehre von der Kirche: Vom Abendländischen Schisma bis zur Gegenwart*, Handbuch der Dogmengeschichte, ed. M. Schmaus, A. Grillmeier, L. Scheffczyk, Bd 3, Fasz 3d (Freiburg: Herder, 1971), 115–120. Even the lovely work of Geoffrey Preston, *Faces of the Church*, ed. Aidan Nichols (Grand Rapids: Eerdmans, 1997, posthum.), speaks this way; apart from that, it is the best presentation of the biblical "images" of the church known to me.

2. It perhaps needs to be repeated in this volume: I am well aware of the sense in which all language may be said to be metaphorical in its origins. But this trivial observation has recently been widely used to escape the necessary distinction in actual usage between concepts and tropes. Both concepts and tropes are "functions," sentences with holes in them. A concept is a function that, if the hole is filled in, yields a sentence that can be a premise in valid argument. Thus "The church is the temple of the Spirit" is a properly metaphorical proposition precisely because it will not, together with "All temples are containers for a god or gods," yield "The church is the container of a god."

3. E.g., in critique of *Lumen gentium*, Roger Mehl, "En marge de l'ecclésiologie catholique romaine," *Oecumenica 1966*, ed. F. W. Kantzenbach, V. Vajta (Neuchâtel: Delachaux et Niestlé, 1966) 121: "Catholic theology has always in the past insisted on the images of body and spouse; but if we are to grasp the precise relation between Christ and the church it is the multiplicity of images that we must recognize."

cepts. But although "temple" may be a simile when applied to the church, which to be sure is not literally a building or place, "people" clearly is neither metaphor nor simile; and if one pauses to examine Paul's actual use of the phrase "body of Christ," it becomes obvious that neither is it.

If we are to follow this scheme, then it must be the task of systematic theology to take "The church is the people of God, the temple of the Spirit, and the body of Christ" with epistemic seriousness by displaying the conceptual links between these phrases. Here, this will be done by in this chapter bringing "people" and "temple" together in the Augustinian teaching that the church is, literally and indeed paradigmatically, a "polity" and in the next chapter bringing "polity" and "body" together in the ecumenically now dominant teaching that the church is first and last "communion."

II

The second Vatican Council's treatise on the church, *Lumen gentium*, made the description of the church as the people of God a key category in its doctrine, especially in its interpretation of the relation within the church between clergy and laity and its interpretation of the relation between the Roman Catholic Church and those outside it. Moreover, the central use of the category was intended "as an ecumenical bridge."[4]

On the one hand, "people of God" comprehends clergy and laity together and indeed takes its orientation from the laity;[5] making this a primary interpretation of the church responds to Reformation and Eastern fears of clericalism. On the other hand, the concept draws the church's boundaries more flexibly— not more vaguely—than had been usual in Roman Catholic teaching, since inclusion in a "people" always shifts somewhat depending on viewpoint;[6] of the church considered as a people the council could say that she "subsists in"[7] the Roman Catholic Church rather than that she simply "is" the Roman Catholic Church, that she is to be *identified as* the Roman Catholic Church without therefore being *identical with* it.[8]

Lumen gentium's second and comprehensive chapter, explicitly titled *De populo Dei*, begins with a dogmatically fundamental narrative:

4. This we have on the highest authority; Joseph Cardinal Ratzinger, *Church, Ecumenism and Politics: New Essays in Ecclesiology* (New York: Crossroad), 16. The initiative was, moreover, immediately received as such; so by a paradigmatic Protestant, Roger Mehl, "En marge," 119.

5. *Laos* is of course Greek for "people."

6. Will, e.g., a five-eighths-Swedish American of the third generation call the people of Sweden "my people"? Is the uncircumcised son of a Jewish mother "Jewish"? It depends of course on the context of discourse.

7. *Subsistit in.*

8. *Lumen gentium*, 8. Joseph Cardinal Ratzinger, *Theologische Prinzipienlehre* (München: Erich Wewel, 1982), 243, interprets the proposition: "The church is there where the successors of Peter and the other apostles visibly embody continuity with the source; but this unmitigated concreteness of the church nevertheless does not mean that everything else can only be not-church. The equals sign is not mathematical."

It has pleased God to sanctify and save human persons not singly . . . but by constituting them a people. . . . Therefore he chose the race of Israel to be a people for himself, and made a covenant with them. . . . He did this, moreover, in preparation . . . for a new and perfect covenant. . . . "Behold the days are coming, says the Lord, when I will make a new covenant with the house of Israel and the house of Judah." . . . This new covenant Christ instituted . . . calling a race from Jews and gentiles . . . to be a new people of God (*novus populus Dei*).[9]

We will simply appropriate this sketch of saving history's communal plot.

A search of the New Testament, however, quickly discovers something rather surprising: when the New Testament refers to the people of God it rarely has the church in mind. The nation of Israel continues to appear as "the people" of God,[10] often in quotation from the Old Testament;[11] and when the New Testament does refer to the church as God's people, this is in every case but one[12] done at least in part to identify her with Israel. These observations must constrain our use of the notion and our appropriation of the council's teaching.[13]

In much of the Old Testament, the formula from Sinai, "I will be your God and you shall be my people," became shorthand for all the promises to Israel.[14] In the New Testament, the formula and its language continue in that function. And then Paul insists in a famous passage: "Has God rejected his people? By no means!"[15] We must be alert to what it means that Paul, whatever he may elsewhere say of "Israel according to the flesh,"[16] here refers to that very entity: it is the Israel who are not in the church and so are *not* descendants of Abraham on account of christological faith[17] who are his problem. Thus the people whom, according to Paul, God has not rejected is Israel constituted a people in her own ancient ways of national continuity, that is, by the unity of tribal descent with certain religious, legal, and civil institutions, most notably effected by circumcision.

Yet Paul can also argue that the cultic community of the Corinthian church, already mostly of gentiles, must maintain her separation from other cultic communities because *she* is "the temple" of the true God, and he can support this

---

9. *Lumen gentium*, 9.

10. Ratzinger, *Church*, 18, tells of making this discovery: "I stumbled on an unexpected finding: while the term 'people of God' occured very frequently in the New Testament, only in a few passages . . . did it mean the Church, and its normal meaning indicated the people of Israel. Indeed, even where it could denote the Church the fundamental meaning of Israel was retained."

11. E.g., Matthew 2:6; Luke 2:32. A notable passage that is not quotation is of course Romans 11:1–2.

12. I Peter 2:9.

13. This is also the position of Ratzinger, *Church*, 14–28. It may be noted that this article was written while Joseph Ratzinger was Prefect of the Congregation for the Faith.

14. So, e.g., Jeremiah 7:23, chosen for citation here more or less at random. The tradition-historical lines may, of course, run the other way.

15. Romans 11:1.

16. I Corinthians 10:18. The translation of the New Revised Standard Version is simply wrong.

17. Galatians 3:7.

contention by citing the very promise "I will be their God, and they shall be my people."[18] How is all this simultaneously possible?

Neither Paul nor other New Testament writers provide a clear or plainly consistent answer to the question.[19] One would hardly have been possible at the time, and perhaps indeed there can be none short of the End. Nevertheless, certain observations are suggestive.

Paul's one other reference to the church as "God's people" is predestinarian and eschatological: the people of God are those whom God has "prepared beforehand for glory—to whom then he has called us, not from the Jews only but also from the gentiles."[20] The perhaps studied ambiguity of the passage must be noted: In view of the uncertain construction "to whom," what exactly does the group "prepared beforehand" include? It must also be noted that the citation from Hosea with which Paul backs up his claim, "Those who were not my people I will call 'my people'" seems to refer, in the Pauline context, simultaneously to the original call of Israel and to the eschatological call of a remnant of Israel, even as it is used to support an assertion about the gentile-inclusive church.

The other clear New Testament references to the church as the people of God are overwhelmingly eschatological. The writer of Hebrews argues that the "Sabbath rest" of "the people of God" is still future, so that there is yet time to enter the church that will enjoy it.[21] In the Revelation, the appearing of "a new heaven and a new earth" and the "coming down" from this heaven of "the new Jerusalem" are angelically proclaimed as the fulfillment of that same promise: "He will dwell with them as their God; they will be his people and God himself will be with them."[22] For the writer to the Ephesians the "Holy Spirit . . . is the pledge of our inheritance toward redemption as God's own people."[23] And in I Peter, the status of the church as "God's own people," supported once again by citation of the passage from Hosea, has as its consequence that believers are "aliens and exiles" in this age.[24]

Thus it is within the bracket of predestination and eschatology that the New Testament refers to the church as the *populus dei*. And Paul's affirmation of Israel after the flesh as still the people of God occurs in the same context. We will let these observations suggest—they do no more—a proposal: the inner relations and exterior boundaries of the people of God are determinate only within Jonathan Edwards's "most general proportion" of God's acts, in which they are "not tied to any particular proportion, to this or that created being, but the proportion is with the whole series of [God's] acts and designs from eternity to eternity."[25]

---

18. II Corinthians 6:16.

19. We may think of the notorious differences among the Gospels in their interpretation of the Law.

20. Romans 9:23–26. The New Revised Standard Version translation is here very likely to mislead.

21. Hebrews 4:9.

22. Revelation 21:1–3.

23. Ephesians 1:14.

24. I Peter 2:9–10.

25. P. 44.

Within any more limited set of historical connections, within any part or aspect of God's history with us, Israel "after the flesh," the believing remnant of Israel, the church of Jews and gentiles, and the continuing synagogue cannot be neatly sorted out with respect to their character as the people of God. The phenomenon is in fact familiar in Scripture. Throughout the canonical history of Israel the relation between Israel as the natural and adoptive descendants of Abraham and the "remnant" of the faithful in Israel[26] was always shifting; and in the time of the New Testament this remained true, with addition of the church to the picture. Now in the time after the New Testament canon it is still the case, with further addition of the rabbinic synagogue.

The observations and considerations just adduced have been available through the history of the church, nor was the eleventh chapter of Romans recently added to the New Testament. What is new in Christian theology is sustained attention to them and the need to use them with a certain bent, provoked of course by Europe's holocaust of Jews. Insight here has been demanded by guilt.

The content of new gentile-Christian awareness should nevertheless not principally be guilt but rather sober recognition of the history and its present mandate. "The destruction of the city of Jerusalem in A.D. 70, the end of the temple worship and the demise of the priesthood, the subjugation of the Land of Israel to the Romans, all of which seemed permanent,[27] led Christians to think that the Jewish way of life had been replaced by Christianity and that the Jews would no longer continue to exist as a people." What the Holocaust has forced on our attention—besides the evil of which humans are capable—was the urgent need for the church to appreciate in practice and theology the in itself manifest fact that "the Jewish way of life" did *not* in fact end. "Recognition of this historical and spiritual fact sets us apart from earlier generations of Christians."[28]

It is what is often labelled "supersessionism" that must be and is being overcome: that is, the theologoumenon—a doctrine it never was—that the church succeeds Israel in such fashion as to *displace* from the status of God's people those Jews who do not enter the church.[29] The church must indeed call Jews to be baptized into the church of Jews and gentiles and think that when this happens it obeys God's will;[30] but she dare not conclude that the continuing separate synagogue is *against* God's will. In this connection too, the second Vatican Council

---

26. Amos 5:15; Isaiah 4: 2–3, 11–16; Jeremiah 23:3.

27. And none of them done by the Christians!

28. Robert L. Wilken, "The Jews as the Christians Saw Them," *First Things*, 73:28. This essay is in general the most lucid and informed presentation known to me of the conditions under which the ancient church made its judgments about Judaism, of how those judgments may be understood *in bonum partem*, and of why they must not and need not be maintained.

29. The most sustained and properly theological investigation of this matter is by R. Kendall Soulen, *The God of Israel and Christian Theology* (Minneapolis: Fortress Press, 1996). The standard work by Paul Van Buren, *A Theology of the Jewish Christian Reality* (New York: Seabury Press, 1980), seems to me to take a fundamentally wrongheaded approach. Developing a less trinitarian Christology is precisely how not to repent of supersessionism.

30. A "mission to the Jews" is of course another question altogether.

has led the ecumenical way: "For the most part the Jews did not accept the gospel. . . . Nevertheless, according to the apostle, the Jews remain . . . dear to God, who never repents of his gifts and callings."[31] Whether the synagogue can in turn recognize the church as belonging to the same people with her is of course another question and one not to be preempted by the church.

Part of the church's difficulty with the continuing synagogue has been a sort of inferiority-feeling on the part of the church: it has been felt that if the synagogue were at all a legitimate heir of old Israel, she would be the *only* legitimate heir. The synagogue's way of life does, after all, more nearly resemble that of Israel as we see it in the Old Testament's later books. This feeling rests, however, on a historical illusion. What we now call Judaism is the Judaism of the rabbis of Mishnah and Talmud, in continuity with the Judaism of the Pharisees. Pharisaism and the church in fact emerged roughly contemporaneously, as two amid a welter of Judaisms around the turn of the millennium, all equally Jewish. When the Romans destroyed common Jewish identity based on land and Temple, Pharisaism and the church were the survivors. From a purely historical point of view, their claims to continue the worship of Israel's God and their claims rightly to read Israel's Bible are precisely equivalent.

The church, it is here suggested, should regard the continuing synagogue as a detour like herself, within the Fulfillment of Israel's hope. Between the end of canonical Israel and the absolute End the church waits by faith in Jesus' Resurrection, and the synagogue waits by study of *torah*, read in a way devised by the old rabbis for just this situation of waiting. Finally, whatever the synagogue may judge about the church's faith, the church must think that the study of *torah* is indeed worship of the one, that is Triune, God.

So who are the people of God? They are the historically actual and just for that reason not always unambiguously delineable people whom God's predestining will is gathering to fulfillment in him. That the church *is* the people of God can be an exclusive proposition only eschatologically. And if we ask *how* God gathers and moves this people, we must point to *torah* in the most comprehensive sense and to the entire ensemble of institutions—in Israel, in the church, and in the synagogue—by which God has maintained the various modes and aspects of this people's historical continuity.

But we said at the beginning of this work: no structures of historical continuity simply as such—and we must here include *torah*, circumcision, and the other national guarantees of Israel—can maintain the continuity of a people who have a mission other than their own perpetuation. Israel would not have remained Israel, nor would the church or synagogue remain themselves, unless God the Spirit *used* these structures to draw his people to their final goal. We have arrived at the necessary transition to our second characterization of the church, that it is the "temple" of the Spirit.

And here we must note a further reason for continuing to other characterizations of the church. The proposition "The church is the people of God" can, if taken

---

31. *Nostra aetate*, 4.

in isolation, become a threat to the church's self-identity. Since the second Vatican Council, Roman Catholicism, and to a lesser extent the more "magisterial" churches of the Reformation, have experienced within their jurisdictional boundaries movements of what amounts to the more sectarian sort of Protestantism. These have seized on the council's language about the "people of God" and from it have derived "ideas . . . of the grass-roots Church, the 'Church from below,' the church of the people," as something *other* than the church of institutions. As a definition of the church, "people of God" has the shortcoming that it can be used "to free oneself from tradition while at the same time enlisting it on one's side."[32]

III

The church's exact continuity and discontinuity with Israel is established and marked by baptism. We have discussed baptism's institution, the mandate of its performance; now we must consider its import as a sacrament, as a visible mode of the gospel-promise. The New Testament presents baptism's promise in strict one-to-one correlation with the two sides of its mandate: Peter paradigmatically exhorts his hearers to "Be baptized . . . for the *forgiveness* of your sins; and you shall receive the gift of the *Holy Spirit* [emphases added]."[33]

John's rite of repentance did not lose its character when the church adapted it as the rite for those whom the gospel-mission brings to repentance. Thus in the Nicene-Constantinopolitan Creed, baptism is "for the forgiveness of sins"; and the Apostles' Creed expects us to understand that the very phrase "forgiveness of sins" denotes baptism. The Council of Florence defined it somewhat one-sidedly: "The effect of this sacrament is the remission of all original and actual guilt, and of all penalty."[34] The one who comes to baptism, Jew or gentile, apprehends the embodied word, "You are forgiven. God puts your old disobedience behind you."

Yet the Jew who is baptized and the gentile who is baptized are not forgiven the same things. The Jew who is baptized repents of unfaithfulness to Israel's God and covenant, as did those who went out to John; the gentile who is baptized repents of all too much faithfulness to his or her gods and their rites. When gentiles "renounce the devil and all his works and ways" they renounce the past as those who have worshipped or but for the grace of already faithful parents would have worshipped Thor or the Dialectic of History or karma or the Invisible Hand or the Goddess or the great Metaphor of class or gender or ethnic *ressentiment* or Nothingness or some other one or selection of religion's panoply of tyrants.[35] For

---

32. Ratzinger, *Church*, 26–27. Ratzinger derives this potentiality genetically from antecedent uses of "people of God" in Western idealist strains that then became more virulent in the Russian notion of *sobornost*. The derivation is perhaps not very convincing and in any case is of doubtful importance.

33. Acts 2:38.

34. Session 8, *Bull of Union with the Armenians*.

35. For this meaning of the renunciation in the ancient practice of baptism and for the following liturgical references generally, Hugh M. Riley, *Christian Initiation* (Washington, D.C.: Catholic University Press, 1974).

gentiles, the sacramental gift of forgiveness is precisely the gift of entry into the people of the true God, despite native idolatry and unbelief.

In the church's mission baptism thus becomes something it was not for John, a rite of initiation, of entry into a new community. A missionary community must have some rite of initiation; when the Spirit launched the church at Pentecost, she recurred to John's baptism for the purpose, since gentiles' coming to Zion and their reception there is in itself an act of repentance and forgiveness.[36]

In its role as a rite of initiation, baptism, according to Peter's sermon, bestows "the gift of the Holy Spirit." Thomas Aquinas, with the tradition, rightly glosses this as admission to be "a member of Christ,"[37] for the remarkable gifts that the New Testament attributes to baptism and sums up as the gift of the Spirit are all in fact "rights and privileges" of the *community* into which the rite initiates. The church is the community in which the righteousness and sanctity of the Kingdom are anticipated; therefore baptism is said to justify and sanctify.[38] The church is a nation of priests and a prophetic community; in this context baptism appears as the requisite initiatory anointing.[39] The church is the body of Christ; thus baptism is said to unite with Christ's bodily fate.[40] It is because the church is rescued from the messianic woes that baptism is said to "save."[41] And when the church is conceived as the bride of Christ, baptism even appears as the bride's toilette.[42]

It cannot be too strongly insisted: the gifts bestowed by baptism are not mysterious endowments somehow inserted into the interiority of the individual; they are the several aspects of the Spirit who gives himself to the church and belong to the baptized individual as and only as a member of the church. The sacramental efficacy of baptism is that it irrevocably initiates into the church and that the spirit of the church is the Holy Spirit himself.

All these privileges of the church and gifts of baptism are eschatological privileges, aspects of the church's anticipation of the Kingdom. It is just so that they can be taken together as "the gift of the Holy Spirit."[43] For the Spirit's animation of the church is the *arrabon* of the Kingdom, the Life given to a community gathered around or to be the gate of heaven.[44] The "Holy Spirit . . . is the pledge of our inheritance toward redemption as God's own people."[45]

---

36. Robert W. Jenson, *Visible Words* (Philadelphia: Fortress, 1978), 126–129. I would not, however, now say what I did there, that the disciples would have recurred to baptism with or without the Resurrection-appearance mandating it.

37. *Summa theologiae*, iii.62.2: "homo moritur vitiis et fit membrum Christi."

38. I Corinthians 1:26–31; 6:8–11.

39. Hebrews 10:22; I John 2:18–27.

40. Romans 6:1–11.

41. I Peter 1:3–21.

42. Ephesians 5:25–27.

43. Eduard Lohse, "Taufe und Rechtfertigung bei Paulus," *Kerygma und Dogma* 2 (1965):308–313.

44. II Corinthians 1:22; 5:5.

45. Ephesians 1:14.

Although baptism bestows the Spirit on both Jew and gentile, again there is a difference. The baptismal coming of the prophetic Spirit upon a Jew who is baptized is of course a great transformation, which doubtless would otherwise have been wholly unexpected. Yet also without baptism it was in principle a possibility; the Spirit has always come to make prophets in Israel, many of whom did not anticipate the role. For gentiles, baptism is initiation into the community where prophecy occurs; it is translation from one communal reality to a very different one. The writer to the Ephesians could not have been more blunt: "Remember that . . . you gentiles by birth . . . were . . . without Christ, being aliens from the commonwealth of Israel, . . . having no hope and without God in the world."[46]

IV

We have effectively already turned to the second of our characterizations of the church. The second Vatican Council stated it: "The Spirit dwells in the Church and in the hearts of the faithful, as in a temple. . . . In them he prays and bears witness to their adoptive sonship. . . . Guiding the Church in the way of all truth . . . and unifying her in communion and in the works of ministry, he bestows upon her varied hierarchic and charismatic gifts."[47]

Martin Luther defined: "It is the proper work of the Holy Spirit, to make the church."[48] And we must add: the Spirit does this by giving himself to be the spirit of this community, by bestowing his own eschatological power to be her liveliness. As Anglican-Orthodox dialogue put it: the church is the community "which is filled by the Holy Spirit, and it is precisely for this reason that every human person has the possibility of becoming a partaker of the divine nature."[49]

The simile of the church as temple is not common in the New Testament, but when it appears it is powerful. Paul asks, not of individuals in Corinth but of the congregation there, "Do you not know that you are God's temple, and that God's Spirit dwells in you?"[50] And the writer to the Ephesians tells his readers that the church is "a holy temple in the Lord; in whom you also are built together by the Spirit[51] into a dwelling place for God."[52]

Both passages reflect subtle trinitarian distinctions. In Corinthians, the Spirit appears in intended analogy to the "glory" or "name" *of* God that inhabited Israel's

---

46. Ephesians 2:11–12.

47. *Lumen gentium*, 4.

48. *Katechismuspredigten* (1523) (WA 11), 53: "Proprium opus spiritus sancti est, quod ecclesiam faciat." To Luther's pneumatological ecclesiology generally, see Jared Wicks, "Heiliger Geist—Kirche—Heiligung: Einsichten aus Luthers Glaubensunterricht," *Catholica* 2 (1991): 79–86.

49. *Faith in the Trinity*, in *Anglican-Orthodox Dialogue*, ed. K. Ware, C. Davey (London: SPCK, 1977), 23–24.

50. I Corinthians 3:16.

51. *En pneumati*. The New Revised Standard Version's "spiritually" disguises the point very effectively.

52. Ephesians 2:21–22.

temple and that was just so God's personal presence.[53] In the passage from Ephesians, the Spirit unites the church as the *totus Christus,* and this structure is then the dwelling place for "God." The church is not in these passages a temple *to* or containing the Spirit but a temple to the *Father* made *by* the Spirit, a temple that is itself one with the risen Christ. The Spirit is not the deity served in this temple nor yet the temple itself but the possibility and energy of service in it.

It is, moreover, exactly the Spirit of prophecy who here appears. We must again recur to the Pentecost narrative. The regathered disciples are made to be the church by being "filled with the Holy Spirit";[54] and the verbal phenomena that are the only described consequence are proclaimed by Peter as the fulfillment of Joel's promise of an eschatological community of prophets.

In Joel's prophecy itself, it is the God of Israel who pours out the Spirit, but in Peter's sermon it is the risen Christ,[55] as the messianic prophet who bears the Spirit in order to give it.[56] Indeed, the Gospels depict Jesus' very conception and birth as a sort of prophesying. In Matthew, Mary's pregnancy occurs "in the Spirit,"[57] and in Luke the Spirit "come[s] upon" Mary, in the very fashion of the oldest accounts of prophecy, to enable the child.[58] With marvelous art, Luke then describes a sort of epidemic of prophecy in the child's vicinity.[59]

Luke again is very deliberate in his interpretations. Thus he provides the content of a sermon only referenced by Mark: the Spirit-filled prophet of Isaiah 6:1–4 is identified with the final prophet of other Isaianic passages, and then this figure is identified with Jesus.[60] And where Matthew has it that Jesus' disciples would be given "good things," Luke specifies these as "the Holy Spirit."[61]

We should not, therefore, be surprised to see the primal church appear in its recorded self-testimony as a sort of congeries of prophetic phenomena. Individual "prophets" led the congregations in a variety of ways, not easily sorted out,[62] and were decisive in establishing the gospel-tradition.[63] In some places, the whole proper congregation may have been a band of prophesying ecstatics, with those not yet so gifted counted as still catechumens;[64] and Acts' account of the apos-

---

53. Pp. 121–123.

54. Acts 2:4.

55. Acts 2:33.

56. To the following, see 1:86–89.

57. Matthew 1:18–20.

58. Luke 1:35.

59. Luke 1:41, 67; 2:225–27.

60. Luke 4:16–30par.

61. Luke 11:13par.

62. Jenson, *Words,* 191–194.

63. To this point, and to the earliest church's charismatic "enthusiasm" generally, see the pathbreaking articles by Ernst Käsemann, "Sätze heiligen Rechtes im Neuen Testament," *New Testament Studies* 1 (1954–1955):248–260; and "Die Anfänge christlicher Theologie," *Zeitschrift für Theologie und Kirche* 57 (1960):162–187.

64. George Kretschmar, "Die Geschichte des Taufgottesdienstes in der Alten Kirchen," *Leiturgia,* ed. K. F. Mueller, W. Blankenberg, vol. 4 (Kassel: Stauda, 1954); Käsemann, "Die Anfänge," 170.

tolic mission is in much the style of the Old Testament's stories of Elisha and Elijah.[65] This may be why in much of Acts the normal consequence of baptism seems to be prophetic seizure.[66] Most decisively for the future, leaders of all sorts understood their offices in material continuity with Israel's prophecy.[67] We hear from Paul: "My speech and my proclamation were not with plausible words of wisdom, but with a demonstration of the Spirit and of power."[68]

If we remember that the gift of the Spirit is made by baptism, that is, by initiation into the church rather than into any of the offices within her, we will not be tempted to identify the church's prophesying with the work of any of those offices nor yet with any particular charism; we will identify it neither with the *magisterium* of the clergy nor with "the priesthood of all believers" nor with the "Spirit-born." We will be warned in the same way by the primal variety just noted. The teaching must be: the church is as a whole a prophesying community.[69] Or even: the church is a single *communal prophet*.

As to what the church is to prophesy, the Word of the Lord has come to her once for all: in the words of many liturgies, "In many and various ways, God spoke to his people of old by the prophets. But now in these last days, he has spoken to us by his Son." The church's prophecy is: "Jesus is risen." Her prophecy is that same message whose hermeneutic is the task of theology, the message labeled "the gospel." The church is to stand in the street or the temple or the palace, like Amos or Isaiah or Jeremiah, and state the truth of the present situation by speaking the Word that evokes the future: "The one who inhabits and sends the future is this Jesus whom you crucified. What is to be expected is what may be expected from him. What may be done is what can be refined by his coming."

It is again time to specify the *power* of the gospel. The church speaks the gospel in the certainty that this word will change its hearers. God says of the Word that comes to the prophet and that the prophet is to speak that "it shall not return to me empty, but it shall accomplish that which I purpose,"[70] for this Word is not other than the Word that "was in the beginning," the Word by which the worlds are created. A creature is what it is said to be in this Word and is nothing else. So if a prophet of the gospel says to me, "You are holy for Christ's sake," that is what I factually am.

In the first volume we analyzed this fact and its coming to be in the terms provided by Bultmann and his followers[71] and in a following chapter will return

---

65. Acts 4:31; 5:32; 6:3–10; 7:55–56; 8:29; 10:19–20; etc.

66. Acts 8:14–18; 11:15–17; 19:2–6.

67. I Peter 1:11–12; Acts 7:51–52; Hebrews 3:9; 9:8; 10:15; Acts 28:25; II Peter 1:21.

68. I Corinthians 2:4.

69. This point does not rest only or even primarily on Acts. The conclusion of Käsemann, "Die Anfänge," 170, rests mostly on form-historical analysis of passages in Matthew: "Die ganze Gemeinde steht, weil sie durch Inspiration ausgezeichnet ist, in der Nachfolge der alttestamentlichen Propheten."

70. Isaiah 55:11.

71. 1:166–171.

to the matter from a different anthropological aspect. Here we may be content with the direct biblical affirmation.

V

In the creeds, Christ "by the power of the Holy Spirit" was "born of the Virgin Mary." Within the system here presented, this is the chief place where we must consider what is to be said about Mary.

The confession cited by Paul, "When the fullness of time had come, God sent his Son, born of a woman, born under the law ," is the earliest scriptural mention of Mary, and is undoubtedly where teaching about her must begin, as it is where the careful and ecumenically attuned teaching of the second Vatican Council begins.[72] Paul's own point, and the first thing to be said about Mary, is christological rather than directly mariological: the Son indeed has a mother. That is, he really is a human being, just as he is a specifically Jewish human being because he has a Jewish mother, because he was "born under the law."

But if the Christology of the ancient councils is true—and assuredly if this work's development of their Christology is true—a startling mariological consequence immediately follows: the person this woman bore is an identity of God, so that, as has been said explicitly since the beginning of the third century,[73] Mary must be "confessed . . . as truly the Mother of God."[74] And if such an epithet is justified, it must also be right for there to be a subdepartment of theology called mariology.

From the traditions incorporated by Matthew[75] and Luke[76] on, it has been taught also that Mary conceived and bore Jesus as a virgin, and the term then appears in the creeds as an assumed epithet. The theological import of Mary's virginal motherhood is that the Son was not born "of the will of the flesh or of the will of man."[77] The question then is: By what will and power *did* Mary conceive? If we are to follow the suggestions of Luke's narrative, the answer must be double. Mary was freed from the short-term continuities of human procreation and descent "by the power of the Holy Spirit"; her pregnancy is one of those events that can be understood only within the total plot of God's history with us. And as the second Vatican Council teaches, she "received the Word of God with her heart

72. *Lumen gentium*, 52.

73. A fine concise statement of the history is provided by Michael Schmaus, "Mary," *Sacramentum Mundi*, ed. Karl Rahner, Adolf Darlap (Freiburg: Herder, 1969), 3/338–341.

74. *Lumen gentium*, 53. It may be noted that John of Damascus specifies that this predicate belongs to Mary both by virtue of the hypostatic union itself and by virtue of the communion of attributes; *The Orthodox Faith*, 56.60–62: "we confess the blessed virgin as Theotokos not only on account of the nature of the Logos but also on account of the deification of the human," 56.60–62.

75. Matthew 1:15.

76. Luke 1:35.

77. John 1:13.

and with her body"—Gabriel being the preacher!—and *so* gave birth,[78] precisely to the Word himself, just as all prophets first receive the Word and then bring it forth.

It is a secondary question, but it of course cannot be elided: Does Mary's virginity as dogmatically taught and here interpreted necessarily mean that Jesus' birth was gynecologically exceptional? Does Jesus' birth by the power of the Spirit and by Mary's reception of the Word necessarily mean that he had no biological father?[79] The question is analogous to the question discussed in the first volume, whether the Resurrection necessarily involved the emptying of the tomb. In both cases it is the state of the tradition itself, as apparent in the texts, that raises the question. And it must therefore be insisted: just as doubts about the empty tomb are not in themselves doubts about the Resurrection, so doubts about Mary's gynecological situation are not merely as such doubts about "born of the virgin Mary";[80] this is not a question of orthodoxy versus heresy.

In the first volume this work somewhat hesitantly affirmed the empty tomb and here less hesitantly affirms Mary's gynecological virginity. Two considerations seem decisive. The first is respect for what the tradents of the creeds of course intended. The second is that if Joseph was the biological father of Jesus, then if it is true that Jesus was not born by the will of man, Joseph must have been a sacramental vehicle of the will of the Spirit; but sexual initiative as sacrament surely comes much too close to pagan nature religion.[81]

We return to the line of our argument. The likeness between what is to be said of Mary and what must be said of the church is immediately apparent.[82] The Johannine passage just cited, appropriated because it so perfectly states the theology of Mary's virginity, was of course written not about Jesus' birth from Mary but about all believers' baptismal birth. It is an ancient theologoumenon, as again

---

78. *Lumen gentium*, 53: "Angelo nuntiante verbum Dei corde et corpore suscepit et vitam mundo protulit." The antecedent tradition on this point is more iconographic than dogmatic-systematic. One may learn the point by wandering through the museums of Italy viewing fourteenth- and fifteenth-century Annunciations. Or by singing the medieval hymn: "Gaude virgo, Mater Christi/Quae per aurem concepisti/Gabriele nuntio."

79. It is perhaps worth noting that the "virgin birth" involved in reproduction by cloning has the exact opposite meaning from the virgin birth we are here considering. A human clone made from cells taken from the mother would indeed have no father, but not because it was not begotten by human will but because it was all too much a product of human will.

80. Wolfhart Pannenberg, *Systematische Theologie* (Göttingen: Vandenhoeck & Ruprecht, 1991), 2:358–360, argues from "the demonstrably legendary character of the [birth] narrative" (359) that only its theological motivations can be taken as authoritative. He claims that his skepticism about a gynecologically virgin birth is not motivated by—in his view illegitimate—a priori conviction that such a thing cannot have happened, as is skepticism about the Resurrection. It is not clear to me, however, that the judgment that the birth stories are "demonstrably legendary" is entirely distinct from precisely such a priori skepticism.

81. As, lamentably, does a fair amount of Marian piety, sometimes quite explicitly.

82. *Lumen gentium* develops the likenesses in §§63–65. The soteriological pairing of Mary and the church goes back to Irenaeus; Schmaus, "Mary," 339–340.

the second Vatican Council has it, that the church "by accepting the Word of God in faith . . . becomes a mother" and that in baptism her children also "are conceived by the Holy Spirit."[83] So Martin Luther: the church "bears children without cease, until the end of this world, as she exercises the ministry of the Word."[84] Cyprian's dictum was intended as a threat but can be read as a promise: "No one can have God as Father who does not have the church as mother."[85]

The likeness between the two motherhoods is not symmetrical. Mary is an individual member of the church; the relation is thus not between two entities of the same type. The relation rather makes Mary a "supereminent . . . member of the church," the member of the church who is what the church is to be, a "type" of the church's essential character.[86]

So far we have followed the tradition closely. But the doctrine so far developed is weak at a decisive point: in the archetypical relation of Mary to the church, as set forth in *Lumen gentium* and in the general tradition, the *tertium comparationis* is only vaguely and eulogistically identified.[87] Yet the point of comparison does not seem hard to locate: Mary is the type of the church in that the church is the prophetic community. The Word of the Lord comes archetypically to Mary, and what she thereupon brings forth, in the very way of the prophets' forthbringing, is the Word in person: "The Word became flesh and dwelt among us."[88] Mary is the archprophet, the paradigmatic instantiation of the church's prophetic reality.

It is in this capacity that the church may and should invoke her. We do not call upon Mary to speak the Word of the Lord to us; this she has already done unrepeatably. But a prophet does not speak the Word to us only but also to God; it belongs to the prophet's office to intercede for the people with God's own Word, as we see in the lives and speech of canonical Israel's prophets and above all in their archetype Moses[89] who indeed makes a better Old Testament pair for Mary than does Eve. If in the time of the church it is possible to speak to the church's saints and solicit their prayer—a point to which we will return, with affirmative results[90]—then of course it is possible to invoke Mary among them. But when

---

83. Ibid., 64.

84. Cited by Eberhard Jüngel, from WA 40/I:464, in the course of an extraordinarily illuminating ecumenical dispute, in which Jüngel argued *against* the notion of "mother church" and argued laboriously that Luther did not mean what he said; "Die Kirche als Sakrament?" *Zeitschrift für Theologie und Kirche* 80 (1983):450–456. To the discussion, against Jüngel, Robert W. Jenson, *Unbaptized God: The Basic Flaw in Ecumenical Theology* (Minneapolis: Fortress, 1992), 92–94.

85. *De catholicae ecclesiae unitate*, 6: "Habere non potest Deum patrem qui ecclesim non habet matrem."

86. *Lumen gentium*, 68: "Imago et initium est ecclesiae in futuro saeculo consummandae."

87. Thus *Lumen gentium* itself, in e.g., §63, has recourse to phrases like *singularibus gratiis*, which indeed have reasonably precise meaning in technical scholasticism but here and in similar contexts give the unmistakable impression of hand-waving.

88. John 1:14. It will be seen that by simply putting Mary at her place in the Johannine equivalent of the birth-narratives, the entire mariological dogma results.

89. Exodus 33–34.

90. Pp. 365–368.

the church seizes this possibility, such an invocation as "Holy Mary, Mother of God, pray for us sinners" becomes something more than a request for a fellow-saint's prayer: Mary intercedes for the church as did Moses for Israel, or rather does so as Moses' prototype, pleading God's own Word to him.[91]

Moreover, Luke's Annunciation scene has points of theological interest not yet noted. An angel is a chief actor, which suggests something about the event; that it is one of those New Testament junctures where the divine narrative might have broken. What if Mary had *not* said "Let it be with me according to your word," the *fiat mihi* of so much iconography? What if Mary had refused her calling? This is perhaps the point from which to make sense of an otherwise puzzling and indeed troubling item of dogmatic history.

In 1854 Pious IX defined it as dogma that Mary was preserved from the consequences of original sin from the moment of her conception. This definition and the next to be considered were made in uniquely unilateral fashion; it remains to be seen what status these definitions may have in a reunited church and so what status they now can have in the ecumene. But the question of the *meaning* of "sinlessness" is even more difficult.

What exactly does the doctrine of Mary's exemption from the consequences of original sin in fact attribute to her prior to resurrection? Probably the proposition should be interpreted by analogy with the sinlessness traditionally asserted of her Son, following the passage from Hebrews.[92] But this teaching itself has been difficult to clarify, nor has this work found it necessary much to invoke it. Jesus' sinlessness clearly does not exclude behavior on his part that in anyone else would be at least ambiguous: anger, evasiveness, filial impiety, favoritism, and so on. Did the baby Jesus like other babies enforce his needs by howling—the behavior that convinced Augustine of infants' sinfulness? If he did not, how did Mary keep him alive?

Jesus' sinlessness is best understood as his unbroken faithfulness to his calling, a faithfulness identical with his reality as the second identity of God. May we say that Mary analogously was at no juncture unfaithful to her calling as Mother of God and archprophet? That the anticipation of purpose, by which any human life occurs, was in her case and the case of this purpose unbrokenly coherent? Christ's human will, we argued, might have broken in Gethsemane or elsewhere; the fact that it did not is the same fact as that his human identity is the second identity of God.[93] May we interpret Mary's assent to the angel's message analogously? And as itself constituting her sinlessness?

If we may set Mary and Jesus in these analogies, then Mary and her *fiat mihi* belong climactically to the Incarnate Son's preexistence in and as Israel.[94] At every

---

91. One interpretation of Mary's special intercession must be simply rejected. Invoking Mary for the sake of a mother's natural influence with her son in fact reduces her role: either to that merely of a privileged saint or to that of a goddess.

92. Hebrews 5:14.

93. 1:134–137.

94. 1:141.

step of the way, Israel's *fiat mihi* was the possibility of the Incarnation; whenever its refusal threatened, judgment had indeed to begin with Israel to bring her to repentance, lest the Son fail of actuality. When Gabriel challenges Mary, the issue is put to Israel once and for all, with no future for repentance. It is for her obedience at that moment, the climactic obedience of Israel, that we not only invoke Mary but revere her.[95]

Finally, we should notice something about all the preceding arguments, their dependence on the prologue of John's Gospel. Should we want "proof" texts of the chief Marian teachings, perhaps it can be this: if one takes John 1 as what it is, John's equivalent of Matthew's and Mark's birth stories, and inserts Mary explicitly into her places in the story, the Marian doctrines immediately result.

VI

A *people* united in a common *spirit*, that is, a people who have become a community, is a *polity*; this we have already learned from Augustine. A political understanding of the church's reality seems, moreover, to have been much of the content of early use of "*ekklesia*" for the Pentecostal community.[96] We have Augustine's paradigmatic theology of the church as polity already before us[97] and may here proceed quickly by simply extracting a summary of its features.

As God's *polity*, the church's great character is peace, the "tranquility of order." In the Kingdom, there will be perfect peace, that is, perfect mutual structured service. The church anticipates this eschatological peace in the imperfect but real concord of her members, situated in mutual and complimentary modes of leading and obeying.

---

95. There is of course a second papal Marian dogma, defined by Pious XII in 1950: at the end of Mary's earthly life she was taken, body and soul, directly into heaven. The meaning of this definition is even more obscure, and perhaps it is impossible to discover any intellectual content in it.

Does it mean that Mary is, like her Son, already risen from the dead? Then she is like him a pioneer of Resurrection. But that would mean that she is a fourth person of the Trinity, an idea indeed consonant with certain excesses of Marian devotion but hardly the pope's intention.

Notably the oldest tradition was that Mary "fell asleep" and was taken to heaven without dying, so that her situation at the Resurrection will be like that of believers then living; and the Roman *magisterium*, also at the second Vatican Council, has refrained from saying whether Mary died or not. But if her situation is like believers living at the Resurrection, she is not among the saints whom the church now invokes.

Perhaps the best interpretation is that the definition in fact attributes nothing to her, *in this respect*, that is not true of the blessed departed generally. In that case it should be read not as a set of propositions but as an urgent recommendation to venerate the icons of Mary's dormition, surely an excellent recommendation.

96. E.g., according to Karl P. Donfried, "The Assembly of the Thessalonians: Reflections on the Ecclesiology of the Earliest Christian Letter," *Ekklesiologie des Neuen Testaments*, ed. Rainer Kampling, Thomas Süding (Freiburg: Herder, 1996), 390–408, Paul in this letter picks up the accustomed use of *ekklesia thessalonikewn* for the public gathering of the city and addresses the assembly of Christians in Thessalonica as a parallel reality. This assembly is then qualified eschatologically, by echoes of Jewish sectarian use of *ekklesia theou* in apocalyptic contexts.

97. Pp. 76–85.

This peace is unbreakable, even when the church is shaken by controversy or tortured by misused authority or rebellion, because it is constituted in communal love of God. That is, it is constituted in right worship, centrally in the Eucharist where one cup and one loaf are shared, also by those who in the world's polities—or even by the politics of the church—are kept apart or even ordained to social or economic or personal conflict. My political or academic or economic foe and I forgive each other as we approach the table, but our situations outside the church may condemn us to need the same forgiveness again the next day; it is the shared cup itself that is our permanent peace.

In this age the *libido dominandi* remains and survives baptism to appear in the church; but in the church it is robbed of its scope. For the *libido* that unifies the church is directed to one who cannot be dominated or recruited to domineering purposes and whose worship compels our sharing. Try as we will, the members of the church cannot be a mere multitude united only by interest and contract.

As a polity, the church has a government. This must be a government that strives to escape the *libido dominandi* and so forswears all coercion. It therefore is a government whose means of governing are merely *torah* itself: the speaking of the law precisely to combat intrusions of *libido dominandi*, and the solicitations of the gospel; in particular the churchly government's means of governing is its ministration of the sacraments. Those who exercise this governance must therefore be the ministers of "word and sacrament"; to their role we must devote a separate discussion.

The canonical charter of churchly governance is a celebrated saying of the Matthean Jesus to Peter: "I will give you the keys of the kingdom of heaven, and whatever you bind on earth will be bound in heaven, and whatever you loose on earth will be loosed in heaven.[98] This power is in a later passage given to the other disciples also.[99] In the first passage it is granted in a context of eschatological expectation, and in the second it has the context of failing peace within the church. Just so its nature becomes clear.

Already the evangelist Matthew's community had faced the necessity of dealing with severe breaches of communion.[100] And in the church's eschatological situation, Matthew hands down the necessary regulations as a direct mandate from the Lord.[101] No community with a specific mission can thrive without discipline at its borders. In the church's case, this necessity is eschatological, since the spirit of the church is the Spirit of God: when members so live as to disprove the church's missionary claim to the Spirit, the church *must* separate herself from them or be herself unfaithful. The practice of excommunica-

---

98. Matthew 16:19.
99. Matthew 18:18.
100. Here, as at each following historical step, I rely on the splendid history by Herbert Vorgrimmler, "Busse und Letzte Ölung," *Handbuch der Dogmengeschichte,* ed. Michael Schmaus, Josef Geiselmann and Aloys Grillmeier, Bd. IV/3 (Freiburg: Herder, 1978), 3–9.
101. Matthew 18:6–22.

tion is thus an absolute if wrenching necessity: "Let such a one be to you as a Gentile and a tax collector."[102]

Nor can the church's disciplinary action and the judgment on which it is based be simply distinct from the judgment and action of God. If the church excludes a member from her communion, this reverses God's baptismal judgment and action; and if the church later re-admits that person, the act can only be a sort of re-presentation of baptism and so again an act on God's behalf.

Throughout the church's history she has struggled to bear these mandates, particularly the burden of judging on behalf of God. The history is dismayingly complex.[103] The ancient church developed a discipline with successive parts: exclusion of apostates, adulterers, and the like from eucharistic communion; confession; admission to a lengthy period of penitential works as a kind of renewed and more rigorous catechumenate; and reconciliation, if allowed, at the end. All actions were public.

This "canonical penance" was undone by the Constantinian arrangement that made Christianity the official religion of the empire and the church the official religious agency. No government can maintain its authority unless the people it governs include a critical mass of those whose obedience to the law of the polity is unforced. When the boundaries of the church and the boundaries of a city of the world were supposed to be nearly the same, and the baptized therefore inevitably came to include great numbers of the unevangelized, the church's authorities faced an intrinsically hopeless task. It is commonly thought that late antiquity and the early middle ages were periods in which churchly authorities ruled supreme. This is far from the case; rather, proper churchly discipline first became a desperate enterprise and then disappeared altogether except in theory.

VII

A true polity, according to Augustine, is a people constituted as such by antecedent justice. In the church—which is thus the only true polity—this justice is the love of God and thereupon the love of one another. That is, it is the justice described by the first and second tables of the "ten commandments," as these live, not as negative prohibitions of crime but in their historical actuality as slogans of the church's specific moral history with her God. The commandments are the remaining task of this chapter. But there is one—not so explicitly Augustinian—step we must first take.

---

102. Matthew 18:17. See also I Corinthians 5:9–11; II John 11. To the Corinthians passage, Hans von Campenhausen, *Ecclesiastical Authority and Spirit Power in the Church of the First Three Centuries*, tr. J. Baker (London: A. & C. Black, 1969), 134–135.

103. For this, Vorgrimmler, "Busse," 100–182; Nathan Mitchell, "The many Ways to Reconciliation," *The Rite of Penance: Commentaries III*, ed. N. Mitchell (Washington, D.C.: The Liturgical Conference, 1978), 20–37. For my own account, Robert W. Jenson, "The Return to Baptism," *Christian Dogmatics*, ed. Carl Braaten, Robert Jenson (Philadelphia: Fortress, 1984), 2:370–373.

A polity's prepolitical and prelegal possibility is, we said, its openness to prophecy. The church's prophecy is the gospel. Thus the church is a creature of the gospel not only in the sense that she comes into being as those who have heard and therefore must tell this message but also in the sense that its speaking within her shapes her as the specific polity she is. We have noted that the commandments work differently in two contexts: as negative prohibitions of crime, they state conditions of any polity's perdurance; but in the specific communal history of Israel and the church they acquire positive meaning as descriptions of virtues. It is the gospel that is the agent of the specific history of God's people and so enables and shapes such meanings.

We turn then to the Decalogue, to the justice by which the church is the true polity. The first table of commandments specifies the constituting justice of God's people, whether we call it their communal love for God or their communal faith in God. Just so it is specific to the life of Israel; and in its application to the church it will assume form specific to the life of the church.

Israel or the church are to worship the one God, as he asks to be worshipped. For the church, as we will see in the next chapter, this means above all that we are to celebrate the Eucharist in accord with its institution; here is where the church's constituting justice occurs.

At this center of the church's life, her virtue is therefore the order of her ministries and her ritual rubrics, as these constitute her *habitus* of doing eucharistic right. The church's virtue in obedience to the first great commandment consists in such habits as this: let "a bishop . . . be married only once, temperate, sensible, respectable, hospitable";[104] let the deacons of the congregation distribute the offerings of the Eucharist without distinctions to the poor and distressed within the church's reach; invoke only Father, Son, and Holy Spirit in your thanksgiving, with remembrance of Jesus; "Let all drink from this cup"; and so on. The first-table virtue of the church is ordinational and liturgical.

Turning to the second table, we may for exposition's sake begin with "You shall not bear false witness." Martin Luther prompted catechumens to ask, "What does this mean?" and supplied an answer: "We should fear and love God, so that we do not falsely accuse, betray or slander our neighbors, or spread evil rumors about them, but rather excuse them, speak well of them and interpret everything about them in the best sense."[105]

Clearly the pattern of life mandated here is much more than mere obedience to the command's literal and negative meaning as a prohibition of perjury. Luther expounds what the command has come to mean in the life of a people that honors the first table of the law, that in fact fears and loves God. He expounds the command's meaning in a polity whose citizens have reason to attribute good to each other, because good is unconditionally and finally promised to the com-

---

104. I Timothy 2:2.
105. "Die zehn Gebote," *Kleiner Katechismus,* 16.

munity we make together.[106] Our neighbors in the church will in the Kingdom be beyond reproach, so that evil witness will be useless; and we may now regard that as the real truth about them. Indeed, we may regard all fellow humans so, since no human has any other actual *telos* than the Kingdom. We are able to proceed so recklessly because we fear and love God only.

"You shall not steal." "What does this mean?" "We should fear and love God so that we do not seize our neighbor's money or other goods, or obtain them by sharp dealing, but rather help him to improve and guard his property and living."[107] The command, so interpreted, is not one that can be enforced in the world's polities. It is what the command has come to mean in a community where we do not need to be economic individualists, because its very spirit is the knowledge that "All these things will be added to you."

"You shall not commit adultery." "What does this mean?" "We should fear and love God, so that we live a chaste and disciplined life in words and deeds, and so that each one loves and honors his or her spouse."[108] Here Luther altogether skips over the universally necessary negative "Do not violate the law of marriage" and evokes instead the specific Jewish and Christian sexual virtue of faithfulness. As the relation of the Lord to his people is interpreted as faithfulness even to an unfaithful spouse,[109] just so marriage is in Judaism and the church understood as the creaturely analogy of divine faithfulness.[110]

"You shall not kill." "What does this mean?" "We should fear and love God, so that we cause our neighbors no bodily harm or suffering, but help and support them in all the exigencies of life."[111] The prohibition of vendetta, the universally necessary civilizing function of the negative command, has vanished altogether. Instead, in the community of the gospel, the commandment calls us to be "good Samaritans" to one another and to all humanity.

At present and in the foreseeable future, the virtues that Christian faith sees in this commandment will perhaps be the most threatened of all and the most in need of thoughtful attention. For humans' ability both to alleviate the neighbor's suffering and to damage her or his humanity are expanding in a way that threatens to turn virtue into horror, putting the human agent in positions that faith cannot occupy. Genetic engineering, prenatal screening, cloning, the generation of human genes, the nurture of tissue and zygotes as independent entities, all are done allegedly to promote dignity and alleviate suffering. But hidden in them is nothing less than the possibility of "the abolition of man." Western modernity's residual morality is observably incapable of mastering, or even stating, the ques-

106. Gilbert Meilaender, *Faith and Faithfulness* (Notre Dame: Notre Dame Press, 1991), 20: "It seems best to describe Christian ethics as a two-tier ethic—in part general and able to be defended on grounds not peculiarly Christian; in part singular, making sense only within the shared life of the faithful community."

107. Ibid., 14.

108. Ibid., 12.

109. Hosea 1–3!

110. Ephesians 5:22–33.

111. Ibid. 15.

tions that multiply under the label of bioethics; it can only be hoped that the church can sufficiently recoup her understanding of human worth to enable her own life to remain faithful.[112]

Three things will be seen about Christian "ethics,"[113] as instanced by such readings of the commandments as just rehearsed.[114] First, in their specific role within the people of God, moral commands are not burdensome constraints, are not the "law" that the Reformers said "always condemns"; rather they can best be called *permissions*. Here Karl Barth must be cited for his pathfinding and massive development of the insight: "The form, by which God's command distinguishes itself from all other commands, . . . consists therein, that it is *permission*, the *grant* of a specific *freedom*."[115]

In the church, moral commands tell what we may reasonably do because Christ is risen, which otherwise could be thought irresponsible. Insofar as it is the gospel that enjoins us, we do what we do because we may, not because we ought. We can even say with Barth that "[e]thics as the teaching of God's command explains the law as a form of the gospel"[116] itself, the form the gospel takes in the communal history moved by it.

This does not mean that the commandments are not to be taught and urged within the church in their universal negative role also. So long as the church remains only at the gate of heaven, her members too will need to be told again and again of the minimal conditions of life together, which constrain them as they do the citizens of lesser polities; the *libido dominandi* will need to be curtailed within the church also. But it is not this sort of ethics that is *specific* to the church.

Second, we must remember the church's missionary character. Those whom the gospel calls into the church are not without antecedent hopes and fears. Each

---

112. The interior wisdom of the church in such matters can be, within recent discussion, exemplified by the work of Stanley Hauerwas in numerous publications; or by William F. May, *The Physician's Covenant* (Philadelphia: Westminster, 1983); or by Gilbert Meilaender, *Bioethics: A Primer for Christians* (Grand Rapids: Eerdmans, 1996), which despite its subtitle is the deepest comprehensive discussion known to me.

113. The "scare quotes" reflect such discomforts as those of Edmund Santurri in an unpublished lecture at St. Olaf College, July, 1994: the vast apparatus of "ethical inquiry" characteristic of late modern societies may be mostly a device to mask corruption. "Ethics" do not in fact often terminate in ethical judgments, but rather in lawyerly cases for judgments already made on other, usually self-serving grounds.

Or perhaps we should say that "ethics" are the world's closest approximation to the gospel, its description of how to be a good person. Just so they are finally idolatry.

114. Although my understanding of ethics is not to be fathered on Stanley Hauerwas, and I will not engage in point-by-point reference or argument, his work provides the template for the following and is at all times in the back of my mind. Of his voluminous writing, see perhaps first *The Peaceable Kingdom* (Notre Dame: University of Notre Dame Press, 1983) and *After Christendom? How the Church Is to Behave if Freedom, Justice, and a Christian Nation Are Bad Ideas* (Nashville: Abingdon, 1991).

115. *Kirchliche Dogmatik* (Zürich: Zollikon, 1948), II/2:650: "Die Form, durch die das Gebot Gottes sich von allen anderen Geboten unterscheidet, . . . besteht darin, dass es *Erlaubnis* ist: *Gewährung* einer ganz bestimmten *Freiheit*."

116. Ibid., 564.

historically or geographically new community that the mission penetrates is moved already by permissions and prohibitions that are the content of its humanity, and if the gospel is to be promise for these hearers it must speak to this existing morality. Thus the moral history of the church is not, as it were, pure; it is not simply other than the moral history of the communities around it. The gospel takes its ethical form just as it *interprets* an antecedent morality of those who at a time and place are there to hear and speak it.[117]

The gospel turns our antecedent hopes into real possibilities by interpreting them as hopes for a Kingdom that is indeed coming. Just so it also reinterprets them materially. So, to take a central and by now familiar instance, all humans hope for something that may be called peace. But most societies have interpreted peace as the success of violence—in the ideology of Western states, as a "security" to be established by "defense." Just so the hope for peace becomes itself the constant occasion of conflict. The gospel promises the actual advent of peace and invites us to its anticipation in the Eucharist. The gospel makes peace a possibility by telling us that we do not have to defend ourselves, since our lives are hid with God in Christ. Just so, the gospel interprets peace as what Christ brings, as the fruit of his self-surrender.

Third, the ethics here described as specifically Christian do not quite fit either standard mold of recent ethical theory: "The first ethical question is neither deontological nor teleological."[118] The good is constituted neither in sheer obedience to commands nor in a cultivation of virtue, of what I am and am becoming. We are ontologically involved in God and so with each other; so and only so we are moral beings. But this God is the triune God whose own reality is "deontological" moral discourse, who is three persons who mutually command and obey. The moral questions thus are, from this point of view: "a) What is the pattern of the divine life and activity? And b) what does it mean to participate in that life and activity?"[119]

My virtue is constituted precisely as my participation in the divine discourse of eternal mandates and free obedience, which I am allowed to overhear. It is thus at once ontological and constituted in hearing and obeying, at once teleological and deontological.

We have just spoken of the Kingdom. Description of the virtues definitive of the church's life may well have a sour ring in many ears; the life of the church manifests them all too incompletely. We are led to the final function of God's commandments: they are descriptions of the life of the Kingdom, which the church only anticipates. "When we teach them to ourselves and our children, this is the last and best thing we are to say: 'God is making a world of love to God and one another. See how fine that world will be. We will be faithful to God. We will be passionate for one another. We will be truthful with one another. We will . . .'"[120]

117. Would Stanley Hauerwas agree with this? I am not sure.

118. Roland A. Delattre, "The Theological Ethics of Jonathan Edwards: an Homage to Paul Ramsey," *Journal of Religious Ethics* 19 (1991):79.

119. Ibid.

120. Robert W. Jenson, *A Large Catechism* (Delhi, New York: ALPB, 1991), 13.

TWENTY-SIX

The Great Communion

I

The teaching that the church is the body of Christ and the teaching with which this chapter will conclude, that the church is above all and decisively *communion* with Christ and among her members, are linked from their origins. Paul to the Corinthians is the parent of both. "The bread that we break, is it not a communion (*koinonia*) in the body of Christ? Because there is one bread, we who are many are one body, for we all partake of the one bread."[1] Here Paul's concern is the question of compatibility between communion established in pagan sacrificial meals and the communion established in the eucharistic meal. But in the next chapter the state of the congregation's own communion brings up the matter: by their violation of fellowship with each other, the Corinthians fail to "discern" "the body" and so incur guilt respecting "the body and blood of the Lord."[2]

We may remind ourselves of earlier exegesis of these passages.[3] The body of Christ that the Corinthians culpably fail to discern is at once the gathered congregation, which is the actual object of their misbehavior and to which Paul has just previously referred as the body of Christ, and the loaf and cup, which are called Christ's body by the narrative of institution he cites in support of his rebuke.[4] John of Damascus summarized deep and precise patristic interpretation

1. I Corinthians 10:16–17. The New Revised Standard Version translation of *koinonia* with "sharing" in this passage is of course linguistically possible but hides the connection between the passage and centuries of theology built on it by suppressing the linquistically equally good, or perhaps better, traditional translation.

2. I Corinthians 11:17–22.

3. 1:201–206.

4. The pathbreaking essay in understanding this dialectic is Ernst Käsemann, "The Pauline Doctrine of the Lord's Supper," *Essays on New Testament Themes*, tr. W. J. Montague (London: SCM, 1964), 119–121.

of the two passages together: the Eucharist "is called 'communion' and truly it is. For through it we both commune with Christ, and share in his body as well as in his deity, and commune and are united with one another. For as we all eat of one loaf we become one body and one blood of Christ and members of one another. Thus we may be called co-embodiments of Christ."[5]

That churchly and eucharistic communion are one, in that both are communion in the body of Christ, has become a standard item of ecumenical consensus, in part because of Orthodox initiatives. "The church celebrating the Eucharist becomes fully itself; that is, *koinonia*, fellowship—communion. The church celebrates the Eucharist as the central act of its existence, in which the ecclesial community . . . receives its realization."[6] "The whole church of Christ participates in our Eucharistic celebration; we are assured of this because the church is the body of Christ."[7]

II

We earlier found: in Paul's use, "is the body of" is a proper concept also when its arguments are the church and the risen Christ. So the recently and posthumously published ecclesiological meditations of Geoffrey Preston: "The relation of the Church to Christ is not 'like' that of a man's body to the man himself. It *is* that of Christ's body to the Lord himself."[8]

It is of course hard for us, who are more ontologically inhibited than was Paul,[9] to see what he can mean by "The church is Christ's body" if not merely that the church is Christ's and is in certain respects like a body. The church is not an organism of the species *homo sapiens*, nor is a human organism a community of persons; and so the church is indeed not what we now first think of as a human body. But Paul was able to think of a "spiritual body,"[10] which according to him *succeeds* the person's "biological body"[11] in the resurrection, as nevertheless providing the same personal embodiment as did the biological body[12] and indeed as if anything more bodily and proper to the person than it was.[13]

---

5. *The Orthodox Faith*, 4.13: *sussomoi tou christou*.

6. *Anglican-Orthodox Dialogue: The Moscow Statement* (1976), ed. K. Ware, C. Davey (London: SPCK, 1977), 24.

7. *Dialogue between Neighbors*, ed. Honnu T. Kamppuri (Helsinki: Luther-Agricola Society, 1986), 50.

8. *Faces of the Church* (Grand Rapids: Eerdmans, 1997), 89.

9. Ernst Käsemann, *Perspectives on Paul*, tr. Margaret Kohl (reprint, Mifflinton: Sigler, 1996), 102–121, destroys any possibility that Paul's "body of Christ" was a metaphor and shows the concept's centrality for Paul's ecclesiology. But then, faithfully to the prejudices of his school, he warns against using the concept metaphysically, lest this lead to results like those that follow.

10. *Soma pneumatikon.*

11. *Soma psychikon.*

12. I Corinthians 15:42–44.

13. So in II Corinthians 5:4, Paul, here using the metaphor of clothing, can describe his wish to leave his biological body and be clothed with a spiritual body as a wish to be more intensively or fully clothed.

Plainly, for Paul the concept of personal embodiment is not itself a biological concept.

We may discover what sort of concept it then is, and simultaneously declare our own usage, by first recalling our general interpretation that for Paul a person's embodiment is his or her *availability* to other persons and thereupon to her or himself and by then again introducing German idealism's subject-object distinction. That the church is the body of Christ, in Paul's and our sense, means that she is the object in the world as which the risen Christ is an object for the world, an available something as which Christ is there to be addressed and grasped. Where am I to aim my intention, to intend the risen Christ? The first answer must be: to the assembled church, and if I am in the assembly, to the gathering that surrounds me. Thus the primal posture of Christian prayer is not involution with closed eyes but an open posture, with eyes intent upon those speaking for the gathering.

Yet we cannot rest with this first answer. In the New Testament, the church and risen Christ are one but can also be distinguished from each other; thus, for example, the church is the risen Christ's "bride"[14] so that Christ and the church are joined as a *couple*. We may not so identify the risen Christ with the church as to be unable to refer distinctly to the one and then to the other. Protestants have for just this reason often feared such language as appears in the previous paragraphs. If we say only that the church is personally identical with Christ, it may seem that the church can never need reform or be open to it.

Our passages from Corinthians have already shown how this concern is satisfied. The object that is the church-assembly is the body of Christ, that is, Christ available to the world and to her members, just in that the church gathers around objects distinct from herself, the bread and cup, which are the availability *to her* of the same Christ. Within the gathering we can intend Christ as the community we are, without self-deification, because we jointly intend the identical Christ as the sacramental elements in our midst, which are other than us. Yet again invoking the distinction between community and association, we may say that the church as community is the object-Christ for the world and her own members severally, in that the church as association is objectively confronted within herself by the same Christ.

Indeed, that the church is ontologically the risen Christ's human body is the very possibility of the churchly reform for which Protestantism is concerned. We cannot reform the church, any more than we could create it. But every living person can and sometimes must discipline his or her own body. If there is to be churchly reform, the Spirit must do it; it must be done by the triune person who frees the church to be the own body of Christ. And that is to say, it must be an event within the reality of the living Christ, an act—we may go so far as to say—of his own asceticism. Churchly reform is the risen Christ's self-discipline in the Spirit.

But now a question can no longer be repressed: Why must Christ be embodied for us at all? Why is not a "spiritual"—in the vulgar sense—communion

14. Ephesians 5:31–32.

enough? That is, why is it not enough privately to think and feel Christ's presence and to know that others in their privacies do the same? Why do I need to live in the assembled church? Or indeed why is it not enough that the bread and cup move me to inward awareness of the risen Christ and to a deeper feeling of communion with him—as is the understanding of most Protestants and not a few Catholics, whatever the official teaching of their churches? Why must we say the bread and cup *are* his objective intrusion, his body?

Few have probed this question with such passion as Martin Luther. Were Christ's presence in the assembly disembodied, it would be his presence as God but *not* his presence as a human, for as a human he is a risen body. And to the posit of Christ's presence as sheer God, abstracted from his embodied actuality as Jesus, Luther can react only with horror: "Don't give me any of *that* God!"[15] It is God's hiding in human embodiment that is our salvation; Christ's naked deity— were there in actuality such a thing—would be "nothing to do with us"[16] and just so destruction for us.[17] Our salvation is "God incarnate . . . in whom are all the [divine] treasures . . . but *hidden* [emphasis added]."[18]

It is this theme that Hegel then analyzed in the famous "Domination and Slavery" passage of his *Phenomenology of Spirit*, earlier invoked in a related connection. If in the meeting between us you are a subject of which I am an object but are not in turn an object for me as subject, you insofar enslave me. Only if I am able to intend and so grasp and respond to you as you intend and grasp me can our relation be reciprocal.[19] A disembodied personal presence to me could only mean my bondage, no matter how benevolent in intention; and were the person in question God, the bondage would be absolute. Were Christ not embodied in his community, were his presence there merely to and in thought and feeling, he would be the community's destruction, however fond the thoughts and feelings; and were he not embodied for the world in his community, his presence in the world would be the world's damnation.

Finally we may ask how it can be *true* that the church with her sacraments is the body of the risen Christ, the object as which this human person is there for us. The answer is very simple, though it overturns the whole inherited structure of Western thinking. We have given it in other connections: for it to be true that the church gathered around her sacraments is Christ's body, all that is needed is that the risen Christ's personal self-understanding determine what is real, that is, that he be the *Logos* of God.

The church with her sacraments is truly Christ's availability to us just because Christ takes her as his availability to himself. Where does the risen Christ turn to find himself? To the sacramental gathering of believers. To the question

15. Martin Luther, *Vom Abendmahl Christi, Bekenntnis*, WA 26, 332: "Mir aber des Gottes nicht!"
16. *Nihil ad nos.*
17. E.g., *De servo arbitrio*, WA 18, 685–686.
18. Ibid., 689.
19. 1:155–156.

"Who am I?" he answers, "I am this community's head. I am the subject whose objectivity is this community. I am the one who died to gather them." And again: "I am the subject whose objectivity for this community is the bread and cup around which she gathers." The church with her sacraments is the object as which we may intend Christ because she is the object as which he intends himself. The relation between Christ as a subject and the church with her sacraments is precisely that between transcendental subjectivity and the objective self, as we analyzed it in the chapter on human personality; the church is the risen Christ's Ego. And as he is the Word of God by which all things are created to be what they are, no further explanation of his eucharistic presence is needed or possible.

The metaphysics of Mediterranean antiquity, and for the most part those of subsequent Western tradition, of course do not allow for this simplicity. Therefore they are in error. The usual metaphysics suppose that what can be and what cannot be are determined by abstractly universal principles and never by a particular; thus the question of how the church with her sacraments can be the actual body of the individual human person Jesus can be settled only by argument that does not itself mention his particular personhood or the specific communion of the church. But this supposition of the Greek pagan thinkers is neither revealed nor an otherwise inevitable position.

If the gospel is true, precisely the specific personhood of the individual human person Jesus *is*, by the initiative of the Father and in the freedom of the Spirit, the material determinant of what generally can be and cannot be. We have been revising inherited metaphysics on these lines throughout the present work; this discussion of the church's reality and that of her sacraments merely continues the development.

III

It is time to examine the *promises* embodied by the Eucharist, as in the previous chapter we did those embodied by baptism. We have now several times discussed the one chief group of texts from I Corinthians and need not repeat what was found. But before we turn to those embedded in the narrative of institution itself, we must look at one other passage, John 6:51–59.[20]

The passage follows the discourse in which Jesus says, "I am the bread of life," that is, claims that he is the Revelation from God that fulfills human life. This offends his hearers: such "bread" must come from heaven, and Jesus does not look heavenly, while his earthly origins are known to them. The faith then demanded by Jesus is the overcoming of this offense.

Those for whom John writes, however, do not apparently hear or see the man Jesus, nor do they know his family. What is their occasion of offense, and so of faith? It is the bread of the Eucharist, which appears of no more heavenly or mysterious

---

20. To the passage, Eduard Schweizer, "Das johanneische Zeugnis vom Herrenmahl," *Evangelische Theologie* 7 (1948): 263–266.

origin than did Jesus to his neighbors. For John the offense and possibility of faith is the same in both cases—it is for this reason that "bread" was the metaphor of the initial saying. The act of faith "in" the Revealer—whose Johannine explication we have rehearsed[21]—is for later believers the taking and eating of the Eucharistic elements as saving revelation, in defiance of their earthly appearance. The promise embodied by them is: "You do hear and see God's Word, hiddenly."

Of the promises in the institution narrative itself, a first set evokes the eschatological, Spirit-established reality of the Eucharist. "I will never again drink of the fruit of the vine until that day when I drink it new in the Kingdom of God."[22] "I have eagerly desired to eat this Passover with you . . . for I tell you, I will not eat it again until it is fulfilled in the kingdom of God."[23] These texts display the eschatological joy of the primal church's meals[24] and give the narrative content of the cry that is the core of all Christian worship, *Maranatha*, "Come Lord."[25] When the Eucharist is celebrated, Christ's promises of the Kingdom and of his presence in it are in fact fulfilled: even though the Kingdom is still future so long as we are not risen, each celebration is already a wedding feast.

Anticipation, we may say, is visible prophecy; so in the Eucharist we come together to live the Kingdom's fellowship beforehand. But our coming together, however faithful and pious, does not locate us at the gate of heaven, unless God puts us there. That he does is the content of faith that has the Supper itself as the external object to which it clings. That is, it is the content of faith in those other promises: "This bread is my body. This cup is my blood of the new covenant."

Before we can directly approach these words, however, we must return to the mandated rite itself, at slightly greater length and in a particular connection. For "This is my body" and similar promises in the narrative of institution do not in the New Testament appear as mere propositions to be explicated and justified, as they have too often been taken. They appear with a specific function; they interpret the mandated rite.

This rite is a sacrifice of thanksgiving, made with words embodied as the bread and cup. It must be the initial rule of teaching about the Eucharist: when the prescribed action[26] is not in fact carried out, there is nothing for the promise to be about. When thanksgiving is not offered to the Father for his saving acts, and therein specifically for Jesus, or when this thanksgiving is not embodied in the ritual presenting and sharing of bread and cup, nothing happens about which "This is my body and blood" could be true.

---

21. Pp. 68–72.
22. Mark 14:25par.
23. Luke 22:15–16. See J. B. Higgins, *The Lord's Supper in the New Testament* (London: SCM, 1952), 41–44.
24. Acts 2:46.
25. I Corinthians 16:23; Didache, x.6.
26. That the promises are about an *action* is ecumenical teaching. So the standard Lutheran dogmatician, Johann Gerhard, *Loci theologici* (1657), xviii.24: "Sacramenta nos ponimus in praedicamento actionis." The only arguable question is: What is this action?

The Eucharist has been the subject of more controversy—at least within the Western church—than has any other fact of the church's life. And much of that controversy has centered around the Eucharist's character as sacrifice, particularly in the aftermath of the Reformation.

One might have thought the matter obvious: phenomenologically, a "sacrifice" is a prayer made not only with language but also with objects, and the Eucharist mandated by the narrative of institution is plainly just that. But the objects here in question are the bread and cup, which the same narrative of institution says are the body and blood of Christ. It follows that if the Eucharist is a sacrifice, what we here offer is Christ himself, and moreover as he is body and blood "given and shed" for us, that is, as he is sacrificed. But Christ was sacrificed on the cross "once for all." It seems we must ask: Can Christ's sacrifice be *repeated* or *supplemented?*

The problem of course is that if the Eucharist is in any sense a *repetition* of the sacrifice on the cross, it is a sacrifice insofar distinguishable from the sacrifice of the cross. And then, if there is to be any point in making this other sacrifice, it must somehow be supposed to supplement or add to the sacrifice on the cross. But this last no one wishes to claim.

In the dialogues, Catholic representatives have regularly agreed that at the time of the Reformation there were "misunderstandings . . . in popular piety and theories of the mass in theology," which indeed thought of the sacrifice of the mass in this way.[27] Over against such phenomena, the Reformation rightly insisted that the mass is *not* a repetition of Calvary and adds nothing to it. But to sustain that answer most of the Reformation thought it had to deny altogether that the mass is a sacrifice of Christ.

From the other side, Catholics at the time of the Reformation, and definitively at the Council of Trent, were rightly determined above all to maintain the hitherto universal recognition that the Eucharist is indeed a sacrifice and that Christ is its content.[28] They acknowledged the "abuses" of which the Protestants complained[29] but found no way to say simultaneously and with conceptual clarity that the sacrifice of the mass is a real sacrifice, that Christ is there sacrificed, and that Christ's past sacrifice is not repeated or added to. According to Trent, Christ at the Last Supper "left" to his church a sacrifice by which the sacrifice done on the cross should be "represented."[30] In the church's sacrifice "the same

27. The citation is from the statement by the Catholic members of the Arbeitsgruppe der deutschen Bischofskonferenz und der Kirchenleitung der Vereinigten Evangelisch-lutherischen Kirche Deutschlands, in *Kirchengemeinschaft in Wort und Sakrament* (Paderborn: Bonifatius, 1984), 42–43.

28. Session 22, *Doctrina et Canones de sanctissimo missae sacrificio*, 1: "If anyone says that a sacrifice, in the true and proper sense of the word, is not offered to God, . . . let him be anathema."

29. To this, Ökumenischer Arbeitskreis evangelischer und katholischer Theologen, "Das Opfer Jesu Christi und der Kirche: abschliessender Bericht," *Das Oper Jesu Christi und seine Gegenwart in der Kirche*, ed. Kalr Lehmann, Edmund Schlink (Freiburg: Herder, 1983), 3.3.1–4.3.

30. Sessio 22, *Doctrina et canones*, ch. 1.

Christ is . . . immolated without the shedding of blood, who on the cross offered himself once and bloodily."[31] But what exactly does this mean?[32]

The most decisive of the Catholic-Protestant dialogues was established by the Catholic and Evangelical German bishops to review the mutual condemnations of the sixteenth century. This group devoted a separate study to the controversy about eucharistic sacrifice.[33] They concluded that at the time of the Reformation both sides were hindered by a shared lack: of properly "sacramental" concepts, that is, of concepts by which to grasp the specific ontological character of the eucharistic sacrifice in its identity with and distinction from the one sacrifice on the cross. The passage "Do this for my remembrance"[34] contains, they found, the needed concept, but at the time of the Reformation neither party was able to understand remembrance as anything more than subjective recollection nor then representation otherwise than as either mere symbolic pointing or repetition.[35] Thus Protestants thought they could preserve the uniqueness of the cross only by denying eucharistic sacrifice, and Catholics thought they could affirm eucharistic sacrifice only by positing some, however minimal, distinct identifications of eucharistic sacrifice and of the one sacrifice of the cross.[36]

We will return to a constructive interpretation of the Eucharist as anamnetic sacrifice. At this point, our concern is the liturgical consequences of the mutual denials. For the controversy has not been conducted only with teaching *about* the Eucharist.

Protestants have tried by liturgical truncations to make it impossible to experience the Eucharist as sacrifice by removing those parts of the traditional rite that are plainly directed to God; often in the process they have in fact obliterated the biblically mandated rite. A ceremony consisting of recitation of the narrative of institution and distribution of bread and wine[37] is not the rite about which the narrative of institution says "This is my body. This is my blood." Insofar as such ceremonies have been perpetrated, we can only say they should not have been, leaving unanswered the question of what their communicants have communed in. For much of Protestantism, "We will not commit the sacrifice of the mass" has in practice meant "We will not obey the Eucharist's institution."

Conversely, between the council of Trent and the second Vatican Council, Roman Catholicism sometimes seemed bent on proving that it did indeed commit "the abomination of the mass-sacrifice." If we ask what Martin Luther and

---

31. Ibid., ch. 2.
32. Were "representation" an ontological category.
33. Ökumensicher Arbeitskreis, *Das Opfer Jesu Christi.*
34. *Anamnesin.*
35. *Das Opfer Jesu Christi.*
36. Ibid., 3.3.1–4.3.
37. It must be noted that the theological justification for this reduction was provided by the thoroughly medieval Council of Florence (1439–1443) in its Decree for the Armenians: "*Forma huius sacramenti sunt verba Salvatoris: . . . sacerdos enim in persona Christi loquens hoc confecit sacramentum.*"

others meant operationally by such phrases,[38] we find that Luther himself adduced just three things.

First is the particular text of the old Roman canon, which indeed seems to speak of the sacrifice to be offered as an event distinct both from the sacrifice of the cross and from the offering of thanksgiving. Second are private masses, which in the late middle ages provided the dominant paradigm for popular understanding of the mass. Where there is no shared eating and drinking, the bread and cup are robbed of their character as embodiments of meal-thanksgiving, and their offering cannot then be the mandated action. Thus free-floating, the offering can indeed easily be preempted by our self-directed effort to placate God. Third is the inaudible recitation of the narrative of institution. In the Western liturgy, the narrative of institution had become the one place where the promises embodied by the elements were spoken. When it was silenced, so were the promises, again leaving the sacrifice to be our self-chosen work. Precisely these features of medieval practice were aggressively emphasized in post-Tridentine Catholic practice.

On the supposition that the mandated rite *is* enacted, what is promised about it? We may begin with the Pauline "This cup is the new covenant in my blood."[39] Any cup shared in meal-thanksgiving, or a loving-cup in many other contexts, is in itself a "covenant." What is specific here is that this cup is the "new covenant" of Jeremiah[40] and that the blood in which this covenant is sacrificially sealed[41] is shed by Jesus. The promise that "comes" to the cup is therefore Israel's entire eschatological hope, as it is now sealed by Jesus' sacrifice.

Since Paul's word for the cup is thus independently meaningful, "This is my body which is for you" must in his text also be read for itself, and "body" must therefore be taken in its usual Pauline sense.[42] The bread is Jesus' availability to those gathered, for them to see, touch, address, and even finally take into themselves. The phrase "for you" is again sacrificial language: Jesus is here thus available as his sacrificed self.

Mark's and Matthew's versions of the institution narrative reflect a later liturgical form than does Paul's and perhaps Luke's. The ceremonial courses of bread and cup have come to be eaten together, whether after a meal for nourishment or altogether without one, so that the word for the bread and the word for the cup are now paired. The pair for "body" is "blood," already present in the earlier form; thus now we have "This is my body. This is my blood." The promise

38. To the following with documentation, Robert W. Jenson, "The Supper," *Christian Dogmatics*, ed. Carl E. Braaten, Robert W. Jenson (Philadelphia: Fortress, 1984), 2:352–354.

39. To this, Oswald Bayer, "Tod Gottes und Herrenmahl," *Zeitschrift für Theologie und Kirche* 70 (1973): 35–38.

40. Jeremiah 31.

41. See Ferdinand Hahn, "Die alttestamentlichen Motive in der urchristlichen Abendmahlsüberlieferung," *Evangelische Theologie* 27 (1967):358–373.

42. To this and the immediately following, Robert W. Jenson, *Visible Words* (Philadelphia: Fortress, 1978), 80–83.

of the new covenant is moved to a subordinate clause. "Body" and "blood" therefore here say together what in Paul's version "body" said by itself.

If now we look back over all the New Testament's promises about the Eucharist, we will see that together they promise the reality and life of the church herself, as we have been describing it. And just this recognition has been Orthodoxy's constant concern in the dialogues. The chief East-West dialogue can say: "When the Church celebrates the Eucharist it becomes itself, realizing that which it is—the Body of Christ. . . . [T]he Eucharist creates the Church, since it is in the Eucharist that the Holy Spirit makes the Church the Body of Christ."[43] The teaching is in fact traditional and ecumenical also in the West. Thomas Aquinas defined the blessing accomplished in the mass as "the mystical body" of Christ;[44] and Martin Luther defined it as "the universal fellowship of saints," which "consists in this, that all the spiritual possessions of Christ and his saints are shared."[45]

What then does "This is my body" say about the Eucharist that we have not found true about the entire embodied life of the church, of which it can also be said that it is Christ's body? Recognizing that every linguistic translation of a sacramental sign must be a distortion, we may propose the following. The Eucharist promises: *there is* my body in the world, and you here eating and drinking commune in it. It promises: *there is* the actual historical church, and you are she. That the risen Christ is not present merely "spiritually" is itself a vital promise of the gospel, and the one made specifically by the bread and cup.

IV

A body that is a polity is a communion. Only as a *shared* body could a body be a plurality and so perhaps a polity. Or conversely: a polity that is also a personal body must be a communion. Only as its justice is constituted by participation in one person's justice, could a polity be someone's body. These relations are of course not established by a priori linguistic argument; it was in their context that the language of *koinonia*, "communion," entered the church's specific discourse in the first place, in those same passages of Corinthians that have dominated our discussion.

The biblical understanding of founding *koinonia* with Christ and founded *koinonia* with one another has been preserved in the theological tradition. Thomas Aquinas, having defined the *res* of the Eucharist as the mystical body of Christ, continues that we are nourished in this body "through union with Christ and with his members."[46] And to point the ecumenicity of such insight, we may cite a chief theological architect of Lutheran separation from Rome:

43. Archbishop Kirill of Smolensk, "The Significance and Status of Baptism, Eucharist and Ministry in the Ec. Move.," *Orthodox Perspectives on Baptism, Eucharist and Ministry*, ed. G. Limouris, N. M. Vaporis (Brookline: Holy Cross Orthodox Press, 1985), 86–87.

44. *Summa theologiae*, iii.73.1; 79.4.

45. *The Blessed Sacrament of the Holy and True Body of Christ*, WA 2:743.

46. *Summa theologiae*, iii.73.1; 79.5.

> In the Supper . . . we all receive one and the same Body of Christ. . . .
> And because in this way the members of the church are joined together
> to one Body of Christ, they are also joined with one another and become
> one Body whose head is Christ. So also, when in the Supper we receive
> the body of blood of Christ, we are intimately joined with Christ him-
> self . . . and through Christ we are united to the Father. . . . Thus we are
> made fellows (*koinonoi*) with the Father, the Son and the Holy Spirit.
> All these result from the . . . communion (*koinonia*) of the body and
> blood of the Lord.[47]

Ecumenical *communio*-ecclesiology explicitly so called is a specific and systematic recollection and exploitation of these biblical and traditional themes.[48]
It has been authoritatively called the "heart"[49] of the second Vatican Council's
work on the church.[50] It has been developed and then presupposed in the dialogues,[51] under decisive encouragement from Orthodoxy.[52] Indeed it has become
modern ecumenism's chief theological achievement, to which the present work
hopes only to contribute a few items.

The communion-ecclesiology may be said to comprise three parts: a doctrine of the church's being, a doctrine of the church's proper structure, and a
doctrine of the church's essential office. We will consider the first two here and
the third in the next chapter.

The *communio*-doctrine of the church's being is in part christological and
eucharistic, and insofar is already before us. So, for example: "*Koinonia* with one
another is entailed by our *koinonia* with God in Christ. This is the mystery of the
church."[53] We will here note only one further matter in this connection, a logical
twist not generally noticed, perhaps also not by the dialogue just quoted.

It will not do merely to say that the communion of believers with one another is constituted by the fact of shared communion with Christ. For the body
of Christ received in the Eucharist is, according to our recurring passages from

---

47. Martin Chemnitz, *Fundamenta sanae doctrinae de vera et substantiali praesentia . . . corporis
et sanguinis Domini in Coena*, ix.

48. The compendious systematic presentation of this teaching in its standard form is by
J.-M. R. Tillard, *Église d'Églises* (Paris: Cerf, 1987). But the enormous and founding contribution of Yves Congar, whose work I cannot pretend sufficiently to have studied, must at least be
acknowledged.

49. Joseph Cardinal Ratzinger, "Die Ekklesiologie des Zweiten Vatikanums," *Communio* 15
(1986): 44: the communio-ecclesiology "became the actual heart of the second Vaticanum's teaching about the church."

50. In *Lumen gentium*, see 4, 8, 13, 18, 21, 24–25.

51. A typical statement can be that of Anglican–Roman Catholic International Commission,
The Final Report (Windsor, 1982), introduction, no. 4: "Fundamental to all our statements is the
concept of *koinonia*."

52. Here I must note the extraordinary influence, in the otherwise most various ecclesial quarters, of one book; John D. Zizioulas, *Being as Communion: Studies in Personhood and the Church*
(Crestwood: St. Vladimir's Seminary Press, 1985).

53. Anglican–Roman Catholic International Commission, *Final Report*, introduction, no. 5.

Corinthians, itself identical with the community it creates. Moreover, the shared food and passed-around loving-cup are antecedently means of human fellowship, with or without the New Testament's special promises about them, and just as such are the elements to which these promises "come."

Thus it is not merely that we all have the same communion with Christ and so have this much in common with one another;[54] the church is not a plurality of persons held together by common commitment, like a club or an interest group, not even when the commitment is to Christ.[55] *We* do not create our communion, moved by our—in itself very real—affinity. We receive one another with Christ and Christ with one another; we at once receive Christ and the church in which we receive him. That is, at Eucharist, we are precisely "coembodiments" of Christ.

What is, however, most characteristic of the communion-ecclesiology and makes it so fully integral to this work is its *trinitarian* understanding of the church's communion. Thus the dialogues commonly characterize churchly communion by such phrases as "rooted in the Triune God"[56] or "created in the image and likeness of the Triune God" or "lived in personal fellowship with the Triune God."[57] With dogmatic stringency: the "unity in love of plural persons . . . constitutes the . . . trinitarian *koinonia*, which is communicated to humans in the church."[58]

The church, we have said, exists as anticipation. What she anticipates is inclusion in the triune communion. In the End, the *koinonia* that the risen Christ and his Father now live in their Spirit will become the mutual love in which believers will limitlessly find one another. The church exists to become that fellowship; the church's own communal Spirit is sheer *arrabon* of that Community.

Thus the church's present reality anticipates, in all brokenness and fallibility, the end of all things, exactly as the end is the Trinity's embrace of "all in all." We may say: the communion that is now the church is itself constituted by an event of communion or participation, with the communion that is the Trinity. It is this last twist that locates the church at the gate of heaven.

We may again note the biblical scene in which some of the fathers most distinctly perceived God as Trinity,[59] the Baptism of Jesus:[60] the Father speaks love to the Son, the Son submits to the Father, and the Spirit appears as the hypo-

---

54. It seems to me that the doctrine developed just at this point by Wolfhart Pannenberg, *Systematische Theologie* (Göttingen: Vandenhoeck & Ruprecht, 1993), 3:115–130, displays this error and is in fact subtly sectarian.

55. It was in large part the perception that many enthusiasts for "Vatican II" were coming to see the church just in this way that led to the document from the Congregation for the Doctrine of the Faith, *Letter to the Bishops of the Catholic Church on Some Aspects of the Church Understood as Communion.* See. esp. no. 11.

56. Ibid., 3.

57. Gemeinsame römisch-katholische evangelisch-lutherische Kommission, *Wege zur Gemeinschaft: Alle unter einem Christus* (Paderborn: Bonifacius, 1980), 44–46.

58. International Roman Catholic-Orthodox dialogue, *Le mystère de l'église et de l'eucharistie à la lumiére du mystère de la Sainte Trinité* [the "Munich Document"] (1982), ii.2.

59. E.g., Tertullian, *Adversus Praxean,* xi.9–10.

60. Matthew 3:13–17.

static gift of their communication. Here personal discourse and meeting between Father and Son and Spirit, and their unity in action and being, are equally manifest. And then we should note how Matthew[61] directs the Father's word of love for the Son also to those who are summoned to hear the Son, that is, how the loving converse of the Trinity opens to include the Son's disciples.

We may close these considerations by citing the passages of Scripture that are the implicit texts of all this work's ecclesiology. The "elder John" wrote to his churches: "We declare to you what we have seen and heard so that you also may have fellowship [*koinonia*] with us; and truly our fellowship [*koinonia*] is with the Father and with his Son Jesus Christ."[62] And whether the Evangelist was the same John or not, he records Jesus as saying: "As you, Father, are in me and I am in you, may they also be in us. . . . [May they] be one, as we are one" (John 17:21–22). As we have noted before, the Johannine discourses must be interpreted either as blasphemy or as the inner converse of the Trinity apocalyptically opened to our overhearing.

V

We turn to the *communio*-doctrine of the church's structure. In the previous chapter we discussed the church as a polity but did not discuss the organism of that polity; now we can. We may cite the late Cardinal Willebrands, a pioneer of Catholicism's modern ecumenical effort: "The church becomes a sacrament of the trinitarian *koinonia*. She finds her origin, her model, and her goal in the triune mystery. It is from this insight of faith that we may plumb the secret of 'one in many' for the relation of local churches to each other and so to the universal church."[63] The great principle of the church's polity, according to the insight we are now developing, is that any level or organ of ecclesial actuality that can truly be called church must itself be constituted as communion and that these communions are in perichoretic communion with each other. This insight begins a doctrine of church polity drawn from the nature of the church herself, rather than by imitation of the worldly collectives around her.

Notoriously, *ekklesia* in the New Testament—and notably in I Corinthians itself—can denote a local fellowship, or all such fellowships as a class, or all such fellowships as one great fellowship.[64] If each of these is a communion, then it must follow, as Orthodox–Roman Catholic dialogue has stated: "Most profoundly, because the one and only God is the communion of three persons . . . the one

61. Mathew 3:13–17.
62. I John 1:3.
63. Joseph Cardinal Willebrands, "Die Bedeutung der Verhandlungen der römisch-katholischen Kirche mit den Orthodoxen Kirchen und der Anglikanischen Gemeinschaft für die Lehre von der sakramentalen Struktur der Kirche," *Die Sakramentalität der Kirche in der ökumenischen Diskussion*, 3rd ed., Johann-Adam-Möhler-Institut (Paderborn: Bonifacius, 1983), 17–18.
64. I Corinthians 1:2; 7:17; 12:28.

universal church is a communion of many communities and the local church a communion of persons."[65]

It is ecumenically muddled whether "the local church" in such formulations denotes the "diocese," that is, the internally complex metropolitan or regional congregation whose pastor is—in the ancient and ecumenical vocabulary—a "bishop," or denotes the "congregation" or "parish," that is, the geographically and structurally simpler assembly whose pastor is—in the only generally appropriate vocabulary—a "presbyter." We will return to this. In the more immediately following we will use circumlocutions to avoid confusion.

We should unpack this logic just a little, using our own warrants. Because the identities of the triune God are mutually one God, and because believers assemble with the Son before the Father and in their Spirit, these believers are one. And because their fellowship is thus founded in the one God, there can finally be only one such fellowship: one people and one body and one temple. But only at the end can this fellowship assemble face to face; in the church's interval, therefore, each local fellowship can know itself as the one church of God only by virtue of its fellowship with all those other fellowships who know themselves in the same way and with which it will at the End be identical. Or we may say: precisely this mutual recognition *is* the anticipation by which the church is what she is.

This aspect of *koinonia* was particularly determinative for the self-understanding of the most ancient church. The congregation whose prayers are recorded in the *Didache* summons her members to the local Eucharist "from the four corners of the earth."[66] That the local gathering is in its self-understanding thus identical with the one gathering of all must find expression in practiced fellowship; in the ancient church this was accomplished by the solemn and carefully granted exchange of communicants and celebrants between local fellowships and by the communion among themselves of the bishops who cared for these exchanges.

One powerful aspect of the communion ecclesiology is thus its insistence on the integrity and wholeness of local churches, that is, of continuing Eucharistic assemblies whose members are individual persons. So, again from the East: "Each local congregation, that celebrates Eucharist, is the one and entire church, as Christ on the altar is the one and entire Christ."[67] A local church is not a part of some larger entity, the universal church; in her place she simply is the church, just as Paul addresses the local churches.

If then besides the plurality of local churches, which are each the one church, this one church is herself a singular universal church, this too must be a communion, and indeed a "communion of many communities," established in Eu-

65. Joint Commission for Dialogue between the Roman Catholic Church and the Orthodox Church, *Le mystère de l'église et de l' eucharistie à la lumiére du mystère de la Sainte Trinité* [the "Munich Document"] (1982), iii.2.

66. X.5.

67. Georg Galitis, "Is the Dialogue Acceptable from an Ecclesiological Point of View?" *Les Dialogues Oecumeniques hier et Aujourd'hui*, ed. Centre Orthodoxe du Patriarahct Oecuménique (Chembésy: Centre Orthodox, 1985), 345.

charistic fellowship among them and in the fellowship of pastors, liturgies, and disciplines that sustain this. And if there are regional or disciplinary intermediate entities, the same rule applies. A slogan derived from *Lumen gentium* is now enshrined in ecumenical usage: the singular universal church, the *unica . . . ecclesia*, exists *in et ex ecclesiis*, "in and from" the plural churches[68]—whether these local churches are dioceses, as *Lumen gentium* itself had in mind, or smaller congregations or even perhaps regional or disciplinary entities. But just here a possible rupture of the communion ecclesiology's consensus appears.

If the one church is constituted "*in* and *from*" the local churches, is she also established *by* their fellowship with one another? Is it enough to say simply that each local congregation, because it celebrates Eucharist, "is the one and entire church" if one does not quickly say something else? There are formulations of communion ecclesiology that seem to say that "every particular church is a subject complete in itself, and that the universal church is the result of a reciprocal recognition on the part of the particular churches."[69] And indeed there is a remarkable sort of backhanded congregationalism in some Orthodox thinkers and their Western disciples: "Whenever the people of God are gathered together in a certain place . . . in order to form the Eucharistic body of Christ, the church *becomes* a reality. . . . The church, therefore, is *primarily* identified with the local Eucharistic community in each place [emphases added]."[70]

Such suggestions must be rejected. If believers do not create local communion by their affinity, then no more do local communions create by their comity the communion of whatever other levels are properly called church, whether the one universal church or regional or confessional churches. A saying chiastically paired to "the one church in and from the churches," *ecclesia in et ex ecclesiis*, suggests itself so clearly that it would hardly have needed a pope to provide it, though in fact one has: "the churches in and from the one church," *ecclesiae in et ex ecclesiae*.[71]

If the one church is constituted in and from the local churches, the local churches are constituted in and from the one church. The catholic church is indeed a communion of local churches. But the trinitarian-perichoretic dialectic of *koinonia* demands another flip: the local churches are churches at all only as they participate in the one catholic church. The one church that each local church *is* in its place just so cannot be simply the aggregate or creation of the local churches. Thus in the complete proposition of *Lumen gentium* from which the first slogan is derived, the local churches are antecedently described as "formed to the image of the universal church."[72]

---

68. The actual text of *Lumen gentium*, 23, is: "ecclesiis particularibus, . . . in quibus et ex quibus una et unica ecclesia catholica exsistit."

69. Congregation for the Faith, *On Some Aspects*, no. 8; disapproval of this position is a second motive of the document.

70. "The Ecumenical Nature of the Orthodox Witness" [the "New Valamo Statement"] (1977), *Apostolic Faith Today*, ed. H.-G. Link (Geneva: WCC, 1985), 176.

71. John Paul II, *Address to the Roman Curia*, December 20, 1990, no. 9, cited to this purpose by the Congregation for the Faith, *On Some Aspects*, 9.

72. *Lumen gentium*, 23: "ad imaginem ecclesiae universalis formatis."

When the church was born in Jerusalem at Pentecost, she was at once singular and local. Nor can she have ceased to be singular when, with the incorporation of other local groups of Jesus' disciples and with the mission, she became locally plural. Short of the Kingdom, the one communion of God cannot meet as one body, and yet she is one body or she is nothing. Therefore the church's communion as the one universal church can now indeed consist only in the fellowship between local churches and the means of that fellowship, but it was and is not created *by* the local churches or their mutual arrangements.

Perhaps we may make the point most simply by asking: Who is the pastor of an individual believer? The presbyter of her or his congregation that assembles every Sunday? Or the bishop of the more comprehensively local church? Or the primate of a regional or confessional church? Or the holder of a universal pastorate? And by answering: that depends entirely on the context in which the question is asked. Each of them is this believer's pastor, yet nor are believers shepherded by a committee. Each pastorate, we may say, penetrates the others.

VI

Our discussion of the church as communion has so far been cast mostly in christological concepts, as the ecumenical discussion has been. To end at this point would, however, be highly misleading. For the communion of the church is a communion animated by the Spirit and having its object in the Father.

We have already said nearly all of what must be said about the Spirit's role in the triune communion and in the thereby enabled communion of the church. The Spirit is the freedom by which the triune identities are a communion; just so the Spirit is the common Spirit in which the church is communion. And that "the divine life, which the Spirit bestows, is that of a community of persons," so that therefore the Eucharist's gift is personal community,[73] should also be plain from earlier discussion. But the centrality of the Eucharist for our understanding of the church as communion requires us to note one further point.

As at every step of the ecclesiological way, Orthodoxy insists on the agency of the Spirit also with respect to eucharistic communion. So a typical response to *Baptism, Eucharist and Ministry*: "In the Eucharistic memorial 'Christ himself with all he has accomplished for us . . . is present . . . granting us communion with himself.' . . . [T]his important part of the text . . . should speak explicitly about the action of the Holy Spirit and state clearly that *anamnesis is essentially inseparable from epiclesis.* The Holy Spirit in the Eucharist actualizes that which Christ has performed."[74] Or again: "The Triune God . . . becomes . . . one with us, one body. This oneness is seen during the Epiclesis, the Eucharist being the climax of such communion."[75]

73. Johannes Mabey, "Das Charisma des apostolischen Amtes im Denken und Beten der Ostkirchen," *Catholica* 27:285.

74. Archbishop Kirill, "Significance and Status of BEM," 85.

75. Metropolitan Emilianos Timiadis, "God's Immutability and Communicability," *Theological Dialogue between Orthodox and Reformed Churches*, ed. T. F. Torrance (Edinburgh: Scottish Academic Press, 1985), 22.

The old East-West controversy about the "moment of consecration," in the eucharistic liturgy, whether it is the recitation of the narrative of institution or the explicit invocation of the Spirit at the Epiclesis, is in abeyance and we may hope will remain so. But Orthodoxy's insistence that there *be* the Epiclesis—as in many Protestant rites and in the old Roman canon there lamentably has not been—has vital content. For indeed also the elements and the community gathered around them must be freed from their merely historical reality if they are to be the body of the risen and coming One; just that, as we have seen at several points, is a role of the Spirit.

Finally, we must turn to the Father. As the church shares in the life of the triune identities, she shares in the relation of the Son and the Spirit to the Father. As the Son and the Spirit come forth from the Father, so their agency is toward the Father. Therefore the body of the Son and the temple of the Spirit is directed to the Father. We must yet again cite I Corinthians: "Then comes the end, when he delivers the kingdom to God the Father."[76] The great goal of our *koinonia*, for which the Son works and to which the Spirit draws us, is the Father's Kingdom.

The church as she is determined by the Father's triune role is above all a *koinonia* of prayer. The church gathers with the Son and in the Spirit to petition and adore the Father. As the christological and pneumatological center of the church's *koinonia* is the Eucharist, so the central act of the church at Eucharist is the great prayer of thanksgiving, or *Anaphora* or "canon," in which the church recites and glorifies the saving actions which the Father has performed in the Son by the Spirit and in which she gives her praises the explicit form of the triune relations, as Praise, *Anamnesis*, and *Epiclesis*.

It is on this pattern that the church lives in the world. If the church's christological and pneumatological realities can be comprehended as her mission, so the church's specific direction to the Father is her *intercession*. Agitated by the Spirit and implicated, as the Son's created body, with all creation as it is made through and for the Son, the church's petition and praise represent before the Father the petition and praise of all creation.

That is to say, the church's vocation before the Father is *priestly,* and her service before him *sacrificial.* At Eucharist and throughout her life, the church offers petition and praise, with the Son and in the Spirit, to the Father. "When you pray," our Lord taught us, "pray so: Our Father . . ." It belongs to our obedience that we make intercession also for those who cannot so address him, with words and with the eucharistic embodiment of words.

---

76. I Corinthians 15:24.

TWENTY-SEVEN

The Office of Communion

I

As theology has turned its intention to the church, it has necessarily turned its attention to the church's specific office. And since the status and structure of ecclesial office have provided the occasion or justification of much division in the church, the dialogues have necessarily devoted much time to them. Within the communion ecclesiology, an ecumenical doctrine of office has developed.

Since no later than the writing of the Pastoral Epistles,[1] there have been officers in the church who were initiated by a rite of prophetic address and the laying on of hands. So Timothy is exhorted: "Do not neglect the charism that is in you, which was given to you by Spirit-filled utterance with the laying on of hands by the council of elders."[2] Again: "I remind you to rekindle the charism of God that is within you through the laying on of my hands."[3] It is the rite here adduced that has historically come to be called ordination, whatever other rites in the church could have been so labelled. So also the office therewith bestowed is the one conventionally called "ordained ministry," again whatever other ministries in the church may be said to have been ordained by God. It is this rite and this office that are the matter of this chapter.

---

1. To the Pastorals and ordination as it appears in them, Herman von Lips, *Glaube-Gemeinde-Amt* (Göttingen: Vandenhoeck & Ruprecht, 1979).

2. I Timothy 4:14.

3. II Timothy 1:6. I have altered the New Revised Standard Version translation of these passages to make their import for our concern clearer. "Charism" has become an English word. And "prophecy," while literal, is too specific in this passage. Other references to this rite are I Timothy 1:18; 5:22; II Timothy 1:13; 2:1–2; Titus 1:5.

The congregations to which the Pastoral Epistles were addressed had a definite official structure, though its precise form is hard to discern.[4] We read of "bishops," "presbyters," "deacons," and "widows"; it is evidently bishops and presbyters who were initiated by the rite in question. The two *terms* probably derived from different modes of leadership in different parts of the primal church.[5] Bishops undoubtedly had been in some sense what the title suggests, "overseers," while elders made a spiritual council of some sort, as can be seen from the first text just cited. Whether bishops and presbyters were now in these congregations always or sometimes the same or different persons is obscure.

Bishops and presbyters were, as appears in our texts, initiated by a word of the Spirit embodied in the gesture of laying on of hands, in a public ceremony. The rite, Timothy is told, bestowed a "charism." We are familiar with charisms from Paul's letters, but here they appear much modified. Initially, at least in Paul's congregations, charisms were particular manifestations of the Spirit's actuality in the church, which were differentiated and granted solely by the unpredictable choice of the Spirit; possession of a charism was certified by the sheer occurrence of the activity or, in cases of conflict, by a further charism of testing. In the Pastorals a charism is again a specific manifestation of the Spirit and determines the churchly role of the recipient, but the charism in question is bestowed by a fixed communal ritual, which even has legal force.[6] As in the earlier situation, a charism is the unity of a specific authority in the congregation and a specific ability to serve the congregation, but here these constitute a regular office.[7]

The content of the office is partly explicit in the letters: its holders are to care for the identity of the church's teaching with that of the apostles.[8] This responsibility necessarily includes care for the choice and legitimacy of their own successors in office.[9] We may say that the charism of bishop or presbyter is insofar a charism of diachronic concord with the apostles. If we now consider that the title "bishop," with its Old Testament background and its other New Testament uses, suggests one who shepherds a flock and disciplines its members,[10] who holds it together against external threats and inner centrifugal forces, we obtain this description: the concern of one of the Pastoral Epistles' bishops or presbyters[11] is the unity, both synchronic and diachronic, of the community. The charge of these bishops and presbyters is the church precisely as communion.

---

4. A good brief account of this and the following history through the emergence of the monarchical episcopate is provided by Reginald H. Fuller, "The Development of the Ministry," Lutheran-Episcopal Dialogue, *A Progress Report* (FM Maxi Book, 1972), 76–93.

5. Briefly and compendiously, Klaus Berger, "Episkopat, . . . Biblische Grundlegung," *Sacramentum Mundi*, ed. Karl Rahner, Adolf Darlap (Freiburg: Herder, 1967), 1:1073–1077.

6. Von Lips, *Glaube-Gemeinde-Amt*, 240–265.

7. Ibid., 184–223.

8. Ibid., 106–161.

9. E.g., I Timothy 3:1–8.

10. Berger, "Episkopat," 1074.

11. "Presbyter" makes no specific such suggestion.

If the Lord's delay did not refute the Lord's promises, if the church was to continue beyond the apostolic generation, such an office, particularly in its diachronic dimension, was the one strictly necessary office. It is of course a historical contingency that the office that emerged to meet this need was constituted in an adaptation of the Pauline congregations' charisms and bestowed by the particular ritual described. Moreover, the appearance of these things in the Pastorals includes no "Do this" directed beyond the letters' recipients. The effective institution of ordination and of the office granted by it is therefore the subsequent choice of the church to take the exhortations of the Pastoral Epistles as directed to her own ordained ministry, as this had continued to develop on the lines that there appeared.

Has such an institution dogmatic status? The question is at the heart of considerable ecumenical difficulty. Granted that most of the church has for most of her history had this office, is it constitutive of the church under, let us say, "the same rubric as are the word and the sacraments?"[12] The question becomes most acute when we consider episcopacy as a specific form of this office, and we will leave it for then.

Is ordination "a sacrament"? We have said that little depends on use of the indefinite article. But the question has of course been divisive in the church, and we may here rejoin the dialogues. Considerable reluctance and confusion remain,[13] but the more developed dialogues have recognized that what is described by the Pastorals is just what is usually meant by a sacrament. Here as at many points, the leader was the unofficial Catholic-Protestant Groupe des Dombes: "The ministry of the word and sacraments is not reducible to ecclesial . . . organization; it is a gift of the Spirit and is signified and realized by a sacramental act of ordination."[14] In dependence on the Groupe des Dombes, the international Catholic-Lutheran dialogue could say: "Through the laying on of hands and through prayer . . . the gift of the Holy Spirit is offered and *conveyed* [emphasis added] for the exercise of ministry."[15]

II

From this point we may follow the path of the dialogues, particularly the main multilateral dialogue.[16] The starting point is the Pastoral Epistles' teaching: ordained ministers are distinguished as those who "have received a [particular]

---

12. André Birmelé, *Le salut on Jésus Christ dans les dialogues oecuméniques* (Paris: Cerf, 1986), 194.

13. For the dreary details, Robert W. Jenson, *Unbaptized God: The Basic Flaw in Ecumenical Theology* (Minneapolis: Fortress, 1992), 48–50.

14. Groupe des Dombes, *L'Esprit Saint, l'Église et les Sacraments* (1970), 79.

15. International Lutheran–Roman Catholic Dialogue, *The Ministry in the Church*, 32.

16. Faith and Order, *Baptism, Eucharist and Ministry* (Geneva: World Council of Churches, 1982), i.5.

charism."[17] *Baptism, Eucharist and Ministry* is more reluctant than some bilateral dialogues to say in so many words that the charism is *bestowed* by ordination, that is, that ordination is sacramental, but it does say so in substance:[18] "Ordination is a sign performed in faith that the spiritual relationship signified is present in, with and through the words spoken, the gestures made and the forms employed."[19]

The charism is essentially *pastoral.* Persons are ordained "to provide . . . within a multiplicity of gifts, a focus of unity."[20] They "assemble and guide the dispersed people of God."[21] And since, in line with the communion-ecclesiology, the church is one in that she is one with Christ, the ordained are primally "representatives of Jesus Christ to the community," whose office points to the church's "fundamental dependence on Jesus Christ."[22]

Since the church *is* communion, the office that cares for her unity must be "*constitutive* for the life . . . of the church [emphasis added],"[23] even though it would not a priori have been necessary that the existent office in all its determinants be this constitutive office. Here is an ecumenically groundbreaking consensus.

Baptism, Eucharist and Ministry displays a necessary caution in formulating the new consensus: what is constitutive is the ministry of "persons who are . . . responsible for pointing to [the church's] fundamental dependence on Jesus Christ" and who "thereby provide . . . a focus of its unity" and who "*since very early times have been* ordained [emphasis added]."[24] For the rite we see in the Pastorals was evidently not practiced in all apostolic churches,[25] yet these churches were surely fully constituted. The question then is of course whether the constitutive pastoral functions, once historically vested in ministry granted by this rite, must always be vested there. A third time we will postpone the discussion.

17. Ibid., 7.

18. The Roman Secretariat for the Promotion of Christian Unity and the Congregation for the Faith, making the official Catholic response to *Baptism, Eucharist and Ministry,* were understandably urgent for less evasive language, but finally judge that "the essentials of a sacramental understanding can be recognized in the broad treatment . . . in this text;" *Churches Respond to BEM,* ed. Max Thurian (Geneva: World Council of Churches, 1988), 4:34.

19. Ibid., 43.

20. Ibid., 8.

21. Ibid., 11.

22. Ibid., 11. Again the Groupe des Dombes, *Pour une réconciliation des ministères* (1972), 20–21, has led the way: "The property of the pastoral ministry is to assure and signify the dependence of the church over against Christ, who is the source of its mission and the basis of its unity. . . . [The ordained minister's] functions mark . . . the priority of the divine initiative and authority, the continuity of the mission in the world, the bond of communion established by the Spirit between the many communities."

23. Ibid., 8.

24. Ibid.

25. Agreement to this by Roman Catholic, Orthodox, and Reformed representatives in "Ministry," *Baptism, Eucharist and Ministry,* 19, is an important item of ecumenical consensus: "The New Testament does not describe a single pattern of ministry which might serve as a blueprint or continuing norm for all future ministry in the church."

The charism described must burden its carriers with two functions above all. First, since the communion of the church is established in eucharistic communion with Christ, the one mandated in the Spirit to tend the congregation's communion and in it to represent Christ necessarily occupies the place in the eucharistic celebration from which this unity can be tended and where Christ is most clearly represented. That is, the host of the meal, the one who offers the thanksgiving and admits to communion by administering the loaf, must be ordained. This is generally recognized in the dialogues, if sometimes with a bit of softening: for example, "It is right that he who has oversight in the church and is the focus of its unity should preside at the celebration of the eucharist."[26]

Second, since the initiating necessity of the pastoral charism is for care of threatened diachronic consensus with the apostles' teaching, those gifted in the Spirit to tend the church's communion must have authority to say, "This is/is not the gospel." That is, what we earlier labeled the *magisterium* belongs to the pastoral charism; the ordained have the duty to say what is and is not to be taught in the church and the right to depend on the Spirit as they do so. "The pastors who are responsible for the well-being of the community have a special responsibility regarding its common confession of faith. When conflicts arise as to the terms of its creed . . . those with pastoral responsibility must have the authority to judge which of the conflicting opinions is in accord with the faith of the church."[27]

In substance, also this manifestation of the pastoral charism is widely recognized in the dialogues. So again the Groupe des Dombes: ordained ministers have "the authority which corresponds to their pastoral responsibility, to set forth through the faith of the church the sign of Christ's act."[28] But so soon as the *word magisterium* falls, Protestant consent often becomes shaky.[29] This undoubtedly results from the historical connection between the term and the episcopal mode of pastoral office. We are yet again at our postponed question.

Before we can turn to it, however, two further matters must be dealt with. First, there is a question surprisingly little raised in the dialogues: If the charism bestowed by ordination is pastoral authority and the presence of the Spirit in pastoral action, what distinguishes ordination from installation into a particular pastoral office? Why should not someone who has been in one pastoral office and is now to take a different one be ordained again? Or why should not someone who was a pastor but is now an accountant be regarded as a lay person—as indeed is the ideology,[30] if more rarely the practice, of some Protestant groups?

Insight here depends upon clear awareness of the one universal church and its reality. Persons are ordained to tend diachronic continuity of teaching with

---

26. Anglican–Roman Catholic International Commission, *Ministry and Ordination* (1973), 12.

27. Francis A. Sullivan, *Magisterium: Teaching Authority in the Catholic Church* (New York: Paulist Press, 1983), 30.

28. Groupe des Dombes, *L'Esprit Saint*, 108.

29. For samples, Jenson, *Unbaptized God*, 58–59.

30. So the North Elbian German Evangelical Church, in response to *Baptism, Eucharist and Ministry, Response of the Churches*, 1:50–51.

the one church of the apostles and to tend diachronic continuity of the future church with the one[31] church of their own time; and they are ordained to tend a synchronic communion that constitutes precisely the one body of Christ, a body that does not become plural by identification with local churches. Therefore ordination is not to a "local" entity as such, even when this is a regional or confessional church, but to the one universal church. But the one church will assemble only at the End and so has as such no location now of its own. Therefore ordination is, if we may put it so, portable from one pastoral location to another and is just so vested in the ordained person.

Second, there is a question that *is* agitated in the dialogues: Is *succession,* that is, the ordination of new pastors by those already ordained, really so essential to the office?[32] One would have thought the matter obvious: surely, as in the Pastoral Epistles, it is logically included in responsibility for the church's historically continuing consensus that those who bear it are responsible for their own successors. If this choice is concrete as an initiatory rite, then they must be the ministers of the rite.

That the succession is "apostolic" is tautologous, since its whole point is continuity with the church of the apostles. But there is an initial point to be made here, which is in fact general in the dialogues: the phrase "apostolic succession" should not be used only or indeed primally of the sheer chain of ordinations. For it refers in a "substantive sense to the apostolicity of the church in faith." And it is *this* apostolicity that must be "the starting point." "The basic intention of the doctrine of apostolic succession is . . . that . . . the church is at all times referred back to its apostolic origin."[33] So long as the church is the church, she has the same faith as the apostles, celebrates the same essential rites with them, and makes one fellowship with them and with all believers who have followed after them; so that Orthodox theology in enthusiastic moments can say, "The church is the place of truth's continuous incarnation."[34]

Within this substantive continuity of the church with the church of the apostles, succession in office is one essential factor. We may here reappropriate a position affirmed at the very beginning of this work: succession in office is the *personal* aspect of the church's institutionalized self-identity through time.[35] A personal aspect is essential because the continuity in question is personal communion and not mere legal perdurance or even agreement in formulated doctrine. Moreover, the church cannot "like worldly institutions . . . hand on in its own right that authority which is decisive for it as the church; . . . it can do this only in a spiritual, that is, sacramental way." With its practice of the rite of ordi-

---

31. Which is one precisely because of her unity with the one church of the apostles.

32. I will desist from following twists of ecumenical consent and dissent. See Jenson, *Unbaptized God*, 52–55, 71–75.

33. International Lutheran–Roman Catholic Dialogue, *Ministry in the Church*, 59–60.

34. Metropolitan Damaskinos of Tranoupolis, quoted from recorded discussions between the Evangelische Kirche im Deutschland and the Ecumenical Patriarchate, *Evangelium und Kirche*, ed. Kirchliches Aussenamt der Evangelischen Kirche im Deutschland (Frankfurt: Otto Lembeck, 1983), 97.

35. 1:41.

nation as its "form of granting office, the church expresses faith that she is a creature of the Holy Spirit, who forever continues to live by his gifts."[36]

The dialogues agree that the beginning of differentiated roles in the church was the apostolate.[37] The apostolate in its specifically defining function is unrepeatable.[38] But "In addition to their unique function in founding the church, the apostles also had a responsibility for building up and leading the first communities, a ministry that had to be continued. The New Testament shows how there emerged from among the ministries a special ministry which was understood as standing in the succession of the apostles." Indeed, it can be said that in the New Testament, the ministry "established by Jesus Christ through the calling and sending of the apostles" continues as the essential ministry of the church.[39]

We may conclude these considerations with the teaching of the second Vatican Council: "That divine mission, which was committed by Christ to the apostles, is destined to last until the end of the world . . . since the gospel, which they were charged to hand on, is for the church the principle of life for all time."[40] Just so there must always be pastors and just so they must pass on their office in succession.

III

There are local churches, each of them the church, and there is the one church which each of the local churches is. The church is *in et ex ecclesiis* and the churches are *in et ex ecclesiae*. If now it is established that the pastoral office is constitutive of the church, it follows that both the one church and the many must have pastors. It may be taken as a chief and necessary—though sometimes evaded—theorem of the communion-ecclesiology: at whatever level in a hierarchy of synchronic inclusion[41] we may speak of a church or churches, there must be a pastor or pastors specific to that communion.

The slogans of the communion-ecclesiology initially suggest just two levels: the many local churches and the one universal church. But it is plain that the principle is more flexible. If there are groupings between the local churches and the universal church, and if there is sufficient reason to call these churches, then these are in and from the local churches and the one church is in and from them. And at each of these levels there will then be appropriate pastors.

We may finally turn to the matter of "the episcopate," of the structure of office that "since very early times" and until the Reformation was universal in the

36. Joseph Cardinal Ratzinger, "Fragen zur Sukzession," *KNA-Kritischer Ökumenischer Informationsdient*, 28/29:5.

37. "Ministry," *Baptism, Eucharist and Ministry*, 11.

38. Ibid., 10.

39. International Lutheran–Roman Catholic Dialogue, *Ministry in the Church*, 17.

40. *Lumen gentium*, 20.

41. The scare-quotes are intended to direct readers to the following caution. The word "levels" is very likely to be misleading, but I have been unable to find a better for use in the following paragraphs. I must therefore like Humpty Dumpty decree: in the following, "levels" carries purely topographical and no hierarchical sense.

church. A first step in the history is the emergence and spread, very shortly after the time of the Pastoral Epistles, of the "monarchical episcopate" within "threefold ministry." These terms may suggest something more clear-cut than has ever actually existed, but there are indeed identifiable structures for which they can be our labels. The first clear literary appearance of the single bishop with his presbyters and deacons is in letters written by Ignatius of Antioch on his way to martyrdom; and these letters have established the permanent ideology and image of episcopacy.

The bishop is now definitely a single shepherd of the congregation and the presbyters a distinct college of spiritual leaders. The bishop's authority is God's own, and indeed it and the congregation's obedience to it participate in the triune life: "Let all obey the bishop as Christ Jesus obeys the Father." The bishop is the christological focus of the congregation's unity: "Where the bishop appears, there let the people be present, just as where Christ Jesus is there is the catholic church."[42] This unity is enacted specifically in the Eucharist: "Take care to have but one eucharist. For there is one flesh of our Lord . . . and one cup to unite us in his blood, and one altar; and just so there is one bishop, with the presbyterium and the deacons."[43]

The one great theme of Ignatius's vision of ecclesial order is *koinonia*, under a repertoire of images. So he writes to the Ephesians: "You must be of one mind with the bishop—as indeed you are, for your . . . presbyterium resonates with the bishop as do the strings with a lyre. Thereby, in spiritual unity and harmonious love, the praise of Jesus Christ is sung."[44] Ignatius's image has persisted through subsequent history: of the bishop ministering in the midst of the people, flanked by the college of presbyters and assisted by the deacons, the whole making a sort of choir. The bishop, says Ignatius, is as the Father, the presbyters are as the apostles, and the deacons in their humble serving are as Christ.[45] The unity thus created is mandatory: "Without the bishop, let no one perform any of the church's proper acts."[46]

The episcopate did not long remain quite as Ignatius envisioned.[47] Just how soon the presbyters became pastors of their own eucharistic assemblies does not matter for our purpose. So soon, anyway, as city dioceses came to encompass so many believers that only subsidiary presbyteral congregations could in fact function as eucharistic communions every Lord's Day, or as episcopal charges in thinly populated missionary territories embraced great regions with the same result, the "local" place of the bishop became ambiguous.

In what we now know as episcopal order, the bishop retains control, but only control, of the pastoral office's key functions: presbyters are ordained to celebrate

---

42. *To the Smyrneans*, vii.
43. *To the Philadelphians*, iv.1.
44. *To the Ephesians*, iv.1.
45. E.g., *To the Smyrneans*, vii; *To the Trallians*, iii.1.
46. *To the Smyrneans*, vii.
47. To the following in much greater detail, and particularly to the ecumenical problematic, Jenson, *Unbaptized God*, 61–75.

Eucharist but do so as the bishop's vicars, and in case of conflict between theo-logical judgments the bishop holds "the teaching office." It will be seen that the bishop's responsibility thus becomes in part what now is called management; and this will necessarily bring legalities and administrative structures with it. Churchly language speaks of "jurisdiction."

On the other hand, pastoral care for communion of communions, earlier given in and with eucharistic presidency and magisterial authority, now becomes more a function of its own and defines the bishop over against the presbyteral pastors. The bishop cares for the communion among themselves of the presbyteral congregations of the diocese, and he cares for the communion of the diocese with others, as the presbyters cannot. Indeed, quite early in the church's history the episcopate came to be seen as a single collegiate entity, whose unity is constitu-tive of the unity of the church.[48] And one function of the Pastoral Epistles' office is now necessarily the bishop's alone: ordination of successors in churchly office.

Two questions immediately pose themselves. First, which is now the "local" church, the presbyteral congregation or the diocese? Or in the other direction it might be asked: Since, for example, the autocephalous Church of England is a particular church, can it be thought of under the rubric of "local" church? In one way it does not matter what usage is adopted, so long as different terminologies are not allowed to generate ecumenical cross purposes. With the division of Ignatius's ideal episcopal-presbyteral assembly, there are in any case three or four levels of church: presbyteral congregations, episcopal "dioceses," perhaps inter-mediate jurisdictions, and the one church—and approximations of at least the first three levels appear under some title in almost all confessional groups, how-ever otherwise alienated from the historic ministerial succession. But there is good reason to treat the diocese as the local church, which is provided by the answer to the second question.

This question is: Do presbyters and bishops now hold one office or two dif-ferent offices? The matter has been historically unclear in the chief episcopal churches. Churches coming from the Reformation have insisted that there is only one churchly office, so that one ordained to presbyteral ministry possesses the office and does not acquire another if made bishop, and so that churches lacking administrative bishops in succession need not therefore lack chief pastors in suc-cession.[49] Roman Catholicism has now clarified its position; according to the second Vatican Council there is a single "divinely instituted ecclesiastical minis-try" that is "exercised at different levels[50] by those who from ancient times have

---

48. Cyprian, *De catholicae ecclesiae unitate*, 5: "Quam unitatem tenere firmiter et vindicare debemus, maxime episcopi qui in ecclesia praesidemus, ut episcopatum quoque ipsum unum atque indivisum probemus . . . episcopatus unus est, cuius a singulis in solidum pars genetur."

49. So the the Lutheran participants in the Arbeitsgruppe der deutschen Bischofskonferenz und der Kirchenleitung der Vereinigten Evangelisch-lutherischen Kirche Deutschlands, *Kirchenge-meinschaft im Word und Sakrament* (Paderborn: Bonifatius, 1984), 75: "The evangelical-Lutheran Kirche speaks only of *one* ordination to churchly office."

50. In this text, *ordo* is used interchangeably with *gradus*. To avoid confusion, it seemed best to translate as I have done.

been called bishops, priests and deacons."[51] The pastoral office is one office, according to both Catholicism and Protestantism.

It is then, according to the council, the bishops who are "invested with the fullness" of this office.[52] This doctrine would once have been again an ecumenical problem but is not in context of the present ecumenical teaching, in which the council shares, that the bishop's office is definitively pastoral.[53] If the Reformation has always seen churchly office exemplified by the shepherd in the midst of the flock, so does the council, when the diocese is seen as the local flock.

There is also independent reason to see the diocese as the local church. It incorporates in itself a certain miniature communion of communions, to mirror in this way the nature of the church it is. And its ministry encompasses both bishop and presbyters, thus preserving the ancient image of episcopally led eucharistic assembly. The question is, of course, whether this image is indeed to be preserved.

IV

We must finally turn to our postponed question, with its full difficulty before us. The classic structure of churchly office is the result of a long series of postapostolic contingencies: the appearance in one part of the immediately postapostolic church of the rite alluded to in the Pastoral Epistles; the application to the whole church's ministry of the Pastoral Epistles' exhortations about this rite and the office determined by it; the emergence of the monarchical episcopate; and the subsequent separation of the bishop's local church into two levels each with its pastors. Can such a drawn-out postapostolic institution have dogmatic force? Is episcopacy an irreversibly instituted structure of churchly office? If it is, the prior question, whether the ordained office as such is irreversible in its role, is of course also settled.

It is possible to construct a pragmatic argument that ordination provides the office best suited to the church, that its evolution into episcopal and presbyteral ministries provides the political form best suited to the church, and that the history that led to the classic structure was therefore by and large on a right track. We have just done something close to that. But such argument cannot justify ordination and episcopacy dogmatically, cannot indeed justify this chapter's appearance in a work of systematic theology.

The theological question has historically been framed: Is episcopacy mandated *iure divino* or *iure humano*, by divine law or human? Both sides of the Western schism supposed at the time of their division that for a churchly institution to be *iure divino* it had to be impossible for the church to be herself without it. They further thought that this meant the institution must always in fact have been present in the church, and that is, that it must have been instituted by Pen-

---

51. *Lumen gentium*, 28.
52. *Lumen gentium*, 26.
53. Jenson, *Unbaptized God*, 68.

tecost at the latest, and so—since nothing decisive was thought to have happened between Ascension and Pentecost[54]—by the Lord himself. Papal theologians thereupon insisted that the episcopacy was dominically instituted, and the continental Reformers that it was not.

Historical scholarship makes it impossible to assert institution of the episcopate—in any plausible sense of the terms—at or before Pentecost. But this is no triumph for the old Protestant position, for the same historical consciousness makes it impossible to assert dominical or scriptural institution of much that especially Protestantism must regard as *iure divino*:[55] for example, the canon of Scripture itself. If the canon is divinely mandated, then something can appear in the already existing church's history and still be *iure divino*; if the Bible belongs to the church's foundation, then something can emerge in the already founded church and still belong to her foundation.

The traditional way of deciding what is or is not *iure divino* is in fact irrecoverable.[56] And the church cannot well do without a replacement, since every phenomenon of the church's historically developed life can hardly be divinely mandated. A new concept of the relation between the church's historic decisions and divine command is needed; and one has been offered in the dialogues.

It has been proposed that "historically relative and conditioned" institutions may be considered as divinely instituted if two conditions are fulfilled. First, they must be "contingently but really necessary 'for the sake of the gospel.'"[57] In this work's concepts, they must be *dramatically* necessary in the church's history, not mechanically determined beforehand but nevertheless once there the very thing that had to happen. And second, their appearance must be irreversible.[58] This proposal, made from the Protestant side of the dialogues, seems acceptable to Catholicism at its highest level; according to the Congregation for the Faith, "what '*iure divino*' means" is that something is "inalienable."[59]

But what constitutes irreversibility in the church's life? In volume 1, we said that an irreversible creedal or liturgical or canonical choice was one by which the

---

54. At least in the account in Acts.

55. Two articles by the same author are decisive both in the ecumenical discussion and for the matter: George Lindbeck, "Papacy and the Ius Divinum," *Lutherans and Catholics in Dialogue*, ed. Paul C. Empie, T. Austin Murphy (Minneapolis: Augsburg, 1974), 193–202; "Doctrinal Standards, Theological Theories and Practical Aspects of the Ministry in the Lutheran Churches," *Evangelium-Welt-Kirche*, ed. Harding Meyer (Frankfurt: Otto Lembeck, 1975).

56. The insight is ecumenical. From the Catholic side, J.-M. R. Tillard, *Church of Churches: The Ecclesiology of Communion*, tr. R. C. De Peaux (Collegeville: Liturgical Press, 1992), 304: "No clear boundary exists which permits us to say: 'What is on this side has been positively willed by God, what is on that side is entirely dependent on human freedom.'"

57. Lindbeck, "Papacy and Ius Divinum," 202.

58. Ibid., 203. The Catholic Tillard, *Church of Churches*, 304, can agree with both this point and the previous one: "It is not a question of searching to see if such or such a structure is or is not explicitly certified . . . in the Scriptures. . . . It is a question of disclosing if it is not only useful but *necessary* for the Churches, based on what Revelation specifies as the nature of them, and because of that willed be God . . . and destined to *last*."

59. "Observations on the ARCIC Final Report," b.ii.2, *Origins* 11 (1982):752–756.

church so decided her future that if the choice were faithless to the gospel there would be no church thereafter extant to reverse it. Crudely put, an irreversible decision is one on which the church bets her future self-identity. And that tells us in what direction we must look for understanding: to the church's future fulfillment, and to the Spirit who is the *arrabon* of that fulfillment.

We can make the previous paragraph's argument with particular reference to the episcopate, turning the argument on the *magisterium*. The ordained pastoral office has in fact been made to bear the *magisterium*, and as the office divided the bishops were in fact burdened with its "fullness." But then the argument must hold: "When we are talking about the universal reception of bishops as authoritative teachers whose decisions on matters of faith were recognized as binding on the faithful, we are talking about the reception by the Church of a *norm* [emphasis added] of its faith." But if the church made *that* decision wrongly, she is not only materially but methodologically separated from her truth. A church guided by the Spirit cannot "have been mistaken when it determined what was going to be the norm of its faith."[60]

The argument can be made more bluntly, in a form aimed at Protestant hesitations: "It is to [the] episcopally united church . . . that all . . . Christian traditions owe their creeds, their liturgies, and above all their scriptural canon. If these latter are unexpungable, why not the episcopate?"[61] Canon, creed, and episcopate were but parts of a single norm of faith, discovered in response to a single historical crisis; if one of the three is alienable, how are the other two not? It was precisely in their interaction that they were to guard the apostolicity of the church's teaching; what justifies separating one as dispensable?

As at many points before, we are left with faith in the Spirit's past guidance of the church. But we may still be unsatisfied dogmatically. For the argument just concluded operates with a certain ad hoc compulsion: if you dismiss episcopacy you must be prepared to dismiss more than you will like.

The judgment "The church has acquired institution x by the leading of the Spirit" must in any case be after the fact; dramatic necessity can be perceived only when the event is there. The church's beginning, it appears, provides no paradigm by which to make such judgments. We may now say: that is appropriate, since it is the church's end that must properly provide the paradigm; a coherent narrative hangs together by anticipations of its conclusion. The church is what she is as anticipation of her transformation into God. Thus even if the church's beginning were uniform, we should still look forward to see her true shape.

The proposal to look to the future rather than to the past for a norm of development in the church's life is not a proposal to relativize the past.[62] We will

---

60. Francis A. Sullivan, *Magisterium*, 30–31.

61. It should be noted the person cited is perhaps Protestantism's single most experienced and knowledgable ecumenical participant; George Lindbeck, "The Church," *Keeping the Faith: Essays to Mark the Centenary of Lux Mundi*, ed. Goeffrey Wainwright (Philadelphia: Fortress, 1988), 199.

62. It is to be feared that Jürgen Moltmann's theology has tended this way from the book that first established his position, *Theologie der Hoffnung: Untersuchungen zur Begründung und zu den*

look to the gospel's vision of fulfillment to provide clues by which to perceive precisely the dramatic continuity of the Spirit's leading in past history: for a way to tell how the church's past is authoritative for future decision, how past decisions guide future choices and can prohibit certain paths.

We have, of course, no simple description of the Kingdom or of the church's entry into it, only certain limiting propositions and the iconic visions of apocalyptic. But for after-the-fact judgment of dramatic coherence, these are exactly what we need. We cannot in advance read one mandatory pattern of ecclesial office, or of ecclesial structure generally, from the gospel's promise of the church's fulfillment. For part of what is promised is freedom, which the church in her history anticipates by making her own contingent choices. But by the character of the gospel's promise we *can* judge after the fact between historical turnings dramatically appropriate to the church's fulfillment and others inappropriate to it and so discern when the Spirit can or cannot have been leading.

If the Spirit has been leading the church, then if the episcopate has been in fact established in the history of the church, and if this establishment *can* dramatically have been the leading of the Spirit, then we must judge that the establishment *was* the leading of the Spirit. And, as we have just argued, given the scope of the decision made as the episcopate became established, if this particular decision was in its time proper it is also irreversible.

We begin with the limiting propositions. The church's end will be perfect inclusion in the triune life. A proper ordering of the church is one that can accept this inclusion, that can fit into the triune life, audacious as that claim may seem. This immediately provides three norms relevant to the judgment we have here to make. A possibly Spirit-instituted structure of churchly office will be differentiated, perichoretic, and reciprocally hierarchical. The office will encompass different roles; these will have agency only in and by their interaction; and they will be unequal, but so that the direction of subordination depends on context. For example of the first two principles' application: the reduction of the ordained office to the solitary figure of "the minister" standing before "his" or "her" congregation in much of Protestantism, and in practice in much of Catholicism, cannot have been the leading of the Spirit. For illustration of the third principle: in the threefold ministry, the bishop is the "monarch," but it is the humble deacon whom Ignatius coordinates to Christ.

Could not structures of office other than the traditional one have satisfied these requirements? Of course, but if the kind of reasoning here being developed is appropriate, that is now beside the point. The "threefold ministry" did come into being, and nothing about the destiny to which the Spirit is leading the church requires us to say that this emergence was outside his intention. The question has

---

Konsequenzen einer Christlichen Eschatologie (Munich: Kaiser, 1965). What according to Moltmann makes the future the *future* is its contradictions to whatever is already there. This is an important insight about the relation of Christian hope to the orders of the world. But applied to the history of the church it is false, and its falsity is of a peculiarly destructive sort.

sometimes been posed so: Does the episcopate belong to the church's *esse* or to her *bene esse*, to her being or to her well-being? But if our sort of reasoning is appropriate, no such distinction can obtain.[63]

Apocalyptic iconography of the End is, however, perhaps more at the heart of the sort of the reasoning here advocated than are abstract propositions about the End; a judgment of dramatic coherence is, after all, an aesthetic judgment. We must ask: Does the picture of the bishop among the people, with flanking presbyters and serving deacons, *harmonize* easily with Scripture's evocations of the Kingdom? Can we, for example, call up the Revelation's scenes of eternal worship and sketch Ignatius's vision into them? Surely we can, and very satisfyingly.[64] We could perhaps devise a different picture that fit, but again that can no longer be to the point.

It remains to note that the mandate we have discovered for the church's existing structure of office makes demands on practice, even demands for reform. Two must be mentioned.

First: if the monarchical episcopate is to answer to its historical-eschatological legitimation, as we have just argued it, bishops must be in fact the pastors of plausibly "local" churches. Dioceses must be demographically able actually to function as continuing even if infrequent eucharistic assemblies.

Recognition that this is not generally the case is widespread. So an Orthodox-Roman Catholic consultation, in criticism of the "Munich" document's romanticism: "The way in which the document sees the local church, led by the eucharistic ecclesiology, does not really correspond to the current actual situation of the bishops and their churches. Even though the model proposes certain useful perspectives, the numerical size and geographical extent of these local churches makes the application of the model problematic.[65] It must be said: if episcopal churches rest content with malformation of the bishop into a sort of branch manager, there can be no very strong mandate for churches now without episcopal succession to restore it by joining the existing system.

Second: if the monarchical episcopate is to answer to its legitimation, the work actually prescribed for bishops must be sacramental and instructional and be administrative only in necessary consequence. Reform in this direction is needed both for the guidance of bishops in office and to turn the choice of new bishops toward the church's theologically and liturgically more gifted clergy. Every bishop who has to be guided through a service or refers every theological question to advisers is a walking refutation of episcopacy.

---

63. When Orthodoxy falls into use of this distinction, the results are particularly wooden. See e.g., Robert G. Stephanopoulos, "The Lima Statement on Ministry," *St. Vladimir's Theological Quarterly* 27 (1983), 278.

64. P. 340.

Indeed, the picture in Revelation seems to have been cast on the image of worship in congregations like Ignatius', which would push monarchical episcopacy back several steps.

65. "Bilateral Catholic-Orthodox Consultation in USA, to Munich 1982," *Episkepsis* 14 (1983), 304:11.

Finally, what of churches that at the Reformation were deprived of episcopal succession? It must first be noted that in some instances this perhaps could not be averted, precisely in fidelity to the church's "substantial" apostolicity. The first and theologically decisive round of Anglican-Lutheran dialogue in the United States concluded:

> At the time of the Reformation, one of our communions in its place experienced the continuity of the episcopally ordered ministry as an important means of the succession of the gospel; in various ways the other in its place was able to take its responsibility [for][66] the succession of the gospel only by a new ordering of its ministry. We agree that by each decision the apostolicity of the ministry in question was preserved."[67]

But even if we accept this judgment, how are we now to understand the latter church's situation?

A word of the Roman Congregation for the Faith is perhaps the best that could be found: churches lacking episcopal succession are "wounded."[68] It is anyway true, both pragmatically and theologically: "Not by episcopal succession alone, but certainly not without episcopal succession, can there be any discussion of the recovery of true unity in the one Church."[69] The final mandate of this section must be healing: of the practice of the episcopal churches; of the wound of the nonepiscopal churches, by restoration of the mandated order; and of the division between them.

V

The biggest ecumenical stone of stumbling presents the easiest theological assignment, at least at the main point. At the beginning of modern Roman Catholic ecumenism Paul VI said: "We are aware, that the pope is undoubtedly the greatest obstacle in the path of the Ecumene."[70] But if the communion ecclesiology is anywhere close to the truth, then plainly the "one church" of its slogans must have her own pastor.

What then should be said about such a universal pastorate? The first Vatican Council has already said a great deal.

In reading this council's texts, one must tolerate a great deal of bombastic and legalistic language. And the sense of its decrees must be, here as in other cases, carefully and historically studied.[71] But what this council actually said about the

66. The published text has "of" here, a typographical error.
67. Lutheran-Episcopal Dialogue, *A Progress Report*, 21.
68. Congregation for the Doctrine of the Faith, *Letter to the Bishops of the Catholic Church on Some Aspects of the Church Understood as Communion*, 17.
69. Stephanopoulos, "The Lima Statement," 278.
70. Acta apostolicae sedis 59 (1967):498.
71. This is done exhaustively by Gustave Thils, *Primauté et infallibilité du pontife romain à Vatican I* (Louvain: Peeters, 1989).

universal pastor is, when one gets through to it, in itself unproblematic and even tautologous, if the universal church is herself real.

The council spoke first of the universal pastor's "jurisdiction." This jurisdiction is defined as "truly episcopal"[72] and its purpose as the communion of "one flock under one supreme pastor"; the jurisdiction so described is then said to be "ordinary" and "immediate."[73] That is, the pope's role in the univeral church is of the same *sort* as that of a pastor in a local church; and therefore its functioning is "ordinary," not granted by the local bishops, and "immediate," not necessarily exercised through them. If there is a pastorate of the universal church and if the universal church is indeed a church, then of course these propositions must be true of that pastorate as they are *mutatis mutandis* of any.

There are, to be sure, restrictions on what might easily be deduced from the council's propositions. The only *sacrament* here in question is ordination; therefore "the papacy is not a sacrament" in addition to the sacrament of ordination bestowed on all bishops and presbyters "or even a degree in the fullness of the sacrament of orders," as is the presbyterate or the episcopate. The papacy "is a particular way of putting into operation" the charism common to all bishops.[74]

So also the pope is not "a 'super-bishop'" but a local bishop with a specific universal responsibility.[75] Nor, despite what many fathers at the first Vatican Council may have intended, may we combine the papal pastorate's universality with its "truly episcopal" character in such fashion as to derive the notion of a universal bishop, who "would concentrate all ecclesiastical authority in his person"—not if we are at all to reckon with patristic and Orthodox understanding.[76] We should remember that the "fullness" of the pastoral office is, as the second Vatican Council made plain, located in the episcopacy and so not in the papacy simply as such.

Then the council spoke of "infallibility."[77] The text is forbidding: "When the Roman pontiff[78] speaks *ex cathedra*, that is, when in the exercise of his office as shepherd and teacher of all Christians . . . he defines a doctrine . . . to be held by the whole church, he possesses . . . that infallibility which the divine Redeemer willed his church to enjoy. . . . Therefore such definitions of the Roman pontiff

---

72. "Quae vere episcopalis est."

73. *Constitutio dogmatica prima de ecclesia Christi*, iii. For the understanding of this language in its historical context, and so for the following, Thils, *Primauté*, 61–106.

74. Tillard, *Church of Churches*, 257.

75. Ibid., 260.

76. Metro. Chrysostomos Konstantinidis, "Authority in the Orthodox Church," *Theological Dialogue between Orthodox and Reformed Churches*, ed. T. F. Torrance (Edinburgh: Scottish Academic Press, 1985), 70: "The *episcopus universalis*, who would concentrate all ecclesiastical authority in his person, does not exist in Orthodox theology."

77. To the following, Thils, *Primauté*, 117–228.

78. Perhaps the single greatest stroke toward reunion of the church would be if the Vatican could accustom itself to less pompous and inappropriate terminology. One understands how "pontiff" came to be a term for the Roman bishop, but it can hardly help but mislead even its users; and there is other terminology that is worse.

are irreformable in their own right [*ex sese*] and not by the consent of the church."[79]

The more one contemplates this passage, the harder it is to fix its scope. It surely cannot mean that a pope never errs when claiming to define doctrine. For—to take the most blatant and always cited case—in the midst of the explicitly dogmatic struggle over monotheletism,[80] Honorius I formally propounded the monothelite position; an undoubted ecumenical council[81] defined monothelitism as heresy and explicitly rebuked this pope; and a subsequent pope confirmed the council's judgment.

The first Vatican Council did—or so it appears—lay down a *condition* for the infallibility of a papal decision: it must be made *ex cathedra*, that is, from the metaphorical throne that the bishop of Rome ascends in order to act specifically as universal pastor. Where conditions need to be stated it must be possible that they are not always fulfilled. Perhaps, therefore, the solution of our puzzlement is that a Roman bishop's claim in a specific case to act as universal pastor does not by itself guarantee that he then does so.[82] There may be conditions of a papal pronouncement's infallibility beyond its own claim to it. Intrinsically, after all, papal promulgation of a doctrinal or moral teaching and papal assertion of that promulgation's *ex cathedra* character are two different things; perhaps the former are sometimes infallible, that is, when in fact *ex cathedra*, but the latter are not.

The interpretation is at least possible[83] that "two different questions" are in play. The one is: "What conditions are objectively required for an infallible . . . definition?" What must be the case for a papal promulgation to be in fact *ex cathedra*? And the other is: "How can we know in any particular case, that all of these conditions have been fulfilled?"[84] The ascertainable consent of the church is, according to the council, not among the conditions of infallibility itself, but it nevertheless may be a necessary sign that those conditions are fulfilled. Thus Boniface VIII used every conceivable formula of final definition, "We declare, teach and define," in proclaiming that political submission to the papacy is "necessarily" a condition of salvation, yet no one, including the pope, seems now to believe this.

---

79. *Constitutio dogmatica prima de ecclesia Christi*, iv.

80. 1:134–137.

81. The sixth.

82. Unom Sanctum (1302). Francis A. Sullivan, *Magisterium: Teaching Authority in the Catholic Church* (Mahwey: Paulist Press, 1983), 108: "Does the fact that the pope has used an *ex cathedra* formula in making a particular statement, absolutely rule out any question as to whether all the conditions objectively required for an *ex cathedra* definition of faith were actually fulfilled in that act? I am inclined to agree with a number of Catholic theologians who give a negative answer." Sullivan lists as such theologians Joseph Ratzinger, Heinrich Fries, and George Tavard.

83. For the following argument I continue with Sullivan's celebrated if also controverted *Magisterium*.

84. Ibid., 99.

And that seems to be the teaching of the second Vatican Council, though its elaborately deferential attitude to its predecessor prevents complete certainty.[85] Having confirmed the former council's teaching that the pope's—or an ecumenical council's—irreformable decisions are so in their own right and do not become so by the assent of the church, the council then exegetes this by saying that when a decision is in fact irreformable the "assent of the church cannot fail" to be forthcoming.[86] In this teaching, the church does appear as something other than the pope by himself or a council by itself and the assent of the church as something other than the papal or conciliar claim itself.[87] What then if in fact a papal or conciliar promulgation is in the long term ignored or contravened in the common teaching of the church? This can only mean, in the council's logic, that the promulgation was not in fact irreformable.

Nor does this empty both councils' teaching that irreformable papal and conciliar decisions are so in their own right. An appropriate positive interpretation of papal infallibility is in fact at hand:

> The first Vatican Council said that the Pope could make definitive decisions not only on the basis of the church's agreement, but also by himself . . . *ex sese*. . . . Although . . . there were many efforts to interpret this blunt and easily misunderstood formula so as better to bring out its real content, this could not then be done. . . . Now what then remained a wish has been accomplished [by the second Vatican Council]. . . . It is now said that the work of the teaching office always takes place on the background of the faith and prayer of the whole church. Yet at the same time it cannot be restricted only to the expression of an already established common opinion but . . . must under certain circumstances take the initiative . . . over against the confusion of a church without consensus.[88]

Exactly the same must be said, *mutatis mutandis*, of any pastorate; were it not so, it should not be said of pope or council. In this matter, to be sure, the *mutandi* are considerable. For a presbyteral pastor or a bishop in the local diocese of course cannot say "This is what *the* church teaches" in such fashion as to settle the matter, unless *the* church has in fact taught it. All pastors sometimes must speak with "that infallibility which the divine Redeemer willed his church to enjoy," but they do so as they speak in concord with the whole church, a con-

---

85. This matter has of course been elaborately debated among Roman Catholic theologians, and many magisterial pronouncements are relevant to its decision. I have neither the space nor the knowledge even to dip into that ocean. I can only work with the council's actual text and make such contribution as exegetical skill may provide.

86. *Lumen gentium*, 25.

87. "*Istis autem definitionibus assensus ecclesiae numquam deesse potest propter auctionem . . . Spiritus sancti.*"

88. Joseph Cardinal Ratzinger, *Theologische Prinzipienlehre* (Munich: Erich Wewel, 1982), 247.

cord ascertainable only as the one church speaks through her organs of unity. This does not empty the charism of individual bishops and presbyters; in actually addressing the church's teaching to a local church's unique concerns and questions, a bishop or presbyter cannot simply recite dogma but must explain and apply and therein must rely on the same promise of the Spirit as does pope or council. And a local pastor's teaching about a matter not dogmatically settled may determine the church's eventual, and perhaps then irreversible, consensus.

We have in these paragraphs again mentioned councils. That what has just been said of the pope is anyway true of universal councils has been a supposition of this work from the beginning. The decisions of the ecumenical councils—found to be ecumenical by assent of the church!—have all along provided our model and rationale of strictly dogmatic teaching.[89] The theological reason of this policy has just been provided; it is the same as the reason of the more controversial papal *magisterium*.

In this connection too, and indeed paradigmatically, we may ask: Can a council err? Obviously it can, in the sense that it is always possible for a gathering of bishops and other dignitaries to fall into conflict with Scripture or existing dogma, even when that gathering understands itself to be and claims to be a council of the church. But then it is not one. This will be discovered, if the Spirit guides the church, and the church's assent "cannot fail" to be refused; just this happened in the case of the famous "Robber Council" at Ephesus, which in its mere formalities differed little from the ecumenical "Council of Ephesus."

The definitions of the first Vatican Council were thought by many to have made councils obsolete; it is a further achievement of the second to have overcome this temptation. *Before* its reaffirmation of papal infallibility we find: when the bishops, "maintaining the tie of communion among themselves and with Peter's successor, join in one opinion as something to be definitively affirmed, they pronounce Christ's doctrine infallibly. And this is most plainly the case when they are joined in an ecumenical council."[90]

Two matters remain, for this section and for this chapter. The first is a question so far skirted: Granted that there must be a universal pastorate, why should it be located in Rome? Why not, for example, Jerusalem? The question is odd, since Roman primacy developed first and the theology thereof afterward. But it nevertheless must be faced.

Pragmatic reasons are not hard to find, and the dialogues have gone far with them. So international Catholic-Anglican dialogue: it occurred "early in the history of the church" that to serve communion between local diocesan churches "a

89. Metropolitan Johannes of Helsinki, as recorded in protocol of dialogue between the Evangelical Church in Germany and the ecumenical patriarchate, *Evangelium und Kirche*, ed. Kirchliches Aussenamt der Evangelischen Kirche im Deutschland (Frankfurt: Otto Lembeck, 1983), 102: "The ecumenical councils . . . certainly on the one hand first become ecumenical councils when their decisions are accepted by the whole church; on the other hand we know that they did their work in the consciousness that they were making final decisions."

90. *Lumen gentium*, 28.

function of oversight . . . was assigned to bishops of prominent sees."[91] And within this system of metropolitan and patriarchal sees, "the see of Rome . . . became the principal center in matters concerning the church universal."[92] And so finally: "The only see which makes any claim to universal primacy and which has exercised and still exercises such *episcope* is the see of Rome, the city were Peter and Paul died. It seems *appropriate* [emphasis added] that in any future union a universal primacy . . . should be held by that see."[93]

It is clear that the unity of the church cannot in fact now be restored except with a universal pastor located at Rome. And this is already sufficient reason to say that churches now not in communion with the church of Rome are very severely "wounded." Just so it is sufficient reason to say also that the restoration of those churches' communion with Rome is the peremptory will of God. Yet such considerations do not provide quite the sort of legitimation we look for in systematic theology and that we found for the episcopate and for the universal pastorate simply as such.

The historically initiating understanding of Roman primacy[94] is perhaps itself the closest available approach to what is wanted. For in the earlier centuries of the undivided church, it was precisely the local church of Rome, and not the Roman bishop personally, that enjoyed unique prestige. The bishop of Rome enjoyed special authority among the bishops because their communion with him was the necessary sign of their churches' communion with the church of that place.[95] If the pope's universal pastorate is based on a unique prestige of the Roman congregation, then obviously in Rome is where it must be exercised.

In the fathers' understanding of the apostolic foundation of the church, the founding history of each apostolic local church was a different act of the Spirit. This act was thought to live on in a special character of that church, in what one might perhaps call a continuing communal charism: the continuing life of each apostolically founded church was experienced as an enduring representation of her role within the Spirit-led course of the apostolic mission. The specific authority of the church of Rome derived from her honor as the place to which the Spirit led Peter and Paul, in the book of Acts the Spirit's two primary missionary instruments, for their final work and for their own perfecting in martyrdom; the Spirit was therefore expected to maintain the Roman church as a "touchstone" of fidelity to the apostolic work and faith.[96]

---

91. Anglican–Roman Catholic International Commission, *Authority in the Church* (1976), 10.

92. Ibid., 12.

93. Anglican–Roman Catholic International Commission, *Elucidations* (1981), 8.

94. To the following, see the fundamental work by J.-.M. R. Tillard, *The Bishop of Rome*, tr. John de Satgé (Wilmington: Michael Glazier, 1983).

95. Ibid., 86: "The successors of Linus . . . will have had a place within the communion of bishops commensurate with the place of Rome within the communion of churches. . . . Because he was bishop of the church which had the *potentior principalitas* among the churches, the bishop of Rome would have been the first among the bishops."

96. Ibid., 67–119.

But one need not enter the realm of science fiction[97] now to imagine a time in which Rome, with its congregation and pastors, no longer existed. Yet the role that initially developed around that church, once developed and theologically validated, would still be necessary. Surely an ecumenical council or other magisterial organ of the one church could and should then choose a universal pastor, elsewhere located. The new ecumenical pastor might of course still be styled "bishop of Rome," but this is neither here nor there to our problem. Probably we must judge: identification of the universal pastorate with the Roman episcopacy is not strictly irreversible. On the other hand, hard cases make bad law.

Finally in this section, we must recognize that also the mandate of a universal pastorate—whatever the truth about its location—makes demands on the practice of that pastorate and may demand its reform. Two matters demand attention.

First, the medieval period's "ever wider separation of sacrament and jurisdiction,"[98] and the resulting interpretation of office in terms of legalistically and managerially construed jurisdiction, has been identified as the chief false development in the West's understanding of churchly office.[99] Moreover, the bishop of Rome is at once universal pastor and patriarch of the West, which latter is a mostly juridical office. The East-West schism made the boundaries of the patriarchate identical with those within which the pope's universal care can now actually function; in this situation the two offices are easily confused and the papacy's universal mission understood administratively.[100] It can hardly be denied that both these temptations have often afflicted papal practice and that experience with such practice[101] is in considerable part responsible for Protestantism's and Orthodoxy's continuing fear of papal jurisdiction.

Second, the difficulty in setting the boundaries of papal infallibility obviously pose a temptation. For the bishop of Rome does not cease to teach as a bishop when he descends from the universal *cathedra*. What of those in the universal church, but not in the diocese of Rome, who for theologically plausible reasons disagree with something he then teaches? Do they thereby dissent from the universal pastor? It must be very easy for the papacy to think that they do. But precisely if the papacy is to fulfill its defining mission of unity, this temptation must be firmly resisted.[102]

---

97. In *A Canticle for Leibowitz*, by Walter M. Miller, it having become nearly certain, after millenia of repeated nuclear catastrophes and repeated slow rebirths, that this time nuclear warfare will render the earth permanently uninhabitable, three cardinal bishops are sent to the small human colony on Mars.

98. Ratzinger, *Prinzipienlehre*, 267.

99. Ibid., 263–270.

100. Tillard, *Church of Churches*, 264–272.

101. For a rather major example, that Martin Luther's reforming polemics led to schism was the result of (1) Luther's apocalyptic eschatology, (2) the involvement of the case in Italian-German conflicts, *and*, probably most decisively, (3) Leo's use of doctrinal argument and churchly excommunication for purposes of business administration and international politics.

102. It has to be said that recent promulgations of John Paul II and the Congregation for the Faith are very alarming in this respect. So, immediately of this writing, *Ad tuendam fidem* and its attached exegeses.

The present pope feels all this and has proclaimed his hope to "find a way of exercising the primacy which, while in no way renouncing what is essential to its mission, is nonetheless open to a new situation." And with potential immense significance, he has made an invitation: "Could not the real but imperfect communion existing . . . persuade Church leaders and their theologians to engage with me in patient and fraternal dialogue on this subject?"[103] Theology must for the present rest the matter with hope for this invitation.

VI

Such necessary discourse as that to which this chapter has been devoted—analysis of the churchly office and its roles and authority—can by itself, however carefully stated, easily suggest a picture of the church very different from that which earlier chapters evoked. The church is not a populace ruled by various local dignitaries, with a federal senate of bishops and a Gaullist-style presidency. The church is the people of God, the polity of justice, and the place of Christ's availability; the church is communion. We must, to end this chapter, remind ourselves of Augustine's great insight: the church is the polity in which the *libido dominandi* need not rule and indeed cannot successfully do so.

Orthodoxy's vision of the hierarchy as *itself communion*[104] may therefore conclude this discussion. In a typical formulation: "Just as the triune oneness implies a fatherhood which is not domination but sharing, the exchange of an 'eternal movement of love,' so episcopal conciliarity shapes itself around 'centers of harmony' (in the profound expression of Father Schmemann), whose own hierarchy culminates . . . in a center of universal harmony that does not exercise dominion *of* the church but a 'primacy of love' *within* the church."[105] So long as the church is not yet translated into God, such a vision of office and its jurisdiction will be failed again and again at all levels. But it must shape the hopes of all pastors.

---

103. John Paul II, *Ut unum sint*, 95–96.
104. Perhaps, lamentably, realized least of all in Orthodox churches.
105. Olivier Clément, "Quelques remarques d'un orthodoxe sure la Constitution De ecclesia," *Oecumenica 1966*, ed. F. W. Kantzenbach, V. Vajta (Neuchâtel: Delachaux et Niestlé, 1966), 111.

TWENTY-EIGHT

The Mysteries of Communion

I

As the dialogues have struggled with the division of the Western church, they and theologians connected with them have sometimes lamented a Western late-medieval and modern lack of categories for specifically sacramental reality. To say that Christ is sacramentally present is claimed to attribute to him a "special sort of reality" with its own laws:[1] to be something sacramentally is to *be* it in a certain way. We have, it is said, lacked means to speak of such being, and this has been an important cause of our mutual misunderstandings.[2]

This work shares the goal posited by this lament, though with a caution. The effort cannot be to construe an ontological sort on general principles, in order then to classify the church's sacramental events as of that sort. Thus it can be very misleading to speak of a special "sacramental universe" within which sacraments have their being[3] or of some generally sacramental character of created being, which enables the church's specific sacramental life.

The effort must rather be to interpret the being of a particular person, the risen Jesus, insofar as we truly say of him such things as that he is "really present" as the eucharistic elements or that he "speaks" when the Scriptures are read in the midst of the people or that he "re-presents" himself by an icon of the Pantokrator. If the interpretation succeeds, it will state a key ontological fact; but

---

1. The citation is from a chief architect of much ecumenical consensus, J. M. R. Tillard, "Catholiques romains et Anglicans: l'Eucharistie," *Nouvelle Revue Théologique* 103 (1971):607.

2. Most decisively, Ökumenischer Arbeitskreis evangelischer und katholischer Theologen, "Das Opfer Jesu Chrsti und der Kirche: Abschliessender Bericht," *Das Opfer Jesu Christi und seine Gegenwart in der Kirche,* ed. Karl Lehmann, Edmund Schlink (Freiburg: Herder, 1983), 4.2.3.

3. Ibid.

here as always when metaphysical questions arise, the direction of thought—what one takes as given and what one may then have to reinterpret—is decisive.

We start therefore with the risen Jesus, in the present tense. The question about someone's *present* tense is: Where is he or she? Jesus, according to Scripture, is now located in heaven. Heaven, we saw, is the place of the future as this is anticipated by God. To our present concern, what is in heaven is therefore Jesus *as* the head of that communal body that itself will be whole only at the End.

Continuing with earlier results, sacramental events make the boundary between our world and heaven, marking it by the "visible" objects they involve. Just so they are the embodied presence to our world of what is in heaven; in the present context, they are the embodied presence of the risen Jesus and the Kingdom he presents to the Father in the Spirit, as these are anticipated for the Father by the Spirit.

So far one conceptual framework for our present assignment. Thomas Aquinas perfected the standard Western interpretation of sacraments within a very different and more abstractly analytical framework. We will in this section try to join the two. We will first lay out Thomas's scheme itself as he uses it to interpret baptism and the Eucharist and as it has been used to interpret ordination. Thereby we will also continue the discussion of these sacraments.

In Thomas's Augustinian terminology, which we have already invoked in several connections, the bread and cup are *signa*.[4] "Signs" in this technical use are things "available to sense"[5] that point to something other than themselves, a "something," *res*, that needs signifying just because it is not thus available.[6] When what the signs point to is divine, "they are called sacraments."[7] In the case of the bread and cup, the *res*, according to Thomas, is "the mystical body" of Christ,[8] the Kingdom's fellowship of Christ and his saints insofar as this is anticipated in the church's communion.

There are of course many sorts of signifier-signified relations, most of them involving nothing remarkable beyond the wonder of language itself. The relation between the bread and cup as *signum* and Christ's mystical body as *res* is exceptional in the way called sacramental in that there is a middle reality between what is simply sign and what is simply *res*; this is the body and blood of Christ. The body and blood are at once *signum et res*: they are the thing the bread and cup signify but in turn they are signs, the visible Word of God that promises our communion with God and with one another.[9]

---

4. In Thomas's own more usual language, *sacramenta*.

5. *Summa theologiae*, i.73.1.

6. Augustine, *De doctrina christiana*, 1.2: "Omnis doctrina vel rerum est vel signorum, sed res per signa discuntur. . . . Ex quo intellegitur, quid appellem signa, res eas videlicet, quae ad significandum aliquid adhibtentui."

7. Augustine, *Epistola 138*, 7, in lapidary formulation: "Cum [signa] ad res divinas pertinent, sacramenta appellantur."

8. *Summa theologiae*, iii.73.1; 79.4.

9. *De articulis fidei et ecclesiae sacramentis*, 255a–b: "Sic igitur in hoc sacramento est aliquid quod est sacramenentum tantum, scilicet ipsa species panis et uini, et aliquid quod est res et sacramentum, scilicet corpus Christi uerum, et aliquid quod est res tantum, scilicet unitas corporis mistici, id est ecclesie."

To be signs Christ's body and blood must be *there*, available to our apprehension. Yet they are no more apparently present than is the mystical body they signify; they are visible only as the bread and cup that signify them. It is this identity between being visible only as signified and being visibly present so as to signify that makes the peculiar sacramental reality.

With baptism, the washing is the sign and justification is the *res*.[10] But justification is by faith; if then the baptized person does not believe, does nothing happen? If lack of faith cannot make the washing an ineffective sign, this must be because there is a gift signified by the sign that like the sign itself can be present without faith, precisely to *be* believed.[11] This, says Thomas, is "the baptismal character, which is the thing signified by the external washing and is the sacramental sign of inward justification."[12]

A sacramental "character,"[13] in Thomas's use, is not a quasi-physical impression on the soul[14]—as some Protestant polemics have supposed. A character is a ritually granted personal potentiality[15] of a specific kind, rather like the Pastorals' "charisms" but more restricted in scope. Thomas's material definition of sacramental characters is that they "are nothing other than different participations in Christ's priesthood."[16] The participation that baptism grants is the general one within this group; it is what the Reformation called "the priesthood of all believers."[17] Thus the *res et signum* of justification is true membership in the church.

Yet true membership in the church is a sign that is visible only as the baptism that signifies it. That I am numbered among the elect is visible only as my washing in the triune name; no amount of churchly activity will make it certain nor any amount of vice quite certainly disprove it. Am I or will I be justified? When the question becomes serious, my only assurance is that I belong to God's people, and my only assurance of this is that I am baptized. As with the Eucharist, the middle reality by which the signifier-signified relation is sacramental is something really and visibly present yet visible only with something else's visibility.

Ordination has been in the main tradition interpreted in parallel with baptism. What exactly the sign is has been confused through history;[18] it now seems

---

10. Ibid., iii.66.1.

11. Martin Luther, "Taufe," *Grosser Katechismus*, 53: "Wenn das Wort bei dem Wasser ist, so ist die Taufe recht, obschön der Glaube nicht dazu kömmpt; denn mein Glaube machet nicht die Taufe, sondern empfähet die Taufe."

12. *Summa theologiae*, iii.66.1.

13. The term is likely to be a fruitful source of confusion. The meaning for which the word has been taken into English is not its meaning in Latin; and the Latin word is itself a transliteration of a Greek word.

14. Ibid., iii.63.4: "Character non est sicut in subiecto in essentia animae."

15. Ibid.: "sed in eius potentia."

16. Ibid., iii.63.3.

17. Bukhard Neuenheuser, *Handbuch der Dogmengeschichte* (Freiburg: Herder, 1956), VI/2:88–92.

18. For a quick sketch of the history, with bibliography, Robert W. Jenson, *Christian Dogmatics*, ed. Carl Braaten, Robert Jenson (Philadelphia: Fortress, 1984), 2:380–382.

ecumenically agreed[19] that since the Pastoral Epistles are the warrant for ordination in the first place, their sign of the laying on of hands is the one mandated. The *res* is the edification of the church. And the character, which again is *signum et res*, is the specific participation in Christ's priesthood that determines the office.[20]

II

We may begin the attempt to plot these two frameworks on one another by asking: *Where* does Christ exercise his priesthood? Where does the sacrifice occur in which sacramental characters are participations and of which the eucharistic body and blood are the offering? The risen Christ now offers himself and his church, the *totus Christus*, to the Father. This offering anticipates his eschatological self-offering, when he will bring the church and all creation to the Father that God may be "all in all." Thus the present reality of Christ's priesthood occurs in God's anticipation of the Kingdom, that is, in heaven, which is where the New Testament anyway locates it.[21]

The next step is to ask: How does this participation in Christ's priesthood work? How does it happen that there is a middle reality, a simultaneous *signum et res*? We may answer: all sacramental *koinonia* is some aspect of the fact that the church on earth is the embodiment of the Christ who is in heaven. But how does *that* work? Here is the place where Johannes Brenz and his fellows, adduced in the first volume of this work,[22] come into their right.

The outcome of the first volume's christological reflections may be summarized: the human person Jesus is actual just as the identity of God called the Son.[23] That is, the human person Jesus occurs only within the perichoretic event that is the triune God, as one identity of that event. And while the triune God does *not* simply transcend the temporal distinctions between origin, goal, and present reconciliation but rather their mutual alienation as lost past, unavailable future, and vanishing present, just so he does wholly transcend spatial distances.[24] What

---

19. For Roman Catholicism with the encyclical of Pious XII, *Sacramentum ordinis*; and *The Rites of the Catholic Church*, series 2 (New York: Pueblo, 1980), 60–69; this had always been the position of most Protestants.

20. Thomas Aquinas, *Summa theologiae*, Supp.34.2. The description of this participation has of course been controversial. The Council of Trent, Session xxiii, ch. 1, defined it as "the power . . . to consecrate, offer and administer [Christ's] body and blood, and to demit or retain sins." It is doubtful that this definition would now be considered in conflict with the primal text among Reformation documents, the Augsburg Confession, art. v: "the ministry of preaching the gospel and administering the sacraments."

21. Hebrews 8:1–2.

22. 1:203–205.

23. 1:136–138.

24. Since for something to be at a place distant from the one where I am is to be where I cannot *now* reach it, that is, is to be a future unavailable to me. It must be noted, in fairness to the opponents of Brenz and fellow enthusiasts, that their argument at this point worked very differently.

Thomas says must be true, precisely within the doctrine of God offered in this work:[25] "Wherever something is at work, there it is. . . . But this belongs to the supreme power of God, that he acts immediately in all things. Thus nothing is distant from him."[26] For God there are only two places: the place that he is and the place he makes for creatures, immediately and inwardly adjacent to him.

Thus the creation is for God just one place.[27] And the one creation is heaven and earth together, however otherwise they differ. Therefore the difference between God's being in heaven and his being on earth can only be a difference between styles of his presence;[28] for him to "come" from one to the other does not require him to leave where he was or arrive where he was not. When the Lord rends the heavens and comes down, he comes to his Temple, where he is all along, and does not cease to be in heaven.

The person of the risen Jesus occurs as one identity of this God, without whom indeed this God would neither create space nor transcend it. Thus the risen man Jesus not only transcends space but is constitutive of God's transcendence of it. Therefore his total self is located in God and in creation, and in either only because also within the other; within creation he is located in heaven and on earth, and in either only as within the other. God is in his heaven and has the Temple as the place of his habitation, and vice versa, and is contained by neither.[29] Christ, as the second identity of God, is at the right hand of the Father and just so can find his Ego in a community of earthly creatures and have that community as his body. Nor is the one human personality Jesus thereby divided or separated.

But now it must be recognized that the propositions of these last paragraphs are not usual theologoumena of the Western church. The first volume of this work referred to the "privations" of Western Christology, which has continued on the path pointed at Chalcedon by the *Tome* of Leo.[30] It is at just the present juncture that those privations appear. A Christology that does not transgress Leo's principle that "each nature" is the doer or sufferer only of what is naturally proper to it cannot affirm the actuality of the human Christ in God's transcendence of space. Therefore it cannot itself account for the presence of the human Christ at once in heaven and in the church. That means it cannot account for sacramental reality, for identity between a reality being present only as signified and a reality being availably present so as to signify. And that means it cannot account for a chief feature of any catholic understanding of the church: that Christ is embodied for and in it.

---

25. Problematic though what he says of God and time may be.

26. *Quaestiones de veritate*, 1.8.1.

27. As Thomas has it, ibid., 1.52.2: "Universal being relates to the power of God as one single thing."

28. Let me cite the great Theodore of Mopsuestia approvingly for once, *On the Incarnation*, fr. 10: "For what in our case is spoken of according to its disposition in space is spoken of in the case of God according to the disposition of his will. As we say of ourselves, 'I was in this place,' so also we say of God that he was in this place, since what movement brings about in our case is effected by will in the case of God."

29. Pp. 121–123.

30. 1:133.

In standard Western Christology,[31] the "communion of attributes" provides such content as "the hypostatic union" is allowed to have.[32] And in standard doctrine the communion of attributes does not include a role for the man Jesus in any defining attribute of deity. Thomas Aquinas teaches that a relation of the human Jesus to God that "exceeds the natural power of a creature" requires something "*other than* [emphasis added] his personal union with the *Logos*." For Jesus to be savior he must indeed be enabled to do what a human cannot naturally do, but these gifts, says Thomas, are *not* given in the hypostatic union. And they remain "*created* [emphasis added] grace;" they do not involve Christ's human nature in the divine perichoresis as such[33] and so do not extend to such things as having God's relation to space. We may analyze the standard doctrine so: the sentence "Jesus is God" is indeed true, but for it to reflect in its form the fact *to* which it is true it must be rephrased, "Jesus, who is a man, subsists in the *Logos*, who is God." Therefore within the restrictions of the standard doctrine we cannot in fact draw all the conclusions about Jesus that would seem to follow from "Jesus is God,"[34] including, to present concern, "Jesus transcends space."

Thus in standard Western teaching, the risen Jesus' embodiment in the church has to be accounted for despite received Christology or denied on account of it. In the course of the Reformation, the issue was raised and the resulting theologoumena became occasions of confessional division. Catholic scholasticism had taught and continued to teach that the identity of Christ's body with the

31. A remarkable and precise, if untranslatable, statement of standard Western Christology's weakness is provided by Karl Rahner, *Schriften zur Theologie* (Einsidelen: Benziger Verlag, 1956–), 4:122: in standard scholastic doctrine the human nature has to the *Logos* as *Logos* no other relation than that which any creature has to its Creator, "abzüglich eines formalen Subsistierens in ihm, so dass sie von ihrem Subjekt zwar 'gesagt' ist, aber dieses Subjekt in ihr doch nicht *sich selbst* wirklich 'aussagt.'"

32. So Duns Scotus, *Parisiensia reportata, Opera Omnia*, vol. 23, ed. L. Vives (Paris, 1894), iii.xii.1: "Natura non est elevata ex hoc quod assumpta, ad idem esse formaliter cum Verbo, nec potentia ad idem operari formaliter, sed *tantum* [emphasis added] per communicatio idiomatum."

33. Here citing, from among many possibilities, the *Quaestiones de veritate*, 29.1.

34. This is most clearly explicated by Duns Scotus. The subsistence of one person in another is a purely "metaphysical" relation. That is, that the human Jesus has his hypostasis in the Son means that were it not for the existence specifically of the *Logos*, there would be no man Jesus, for in his case his individual human nature is not as with other creatures identical with its own "*suppositum*"; that is, he lacks the relative independence of existence that other creatures have. So, for example, *Parisiensia reportata*, iii.i.2–5. This metaphysical circumstance is "metaphysical" precisely because it involves nothing material for either the *Logos* or Jesus. "New" to the human nature or the *Logos* is only the actualization of the one's possible dependence on the other, a relation that is extrinsic and adventitious; ibid., iii.i.2. Therefore, ibid., iii.xii.1: "Formaliter . . . manet esse proprium naturae humanae aliud ab esse propria Verbi." The lengths to which this thinking can go may be instanced at some random. Ibid., iii.xx.1: A human person who was *not* hypostatically one with the *Logos* could do and be everything Christ in fact is or does. On the other hand, ibid., iii.ii.2, a human nature could have been united hypostatically with the *Logos* and remained unable to save or even indeed to be saved. Nor should one make out Scotus's Christology to be exceptional by deriving it from his peculiar doctrine of divine *potentia absoluta*; on the contrary, the doctrine of *potentia absoluta* is developed in the course of his extraordinarily profound analysis of the traditional Christology.

Eucharistic elements was sheerly "supernatural," that is, true in exception to everything otherwise true of bodies, his included.[35] This exception must nevertheless
be predictable; as we participate in the Eucharist we cannot be wondering whether
this time it is happening. The miracle is guaranteed by a character of the church's
ministry: God grants the ordained minister authority to say, "This is my body"
and have it be true in that it is said.[36]

Reformers in the line of John Calvin in effect substituted the faith of the individual for the power of the church. Thus according to Theodore Beza's classic
teaching,[37] the bread and cup in their eucharistic use as visible *signa*, together with
the verbal promises of Scripture, bring the *res* of the Supper before the soul. The
Spirit uses this presence to open the soul and create faith. And to faith, local separation is no more real than it is to the Spirit who creates it. Thus in the Eucharist
the believer is joined to Christ in heaven, body and soul.[38]

Other Reformers, the power of dogma once broken, abandoned "real presence" altogether. Ulrich Zwingli simply maintained Leo's rule[39] and drew the
conclusion others repressed.[40] He maintained against Catholics, Lutherans, and
Calvinists alike: "We rely on the testimony of the angel, who said, 'He is risen, he
is not here.' Christ's body is not everywhere, even if his divinity fills all things;
and nor then is he bodily present where there is faith in Christ."[41] And in Zwingli
we see clearly that it is not the human Christ's presence particularly in the Eucharist that is at stake but all aspects of his presence in the church, which according to Zwingli can be a presence of his divine nature only: "According to his divine nature Christ . . . is everywhere. Where two or three are gathered in his name,
he is [in this nature] among them. In his human nature . . . he is departed."[42]

It is perhaps the chief strictly theological achievement of the Lutheran wing
of the Reformation, in the conceptual turmoil of the time, to have seen how these
expedients were provoked by inadequate Christology. Martin Luther, here a dis-

---

35. Thomas Aquinas, *Summa theologiae*, iii.75.4: "Est omnino supernaturalis, sola Dei virtute effecta."

36. Ibid., iii.78.4–5; 82.1–3.

37. My description is summarized from Jill Rait's remarkable study of the structural similari-
ties between Tridentine scholastic and Calvinist doctrines of the real presence: *The Eucharistic
Theology of Theodore Bez* (Chambersburg: American Academy of Religion, 1972).

38. Let me comment here that I do not regard the differences between Catholic, Calvinist, and
Lutheran theologoumena here as legitimately church-divisive.

39. E.g., *Eine klare underrichtung vom nachtmal Christ, Sämtliche Werke* (Leipzig: Zwingli-
Verein, 1927), 4:828: "I know of course that . . . on account of the two natures that nevertheless are
but one Christ, we often say of the one what nevertheless belongs only to the other . . . as when one
says 'God suffered for us.' Such speech is now and then allowed by Christians, and does not offend
me. But it is not that deity can suffer, but because the person who in human nature suffered, is as
truly God as he is human [that such things can be said]. Thus suffering, if we speak properly, belongs only to the humanity."

40. The parallel between Zwingli's historical role and that of Arius is quite remarkable.

41. *Amica exegesis, id est expositio eucharistiae negocii, ad Martinum Lutherum*, ibid., 5:583.

42. *Eine klare underrichtung*, 827–828.

ciple of his disciples,[43] taught that Christ, the one divine-human *person* as whom
his divinity and humanity have their only actual existence,[44] is not delimited by
space. Thus we are to locate the divine-human Christ where he directs us to find
him, where he has "defined" his presence.[45] It was this Christology that rescued
Luther from the horror of a naked deity: "No, my friend! Where you set God before
me, there you must set his humanity with him!"[46] What Luther and others in fact
did was to provide a christological and so catholic understanding of the church
with a basis that is not circular—that is not itself a claim about the church.[47]

It does not follow that the doctrines that Catholic and Calvinist theologians
recruited to supplement Christology may not be in themselves true and necessary. As we have seen, the reality of the church, and so its reality as the embodiment of Christ, is indeed not separable from the presence in the church of the
ordained ministry's charism or "character."[48] Nor is Christ's embodiment in the
church a corpse; if the Spirit did not enliven the assembled church and rest upon
the eucharistic elements the risen Christ indeed would not be present. Moreover,
that the Spirit uses the elements to gain access to the assembled persons and create faith is certainly true and essential.

We come to a further question. It is *Jesus'* priesthood in which we participate sacramentally and not someone else's. "Jesus" is the name of a known historical figure; the name *identifies* the one present in the church and at God's right
hand. How is the one in whom we now participate identical with the past historical figure? The question makes also a necessary transition back to temporal
categories.

---

43. The so-called *Syngramma Suevicum*, a joint manifesto by Johannes Brenz and other young
pastors, many of whom had been students at Heidelberg when Luther came there for the famous
disputations, preceded and set the pattern for Luther's writings on the matter; Johann Brenz, *Werke*,
ed. Martin Brecht, Gerhard Schäfer (Tübingen: 1970), I/1:207–218.

44. The root of Luther's Christology is his insistence that the *Logos* is God's actual speech. The
saving fact of Christ is his "preaching office," that he speaks a word that reveals God. This office is
not deduced from the existence of the eternal Word; it is a human task and effort. But *what* is
"preached" is precisely *that* God speaks, that is, the *Logos*. To this, Ian D. Kingston Siggins, *Martin
Luther's Doctrine of Christ* (New Haven: Yale University Press, 1970), 13–78.

In his use of Chalcedon's language, Luther barely skirts violating its dogma. The one person
is the reality of the two natures on account of their mutual participation. So the *Disputatio de
divinitate et humanitate Christi* (1540), WA39/11:101–102: "Distinctae sunt naturae, sed post illam
communicationem est coniunctio, id est una persona. . . . Da gehets ineinander humanitas et
divintas. Die unitas, die helts." Thus he can say, ibid., 110, of the divine *nature,* "when it is taken of
the person," that it was "born, suffered and died." And he can read Christ's reply to Philip, "He
who has seen me has seen the Father, to mean, ibid., 106, "Whoever touches the Son of God touches
the divine nature itself."

45. *Vom Abendmahl Christi: Bekenntnis*, WA 29: 324–342.

46. Ibid., 338.

47. Though remarkably few later Lutheran theologians have noticed this.

48. Is a Eucharist celebrated by an unordained person really the Eucharist? The question is
perhaps unanswerable. Something happens, and we cannot know what, in the mercy of God, that
may be. But the event should not have happened; a "valid" Eucharist it certainly is not.

Particularly when interpreting the Eucharist, the advanced dialogues have all looked to the same resource for ontological insight: they have called for "return to . . . the notion of *memorial*"[49] that appears in the narrative of institution, and they have construed this notion on the background of the Old Testament's understanding of memorial events. When we give thanks and share the bread and wine, we do it for the sake of Christ's "remembrance." To avoid modernity's subjectivist associations with this word, recent discussion often simply imports the Greek of the narrative, *anamnesis*, or employs a neologism, "re-presentation."[50] *Anamnesis* or re-presentation is "the making effective in the present of an event of the past," as each Passover celebration makes the Exodus present in the life of Israel.[51]

But "Do this for my remembrance," however ontologically weighty *anamnesis* may finally turn out to be, must initially say that when we celebrate the Eucharist we *remind* someone of Jesus. As Catholic-Protestant dialogue has observed about the historic controversies,[52] both the Reformation and the Counter-Reformation presumed *we* must be the ones to be reminded and therefore could make nothing ontologically weighty of the reminding. But there is another possibility, then— and often still—excluded from view by inherited metaphysical prejudice: that we are to remind God.[53] Since "Do this for my remembrance" in the narrative mandates inclusion of Jesus in the content of the thanksgiving-*prayer*, this is in fact the only exegetically possible reading.

In the Old Testament, God's being reminded and remembering are pivotal theological concepts. For the central example: "And God heard [Israel's] groanings [in Egypt] and God remembered his covenant with Abraham."[54] It is a standard beginning of Israel's prayer: "Remember your mercy, O God, and your steadfast love from of old."[55] This divine "remembering" is not an act enclosed within divine subjectivity; it occurs precisely as his hearing of Israel's cries and as his answering intervention. The remembering that prayer solicits is that God answer the prayer.

When someone remembers, this is a present act. When it is God who remembers, his answer creates what it mentions, as do all his addresses. But since in this instance the creative address is response to a reminder, it creates the present tense of a past event. We may generalize: anamnetic being is present reality created by a word of God that simultaneously evokes a past event and opens its future, to make it live in the present.

---

49. Tillard, "Catholiques romaines," 607.

50. To what extent the invention of this word is intended to make an implicit interpretation of the Council of Trent is hard to say.

51. Anglican–Roman Catholic International Commission, *Eucharistic Doctrine* (1971), 5.

52. Pp. 217–218.

53. The classical exegetical presentation of this possibility is Joachim Jeremias, *The Eucharistic Words of Jesus*, tr. Norman Perrin (Philadelphia: Fortress, 1977), 244–255.

54. Exodus 2:24.

55. Psalm 25:5.

Martin Luther prompted a catechetical question about baptism: "How can water do such great things?" And supplied the answer: "Water indeed does not do them, but God's word in and with the water."[56] Baptism's washing is not in "just any water, but in water specifically grasped and sanctified by God's Word."[57] Specifically sacramental being is created by envelopment in God's converse with and in the church, in the narrative recollection of the biblical story, and in the making of its promise.

To be, we have maintained, is to be spoken of by God. Therefore, to be located is to be referred to by him in a specific network of relations of otherness. Christ the high priest's location is where his converse with the Father and the church puts him in relation to the congregation and the world. The middle being that is specific to sacramental reality, in which the difference is transcended between the earthly location of the sign and the heavenly and then eschatological location of the reality, is thus constituted in the logic of the triune God's conversation with his people.

III

With discussion of "memorial" or "remembrance," we moved from spatial to temporal categories. This is the move that indeed must conclude analysis of "sacramental" being. For, as we have seen, space is but time's present tense. The relations between the place that God is and his heaven and our earth are founded in relations between the future and the present and the past. And it is these temporal relations that *words* open and maintain.

The conversation that envelops and carries the sacramental situation is the converse of God and the congregation—this work's invariable topic in one way or another. In this conversation what is said is always somehow "Jesus is risen"; its narrative content is Israel and the one Israelite, and its import is final promise. Whether as God's address to us or as our address to God, the word in the church is at once narrative of the past and promise of the eschatological future. It is the "at once" that is ontologically crucial: the past is narrated just *as* the identity of the promised goal.

If this discourse is true, in it a word that opens the future "comes to" the remembered past to do this and so makes the past alive. Just so, in this word the past identifies the future. Thus the occurrence of this word is itself the unitary present event of both; in christological concentration, this word-event is the event of the remembered Jesus as the presence of the coming one.

Insofar as this converse visibly embodies itself in the objectivities of the church's life, these become signs with specific meaning, given by the gospel narrative. The narrated past is "re-presented" in them by the power of that promise that the narration simultaneously is. But this presence is hidden in them, by their

---

56. "Die Taufe," *Kleiner Katechismus*, 9–10.
57. "Taufe," *Grosser Katechismus*, 14.

own visible appearance as, for example, mere bread and cup or gesture of friendship or painted surface, or indeed as a mere human preacher's sentences. And the presence given in this representation is itself promise, is itself sign of what is not yet, of the last Fulfillment.

The last paragraphs have widened the discussion's scope. We have not talked of enumerable sacraments only, by whatever principle we may set their number. To whatever extent we have succeeded in developing and presenting a theory, it is a theory about the ontological heart of the church's life, encompassing *all* its great and small sanctifying events. It is for this reason that the title of this chapter uses Orthodoxy's favored word for such things as sacraments—as would that of the next chapter also were the result not overly long. The flexible denotation of "mysteries" is just what commends it.

The liturgical or devotional reading of Scripture is not "a sacrament," by any usual enumeration, but the coincidence of heaven and earth, future and past, sign and *res* is the truth of Scripture's role and power: Scripture is indeed a "mystery." Liturgical processions and blessings at family meals and signs of the cross and greetings in Christ's peace and invocations of saints and parental example in the faith and testimony before Caesar and kissing the crucifix and household reverence for the Book's place of honor are not sacraments by any counting likely to be adopted; but they are all minor or major mysteries of communion. A missionary sermon is not "a sacrament," but if the preacher manages to speak the gospel, human vocables are the Word of God. Icons and officially rostered sacraments no doubt differ in significant ways but not in respect of their place in the mystery of the church's life.

IV

The remainder of this chapter will thus be a miscellany. This is not a flaw; the profusion of the church's mysteries is historically rather than systematically determined and so can be captured by no merely conceptual structure. Systematic theology can only discuss the few that need separate mention. Two foundational and very profound mysteries must first merely be named, since we have already interpreted them: the name of God, whether JHWH or "Father, Son, and Holy Spirit"; and prayer, especially the "Our Father." Given the history this chapter will for the most part occupy itself with those of "the" sacraments not yet discussed.

Lists of "the" sacraments vary historically and confessionally; and any but the shortest again encompasses rites in themselves quite different from one another. The historically dominant enumeration of sacraments is that of the later medieval Western church and the Council of Trent.[58] The list is in fact appropri-

---

58. Session vii.primum: "Si quis dixerit, sacramenta novae legis . . . esse plura vel pauciora, quam septem, videlicet baptismum, confirmationem, eucharistiam, poenitentiam, extremum untionem, ordinem et matriomonium . . . anathema sit."

ate to our purpose: its seven rites are ecumenically practiced, and if we allow Trent its own use of the phrase "a sacrament," each of them can indeed be so named. To be sure, a different linguistic decision would grant the title to fewer or more rites; thus the Reformation lists of two or three result from preferring more conceptually circumscribed uses of "a sacrament." There is no necessary dogmatic dissensus here.[59]

We have already discussed baptism, the Eucharist, and ordination at considerable length. That leaves confirmation, penance, healing, and marriage.

"Confirmation" is one part of baptism's third- and fourth-century dramatic whole, gone off on its own. Its separation was part of a general dismantling of baptism's structure, inflicted by Christianity's late-antique and medieval situation as Western civilization's official religion.

When everybody was supposed to belong to the church, baptism of course came to be performed mostly on infants; this destroyed baptism's first act, the catechumenate.[60] First communion long continued to be the conclusion of baptism even after most neophytes were infants; in the East it still is. But in the West,[61] the practice of communing infants was ended by a coincidence of twelfth-century circumstances for which the leading of the Spirit can hardly be claimed. In a frugal society, infants were weaned late and many could not be trusted to swallow the bread; this led to the custom of communing infants with wine only. When the cup was then taken from the laity, the infants were thus left with nothing.[62] Recently there has been movement toward repairing this disaster.

Baptism's special rite of the Spirit[63] was turned into detached "confirmation" by a similar worldly coincidence: in this case, of large dioceses, bad roads, and high infant mortality. It had not been the bishop's specific role to conduct the bath; his was the concluding rite of the Spirit. When the bath came routinely to be done altogether in the bishop's absence, because haste was wanted and the bishop was distant from most of his flock, the rite of the Spirit was in the West kept for his later availability. Once there, the interval has expanded or contracted in response to social and pietistic pressures.

If we suppose the medieval and modern practice, the bath and the detached rite of the Spirit indeed appear as two "sacraments," in Trent's use of the word.

---

59. If Protestants allow the council to speak of "sacraments" with the council's own conditions for the term's application, all will affirm the seven; if Catholics allow Reformation traditions to speak of "sacraments" with their own conditions for the term's application, all will affirm but the two or three. One must, of course, wish that Trent had not been quite so enthusiastic in its use of the anathema.

60. Aidan Kavanaugh, *The Shape of Baptism* (New York: Pueblo, 1978), 54–86.

61. To the following J. D. C. Fisher, *Christian Initiation: Baptism in the Medieval West* (London: SPCK, 1965).

62. The classic account of this and related disasters is Fisher, *Christian Initiation*.

63. To the following, Nathan Mitchell, "Dissolution of the Rite of Christian Initiation," *Made, Not Born*, ed. Murphy Center for Liturgical Research (Notre Dame: Notre Dame University Press, 1976).

Should the decades-long effort of ecumenical liturgical theology to reunite them continue to bear fruit, there would be only the one continuous rite, though in deference to Trent we doubtless should still speak of two "sacraments." There is anyway no theological excuse for the separation as such. Acts' evidence that the manifest "coming" of the Spirit was in some quarters an expected consequence of initiation, and that this required the laying on of hands,[64] provides biblical support for the action of laying on of hands for the gift of the Spirit, but in no way supports its practice separately from the bath; on the contrary if it suggests anything it is that baptism without the rite of the Spirit is defective.[65] As for what a blessing bestowed by isolated confirmation might be, Thomas Aquinas doubtless says what little can be said: the Spirit is so given as to enable more "robust" Christian life.[66]

Penance[67] is a much less ambiguous matter. Its necessity is clearly biblical;[68] as we have seen, already the evangelist Matthew's church had to deal with severe breaches of her communion, and in the community that has the Lord for its center, discipline of such breaches must be *iure divino*, as Matthew in fact presents the rules followed in his congregation.[69] The *mystery* of penance is then the famous and already cited saying: "Whatever you bind on earth shall be bound in heaven, and whatever you loose on earth shall be loosed in heaven."[70]

The rite Trent had in mind as one of its seven is the result of a relatively late synthesis:[71] between the lingering theory of canonical penance and the actual practice of "Irish penance." The latter was a routine of daily pastoral care developed in the Irish church of the early medieval centuries, where monasticism provided the paradigm of churchly life, and then carried by Irish missionary monks

---

64. Acts 8:4–20; 19:1–7.

65. Any more than it supports a Pentecostalist separation of "water baptism" from "Spirit baptism." The struggles of earlier Catholic theology to justify biblically an indepedent sacrament of confirmation are sad to behold; e.g., a work on whose scholarship I much depend, Burkhard Neuenhauser, "Taufe und Firmung," *Handbuch der Dogmengeschichte*, ed. Michael Schmaus, Josef Geiselmann, Aloys Grillmeier, Bd. 4/2 (Freiburg: Herder, 1956), 19–24. Uncritical reliance on the Acts passages, which is the staple of such efforts, would necessitate the teaching that confirmation that did not immediately result in speaking in tongues had to be repeated.

66. *De articulis fidei et ecclesiae sacramentis, Opera Omnia* (Rome: Editori de San Tommaso, 1979), 254a.

67. The most lucid presentation known to me is a sort of historical-catechetical chapter on "Second Repentance" in Geoffrey Preston, *Faces of the Church* (Grand Rapids: Eerdmans, 1997), 162–170.

68. Here as at each following historical step, I rely on the splendid history by Herbert Vorgrimler, "Busse und Letzte Ölung" *Handbuch der Dogmengeschichte*, ed. Michael Schmaus, Josef Geiselmann, Aloys Grillmeier, Bd. 4/3 (Freiburg: Herder, 1978), 3–9.

69. Matthew 18:6–22.

70. Matthew 18:18.

71. For this, Vorgrimmler, "Busse," 100–82; Nathan Mitchell, "The Many Ways to Reconciliation," *The Rite of Penance: Commentaries III*, ed. N. Mitchell (Washington, D.C.: The Liturgical Conference, 1978), 20–37. For my own account, Robert W. Jenson, "The Return to Baptism," *Christian Dogmatics*, ed. Carl Braaten, Robert Jenson (Philadelphia: Fortress, 1984), 2:370–373.

into the vacuum left in Europe by the decay of canonical penance. The synthesis is often referred to as "private confession."

The medieval and modern practice carries a desperate theological problem. Since the transgressor has usually not been excluded from communion, reconciliation is not so much openly with the church as hiddenly with God. Since the theory of penance had never claimed that works of penance are necessary to placate *God*, and since we would not in any case know when enough had been done, the period of waiting as a penitent drops out. Reconciliation thus follows immediately on confession and is accomplished by an absolution directly on God's behalf. Penitential works are still imposed but not now to prepare for reconciliation. The resulting direct confrontation of confession and absolution made this rite be what the church had not previously had, a rite directly confronting the penitent's sin and God's forgiveness. This is undoubtedly very much to the good. But the question is now desperate: *What* achieves the reconciliation?

Theory carried over from the ancient church's penance said: the works of penitence achieve reconciliation. In the ancient church, however, reconciliation had been with the congregation's Eucharist. Now the only works done before the reconciliation are the sinner's subjective and oral confession, and the reconciliation is with God and not necessarily with the Eucharist, from which in most cases there has been no separation. The conclusion seems to follow that contrition earns God's forgiveness.[72] But so blatant a doctrine of justification by works was of course unacceptable, and medieval theology labored to correct it.[73]

Thomas Aquinas can again state a classic position. The *signum* is the sinner's apparent contrition, his or her confession and subsequent satisfactions, and the confessor's absolution.[74] The absolution effects the reconciliation.[75] Thomas accommodates this to the ancient understanding that it is contrition that obtains reconciliation by making true contrition the *signum et res* of this sacrament, the direct effect of the absolution as sign[76] and itself the effective sign of reconciliation.

The doctrine is analytically penetrating and no doubt descriptively accurate. But in the subjectivity of the penitent, a dire religious problem can still appear. The doctrine assures me that in the moment of absolution my true contrition cannot be lacking. But for all I can be assured, this moment may be the only moment of contrition's reality. In canonical penance, the eucharistic communion of the church, into which the penitent was restored, was itself the continuing assurance of worthiness; but here eucharistic fellowship was never terminated, and just so eucharistic fellowship is experienced as compatible with lack of contrition. Thus the introspective question, "But am I really contrite?" is not finally checked. Mixed canonical-Irish penance must often undo precisely those whose

---

72. Vorgrimmler, "Busse," 104–131.

73. Ibid., 129–130.

74. *Summa theologiae*, iii.84.1–2.

75. Ibid., iii.84.3.

76. Edward Schillebeeckx, "Transubstantiantion, Transfinalization, Transignification," *Worship* 40 (1966):334–338.

prickly consciences most need it; it was, after all, over questions of penitential practice that the conflict of the Reformation first broke out.

There are two possible resolutions of the problem. Perhaps the church will recover a public discipline, so that something like the practice of the ancient church reappears, which the theology of the ancient practice will again fit. The continuing collapse of Christianity's established position holds out some possibility of this. Otherwise, the theory left over from canonical penance must no more be applied to "Irish" penance, so that penance can be straightforwardly what some Reformation theology[77] makes of it, a concentrated direction of God's *torah* and of the gospel itself to the particular life of the penitent, with no detour by way of prior achievements or failures, inner or outer. Perhaps *both* rites would belong to a proper post-Constantinian practice of penance.

Embodied prayer for the sick is so obvious a thing for Christians to do, that it scarcely needs an explicit institution. The Scriptures from beginning to end see bodily disaster as a chief sign of creation's alienation from God's intention for it. Thus Jesus' proclamation of the immanent Kingdom found embodiment above all in his healings.[78]

A certain sacramental relation appears in Jesus' practice: healing the body is at least sometimes the visible sign of the otherwise invisible forgiveness of sins, which is in turn a sign of the Kingdom's coming, and so *signum et res*.[79] When the disciples were commissioned, such healing was part of their mission also;[80] and Pentecost renewed it as part of the apostles' ministry.[81] According to Mark, the disciples anointed the sick with oil;[82] we find the same rite in what is often taken as an apostolic mandate: "Are any among you sick? They should call for the elders of the church and have them pray over them, anointing them with oil in the name of the Lord." The connection between forgiveness and healing appears again: "The Lord will raise them up; and anyone who has committed sins will be forgiven."[83]

The connection between sin and sickness in the continuing life of the church, and the consequent connection between penance and healing, are illuminated by an observation of Geoffrey Preston: both sin and sickness alienate from the Eucharist. In a proper practice of penance, the sinner is welcome in the service but not given the elements; the sick person may be brought the elements but cannot take his or her part in the celebration to which they belong. "When a person is in either situation . . . the pastoral care of the Church is called for. The sick

77. Apology of the Augsburg Confession, art. xii.
78. Mark 5–6.
79. Mark 2:1–12.
80. Mark 6:6–13parr.
81. E.g., Acts 3:1–10.
82. Mark 6:13.
83. James 5:14–15.

person or the sinner needs to be reconciled to the community" and to the future Kingdom which the eucharistic celebration anticipates.[84]

The church's rite of healing has a convoluted history; since the anointing is to heal both sickness and sin, especially the relation to penance has been uncertain and liturgically confusing.[85] Particularly remarkable was the medieval transformation of a rite of healing into a rite of passage for the unhealable, "extreme unction." But the second Vatican Council reversed this for Roman Catholicism,[86] and the new Roman Catholic rites of healing seem to be providing a pattern for renewal in Protestantism also.

Finally, inclusion of marriage perfects the miscellaneous character even of the short Tridentine list.[87] Marriage itself is not a specifically churchly event at all; it is public entrance into a worldly polity's sanctioned structuring of sexuality, into the nexus between a society's chief synchronic unit and its diachronic continuity.[88] Some form of marriage is therefore a foundation of any functioning society. Christian, "sacramental" marriage is simply marriage that is also an ecclesial reality, because it is between Christians and is blessed by the church—as any created good can be.[89]

Yet marriage is the only instituted event that Scripture explicitly calls "a mystery": "A man will . . . be joined to his wife, and the two will become one flesh. This is a great mystery, and I am applying it to Christ and the church."[90] Throughout Scripture, marriage, in its intrinsic intimacy and permanence, is the chief created analogue of the Lord's relation to his people. The mystery is: when Christians marry, and live in the church that explicitly witnesses to this relation, the analogy itself comes to word. Their marriage becomes as such an embodied word of the gospel.[91]

What is the *signum* here? The couple's promise, or the church's ceremony of blessing, or their sexual union itself, or their churchly witness? Surely all four, each in its way. Does marriage fit the Thomistic scheme, or any other enumerating definition of "sacraments"? Not very well. *Is* it then a sacrament? Nothing serves better than marriage to show how that question poses a mostly linguistic choice. A great mystery of communion with Christ in the church, marriage assuredly is.

---

84. Faces, 172–173.

85. To this Vorgrimmler, "Busse," 127–138.

86. *Sacrosanctum concilium*, 73–75.

87. For the ritual and theological history of Christian marriage, Edward Schillebeeckx, *Marriage: Human Reality and Saving Mystery* (New York: Sheed & Ward, 1965).

88. Thomas Aquinas, *De articulis*, 256: there is a "triple good of marriage: the first is the bearing of children and their education to the service of God; the second is the faithfulness with which the one spouse serves the other."

89. An agreed sign, if the blessing is here to be a sign, there has never been. Schillebeeckx, *Marriage*, 244–256.

90. Ephesians 5:31–32.

91. According to Thomas, *De articulis*, 257, the "sacramentum" here is "the indivisibility of marriage, which obtains because it signifies the indivisible union of Christ with the church."

V

Two more mysteries complete this chapter's miscellany. The first is the as yet undiscussed aspect of the Eucharist, its reality as sacrifice, or as it has been called with honor or loathing, "the sacrifice of the mass."

The most theologically penetrating Catholic-Protestant dialogue has said flatly: "The controversy about 'the sacrifice of the mass' . . . has been left behind";[92] and this is in general the opinion of ecumenists. The understanding of eucharistic sacrifice that makes such surprising consensus possible has been provided mostly by the revival of Roman Catholic sacramental theology before and after the second Vatican Council.[93] We may summarize this theology in several steps.

First: the Eucharist is *sacramentally* a sacrifice, and not otherwise.[94] The dialogues have not in fact had so developed a concept of sacramental being as this chapter has attempted, but even the posit that there must be such a concept seems to suffice for ecumenical consensus. According to the dialogues, if Christ is sacrificed historically by Pilate on Calvary and sacramentally by and in the church, then the first event is neither "continued, nor repeated, nor replaced, nor complemented" by the second,[95] since such is not ever the relation between historical and sacramental being. Christ is sacramentally present in the Eucharist and *so* is "present . . . *as* [emphasis added] the sacrifice which once for all was brought for the sins of the world."[96] The eucharistic sacrifice is the sacramental presence of the sacrifice on the cross.

Second: the specific sacramental relation of the eucharistic sacrifice of Christ to the sacrifice on Calvary is *anamnesis*, "the making effective in the present of an event of the past."[97] Catholic-Reformation consensus is achieved when it is understood on both sides that Trent's word "representation" need not mean "doing again" but as a translation of the biblical *anamnesis* must mean "presenting again."[98] Recovery of a biblical and patristic understanding of memorial has made it "possible . . . to state faith's conviction [both] of the uniqueness and perfection of Jesus Christ's offering on the cross and of the breadth of its *anamnesis* in the church's celebration of Eucharist."[99]

---

92. Ökumensicher Arbeitskreis evangelischer und katholischer Theologen, *Lehrverurteilungen —kirchentrennend?* ed. Karl Lehmann, Wolfhart Pannenberg (Freiburg: Herder, 1986), 1:121.

93. The highly creative and influential J. M. R. Tillard must be explicitly mentioned. Two articles especially show his thought: "Catholiques romains"; "Sacrificial Terminology and the Eucharist," *One in Christ* 28 (1987).

94. The point is in itself not new; Thomas Aquinas, *Summa theologiae*, iii.79.7: "This sacrament is not only a sacrament but also a sacrifice. For *in that* [emphasis added] in this sacrament the passion of Christ is represented . . . it has also the character of sacrifice."

95. Joint Lutheran–Roman Catholic Commission, *The Eucharist* (1978), 56.

96. Ibid.

97. International Anglican–Roman Catholic Dialogue, *Eucharistic Doctrine* (1975), 5.

98. Kent S. Knutson, "Eucharist as Sacrifice," *Lutherans and Catholics in Dialogue*, vol. 3, ed. Paul Empie, T. Austin Murphy (Minneapolis: Augsburg, 1974).

99. Ökumenischer Arbeitskreis, *Lehrverurteilungen*, 121.

Third: it is "above all, the 'rediscovery' of the *communion*-structure of the Eucharist"[100] that enables new understanding of how the church can offer Christ. That is, the understanding of Eucharistic sacrifice that enables consensus is, unsurprisingly, one that is part of the communion-ecclesiology in general.

We may simply summarize and appropriate the results of Catholic-Protestant dialogue devoted specifically to this matter. Jesus on the Cross gave himself to the Father for us and gave himself to us in obedience to the Father; just this is his sacrifice. Thus what he gives us is communion: with him and so with the Father and so with one another. Conversely, what we materially share in this communion is Jesus himself, and specifically his sacrificial self-giving. And insofar as this sacrifice is anamnetically present, so that it is the bread and cup of the Eucharist by which he now gives himself, the eucharistic event itself is determined by these same relations.[101] Therefore it can be said ecumenically, across all previous conflicts: "In the celebration of the memorial, Christ . . . unites his people with himself. . . so that the church enters into the movement of his self-giving."[102]

The whole tendency of this work must lead to agreement with such formulations. Christ unites the church to himself precisely in his sacrificial self-giving to us and to the Father. It is the Eucharist at which this centrally occurs. Therefore, despite centuries of controversy, it is true: when the church in the Spirit offers thanksgiving to the Father for the Son and embodies this prayer as the bread and cup that are Christ's sacrificed body, she is one with Christ in his self-giving and so indeed herself offers Christ. The precise formulation was given long ago, by Augustine: Christ "is both the priest who offers and the one who is offered. It is of this reality [*res*] that the church's sacrifice intends to be a daily sacrament: since she is his body and he her head, she studies to offer herself by offering him."[103]

VI

This chapter's final assignment is the mystery of departed saints' prayer for us. It can hardly be said that ecumenical ecclesiology as yet extends to consensus in this matter.

The church is one communion through time. This communion cannot be broken by time's discontinuities, particularly not by death, for it is founded in the eternal triune communion of God and is constituted in the Spirit who is the Power of eternal life. Thus the church is a single active communion of living saints and departed saints—and indeed of those yet to be born. The second Vatican

100. Ökumenischer Arbeitskreis, *Das Opfer Jesu Christi und seine Gegenwart in der Kirche*, ed. Karl Lehmann, Wolfhart Pannenberg (Freiburg: Herder, 1083), 1.1.

101. Ibid., 4.3–4.

102. Anglican–Roman Catholic International Commission, *Eucharistic Doctrine: Elucidations* (1979), 3.8.

103. *De civitate Dei*, x.20. Augustine's aphoristic Latin is as so often not quite translatable: "Et sacerdos est, ipse offerens, ipse et oblatio. Cuius rei sacramentum quotidianum esse voluit Ecclesaiae sacrificium: quae cum ipsius capitis corpus sit, se ipsam per ipsum discit offerre."

Council taught: "The union of those who are still wayfarers, with brothers and sisters who rest in Christ's peace, is not interrupted but rather . . . becomes stronger by the communication of spiritual gifts."[104] As Jonathan Edwards, no papalist, taught: "The church in heaven and the church on earth are more one people, one city and one family than generally is imagined."[105]

Surely the council's and Edwards's teaching is true. But of course the question is, What is included in this "communication of spiritual gifts"? Do the saints in heaven *do* things for those on earth? And can our "communication" with them extend to requesting such action? Historically dominant actual practice poses the question in specific form: Do the saints in heaven pray for those on earth? And can we solicit their prayers?

Christians certainly may not in the proper sense pray *to* saints, any more than we pray to other creatures; and any practice suggesting such idolatry calls for reform.[106] But on earth we do and should request prayer of one another—which of course we may very well do with the vocabulary of "praying." Therefore there cannot in itself be anything inappropriate in asking Lucia or Martin also to pray for us, or indeed in referring to such requests as themselves prayer. And if there is nothing against the practice, there is surely everything for it. If "the prayer of the righteous is powerful and effective,"[107] we may well ask Joseph or Julian to pray for us. But again the question is, crudely: Can it work? Do the saints in heaven hear and honor such requests?

In decisive part, the question belongs to specific eschatology and will be taken up in the next part of the work; at issue is the ontological status of departed believers. Here we will proceed on the hypothesis that nothing will there be discovered that forecloses the ontic possibility of now soliciting the saints' intercession.

In the meantime, the churches have answered the question by practice. Orthodox, Catholics, and a few Protestants invoke the saints, together and individually, and most Protestants do not; opposite practice at this point is one of most obtrusive signs of churchly division.

There is on both sides very cautious doctrine in the matter, stated by the Council of Trent and by the Apology of the Augsburg Confession, in this matter the paradigmatic Protestant document. Dogmatic condemnation is mutually avoided, while the practical dissensus clearly appears. The *Apology* teaches that the saints in heaven do communally pray for the whole church on earth[108] but that because we have no scriptural warrant for supposing that the saints can be addressed by us, believers cannot be required to invoke them.[109] On the other

---

104. *Lumen gentium,* 49.

105. *Miscellanies,* 421.

106. It will be seen that I do not deal with this question by terminological distinctions, the traditional ones or others. They have been, I fear, less than helpful.

107. James 5:16.

108. Apology of the Augsburg Confession, xxi.8–9.

109. As a notable Protestant ecumenist said, when argument on the point became vigorous, "I don't talk to dead people!"

side, Trent carefully does not *require* invocation of saints but only vigorously urges it as something "good and useful" to do.[110]

The *Apology* is surely right in its precise statement: there can be no rule of faith that believers *must* invoke the saints. Protestant ascesis in this matter belongs to a general pattern of piety[111] whose restraint and biblical criteria must commend it within the church. But the tendency of this work urges the riskier practice. One major control is clear: since the communion of the church is established only by communion with Christ, whatever communion the church on earth has with the church in heaven is also so founded. The saints are not our way to Christ; he is our way to them. Our communion with departed saints, whatever may be included in it, is not fundamentally different from our communion with living saints. We may not ask Mary to bring us to Christ; because we are one with Christ we can address Mary.

But again, Can we indeed? The saints are in heaven; heaven is the presence of the future Kingdom. To speak to the saints would therefore be to intrude in the conversation that is the life of the Kingdom; it would be to call out to Francis as he takes his part around the throne. But the whole life of the church, with *all* its discourse, is anticipation of our inclusion in that same conversation. From our side, it would therefore seem that no other miracle is required than the miracle of the church's existence.

But still there is another condition. For us to address the saints, they from their side must be aware of and interested in us. We here touch the matter that must be reserved for the last part of this work. Supposing the saints' consciousness of us, it must differ from wayfaring saints' consciousness of one another in whatever ways risen consciousness differs from not yet risen consciousness. Later we will speculate about that, but the chief point can be made here: in the Kingdom we will know one another by participation in God's own knowledge of us. If the saints know us at all, they know us infinitely better than we know ourselves; surely this makes them attractive—and fearsome—as intercessors.

---

110. *Session* xxv, "De Invocatione."
111. What one would, were it not for recent use of the term, call "a spirituality."

TWENTY-NINE

The Word and the Icons

I

The founding mystery of the church's communion is the occurrence in her of the Word of God. Three referents of "the Word" are often distinguished: the eternal *Logos*, the church's speaking of the gospel, and the Scriptures. The substance of what this system has to say about the first two is already before us, developed through the whole work; we need here only summarize, with emphasis on certain points.

The eternal *Logos* is God's *address* and not his mere meaning or intention; and in fact this address is Jesus of Nazareth. What God says to himself, to be eternally the triune God, is the word-event reported in the Gospels. What the Father says, to generate the conversation that is God's eternal being, is "I am the Father of the one who . . ." with the ellipsis filled from what Jesus said and did and underwent.

The person who thus determines the Father's personhood cannot himself be other than the Father's perfect counterpart. Thus he is not only speech but like the Father a speaker; then the being of God is conversation. This counterpart speaker of the triune conversation is the human Jesus, again whatever might have been. When the Gospels quote Jesus' reports of his sending by the Father and Jesus' prayers to the Father, they cite exchanges in the conversation by and in which God is God.

This is the first and foundational mystery of communion,[1] that the triune conversation opens to creatures to be the converse of God within a historically

---

1. With this ordering, I dissent from Thomas. Otto Herman Pesch explains Thomas's position; "Theologie des Wortes bei Thomas von Aquin," *Zeitschrift für Theologie und Kirche* 66 (1969):464: "The sacraments' higher rank than preaching [for Thomas] . . . is the final consequence of . . . the circumstance that . . . for the sake of his doctrine of Trinity he had to develop a word-concept according to which the inner, acoustically inaudible word is the word in the richer and more essential sense."

actual human community. The primal mystery of communion is, in a favorite phrase of the Reformation's theology, the *viva vox evangelii*, the event of living human persons speaking and showing God's word and so hearing and seeing it.

Were it—contrary to possibility—God the Father's role to be himself God's word to us, we would either be abolished by this address or originated anew as identities of a pantheon. But it is the Son who is God's word and is so as one of us. God speaks to us and we neither die nor become his rivals because the Son is the speaker, as human and just so as God. God's address does not abolish us, but it does indeed originate us anew, as participants in an identity of the triune life. To adapt an earlier point about the Son's "natures": the transcendental focus from which the human person Jesus speaks is identically that of *the one whose* place in the human narrative and community is that of the one whose body is the church, and that of *the one whose* place in the triune narrative and community is that of the Son of the Father and the defining beneficiary of the Spirit.

That Jesus is risen means that his death does not inhibit his exercise of this trinitarian role. Indeed we have seen that on the contrary Jesus' Resurrection is his "determination" as the eternal Son and so his "determination" as the divine Word *ad extra*.[2]

But we have still only approached the specific identity of *signum et res* here to be interpreted. Augustine states the mystery with precision: "Whether the head speaks or the members, it is the one Christ who speaks."[3] Again: "Christ may thus speak, because the church speaks in Christ and Christ speaks in the church; the body in the head and the head in the body."[4] The trinitarian speaker of God's word *ad extra* is the *totus Christus*.

The church speaks *about* Christ as God and directly *for* God in his name: the church's word is a sign, of which both God's word to us and God's hearing of our word to him are the *res*. *Signum et res* is *Christ's* speech. He is the Speech of the Father; as the Father's speech to us he is embodied in the church and therefore does not, whatever might have been, speak except by this body. When the church pronounces absolution, this is Christ's absolution. When two or three gather as the church to petition the Father, there he is, praying with and indeed through them.[5]

We must still question the *truth* of this mystery. Earlier we asked: How can it be that the risen Christ has a created community as his body? We answered: it is so simply because he takes it so and because the way the *Logos* takes things determines how they are. To the present question we must answer with a like and indeed finally identical simplicity: the gospel-promise spoken in the church must either be spoken by the risen Christ or be utterly false; since it is true, it is spoken by the risen Christ. The gospel's truth is itself the ontological fact we are looking for.

---

2. 1:142–144.

3. *In Psalmos*, cxl.3: "Sive caput loquatur, sive membra, unus Christus loquitur."

4. Ibid., xxx.2,4: "Loquatur ergo Christus, quia in Christo loquitur Ecclesia, et in Ecclesia loquitur Christus; et corpus in capite, et caput in corpore."

5. Matthew 18:20.

The gospel is false if it is not the risen Jesus' own address to us, because it promises what only he in person can truly promise. The gospel promises Jesus himself, that he will eternally be our identity before the Father and our communion with each other. There is much I can promise on someone's behalf; but to promise someone's own self, I must speak not only for that person but *in* his or her person. The apostles and all evangelists of Jesus' love, and liturgical celebrants who plead it before God, thus always claim, with or without explicit assertion, to speak in Jesus' person.[6] If the claim is true, their speech is Jesus' speech; if the claim is false, the gospel is false.

Finally in this section, we must observe that the direction of our earlier interpretation is reversed. This work has to this point used the Old Testament's category of *prophecy* to interpret God's word both in Israel and in the church, as the New Testament itself does. Now, however, we have begun with the church's discourse itself, interpreting it by the trinitarian and christological doctrine this discourse has developed for its own interpretation.

The present order of interpretation traces the ontologically founding order. If Christ's advent is the fulfilling of Israel's story, then his discourse in the church is the possibility of all prophecy, also in Israel. The eternal *Logos* is the one Word of God, whenever spoken. And Christ's preexistence as this *Logos* is precisely *his* preexistence, the preexistence of the very one he is in and for the church.[7] The fathers could read the Old Testament no other way: the Word of God that "came" to make prophets and that was then spoken by the prophets[8] was none other than this Christ.[9] Even the apologetic *Logos*-doctrine had to sacrifice conceptual purity to this conviction. Thus according, for example, to Origen: "By the words of Christ we do not mean those only which he taught . . . when present in the flesh; for also before this Christ was the Word of God in Moses and the prophets."[10] Note that Origen does not revert from "Christ" to "the *Logos*" in the last clause.

II

Christ is the Word of God. The *viva vox* of the gospel is the Word of God. Scripture is the Word of God. This chapter will be disproportionately devoted to Scripture; a full discussion *de scriptura* cannot, given Western theology's history, now be lacking in any intentionally churchly system. The late-sixteenth- and seventeenth-century Protestant development of this *locus* can claim to be the only fully developed proposal so far; it will from time to time be adduced, usually favorably.

---

6. Further to this, Robert W. Jenson, *Story and Promise* (Philadelphia: Fortress, 1973), 160–163.

7. 1:138–144.

8. 1:78–80.

9. Here as in so many places, Jaroslav Pelikan provides a clear and concise statement of the case; *The Christian Tradition: A History of the Development of Doctrine* (Chicago: University of Chicago Press, 1971), 1:110–111.

10. *First Principles*, Preface, 1. Or see Irenaeus, *Against All Heresies*, iv.2.3.

The previous volume brought one part of this work's proposal, discussing Scripture's role as a norm available to theology for judging the church's faithfulness. Along the way, we affirmed a distinction proposed in old Protestantism but not then generally adopted. Johannes Musaeus taught that the authority of Scripture is a "double capacity: one to judge other writings and teachings; . . . another to bring about the assent of faith."[11] In discussing Scripture as a norm of theological judgment, we limited ourselves to the first "capacity." Here we turn to the second.

Scripture is read in all services of the church, and its language and stories and sayings otherwise pervade them; Scripture is read in the devotions of Christian homes and religious communities, where it shapes the minds of sequential generations; Scripture is read by the pious quietly; and even a theologian checking a reference may be moved by it in unexpected fashion. In some traditional rites the reading from the Gospels is introduced by the announcement, "The holy gospel is from the Gospel according to . . ." The repetition of "gospel" gives the exact intent: reading a Gospel-text is to be the saving spoken gospel.

When a text is actually read, it is not merely text but somehow is living address. The reader, if only to him or herself, appropriates and directs the text by selection, posture, acoustic or mental intonation and tempo, and so on. Yet, more importantly, the communal context of reader and hearers—even when these are the same person—directs the text's address into and within the community's living discourse; in eucharistic and preaching services of the church very directly with the homily that follows the readings.

The first and foremost doctrine *de scriptura* is therefore not a proposition *about* Scripture at all. It is rather the liturgical and devotional instruction: Let the Scripture be read, at every opportunity and with care for its actual address to hearers, even if these are only the reader. The churches most faithful to Scripture are not those that legislate the most honorific propositions about Scripture but those that most often and thoughtfully read and hear it.

The more narrowly theological normativity of Scripture can function only within this role in the life of faith. Scripture's fundamental authority is simply the fact that its *viva vox* is present in the church, and so present as to shape her life. Insofar as theology is called to measure the church's faithfulness in this matter also, the decisive questions are therefore questions about elementary churchly practice. What stories, lines of argument, and turns of phrase actually come to furnish the minds of those supposedly instructed in the faith? When prayers and hymns are chosen or written, what vocabulary and what narratives of invocation and blessing come first to hand? Do we witness the preacher struggle to be faithful to the readings, whether successfully or not?

The primary doctrine of Scripture may be stated: *privilege* this book within the church's living discourse. And that of course does pose a theoretical question: *Why* should Scripture be thus privileged? The answer is almost tautologous.

---

11. *Introductio in theologiam* (1679), ii.iii; cited 1:29n.

The gospel is a narrative, and this book is that telling of the narrative from which all others draw, quite apart from any need for their correction by it.[12]

Long before Pentecost the way in which Israel told of God's history with her was by editing and reading and commenting her history-book, and the church was born directly in course of this tradition. The formation of a New Testament was done somewhat more deliberately, as part of the church's general struggle with early heresy, and in particular response to Marcion's creation of the first and heretical New Testament canon.[13] But the collection and its relation to the Old Testament were nevertheless not fashioned to provide proof texts against or for particular propositions but shaped rather to the general plot and understanding of the church's story as she had been telling it all along. Thus the New Testament canon could accommodate Gospels with some plainly discordant orderings of events, because all four were used in the orthodox churches, and accommodate theological letters not easily brought to systematic agreement, because an apostolic witness is an apostolic witness. The New Testament retraced the overall story and mediated an unexpurgated apostolic testimony to the story's high point in Christ.[14]

That is, a narrative general interpretation of the documents that became the New Testament, in their relation to the Old Testament and to each other, was itself the principle of their gathering. The church's continuing practice of proclamation and prayer, and the collection of Scripture as it was gradually shaped, were simply versions in two media of the same story. The old-Protestant doctrine of Scripture rightly made "perfection" or "sufficiency" Scripture's first defining attribute, meaning that its content is the same as that of the church's continuing message, that neither needs to be *added* to from the other.[15] It may not, of course, have been so clear to these theologians as it might have been that each nevertheless needs the other.

Irenaeus of Lyon was perhaps the chief shaper of this material principle. "The frame for his general interpretation was provided by the salvation-historical scheme of divine covenants, which Irenaeus took over from Justin. . . . But Irenaeus . . . had means powerfully to deepen the old notion: here belong his expositions of the relation of creation and redemption, and of redemption and new life."[16]

Also the *language* of Scripture must be privileged in the church; the insight goes back at least to Origen.[17] For in distinction from theories or individual statements of fact, narrative offers little scope for translation of concepts, metaphors,

12. E.g., Johann Gerhard, *Loci theologici* (1610), i.xviii, 367.

13. Hans Freiherr von Campenhausen, *Die Entstehung der christlichen Bibel* (Tübingen: J. C. B. Mohr, 1968), 173–241.

14. Ibid., 237–242.

15. Gerhard, *Loci theologici* (1657), i.xviii.367.

16. Ibid., 240–241.

17. Peter Widdicombe, *The Fatherhood of God from Origen to Athanasius* (Oxford: Clarendon, 1994), 54–57.

or turns of phrase. A physics text loses little or nothing in translation from French to English; translation of Proust from French to English loses a lot; and translation of Proustian diction and allusion into easy reading for unprepared English-speaking students would lose almost everything. Moreover, the translation of a narrative must be guided by its conclusion, from which alone it is intelligible. But the conclusion of the biblical narrative is given only by reference to a person, the returning Christ, and in untranslatable apocalyptic iconography.

Thus even biblical Greek and Hebrew must be familiar somewhere in the life of the church. And the diction and common turns of Scripture, however translated into modern languages, cannot be replaced; even in such highly abstracted theology as this work, we have not done without—to take only very obtrusive cases—"who raised our Lord Jesus," or the "coming" of the Word, or "heaven," or "justification." Among the church's people a casual reference to "Babel" should call up an entire network of story and teaching, and the very jokes and insults turn on the likes of Samson or Ananias. For weighty illustration of the point: the post–Vatican Council recasting of the Roman mass into vernacular languages, and particularly the attempt to provide vernacular hymns for it, has been, at least in English-speaking territories, bane more often than blessing, through neglect of just such considerations.[18]

Finally in this series we must note that it is a *text* that is privileged. Reading a text still differs from composing an address in one's own responsibility: these sentences and paragraphs and documents are given for the reader just as for the hearer. The Word of God always, we have said, contrives somehow to be an "external" word, a word that cannot be absorbed into the hearer's subjectivity. Scripture's character as text is a specific such objectivity, of proclamation and prayer's apostolic givenness. Whatever the church may from time to time make of Scripture or any passage in it, there the pages themselves sit, text-relic of the apostolic gospel.[19]

We return to the justification of Scripture's privilege in the church. This, we said, is almost tautologous, but the tautology is sacramental. How *can* someone's reading a book be the risen Christ speaking? Part of the answer is already before us. Insofar as the reading is living speech, it is the gospel, which promises what

---

18. Such recent enterprises as "entertainment evangelism" or the liturgical and catechical prescriptions of the "church growth" movement are of course on another level of disreputability.

19. This is one reason why attempts to rescue Scripture from whatever at any time are its political incorrectnesses by "translations" that excise them are so fatuous. Thus the editors of *Lectionary for the Christian People*, ed. Gordon Lathrop, Gail Ramshaw-Schmidt (New York: Pueblo, 1986) detect, besides many other shortcomings, anti-Semitism in John. Let them then denounce this; perhaps they are right. But let them not sanitize John by translating *hoi Iudaioi* with "Jewish people" when they are favorably or neutrally mentioned, and "Judeans" when they are unfavorably mentioned. There are of course worse productions than this lectionary; someone uninitiated in current ideology might take *The New Testament and Psalms: An Inclusive Version*, ed. Victor Gold et al. (New York: Oxford University Press, 1995) for a student prank. But the matter is serious: only a church that had forgotten her identity with the apostolic church could stand to use such materials.

only Christ in person can promise; the truth of what is said is thus itself the sacramental relation. But in the case of Scripture the living speech is not that *of* a living person but carries all the baggage of historical conditionings and limitations inherent in millennia of writing and editing and collecting.

For the first volume of this work Johann König provided a statement of the problem that drove old-Protestant doctrine: we may consider Scripture "as it is simply the divine word, in which respect we can say that Scripture is prior to the church; or as it is recorded in writing, in which respect Scripture is subsequent to the church."[20] As Scripture is the Word of God simply understood, it is God's saving gospel, which *creates* the church. But the Scripture as such is a collection of writings put together *by* the church, some of which were written *in* the church. How do we get theologically from the one to the other? In the old-Protestant doctrine, the "way from the *verbum dei* itself to *scriptura* was made by way of 'inspiration.'"[21]

Surely this was initially the right move. It must indeed be the Spirit who frees the composition, editing, preservation, collection, and reading of certain texts by the church to be apt to be the risen Christ's word to his church.

But this doctrine ironically forgot that the Spirit is freedom. The Protestant scholastics made inspiration be a predicate of those events by which the Word of God came to be "written down."[22] The identity of the *verbum dei* with specific writings was supposed to have been accomplished by divine controls that guaranteed the truth and power of these writings by the correctness of what is written in them. This made a sacramental relation between God's speech and their actual reading unnecessary and indeed impossible.

We must reason in just the opposite direction to construe the true mystery of Scripture's living divine voice. How indeed, to take a case not often adduced, can the productions of some civil servant in the Jerusalem court, in part cribbed from Egyptian models,[23] be God's "wisdom" for my life? Not because the Spirit provided exactly the words he one day wrote, thereby guaranteeing their wisdom and power independently of all subsequent history. Rather because the whole event, from that civil servant's memorizing Egyptian and other wise maxims in his youth to his rethinking them in maturity, to the accidents of collecting and editing and preserving, to the way in which we attend the Old Testament reading some Sunday morning, is drawn on by the Spirit's freedom. The Bible is the Spirit's book, who may do with it what he will; and the church as his prophet knows what that is.

---

20. *Theologia positiva acroamatica* (1664), 83: "Sumitur vel praecise qua verbum divinum est, quomodo dicimus scripturam esse antiquiorem ecclesia, vel qua literis consignatum est, quomodo scriptura est posterior ecclesia."

21. Carl Heinz Ratschow, *Lutherische Dogmatik zwischen Reformation und Aufklärung* (Gütersloh: Gerd Mohn, 1964), 1:79.

22. For the doctrine and its development, in its paradigmatic Lutheran form, with texts, ibid., 81–97.

23. E.g., Proverbs 61:19.

III

First of all then, the church is to read the Scripture. But of course even in choosing what to read we interpret the reading. The question cannot be avoided and is indeed a primary systematic-theological question: How is the church to go about interpreting her Scripture?

The first point to be made both reverts yet again to churchly context and relativizes procedural answers to the question. Churchly interpretation of Scripture is not interpretation that obeys some preferred procedure, that, for example, prefers redaction criticism to form criticism or vice versa, or eschews critical methods altogether, or follows any similar prescription. Churchly interpretation of Scripture is interpretation done in course of activities specific to the church: missionary preaching, liturgy, homiletics, catechetics, endurance of suffering, governance, care of souls, or works of charity. And to repeat in this context a point made in a slightly different one: there is no way to list in advance what roles Scripture may play in these different enterprises and their changing historical situations. So the chief hermeneuticist in the recent "Yale school" of American theology, Hans Frei: "It is doubtful that any scheme for reading texts, and narrative texts in particular, and biblical narrative texts even more specifically, can serve globally or foundationally."[24]

There is nevertheless a now overriding methodological question which cannot be avoided. In modernity, "historical-critical" exegesis has become the approved way of reading texts originating at some temporal distance from the reader. The policy is now taught in all mainline schools of theology as the one fully legitimate way to read the Bible. Nor has recent criticism of this curriculum's effects on the church produced any plausible replacement.

It is a specific character of modernity to experience the stretch of time between ourselves and, for example, Socrates' life and teaching as *distance,* though it of course could just as well be experienced as *connection,* and for most of human history has been. "Only with the breakdown of traditional metaphysics . . . did the historicity of existence come fully to consciousness."[25] So long as history is experienced as encompassed within an unchanging structure of cosmic being, the difference between yesterday and today is not felt *as* difference but rather as commendation; Plato's accounts of Socrates are read as if Plato were a well-tested local

24. "The 'Literal Reading' of Biblical Narrative in the Christian Tradition: Does It Stretch or Will It Break?" abr. and ed. Kathryn Tanner, *The Return to Scripture in Judaism and Christianity,* ed. Peter Ochs (New York: Paulist Press, 1993), 70.

This essay, as abridged by Tanner, is perhaps Frei's most straightforward statement of his mature position, and in particular of his judgment of dominant hermeneutical theory and antitheory. The congruence between much of Frei's theory—if he would be willing to have it called that—and what follows here is plain: central to both is the observation that the Bible is the church's book, and that therefore the right rules for reading the Bible must be those that constitute the church's relation to this book. But it is not plain to me that Frei would countenance everything that follows; he is a very determined antimetaphysician, and that must surely make a difference here also.

25. Gerhard Ebeling, *Wort und Glaube* (Tübingen: J. C. B. Mohr, 1960), 33.

reporter and Socrates a revered public personality. The metaphysics of timeless-
ness is the theology of this religion of cosmic enclosure, and it is merely a further
aspect of the gospel's secularizing backslash in Western civilization to have discredited this metaphysics.[26] If the gospel's story is the final truth about being, then
precisely the temporal differences within history are where truth emerges.

It will belong to Western modernity's consciousness and that of cultures
decisively influenced from the West so long as any of these lasts: Socrates, to continue the example, is *not* our contemporary; his Athens was a very different place
from any of our communities; his most decisive references and turns of phrase
depend on knowledge and attitudes alien to us. That is, he and we are historically
conditioned and differently so. A specific policy toward the past and toward the
texts in which we learn of it follows immediately: "When . . . the fact of historical
change, of historical conditioning . . . became clear, the freedom, but also the
necessity . . . was given to consider history in its pure historicity, that is, objectively from a distance."[27] Historical-critical exegesis is nothing more than interpretation steered by determination to find out about Socrates, and Plato who tells
of him, and about Jesus and the apostles who tell of him, and about Moses and
the tradents who tell of him, as they were in their times and places and as they
were conditioned by them, precisely as these were *not* our time or place.

Such historical consciousness and the routines of reading that have developed within it—the various sorts of "criticism"—are in themselves imperative
for the church's interpretation of Scripture. For "the procedure that critically
makes the documents transparent in their historicity and therewith in their distance from the present . . . creates the necessary presupposition for . . . letting them
say something to us."[28] Within Christianity's construal of reality as history, discovery that Paul in his time and place did not necessarily think or experience what
I in my time and place presuppose everyone must is a necessary first step of his
authority over me. Paul cannot enrich my apprehension of the gospel so long as
I presume his apprehension and mine must obviously be the same. Historical-
critical reading of Scripture is, at least where Christianity and modernity or
postmodernity overlap, the necessary "self-criticism by the interpreter with respect to . . . possibilities of self-deception about what the . . . text intends."[29]

But at the same time, historical-critical consciousness and practice make a
crisis of all interpretation, a crisis intrinsic to Western modernity and increasingly disastrous for it, and so far unresolved also within the church. In modernity, scholarly reading of texts becomes labor to build bridges across the historical distance between readers and the time and place from which the texts come,
to overcome a "hermeneutical gap" between ourselves and Jesus or St. Francis or
Socrates. The question had eventually to arise: Can this ever really succeed?

26. The great interpreter of this is again Friedrich Gogarten, *Der Mensch zwischen Gott und Welt*
(Stuttgart: Vorwerk-Verlag, 1956).

27. Ebeling, *Wort*, 33.

28. Ibid., 36.

29. Ibid., 451.

The Western world has come to view the past all too decisively "from a distance." And this alienation has penetrated deeply into the church's thinking also. When we have made it fully clear to ourselves, for example, that the historical Jesus told the parable of the vineyard-keepers[30] as an immediate eschatological threat to first-century Jewish rulers of temple and synagogue, what are *we* then to make of the parable, who are not such persons, nor can feel how they would have heard such a threat, and who moreover know that most of them probably either died in good old age or were killed not by an archangel but by Titus? Ironically, what usually happens is that preachers and teachers are defeated by such questions and relapse to whatever moralistic or theological platitudes they would have proclaimed anyway; that is, they are returned to the very possibilities of self-deception from which historical-critical study was to rescue them. Or for a different sort of problem, when investigation has made it clear that the ancient world had no concept of "sexual orientations,"[31] what use can we then make of Scripture's judgments of sexual practices?[32] The academic exegetes, when queried by the church, have thrown up their hands and responded that historical conditionings prevent Paul or the authors of Leviticus from speaking to us about the matter.

In a crisis of her own modernity, the church is able to live neither with nor without "historical-critical exegesis."[33] And yet the resolution, as it seems to the present writer, is provided by one simple insight. Whatever hermeneutical gaps may need to be dealt with in the course of the church's biblical exegesis, there is one that must not be posited or attempted to be dealt with: there is *no* historical distance between the community in which the Bible appeared and the church that now seeks to understand the Bible, because these are the same community.

Much has recently been made of "communities of interpretation": what a text means in one such community, it is said, may have little relation to what in means in another. Undoubtedly it is so; and this insight must be yet a blow to modernity's assumptions.[34] But the text we call the Bible was put together in the first place by the very same community of interpretation that now needs to interpret it.[35]

The error of almost all modern biblical exegesis is a subliminal assumption that the church in and for which Matthew and Paul wrote, or in which Irenaeus shaped the canon, and the church in which we now read what they produced are historically distant from each other. That is, the error is the subliminal assump-

30. Mark 12:1–9parr.

31. Very much to its credit for realism, by the way.

32. Romans 1:26–27.

33. A set of diagnostic and polemic essays on the matter is provided by Carl E. Braaten, Robert W. Jenson, eds., *Reclaiming the Bible for the Church* (Grand Rapids: Eerdmanns, 1995).

34. Modernity's epistemological foundation is the assumption of a common standard of rationality. And modernity indeed had such a standard but failed to notice that it existed not in abstract endowments of the human neural system but in texts.

35. I do not here draw very directly from the work of Brevard Childs, but his chief work must be named, as a permanent foundation stone of such reflections as those here called for. *Biblical Theology of the Old and New Testaments* (Minneapolis: Fortress, 1993).

tion that there is no one diachronically identical universal church: nearly all modern biblical exegesis in fact presumes a sectarian ecclesiology. But while Athens may perhaps have disappeared into the past and been replaced by Paris or New York, Paul's church still lives as the very one to which believing exegetes now belong. Moreover, this church remains in the same relation to canonical Israel as on the day of Pentecost.

What the most percipient of twentieth-century hermeneutical theory has said must therefore hold in the church and of her Scripture, if nowhere else: our present effort to understand a handed-down text cannot be hopeless, since it is merely the further appropriation of a continuing communal tradition within which we antecedently live.[36] Past and present do not need to be bridged before understanding can begin, since they are always already mediated by the continuity of the community's language and discourse: the concepts and turns of phrase and dominating metaphors and ready-to-hand warrants with which I now try to say what the text says cannot be wholly unsuitable to the task since they were inculcated in me by the very tradition of which the text is a part.[37] "Understanding is not so much an undertaking by the subject as it is further entry into a continuing tradition-event in which past and present anyway mediate themselves."[38]

When academic exegetes say that Paul's opinions are too historically conditioned now to be helpful, or that the parable of the vineyard-keepers cannot itself control what we now make shift to draw from it, they are simply interpreting Scripture as it now will inevitably be interpreted outside the church. Current academic, political, and publicistic elite communities[39] are indeed alienated historically from the community in which the Bible emerged, and this is the reason and indeed excuse of their helplessness before this text. But when the church reads Scripture in course of her own worship and catechetics and preaching, her interpreters cannot give up so easily, because they are themselves at stake.

Those who interpret Scripture in and for the church are compelled to keep trying to say what it says, and by the mere act claim that Scripture does say *something* to us; the struggle itself is the hermeneutical principle. Bishops and parish presbyters and scholars in their service are the ones whose labor to read the text honestly and faithfully, and whose assumption of the labor this means in their office, will maintain the authority of Scripture or whose failure to do so will undercut it. The old-Protestant doctrine of Scripture gave it a second essential predicate: it is "perspicuous," by which they did not mean it contains no obscurities or can be understood without effort[40] but that the effort need not finally be defeated.

36. Hans Georg Gadamer, *Wahrheit und Methode* (Tübingen: J. C. B. Mohr, 1965), 250–290.

37. Ibid., 361–382.

38. Ibid., 275.

39. Including most decisively and destructively those of the "biblical-literature" and "religious-studies" denominations.

40. Gerhard, *Loci*, i.ii, §414: "Non excludi a nobis per assertionem perspicuitatis pium studium in lectione et meditatione Scripturae adhibendum, nec adminicula ad Scripturae interpretationem necessaria."

One consequence of the positions just stated must be noted and emphasized: historical honesty requires the church to interpret Scripture in the light of her dogmas. If the church's dogmatic teaching has become false to Scripture, then there is no church and it does not matter how the group that mistakes itself for church reads Scripture or anything else. But if there is the church, then her dogma is in the direct continuity of Scripture and is a necessary principle for interpreting Scripture, and vice versa. So, for example, the church teaches that the Word that came to the prophets and the Word incarnate by Mary are the same entity; therefore interpretation of the Servant Songs by the Christology of the ecumenical councils is *not* the imposition of an extrinsic rule but is rather vital elucidation of what the text historically says.

This does not mean that every biblical passage must be made to agree with dogma. The Bible is not theologically homogeneous even with itself; nor is point-for-point unanimity the mode of any community's diachronic consensus. Nor does it mean that historical study may not find that particular apparently dogmatic decisions of the church are unsupported by Scripture. If this happens, the church, bound by her faith in the Spirit's leading, will suppose that the dissensus is not fatal and can be overcome. A classic example can be the way in which later ecumenical councils dealt with the Christology of Chalcedon, bending it ever more to Cyril's insight into the unity of the Gospels' narrative.[41]

Nor does such insight, and an exegetical practice based on it, disarm historical-critical study's ability to confront readers of Scripture with the otherness of the texts. Between Isaiah and Paul and between each and a modern exegete there are historical distances enough, and it is the task of historical critique to display them. But they are differences of times and places within the life of one community.

The historical distances that historical-critical reading of Scripture can and must keep open are historical distances *within* the story of Scripture's community; they make the historical *compass* of the one community whose book this is. The historical distances with which interpretation must indeed reckon and of which historical-critical labors must maintain the awareness are the distances between Moses and the later prophets, or between the prophets and Jesus, or between Jesus and Paul and Paul and us, but never between the story as a whole and us, never between the biblical community as a whole and the present church. The church's exegetes need, and indeed are permitted to make, no special exertions to join the community of which Scripture speaks, since they already belong to it, or to connect with its story, since they are themselves characters in it.[42]

John's theology was different from Paul's, and the present author's is different from John's. Mark's expectations of the End were different from Daniel's, and

---

41. 1:131–136.

42. Recently, academic exegetes have worried much about "recovering" such entities as "the Pauline participatory discourse" or "John's subjectivity." All such proposals are oxymoronic, since if such things are once lost they cannot be recovered. In the church, Paul's "participatory discourse" is not lost and does not need to be recovered.

the present author's are different from Mark's. And so on. It is the task of historical-critical reading to mark such differences ever more sharply. But in the church this must be done only to profile the individual moments of one dramatically coherent history and its telling. With any particular biblical event or passage, this preliminary step is necessary; but actual interpretation is then the art of displaying the thus profiled event or teaching or prophecy or prayer in its place within the one story of God with his people.

The church once called this sort of exegesis "spiritual." The true intent of traditional spiritual exegesis was long hidden from the modern church both by irresponsible practice thereof and by historically uninformed polemic against "allegory." But it has been rediscovered, perhaps principally by the work of Henri de Lubac,[43] already our guide in other connections.

"Spiritual exegesis" was primally exegesis of the Old Testament. The church is convinced that the events told in the New Testament are the dramatic conclusion of those told in the Old.[44] Spiritual exegesis, in this following the practice of the New Testament itself, thus reads all events of Old Testament history as what we may call prophetic word-events: "'Allegory' is prophecy inscribed in the events themselves. . . . The historical facts . . . are themselves the 'figures,' themselves contain the mysteries that the practice of allegory seeks to extract."[45] What they prophesy is Christ: the "spirit" to be found in the Old Testament "letter" is Christ.

Contrary to what has often been thought,[46] therefore, spiritual exegesis does not intend to "spiritualize" its texts; the mystery supposed to be hidden in an Old Testament event or testimony "is not . . . a timeless truth. It is . . . an action, the realization of a great plan, and is therefore . . . itself a historical reality."[47] The "letter" is the successive events narrated by the texts; and the best masters of spiritual exegesis, when reading *ad litteram*, labored like any modern exegete to trace the events in their causal sequence.[48] The "spirit" is the meaning of those events, within the gospel's whole teleological narrative.[49] We may say that "literal" reading traces the causal sequences of biblical history and that spiritual reading traces its eschatological plot.[50] Nor need such exegesis be uncontrolled or arbitrary, since it is controlled by the New Testament's accounts of Christ and evocations of the Kingdom.[51]

It is thus not at all clear that the Reformation's principles of biblical exegesis are actually at odds with those of patristic or medieval exegesis. If Martin Luther's

---

43. Henri de Lubac, *Exègése Médiévale: les Quatre Sens de l'Écriture* (Paris: Aubier, 1959–1964).
44. Ibid., 1:400, 498–511.
45. Ibid., 1:493.
46. I must in honesty admit my own previous complicity in this error.
47. Ibid., 1:504.
48. Ibid., 1:479–487.
49. Ibid., 1:425–439.
50. Ibid., 1:515: "On est conduit par une série de faits singuliers jusqu'a un autre Fait singulier; une série d'interventions divines, dont la réalité même est significative, schemine."
51. Ibid., I/1:202–207.

great exegetical maxim was that the Word of God in Scripture is "what confronts us with Christ," the conviction of spiritual exegesis is that everything in Scripture does that, in that the whole Old Testament is a plotted sequence of christological prophecy-events.[52] Luther concludes his introduction to the Books of Moses: "In conclusion I ought also to indicate the spiritual meaning presented to us by the Levitical law and priesthood of Moses. . . . If you would interpret well and confidently, set Christ before you, for he is the man to whom it all applies, every bit of it. Make the high priest Aaron, then, to be nobody but Christ alone," and so on.[53]

The classical system of spiritual exegesis knew, of course, not just literal and spiritual senses, but three modes of the latter: "allegorical," "tropological," and "anagogical." Their differences result from the delay of the parousia, from the church's position *within* the New Testament's fulfillment of the Old. Since the coming of Christ is divided, with time for the church between,[54] three "advents" of Christ fulfill the Old Testament: the Incarnation, his return at the Consummation, and between them his entry into the hearts of the faithful.[55] Allegorical interpretation of a text is christological; it points a text to the Incarnation. Anagogical interpretation is eschatological; it points a text to the End. And tropological or moral interpretation points it to the life of faith.[56] The second and third can thus be applied not only to the Old Testament but also to the Gospels.

Surely this refinement also is in general appropriate. One will not have expounded a passage within the whole biblical narrative unless one has discerned its eschatological dynamic and discerned its import for believers' lives. Yet the temptations posed by thinking of eschatological and moral "senses" *other* than the incarnational are plain: the tropological sense can easily become "what this passage means to me";[57] and the anagogical sense can become untethered mystical or apocalyptic speculation.[58]

Moreover, although allegorical exegesis was in its founding intention interpretation of the Old Testament by the events recorded in the New, medieval exegetes in fact freely allegorized the Gospels also; but since it is the Gospels that control allegorical exegesis, over their own allegorization there can be no control. Nor can it be denied that de Lubac has somewhat exaggerated the historical character of traditional spiritual exegesis; although the sign and its allegorical referent are indeed both historical events, the connections drawn are themselves often ahistorical associations.

---

52. Ibid., II/1:60–64.

53. *Luther's Works*, vol. 38, ed. Theodore Bachmann (Philadelphia: Muhlenberg, 1960), 247.

54. Ibid., 1:416: The three spiritual senses "result from the hiatus . . . between Christ's two advents. When that hiatus is there, the spiritual sense . . . which was an eschatological sense, necessarily devided itself in three."

55. Ibid., 1:621.

56. Ibid., 1:511–643.

57. For somewhat grudging recognition of this by de Lubac, ibid., 1:571–586.

58. Medieval capitulation to this temptation is clearly described by de Lubac; ibid., 642.

What "spiritual" exegesis needs, to prevent its perversion, is precisely that attention to historical locations that we call historical-critical. The churchly exegesis that should now be possible would be as devoted as any medieval homilist to finding a christological and eschatological and moral sense in every last event or testimony of Scripture but would be constrained by historical consciousness from finding them by ahistorical associations. For attempted examples of such exegesis, this work will offer not made-up cases but simply its own pages of scriptural interpretation.

Finally in this section, a special impediment to christological-spiritual exegesis of the Old Testament must be removed. It is often supposed that Judaism's exegesis of Israel's Scripture must be somehow more "literal" or straightforward than the church's and that since Israel's exegesis is of course not christological, christological-spiritual exegesis of the Old Testament must be in comparison imposed from a viewpoint alien to the text. Here an earlier point must be given a particular emphasis.

The paired continuations of Israel—Judaism and the church—have each their defining way of reading Israel's Scripture: the church reads it about Christ; the Pharisaic synagogue reads it about *torah*. As we saw earlier, neither community of interpretation has a historically prior justification or claim on the inheritance of Israel.[59] Theologically, if the church's faith is true, Jesus Christ *is* the *torah*, so that her claim overlaps that of the synagogue. Therefore the church has no a priori reason *either* to defer to rabbinic exegesis *or* to regard it as a priori false. What judgment the synagogue should make of Christian exegesis is of course not to be prompted by Christian theology.

IV

There remain, of the mysteries to be considered in these two chapters, and as a pair to the *viva vox* and Scripture, the icons. They are often taken for a peculiarity of Orthodoxy, which has developed a specific representational technique and special liturgical uses. But the dogmatic definition of icons is broad,[60] and by it icons are common in the West also. The second Council of Nicea in 787 ended the "iconoclastic" struggle and made the appropriateness of venerating[61] icons ecumenical dogma. According to the council, icons are "evangelical exegeses made by spatial depiction,"[62] visual expositions of the gospel narrative for liturgical use,

---

59. Even Hans Frei repeats the common mistake and speaks of the "common scripture which Christianity has usurped from Judaism"; "The 'Literal Reading,'" 79.

60. Some Russians, for whom Orthodoxy has nearly ceased to be a Christian church and has become instead a national spirituality, deny this. Thus a hyper-Platonist like Pavel Florensky simply equates the traditional technique and the Russian synodical canons of representation with "iconpainting" as such and will admit the ancient pagans to salvation but not a Western artist who depicts evangelical events with oils on canvas; *Iconostasis*, tr. Donald Sheehan, Olga Andrejev (Crestwood: St. Vladimir's Seminary Press, 1996).

61. *Proskynesis.*

62. Second Council of Nicea, definition: "euaggelikas exegeseis tas stelographikws ginomenas."

in any representational medium.[63] The church has in fact rarely done without such objects, the most notable periods of abstention being her very first decades, the decades in the East under iconoclastic emperors before 780, and modernity under the more Calvinist branches of the Reformation. From the time of the council, Orthodoxy has of course been the icons' theological champion and expositor.

Followers of a religion that tells a story about identifiable characters will naturally tend to visualize certain characters and incidents. We need not attribute the appearance of "Christian art" as such to any very profound or even reliably Christian impulse. Iconoclasts have always had reason for their suspicion of idolatry. And they have as their weapon nothing less than a commandment fundamental for God's people: "You shall not make for yourself a divine image,[64] whether in the form of anything that is in heaven above, or that is on the earth beneath, or that is in the water under the earth."[65] It is of course icons of Christ that both enable other images' religious significance and are themselves the problem: Since Christ is God, is not use of his representation in worship precisely what the commandment forbids?

Our first step must be deeper understanding of the prohibition of images in Israel. One could not come into *this* God's, JHWH's, presence by orienting to an image of him but only by invoking his name. And not only was this peculiar to him; it was itself a decisive part of his peculiarity, sacred images being an otherwise universal religious phenomenon.

Old Testament polemics and stories make clear what, from the viewpoint of Israel's faith, is the matter with images. First, the existence of the image depends on the self-chosen initiative of the devotees and their artisans: "He plants a cedar. . . . Part of it he takes and warms himself . . . and bakes bread. Then he makes a god and worships it."[66] Second, the image is therefore a *manipulable* access to the god. Samuel's story of the Philistines' capture of the Ark of the Covenant,[67] which they thought must contain Israel's collection of images, displays the pagan attitude as Israel understood it. When Israel brought the Ark into its battle camp, "the Philistines were afraid; for they said, 'Gods have come into the camp.'" And when they nevertheless defeated Israel, they presumed that in carrying off the Ark they were recruiting these gods to their side. An idol you can put where you need it, because you made it or have otherwise gained possession. "They set it in its place, and it stands there; it cannot move from its place."[68] A name you can only speak in appeal to the freedom of its bearer, supposing you have contingently been given to know it.

---

63. Ibid.: "in paints or mosaic or other material."
64. The New Revised Standard Version's translation, "an idol," of course begs the point at issue.
65. Deuteronomy 5:8.
66. Isaiah 44:14–15.
67. I Samuel 4–5.
68. Isaiah 46:7.

What we here again encounter is the fundamental difference on which this work's first volume spent itself: between God as heard and the gods as seen, between the God whose infinity is temporal and the gods whose infinity is spatial, between the God of election and the gods who satisfy. Metaphysically, it is the difference between a doctrine of being as being mentioned and one of being as appearing.

In context of the question about idols, this contrast may be reduced to a point so simple and fundamental as to seem at first unserious: I have flaps on my eyes but none on my ears and can aim my eyes but not my ears. Sight, stretching across space, is a controlled and controlling relation to external reality; hearing, stretching across time, is uncontrollable. I see what I choose to look at; I must hear what is contingently addressed to me. I hear the Lord when he speaks; I see the not-gods who negotiate in the space I make by looking for them.

But must not then the iconoclasts be right? This work's pervasive evocation of sacramentality nevertheless implies that they cannot be. Israel had no holy images; but she did have the Temple and Sinai and the wings of the storm, and prophetic and apocalyptic visions of the "One high and lifted up." That hearing transcends and precedes seeing in the relation to JHWH evidently does not mean our eyes are closed to him. Discourse that liberates rather than enslaves includes, we have argued, availability of each party to the other, "visible" and not only linguistic communication; "the Word" of this chapter's earlier sections was the audible *and* visible Word.

The decisive observation is: Israel herself was a temporally extended moving image of the Lord, within whose life the Temple and all the other "visible" phenomena we have noted made the Lord available; here the dialectic we traced for the *Shekinah* and the Servant and the Word[69] appears again. Israel could not manipulate *this* image because in any actual historical moment she was an incident within it, and its totality as an image was liable at any moment to the Lord's unpredictable action.

What then if an individual Israelite is Israel for Israel? The second Council of Nicaea was precise in describing the possibility then opened: the Son is in obvious fact "delineable,"[70] able to be descriptively depicted, "according to his humanity."[71] It is the specific human personal "history" told by the gospel that is thus representable.[72] And it is in that such depiction *identifies* Jesus and so identifies the Son that the divine Son is venerated in the icon. "He who venerates an icon venerates in it *the hypostasis* [emphasis added] of what it represents."[73]

The Son is identified by his life, which for present purposes runs from his Old Testament preexistence through Mary's womb to the Ascension and to his

---

69. 1:175–182.

70. *Perigrapton.*

71. Second Council of Nicea, Anathemas.

72. Ibid., Definition: "Ectyping by imagining representation" follows "te historia tou euaggelikou kerygmatos."

73. Ibid., Definition.

return in glory. As the story of a human person, this identifying narrative can be told not only in language but also by painting or drawing or mosaic or sculpture. We can identify Christ by depicting an event in his life or a human figure with the emblem of an event: by drawing a man entering Jerusalem on a donkey, or a child with the Virgin, or a figure ruling the biblical universe from the dome of a church. If indeed God the Son and this man are one hypostasis, the conclusion is inescapable: with such visual identifications we depict the hypostasis of God the Son. Nor, if such images are possible, will we avoid making them, any more than we avoid concepts and mental pictures of God. And if, by the standards of this work's chapter on sin, icons are implicated in our idolatry, they are no more so than are theological concepts and pious mental images and will be rescued from our sinful intention by the same contingent divine choice.[74]

What icons may the church make? By the theologoumena just advanced, primarily icons of Christ, and first among these identifying scenes from the Gospels; in the West, the crucifixion itself dominates. If heads or partial figures appear, their emblematic narrative identification must be plain. There must not be *portraits* of the Son, for it is strictly his narrated identity, his "hypostasis," in which the Incarnation transcends the prohibition of images.

There may next be depictions of Old Testament events in their christological interpretation, particularly perhaps those in which "the angel of the Lord" or some similar appearance makes this spiritual sense more easily depictable. Old Testament scenes are even in a way especially suitable, since there is no danger of thinking that, for example, a figure in the sacrifice of Isaac is supposed to *resemble* the Son.

There is a long tradition of icons also of the saints, and most notably of the Virgin, who links the two sorts of icons, figuring decisively as she does in the Gospels. The relation of depictions of saints to depictions of Christ must surely be the same, both as to their foundation and as to their appropriate use, as is the general relation between heavenly saints and Christ in heaven. And finally, we may say that biblical apocalyptic provides untranslatable images of what otherwise could not be depicted at all.

Finally, what should we *do* with icons? A general answer seems clear. The gospel identifies the one of whom it speaks, and the final recourse of identification is pointing, whether by verbal devices or more primitively. In a space furnished with, for example, a "Virgin of the sign" or a crucifixion, one can answer the question "Who is risen?" by pointing and saying, "That one." More experientially: in such a space the risen one is identified by what one is anyway looking at.

It is of course as possible to misdirect with images as it is with words. This will likely be done in one of two ways. One is the attempt to make portraits, particularly of Jesus. A supposed "rendering" of Jesus, if intended to have a religious function, will necessarily try to show his divinity by features of his countenance and expression. Apart from the incurable idolatry of the proceeding, the results

74. Pp. 137–138.

are invariably deplorable. Sallman's "exalted" portrait may have done as much to degrade American Protestantism theologically as any error of the theologians.

Where icons are taken most seriously, their inappropriate use will probably be sheer proliferation. Surely the hypertrophy of the iconostasis in many Orthodox buildings, into a wall shutting out the people from the Eucharist, is very problematic: it is one thing for the biblically mandated action to be interpreted by intervening icons and quite another to be compelled to behold them *instead* of the action. After the fact the wall and its doors have of course been provided with spiritually ingenious justifying interpretations.[75] But precisely Orthodox ecclesiology, centered as this is on the eucharistic work of the people of God, must outweigh these.

What the council called "veneration" should be understood as our allowing the icon to direct our intention of God. We earlier asked where in the assembly we were to aim our intention in order to intend God in Christ and answered that it was to the gathering around us. In a space defined by manifold images of the saints, the full extent of the gathering becomes available for our intention.

Within the assembly, our intention of God in one another is rescued from self-deification by common direction away from ourselves to sacramental objects which we are not. When icons envelop the sacramental events, they complicate and interpret this direction. Thus in the assembly we are moved to bow down before God; we direct our gesture by bowing when the crucifix goes by or a fixed icon is unveiled. Entering an Orthodox church, the worshippers are moved to greet God, and they focus the intention of their greeting by saluting the icon displayed on an easel. And perhaps above all, when we inhabit a place for worship that is richly and with narrative logic adorned with icons, we are ourselves relocated, *within* the "recital of the gospel proclamation."[76]

75. So Florensky, *Iconostasis*, 59–69, interprets the iconostasis as the cloud of saints between the visible world and the invisible, meaning the altar. Thus he turns the Eucharist into an interpretation of Pseudo-Dionysius, instead of the other way around.

76. Second Council of Nicea, Definition. In churches like the Norman-Byzantine churches of Sicily, even a few moments of quiet looking in an otherwise empty or tourist-filled building imbue one with the biblical story embodied in the space.

THIRTY

Anima Ecclesiastica

I

It follows from everything in the previous chapters of this volume: a Christian individual is someone whose nation and polity and communion are the church. The *anima christiana*, the Christian soul, is "the *anima ecclesiastica*, that is, a personal self through whom the integral community of the church expresses itself."[1] Therefore discussion of specifically Christian life belongs to the doctrine of the church, not in a separate department of its own.

Indeed, most of what might even so have been expected in a chapter or chapters with the above title has in this work already appeared. For if the human creature has no other fulfillment[2] than the vision of God, then the baptized person must be the only available paradigm of human personhood. Therefore description and analysis of the *anima ecclesiastica*, though not under that label, was the necessary beginning at every step of this work's anthropology, whether in the doctrine of creation or in earlier chapters of ecclesiology. Humanity within God's people is not a variety of humanity outside God's people; rather the latter is an abstraction from the former. Thus describing humanity's creation by the divine Word posed no special task in the case of the baptized but did when extended to cover those not yet brought to faith.[3] The human creature is an entity whose good is to belong to the *totus Christus* and who exists only in that he or she is directed to that good. Such things as faith, freedom, and love have therefore already occupied us.

---

1. Joseph Cardinal Ratzinger, *Église, oecuménisme et politique*, tr. P. Jordan et al. (Paris: Fayard, 1987), 173.
2. Pp. 66–72.
3. It follows of course that outside of some knowledge of the triune God, humanity cannot understand itself. One is tempted to prove this proposition empirically.

Nevertheless, something remains for a chapter with this title. The main group of remaining questions has in the history of theology appeared under various headings, often overlapping: as the several interventions and modes of "grace"; as the successive moments of "the way of salvation"; or as "justification" and its connections. The East, perhaps wisely, has not much entered these discussions; this chapter will be decidedly Western in its questions, though the positions taken should please the East. Then, to conclude this part of the work, the discussion will be specified for the knowledge of God.[4]

II

Our questions will be marshalled in the last of the ways just noted, as discussion of "justification." There are several reasons for this choice. Supposed dissensus about "justification" has been disastrously divisive in the West, and alleviation of the controversy has been in the center of ecumenical dialogue. It is also sometimes supposed that "justification" and "deification" are antithetical doctrines of the believer's way to salvation, thus construing a conflict between West and East. Moreover, doctrine about "justification," although pivotal for the life of the Western church, ecumenically and in other ways, is badly in need of conceptual sorting out, as it offers a prize example of the confusion of understanding by linguistic illusion.

The language is initially plain enough. In Scripture, righteousness or justice is the mutual responsibility by which a community is faithful to itself; for an individual to be righteous or just is then for him or her to be rightly placed in the community and to accept the duties and privileges of that place as opportunities of service.[5] God "justifies" when he sets things communally right, whether by judgment and reordering of the community as such or by setting an individual right within it. The religious immediacy of the word means that it is richly used in Scripture and the church's language, and in a variety of contexts. This very richness has made it available for theological cross-purposes.

It has been generally supposed that the interrogative sentence "How are we justified?" must state one question or one ordered set of questions, to which there then must be one right answer or ordered set of answers. Thus it has been supposed that different complexes of teaching about "justification," appearing in the teaching of churches or theologians, must be different attempts to answer the same question or questions; and that where they cannot easily be reconciled, this must signal dissensus "about justification." None of this is true.

At least three distinct questions about "justification" have so far appeared in the history of theology. They are related; at the end we will find they are related at a deeper level than has usually been supposed. But they are nevertheless distinct in the sense that it is, at least short of final illumination, possible to agree

---

4. For earlier discussion of the possibility of this knowledge, 1:227–231.
5. 1:71–72.

about any one of them while disagreeing about the rest. Therefore comparison of a church's or theological party's answer to one of these questions with another church's or party's answer to a different one of them, while supposing that both are answering the same question, has been a great source of illusory dissensus, from the Reformation to the present. Before we can investigate the positive relation between the three doctrines "of justification," we must distinguish and then separately discuss them.

We are made righteous in the church; as we have seen, baptism "justifies" because it initiates into the community whose *telos* is righteousness and whose reality is anticipation of her *telos*. The context in which God makes us just is thus the speaking of the gospel, the audible and visible communication by which this community subsists, her specific discourse for and about God. Here the one question about "justification" can arise. It was the Reformers' distinctive and specifically reforming question: How is the church's discourse, audible or visible, to be logically and rhetorically shaped so as not to betray its content? In the dialogues, this has been labelled the "metatheological," "metalinguistic," "hermeneutic" or— more misleadingly—"proclamatory" doctrine.[6]

This question is not the same as the next we must isolate: How does it work, that persons living in this context truly become righteous? How may we tell the human story that ends in God? This was the great Augustinian concern, which has appeared in Catholic scholasticism's analyses of the various sorts and interventions of "grace" and their relations, and in Protestant scholasticism's doctrines of "the way of salvation," the *ordo salutis*. The supposition that this "transformative" doctrine and the "hermeneutic" doctrine must somehow be different approaches or emphases in answering the same question, the first typically Catholic and the second typically Protestant, has confused Catholic-Protestant conversation for four hundred and fifty years.[7] Yet they are clearly logically incommensurate. Augustinian doctrines of "justification" *describe* Christian life under certain terms of analysis; the hermeneutic or metalinguistic doctrine of "justification" describes nothing at all but is rather an *instruction* to teachers, liturgists, and evangelists about certain characters of the language they are to use.

Nor is either of these questions quite the same as the one that agitated Paul.[8] Paul had to maintain against opponents from all sides: the gospel is itself the power

---

6. *Lutherans and Catholics in Dialogue*, vol. 7, ed. H. George Anderson, T. Austin Murphy, Joseph Burgess (Minneapolis: Augsburg, 1985), 88–93; Ökumenischer Arbeitskreis evangelischer und katholischer Theologen, *Lehrverurteilungen—kirchentrennend?* ed. Karl Lehmann, Wolfhart Pannenberg (Freiberg: Herder, 1986), 55.

7. Even the German group, which of all the dialogues so far most clearly understood that these are different modes of doctrine, did not fully grasp the reason, that they are about different things; Ökumenischer Arbeitskreis, *Lehrverurteilungen*, 55.

8. It is quite possible that Paul's thinking never arrived at a coherent solution of the problem posed him by the simultaneous necessity and impossibility of abandoning the Law. For a detailed and ruthless argument that Paul had no consistent conception of the Law, or consistent theology of believers' relation to it, Heikki Räisänen, *Paul and the Law* (Philadelphia: Fortress, 1986).

by which God brings those who hear it to salvation.[9] It does this, he taught, in that its speaking is the apocalypse of God's own righteousness,[10] which is apprehended by and creates faith.[11] God will at the End establish his righteousness for good and all; in the time between the times, he establishes his righteousness by apocalyptically unveiling it in the gospel; this event thus "justifies" those who undergo it.[12] The question that Paul thereby raises for himself and his churches and readers is best seen in his religiously outrageous answer to it: when God thus establishes his righteousness he makes righteous the "one who does not perform works but instead trusts him who justifies the ungodly."[13] How *does* God's righteousness, that is, his utter faithfulness to himself as triune community and just so to his community with his people, establish itself over against unfaithfulness? Or the reality of adherence to false religions?

III

The metalinguistic reforming doctrine has already been described.[14] Here we need only emphasize certain points.

In this context, the sentence "We are justified by faith" stipulates that the church's audible or visible promise of righteousness must be so structured rhetorically and logically that it accepts no lesser response than faith. If the gospel is rightly spoken to or enacted for me, it places me where I can finally say only "I believe, help my unbelief" or "Depart from me." The less drastic response of "works," that is, of deeds or virtues brought forward because they are thought appropriate to the gospel—as in themselves they may well be—does not as such break through my incurvature on myself. For unless this has otherwise been broken, my works, precisely as *my* actions and habits of action, are still "willingly" done within my antecedent rapture into myself.[15] When the church's proclamation appropriately elicits the response of "works," this by itself shows that the gospel has been wrongly spoken.

Only the *promise* of fulfillment in God, and such promise as hides no implicit conditions of its validity, can break the direction of my actions to myself, by opening my place within God's story while offering no handle for antecedent egocentric willingness. When I hear "The one dedicated to your place in God's community with creation, and dedicated to the death, lives as Lord," said with-

---

9. Romans 1:16b.

10. Otto Michel, *Der Brief an die Römer* (Göttingen: Vandenhoeck & Ruprecht, 1955), 45: "In der *dikaiosyne theou* haben wir es mit dem eschatologischen Heilshandeln Gottes, nicht nur mit einer Eigenschaft Gottes zu tun."

11. Romans 1:17.

12. To the establishment of God's eschatological righteousness as the context of Paul's doctrine of justification, Michel, *Der Brief an die Römer*, 13–24, 42–50, et passim.

13. Romans 4:5.

14. 1:13–16, 167–168.

15. Martin Luther, *Von der Freiheit eines Christenmenschen* (1530), WA 7, 23: "Commands . . . indeed advise, but don't help."

out further moralistic or religious qualification, I am bereft of my works and offered my righteousness. It is of course not our logic but the Spirit who frees us, but as we have noted in other connections, not everything can be used by the Spirit in this way.

So long as the last Fulfillment has not utterly banished sin, also the "law" must be spoken in the church: when believers sin the church must tell them they do so and describe the consequences. But so the world also must proceed. The church's *specific* word is the gospel-promise; in all her discourse she must somehow get round to it, and leave her hearers with it.

Precisely for the zealous, it is hard to avoid what the Reformers denounced as "mixing"[16] law and promise, by bringing conditions of the gospel's fulfillment into the gospel promise itself. "But they have to believe it," the faithful preacher rightly thinks, and so ends with the plausible but fatal exhortation, "You only have to believe!" If I do not believe, that is of course that; but to bring this fact into the proclamation as a condition of its application to me undoes the message as promise. Indeed, believing as a condition I have to fulfill is of all "works" the most frustrating and finally irrelevant. Those acquainted with the daily liturgics and homiletics of the church in any confession or period will see how the metalinguistic doctrine of justification regularly acquires a critical function.

The temptation just adduced is strong in Catholicism and Protestantism alike, though typically in different connections. There is also a rather odd and very different temptation that must be mentioned, which was once unique to Protestantism but seems to be spreading: to suppose that adherence to the Reformation doctrine of justification is itself a sufficient condition of faithfulness, that is, to confuse a set of instructions about the gospel with the gospel itself. The short statement of the gospel is "Jesus is risen," *not* "We are justified by faith." The gospel is a story about Jesus and us, not a linguistic or existential stipulation. For this reason, it is possible to dispute the hermeneutic doctrine of justification while in fact proclaiming the gospel according to its intention or to loudly maintain that we are justified by faith alone while never speaking the gospel at all.

IV

For the sake of continuity with the previous section, the ecumenical problematic, and his unique profundity in the matter, we will take Martin Luther for our interlocutor in developing the second, Augustinian, sort of "doctrine of justification."[17] This may surprise some readers, but the study of Luther's thought has taken recent surprising turns.

16. To the Reformation's polemic against this, see, e.g., Philip Melanchthon, *Apology of the Augsburg Confession*, iv.40–47.

17. The following may not much resemble what readers expect from Luther. His texts in fact contain what will here be cited from them, but standard Luther exegesis, conducted mostly by liberal Protestants or philosophical existentialists, has tried to explain these systematics away as too

Theology's problem has always been how to affirm at once the gratuity and the reality of the righteousness or holiness that God gives in the church. On the one hand, I in no way deserve or earn this gift. As Henri de Lubac taught us, the continuity between all my religious and moral strivings and their supernatural and only actual end lies wholly in the freedom of God:[18] I am and will be righteous because God justifies and will justify me, and that is an end of the matter. The results of Catholic-Lutheran dialogue could be summarized: "The central point in which both parties agree involves both an affirmation and a negation. The affirmation is that ultimate trust for salvation is to be placed in the God of Jesus Christ alone. . . . [The negation is that] trust in God alone . . . excludes ultimate reliance on our faith, virtues or merits."[19]

But if, on the other hand, my own faith, virtues, or merits—that is to say, I myself in my religious and moral life—have no grip on this gifted righteousness, how is it *mine?* One must grant Protestantism's typical insistence that the language of "justification" in Scripture is juridical language, so that the righteousness of which it speaks is righteousness established by God's judicial action. But Protestant doctrines of "forensic" justification, by God's decree that gratuitously reckons Christ's merits to my case,[20] seem always on the verge of making this righteousness fictional. Does God judicially declare believers righteous even though he knows they are not? Is justification something like a presidential pardon granted for political reasons?

The in itself obvious answer has often been made, for example, by international Catholic-Anglican dialogue: "God's grace effects what he declares; his creative word *imparts what it imputes* [emphasis added]. By pronouncing us righteous, God also makes us righteous."[21] But how are we to understand this?

In *On the Freedom of the Christian*, Luther begins as perhaps expected: "Believe in Christ, in whom are promised all grace, righteousness, peace and freedom. If you believe, you have it; if you do not believe, you do not have it."[22] But

---

metaphysical and therefore tending to catholicism. Luther is praised, indeed, as theology's great deliverer from ontological thinking. The contrary has now been demonstrated in detail from the texts, by a sustained cooperative research project at the University of Helsinki, sometimes referred to as "the Mannermaa school" of Luther research. Of its many publications, let me mention here just three major works: Tuomo Mannermaa, *Der im Glauben gegenwärtige Christus* (Hannover: Lutherisches Verlagshaus, 1989); Simo Peura, *Mehr als ein Mensch?* (Mainz: von Zabern, 1994); Risto Saarinen, *Die transzendentale Deutung des Gegenwart-Christi-Motivs in der Lutherforschung* (Diss. Helsinki, 1989). The received scholarly understanding of Luther must now be taken as in large part discredited. A forthcoming general study of Luther by David Yeago, who in part draws on the Finnish research, may in fact be expected to refound the whole scholarly discipline.

18. P. 67.

19. George Lindbeck, "Justification by Faith," *Partners* 6 (1985):8–9.

20. E.g., Johann Baier, *Compendium theologiae positivae*, iii.v.1: "Justificatio . . . forensem significationem habet et actum illum denotat quo Deus judex hominem peccatorem adeoque reum culpae et poenae, sed in Christum credentem, justum pronunciat."

21. Anglican–Roman Catholic International Conversation, *Justification*, 15.

22. Luther, *Freiheit*, 24. It should be noted that Luther's tract is theology, not proclamation.

we may ask, as Luther himself does, How does that *work*?[23] Luther answers—as perhaps not expected—by appealing to the moral content of the gospel-narrative and to an ontological mutuality between the word and the apprehending person. The word of the gospel is "true, righteous, peaceful, free and has all good things for its content"; and "the soul of one who clings to the Word in true faith is so entirely united with it that all the virtues of the Word become virtues also of this soul."[24]

According to Luther, the soul *becomes* what it *hearkens to*. If the soul attends to the world's solicitations it becomes itself worldly. If it attends to Satan's councils of despair it is rapt into itself. If it attends to the story of God's righteousness it becomes righteous.

This principle is a remarkable and intentional switch on an old principle of traditional Western metaphysics, made very early in Luther's thinking: "Do not be surprised that I said we must become the Word. For the philosophers too say that the intellect, through the act of knowing, is the known object, and that sensuality, through the act of sensual perception, is the sensed object. How much more must this hold of the spirit of the Word!"[25] The mind, the old metaphysicians held, is open to be formed by objects in that it has no form of its own; in this sense, when it knows something it becomes what it knows.[26] That is, there is nothing material to consciousness but the thoughts and inclinations that shape it; consciousness subsists precisely as consciousness *of* what is known and willed, and as nothing else at all. Since in the tradition the paradigm of cognition was seeing, the old notion was that the mind is formed by what it sees. Luther makes the mind be formed instead by what it hears. He thus bends the old metaphysics to an interpretation of personal life as constituted in speaking and hearing, and beyond that to the apprehension of God's *Logos* as speech.

I become ontically righteous as I hear the gospel—which is in itself true for me independently of my righteousness—and in hearing am formed by the righteousness that its narrative displays, that is, God's own righteousness of love. The believer "needs no works to become pious, . . . and so is liberated from all commands and laws"[27] *not* because the believer is excused from obedience to God's commandments but because as the believer hearkens to the gospel he or she is already actually being formed to the very virtues God commands.

This doctrine might still seem like either fiction on one side or moralism on another, except for a further, christological, step. As the soul is united with the gospel it hears, it is united with Christ whose word this gospel is, so that the two become one moral subject: "Faith . . . unites the soul with Christ, as a bride with her bridegroom. From this marriage it follows . . . that Christ and the soul . . .

23. Ibid., 23: "Wie geht es aber zu?"
24. Ibid., 24.
25. Luther, *Christmas Sermon* (1514), WA 1, 29:15–18.
26. To cite Luther himself on the classic principle, WA 20;26–27: "Ita obiecta sunt eorum [minds] esse et actus, sine quibus nihil essent, sicut materia sine formas nihil esset."
27. Ibid., 24–25.

have everything together: what Christ has belongs to the believing soul and what the soul has belongs to Christ."[28] This is intended not as rhetoric or trope but as a proposition about an ontic actuality. An unexpressed premise, clearly stated in other writings, is another radicalization of a traditional theologoumenon: there is no difference between God's moral predicates, communicated in his Word, and God himself.[29] Thus when God in Christ forms us by his Word to the virtues displayed in it, he forms us to himself, he indeed becomes the metaphysical form of believers' humanity, the defining shape that makes these entities human.

We must here adduce the guiding slogan of Luther's *Commentary on Galatians: In ipsa fide Christus adest,* "In faith as such Christ is present."[30] And we should continue the citation, for its suggestion here and for interpretation in a moment: "Thus faith is an odd cognition, indeed rather a darkness that sees nothing. Yet in that darkness Christ, grasped by faith, is enthroned—just as God was enthroned in the darkness at Sinai or in the Temple."[31]

By this participation in Christ, which occurs as we believe the word of the gospel, we are ontically righteous. For in "the happy exchange" between the believer and Christ, the believer's created unrighteousness is no balance for God the Son's divine righteousness. In the one subject that the believer and Christ make together, the believer's creaturely sin is "swallowed up" in the divine Son's "eternal righteousness";[32] it simply ceases to have any moral weight. In more explicitly trinitarian terms, we may say that our dislocation within the triune and human communities, our unrighteousness, can neither dislodge the Son from his right location within them nor yet separate us from him. And we must here recur to the forensic quality of justification. We may relax our adherence to Luther and let Jonathan Edwards join him in drawing the facit: when the Father judges the believer and says that he or she is righteous, the Father is simply acting as a just judge who finds the facts—about the only moral subject that actually exists in the case, Christ in the believer and the believer in Christ.[33]

Justification is thus "a mode of deification."[34] For Luther's strongest language, we again turn to the *Commentary on Galatians*: "By faith the human person be-

---

28. Ibid., 25.

29. To this, Peura, *Mehr als ein Mensch*, 49–52.

30. This is the theme of the groundbreaking study by Mannermaa already referred to, *Der im Glauben*.

31. *In epistolam S. Pauli ad Galatas*, WA 40/I, 228.

32. Luther, *Freiheit*, 25–26.

33. To Edwards on this matter, Robert W. Jenson, *America's Theologian: A Recommendation of Jonathan Edwards* (New York: Oxford University Press, 1988), 57–62.

The doctrine expounded in the preceding paragraphs is Luther's, but it is not the doctrine of subsequent orthodox Lutheranism, which followed Melanchthon rather than Luther in understanding the righteousness by which we are justified as strictly forensic and the indwelling of the righteous God as a *consequence* of justifying righteousness, to be sharply distinguished from it. So the *Konkordienformel*, 54: "Although by faith . . . God, Father, Son and Holy Spirit, who is eternal and essential righteousness, dwells in the elect, . . . nevertheless his indwelling of God is not the righteousness of faith . . . for the sake of which God declares us righteous."

34. Mannermaa, *Der im Glauben*, 185; see in more detail 52–55.

comes God."[35] Carried along by the Scripture he is expounding, Luther can go beyond even his radical younger followers and make not only Christ but the believer, united with Christ, the subject of a real communion of divine attributes: "Every Christian fills heaven and earth in his faith."[36] Yet this is not dissolution in God or even any usual sort of mysticism or idealism, for the Christ who is one with me so that I am one with God is precisely Christ in "flesh and bones."[37] We may gather Luther's teaching with the remarkable passage: "The 'righteousness of God' [in Romans] . . . is the righteousness by which God is righteous, so that God and we are righteous by the same righteousness, just as by the same word God makes us be and we indeed are what he is, so that we may be in him and his being may be our being."[38]

To be sure, so long as this age endures, we have only a "beginning and some increase" of such participation in Christ and so in God's righteousness.[39] Short of the Kingdom, more than enough room remains for the commandments to rebuke and direct us and for new hearing of the gospel promise. Nor is there any opportunity for moral quietism. So long as I and my neighbors are not in the Kingdom, we live with each other in the conditions of this world; and the Christ who does all for me and lives in me will do all for them also, in part by way of me. Moreover, if I am to be a fit instrument of this divine work, Christ must curb my remaining egocentric longings, and again he will do this through my own agency, through my self-discipline and resolve.[40]

Nor is the "increase" accomplished as progress, but by *return*—by ever new hearing of the promise. Luther's passion for the objectivity of the church's discourse makes him center this return on baptism: "The Christian has enough in baptism for his life's study and practice."[41] It has sometimes been considered a problem: What does the believer go on to, after baptism? The needed insight is surely: short of the End, the believer does not go on to anything after baptism, for baptism is initiation into the gate-community after which there is only the Kingdom. Short of the End, the believer never advances beyond his or her baptism but instead falls behind it and must catch up to it. That is why some peni-

---

35. *In epistolam S. Pauli ad Galatas*, 182.

36. Ibid., 392: "Credens igitur Abraham implet coelum et terram. Sic unusquisque Christianus implet coelum et terram fide sua."

37. To this, Mannermaa, *Der im Glauben*, 39–52. Here is the difference between the doctrine discovered by the Finns in Luther and the thought of Andreas Osiander.

38. WA 2, 259:11–14. it is perhaps at this point that I may find occasion to adduce the remarkable article by David Yeago, "Martin Luther on Grace, Law and Moral Life: Prolegomina to an Ecumenical Discussion of Veritatis Splendor," The Thomist 62 (1998):163–191. With iron adherence to the texts, Yeago disposes of Catholic and Protestant interpretations of Luther that suppose he sees "law" and "grace" as mutually exclusive. Yeago instead identifies a "project shared" by John Paul II and Luther, "of integrating the moral and the mystical, and therefore of relocating the notion of divine law within the context of the perfection of nature by grace."

39. Luther, *Freiheit*, 30.

40. Ibid., 34–36. To this see now Mannermaa, *Der im Glauben*, 95–105.

41. "Taufe," *Grosser Katechismus*, 41.

tential practice or other is always a center of Christian life, for "penance is nothing but a return to and reentry into baptism."[42]

It will be seen that the moves made throughout this section formally retrace
those made in the first volume when affirming Augustine's and Peter Lombard's
doctrine of the Spirit.[43] Augustine and the Lombard taught that as the Spirit was
the bond of love in the Trinity, so he was himself believers' bond of love with
God and one another.[44] All that is actually added in this section is clearer emphasis that the Spirit is the Spirit of Christ, and that therefore the bond of love he
creates is participation with and in Christ. All that is added is a missing trinitarian
specification.

V

Perhaps Luther's teaching that the soul is formed in what it hears provides a sufficient ontology of the soul's christological righteousness. But it will at least further the coherence of this book if we interpret it also on our established schema
of personhood.

It is the unilateral determination of the Father that decrees the sheer existence of any created person, that is, of a particular "transcendental unity of apperception," of a particular perspective on being. This in itself is true of all
created persons. The viewpoint of some persons is from the divine-human community of the church, the viewpoint of faith; this is the particular such determination that is the Father's role in predestination. To recall a previous remark,
the Father himself, considered in his abstracted role as Father, would be a sheer
consciousness, a sheer focus.

Now, when the divine-human community presents such a focused consciousness with an object as its Ego, what does this consciousness "apperceive"? I discover an "I" that is, again as already discussed,[45] one of those for whom Jesus of
Nazareth lived and died and now lives and who is particular in this company
within a network of other possible descriptions, some drawn from location within
the church community and some drawn from other communities in which I find
myself. All this, and nothing else, is *what* I ontologically *am*.

We are still, however, speaking in abstractions. The identity of the one who
can say "I belong to the *totus Christus*" with the "I" of which this is said is not
static but living; their relation is *freedom*. That is, they are liberated for one another by the Spirit—as, we may recall, are the Father and the Son. And this liberation must work both ways: the identified and identifiable Ego presented to me
is a communal phenomenon, and those who make up the communities who

42. Ibid., 76.

43. 1:148–149.

44. As noted in the first volume, this doctrine was too strong for most later medieval and modern theology, which has understood our love for God and each other as a "created" reality, *caused*
in us by the Spirit and just so distinct from the Spirit himself.

45. Pp. 97–105.

present me with myself become in this freedom agents within my life. In the case of believers, this means that the *totus Christus*, as the one as whom I am available to myself, becomes the subject by whose liveliness I am what I am. And that is to say, Christ himself becomes the subject by whose liveliness I am what I am. In the Spirit, the Christ who is *what* I am is the Christ who is *who* I am.

But this person within my personhood is God the Son. Here appears the "darkness" of which Luther spoke, for God is always hidden just by his presence. This person who is "enthroned" as agent of my selfhood can be perceived by me only as another human, and a crucified one at that; the community that is the *totus Christus* and in which I find myself, I can adhere to only as a human religious society and an implausible one at that. Yet just so, God himself is my living Ego, indeed the omnipotent agent of my righteous personhood.

Finally on this line, we must explicitly note the split that has in fact always shown in this work's analyses of human personhood: short of the Kingdom, my Ego is provided by the church *and* by other "public things." In this age, I live in Christ *and* in the polities and other collectives of the world, maintained by the *libido dominandi*. I am, in classic formulation, "the new man" *and* "the old man." I am rapt by the Spirit in freedom and rapt by satanic imbecility. That is, insofar as I am identified by the communities of this age sin still rules, even as in my identification by the church it is past and done with.

Short of the Kingdom, human personality is therefore divided. Even in the personhood of those whose communities are *only* those of the *libido dominandi*, a certain division appears: the focus of their consciousness is given by another community than that in which it finds its Ego. For believers, on the other hand, it is precisely the identity of consciousness that is the sole identity between new man and old. Or, if we will, it lies solely in the Father's determination that I the old man am I the new one.

VI

Paul's problem about "justification" was specifically an apostle's problem. God's eschatological act to set his community in order had occurred in Christ's death and resurrection and was occurring in Paul's own mission, and had taken unexpected courses. Those whom the Father was giving Christ from "Israel according to the flesh" were not only those whose works were righteous. And Paul found himself called to bring in the gentiles, the ungodly by definition, and to do this without compelling them no longer to be gentiles. Thus God was establishing his righteous community in sovereign freedom from what could have seemed appropriate either to Jew or to gentile, gathering it from those who do not "perform works" but instead trust a God who calls them while still ungodly.

How then are we to understand God's justifying initiative? All we can do is pile up tautologies: God justifies us because he loves us; God justifies us because he freely elects us. How are you or I righteous? In that God is God. Our discussion of *this* "doctrine of justification" can be very brief; what is to be said is fundamental and therefore little, and it has moreover been said throughout this work.

VII

The three questions about "justification" which we have just distinguished and tried to answer are separately answerable. Yet links between them will have been apparent. The ecumenical dialogues and their sponsoring churches have been urged to lighten their burden by separating the questions: by saying that Catholic transformational doctrine and Reformation hermeneutical doctrine are about two different things and so do not need to be adjusted to each other, and that Paul's doctrine is a third and confessionally uncontroversial topic, which may be discussed in ecumenical peace. The proposal is right, and necessary if any final clarity is to be achieved ecumenically. But it may be an inchoate perception of a deeper unity between doctrines of "justification" that has kept the dialogues from fully taking up such recommendations.

For there indeed is one thing that the three doctrines of "justification" jointly interpret; they have not been drawn to a common vocabulary by inadvertence only. Their common referent, it is here suggested, is a triune event, a mode of the divine persons' mutual life. Every work of God is begun by the Father, accomplished in the Son, and perfected in the Spirit and has its unity in their *perichoresis*. The three historically occurring doctrines of "justification" clearly suggest interpretation on this pattern. Paul's problem is finally a patrological problem; the Reformation's doctrine of "justification" is a piece of Christology; and the Augustinian concern properly appears under the doctrine of the Spirit.

Justification as an Act of the Father is an absolute beginning, an uninitiated initiative. God the Father mandates and defines righteousness; the fact is underivable and always unprecedented. We are righteous and God himself is righteous simply because there is the Father, because there is a freedom that posits a specific loving community. This is the trinitarian and predestinarian truth controlling Paul's otherwise conflicted statements about "justification." If the Father chooses the Son in community, and chooses that this community shall be a community of good Jews, outcast Jews, and believing gentiles, no further explanations are needed or possible. Protestant scholasticism's forensic doctrines of justification are christological surrogates for missing patrological doctrine and therefore have their air of fiction.

Justification as an act of the Son is the *event* of righteousness. We are righteous as the risen Christ's word is spoken and believed, as the word that he is occurs among us. We are righteous in that Christ the Son unites with us. God himself is righteous in that this same Word occurs as "one of the Trinity": given the Father's decree, if the Word that justifies the ungodly were not in fact spoken, neither God nor we would be righteous, neither the Trinity nor we would be well ordered communally.

The Reformer's hermeneutical doctrine of justification concerns the logic and rhetoric of a discourse that can have this role. It tries to display the structure of proclamation and prayer appropriate to be the audibility in this world of the risen *Logos*. It is thus a pair for such analyses of the visible word as that of Thomas Aquinas, earlier discussed. It might indeed have been better to take up this hermeneutical doctrine in the first part of the chapter on "Mysteries of Communion" and meld it with Thomas's doctrine; it was instead kept for this chapter on account of the historical difficulties about "justification."

Justification as an act of the Spirit is the *achieving* of righteousness. That the Father's speaking of the justifying Word actually creates faith in us, detaches us from bondage to our old selves and moves us toward the Kingdom and its justice, is the work of the Spirit's eschatological liberating. The sending of the Spirit is the movement of our righteousness, is its eschatological liveliness without which it could not be God's righteousness. And again we must even say that the Spirit is the movement of God's *own* righteousness, insofar as this too is not a timeless fact about God but rather a character of his liveliness .

We have at each step spoken not only about our righteousness but about God's. How is God himself righteous? What is the actuality of God's righteousness? What is the fulfillment of God's righteousness? To each question we have found the same answer as to the corresponding question about ourselves. What then is justification? It is the underived event of communal faithfulness in God, as this is set free by the Spirit and is actual in the reality of the incarnate Son. That we are justified means that this history is not only God's but is made to be ours also. And in *this* doctrine of justification, the three earlier discussed do come together.

VIII

In that believers' communion with God occurs in the hearing and seeing of his *Word,* we have with the above already described the structure and possibility of faith's knowledge of God. Believers can know God, as they can love and fear him, only because the church within which they live "sacramentally anticipates the kingdom of God."[46] Within this anticipation Luther's—or others'—analysis of believers' righteousness provides also an epistemology of faith.

This is sometimes made explicit.[47] Thus, according to Luther, Christ as faith's object becomes the form of the believing subject, so that the subject knows God as who he is, as God.[48] And this again is but a switch on a classic theologoumenon: "When . . . a created intellect sees God in his essence, the divine essence becomes the intelligible form of that intellect."[49] Allowing for differences of conceptuality, East and West are at one here: according to Gregory Palamas, it is in *communion* with God that the mind, which in itself *neither* attains to nor is barred from knowledge of God, is in fact "attached to things beyond itself."[50] Also epistemically, deification is the comprehensive relation to God.

---

46. John Meyendorff, "Byzantium as Center of Theological Thought in the Christian East," *Schools of Thought in the Christian Tradition,* ed. P. Henry (Philadelphia: Fortress, 1984), 72–73.

47. To the following, Mannermaa, *Der im Glauben,* 36–39.

48. WA 40/I, 228: "Christus ist jene forma, die den Glauben ornat und informiert. . . . Im Glauben selbst ist Christus anwesend."

49. Thomas Aquinas, *Summa theologiae,* i.12.5.

50. *Triads,* i.3.45.

But now we must bring all this a bit back to earth, lest the vocabulary of communion lead us into dubiously faithful mysticism or into unnecessary dialectical games.[51] God's common life with us once posited, we can understand our knowledge of God much less esoterically than is sometimes done. Within Israel and the church, our knowledge of God proceeds as does our knowledge of each other: God and we share a history, and in its course we become acquainted. Within Israel and the church, we live together with God and learn to know him, as friends or family members or political participants or opposing armies learn to know each other. And here too it holds: of such knowledge we will have in this age only a "beginning and some increase."

To whatever extent we generalize the apocalyptic notion of "revelation," to make it a general category for the possibility of our knowledge of God, we should take it too as calmly as possible. God's self-revelation is that he *introduces* himself: "I am JHWH, your God, the one who rescued you from Egypt. I am the Father, the one who by the freedom which the Spirit is rescued you with Jesus from his tomb." Revelation is simply God's initiative on his side of the dialogue he sustains with us. To be sure, God's self-introduction may not be acknowledged, since God makes himself available only in ways that do not look godly; the gospel may not find faith. But where faith occurs, it is in itself simple recognition of a fact, of someone who presents himself in shared history.

As we live with one another in various communities, our knowledge of one another grows. Just so, as we live with God in Israel and the church, our knowledge of him grows. The difference is that God is infinite as we are not. But since this infinity is, as the first volume argued at such length, temporal rather than spatial, it does *not* remove him into hazy metaphysical distances; the difference between our knowledge of each other and our knowledge of God is not that we know each other clearly from close up and God only obscurely from far away. The difference is that knowing God is an occupation for all eternity.[52] With each other too, we of course never come to an end of mutual knowing, but that is because with finite persons if we press too hard we achieve only mutual triviality.

The knowledge of God enabled in ecclesial communion is the knowledge of *faith*. This does not mean that it is opinion perilously supported by evidence or that it consists in glimpses of deity achieved or given in special moments of experience. The contrary is the case.

Against nearly the whole modern tradition, stemming from Schleiermacher, the first thing to be said is that God is the *object* of faith. As this work has insisted in many contexts, it is central to a Christian grasp of reality that God is ineluctably *there* in his history with us. Next, he is the object specifically of faith in that he is the triune, intrinsically talkative God. We can have *faith* only in a reality

---

51. Karl Barth, *Kirchliche Dogmatik* (Zürich: Evangelischer Verlag, 1948), II/1:1–287, can hardly be forgiven the number of those pages.

52. 1:224–234.

that speaks, that makes promises that may—or by unbelief may not—be relied upon. Next, God does not blither when he makes promises. Therefore faith as personal trust is just so assent to propositions.

Thus there is a sense in which we can and must say: when within the church we know the gospel narrative, we know God and that entirely. We do not know him partially or defectively or in any attenuated sense of knowing. When we hear it said that God raised Jesus or that he desires mercy more than sacrifice, or when we taste and see the bread and wine, these are not clues to God, or evidences of God, or occasions of a cognitive ascent to God, or triggers of an experience in which we will know God; hearing and seeing these things we simply know God. Yet we may still ask: How can it be *God* whom we know in such everyday fashion?

It is the risen Christ who is both God and our object. But he is also the human person who knows this object, himself, as God. God, according to Thomas, is known in his essence by himself and by perfected saints.[53] It is Christ's self-knowledge that is the identity of God's self-knowledge with a perfected human knowledge of God. Thus the saints know God in their perfected communion with Christ, and anticipatory saints know God in their anticipatory communion with Christ.

Thus our knowledge of God depends on the triune *perichoresis* just as our righteousness does. No one "has seen the Father, except the one who is from God; he has seen the Father."[54] The Father does not appear in Israel or the church in his own identity; he is visible only in the triune life itself, to the Son. Yet whoever has seen Jesus "has seen the Father";[55] in our communion with the Son we know the Father with him. And the freedom to know is the Spirit. Knowledge too is always of the Father, with the Son and in the Spirit.

Readers may complain that this account of our knowledge of God is too simple, perhaps even simply too brief. But brevity and naiveté belong to the account being given. This may of course be a sign of its incorrectness. But greater prolixity or argumentative complexity would not improve it.

At the end we must yet again acknowledge God's hiddenness. But we must rightly acknowledge it: God is hidden by and only by the thoroughness of his self-revelation. First, his self-disclosure is perfect and therefore presents us with an infinite person; just so we can never completely know him. He is a figure in the history he shares with us, whom we know as we know other figures in it; but since he genuinely shares it with *us*, this figure is Mary's tortured son within failing and persecuted Israel, and so by our inevitable standards a most ungodly figure; and it is now available to us as the church's sacraments, which do not look like any sort of person. Finally, he speaks to us through every created occasion, none of which resembles him; just thereby he makes of each a mask behind which he hides.

53. *Summa theologiae*, i.1.2; i.2.1.
54. John 6:46.
55. John 14:9.

IX

The last churchly institution of which we must speak is the institution of instruction in this knowledge. The church's *catechumenate*[56] is not an expression of humankind's general inclination to teach but has resulted from specific needs of the church. Indeed, the ancient church posited three kinds of people rather than just two: unbelievers, the baptized, *and* catechumens in between.

In the New Testament itself, we read only of baptism immediately upon confession of faith; thus the Ethiopian eunuch was reading the fifty-third chapter of Isaiah, Philip appeared and said, "That is about Jesus," and the eunuch was baptized in the first available water.[57] But as institutions to sustain the church's faithfulness within continuing history emerged, one was an instructional institution, though its symmetry with canon, office, and creed is not often noticed. It was the experience of the continuing church that baptism and subsequent life in the liturgical and moral life of the church, if granted immediately upon hearing and affirming the gospel, constituted an unsustainable moral shock. Life in the church was too different from life out of the church for people to tolerate the transfer without some preparation.

Converts were used to religious cults that had little moral content, interpreted themselves by myth, and were oriented to the religious needs of the worshiper. They were entering a cultic life oriented not to their religious needs but to a particular God's mandates and devoted to celebrating not myths but alleged historical events. Perhaps most disorienting of all, they were embarking on a religion that made explicit moral demands. The catechumenate was born as the sheer *time* needed to bring people from their normal religious communities to an abnormal one. It was born as liturgical rehearsal and interpretation, as moral correction and discipline, and as instruction in the identity of a particular God, that is, theology of a sort unprecedented in antiquity.

The Constantinian settlement, with its flood of converts, initially intensified this need and resulted in a flourishing and formally organized catechumenate. But eventually it had to turn and destroy the catechumenate altogether. For when the culture's religion and morality and the church's religion and morality are supposed to be more or less the same, no drastic measures will be taken to bring persons from the one to the other. The near-universality of infant baptism was the pivot: you cannot prepare someone to be baptized who already is. So long as infant baptism was only one option, and predicated on the accomplished catechetical discipline of the parents, the catechumenate could coexist with the practice. But when grandparents and great-grandparents have been baptized as infants, the catechumenate loses its space.

---

56. A compendious account of the history is provided by A. Hamman, "Catechumen, Catechumenate," *Encyclopedia of the Early Church*, ed. Angelo Di Berardino, tr. Adrian Walford (New York: Oxford University Press, 1992), 1:151–152.

57. Acts 8:27–38.

And yet the church has never been rid of the feeling that she *ought* to be catechizing, that there *is* a difference between her and the world, however culturally Christianized the latter, so that there is need for training in the difference. When nearly everybody was already baptized, instruction had to take place after baptism and be somehow motivated there. The junctures of life at which such instruction has been undertaken, and its liturgical or other communal contexts, have varied wildly, as has the success of the efforts.

The Constantinian settlement is now manifestly at its very end. Western civilization is still defined by Christianity, but as the civilization that *used* to be Christian, as the civilization indeed whose morale depends on not any more being Christian. The church in the West can no longer suppose that the regular schools or the organs of public opinion or the institutions of the arts or sciences instruct people in a way that is harmonious with the church's instruction. Indeed, we must assume the contrary: that they will inculcate metaphysical mechanism, moral relativism, and the equality and worth of every religion but Christianity. The postmodern church is in this respect returned to the situation in which the catechumenate was born: those to be integrated into the life of the church come from an alien culture; the church's life, if she is faithful, must be a shock and a puzzlement to them.

The church's present position, in the midst of her divorce proceedings from the culture, of course differs from that of the ancient church in a way that inevitably generates confusion: most of those who need catechesis to prepare for life in the church are already members and suppose themselves already qualified for her life. During the time in which the church and the culture are separating but not separated, this ambiguity cannot be avoided or denied.

Much of the late modern church has dealt with the ambiguity by capitulating to it, by mitigating the church's liturgy, morality, and theology to accommodate "seekers" and incompetent members.[58] That way lies apostasy from the faith,[59] which in broad stretches of Western Protestantism has already occurred. However it is to be managed in the time of uncertain boundaries, the church must not dilute or estrange her sacramental culture but instead train would-be believers in its forms, not dispense from God's *torah* but instead reform would-be believers' moral structure, not succumb to theological relativism but teach would-be believers the doctrine of Trinity.

This institution too has its mystery. As the church initiates into her life, into her rites and morality and thinking, she initiates into acquaintance with God. It is not inappropriate to end the doctrine of the church with this proposition.

---

58. There is a splendid study, James Turner, *Without God, without Creed: The Origins of Unbelief in America* (Baltimore: Johns Hopkins University Press, 1985).

59. The recommendations of "church growth" experts will doubtless promote growth, but hardly of the church.

PART VII

THE FULFILLMENT

THIRTY-ONE

The Promise

I

The gospel is a promise. The first volume already argued against Bultmann,[1] and the "dialectical theology" generally, that the gospel must promise a describable something in particular. A promise that we will be able to live by promise and an answering "authentic existence" of perfect openness to a future of perfect openness to the future may be interesting logical and existential constructs but are not the promise that created the church or the fulfillment for which she longs. That fulfillment is rather more dramatic. For example:

> The people who walked in darkness have seen a great light. . . . For all the boots of the tramping warriors and all the garments rolled in blood shall be burned as fuel for the fire. For a child has been born for us . . . and he is named Wonderful Counselor, Mighty God, Everlasting Father, Prince of Peace. . . . And there shall be endless peace for the throne of David and his kingdom. He will establish and uphold it with justice and with righteousness from this time onward and forevermore. The zeal of the Lord of hosts will do this.[2]

We must here turn against the initiating school of specifically twentieth-century theology, whose achievements this work otherwise so much presupposes.[3] "Barth and similarly Bultmann related the Bible's futurist eschatology to the present by concentrating on the reality of God which is its constituting heart. But

1. 1:168–171.
2. Isaiah 9:2–7.
3. It was indeed realization of the dialectical theology's radical insufficiency at this precise point that moderated my perfect loyalty to it.

in the process they stripped it of its specific temporal structure, its drive toward future fulfillment. Its descriptive contents could then only function as metaphors, or as 'mythic' representations that fall away under existential interpretation."[4] Moreover, in this eschatological ascesis, the founding school of twentieth-century theology did *not* break with the mainline Neo-Protestantism against which it otherwise defined itself; in this matter postmodern theology has so far remained bound to its predecessor.

Friedrich Schleiermacher, the great founder of Neo-Protestantism, reports church doctrine about the "return of Christ," the "resurrection of the flesh," the "last judgment," and "eternal blessedness," and then as his own teaching has only a warning. Discourse about such things, he says, is the visionary discourse of the prophets, and such discourse cannot "yield knowledge."[5] Schleiermacher cannot grant prophecy informative power because doing so would involve supposing that the world, as something distinct from the church, could decisively change; we encounter modernity's recurrent mechanism yet again. Salvation according to Schleiermacher is a transformation of human life progressively carried on in the church. The church's "prophetic teachings" promise a conclusion of this trans-formation, but it can in fact never be concluded, because "the church continues . . . to take world into itself, therefore always remains . . . conflicted, and there-fore is never perfected."[6]

Mainline modern and—at least so far—postmodern theology has been char-acterized by inability to attach any descriptions to the proclamation, "See, I am making all things new!"[7] But it is precisely the "contents" that the church hears in this message, "visionary" or not, which demand interpretation, and as some-how informative discourse about a specific future. In Neo-Protestant theology, only a few relative outsiders achieved more robust eschatologies, by a rather strange combination of biblicism with Hegelian or other idealist speculation; and these chapters will try to give some of them the credit that is due.

II

Because Jesus lives, rules, and will judge as the particular person he is, the outcome of history will be different than we could otherwise have expected—also with

---

4. Wolfhart Pannenberg, *Systematische Theologie* (Göttingen: Vandenhoeck & Ruprecht 1993), 3:579. Pannenberg's reference to Barth here is of course to the Barth of the *Römerbrief.*

It is then disappointing that Pannenberg's own treatment of eschatology, in this volume of his sytematics, does not seem fully to emerge from the dialectical theology's eschatological inhibitions. Perhaps this is because these inhibitions were mostly carried over from the mainstream of nine-teenth-century theology, to which Pannenberg is so deeply indebted. Or perhaps it is due to his adherence, after all is said and done, to the traditional metaphysics which through the history of theology have inhibited eschatology. So ibid., 1:644: "God's eternal today . . . needs no remembrance or expections. His day simply remains, . . . in the unmoving and perduring now of his presentness."

5. *Der Christliche Glaube*, 2: §163.

6. Ibid., §157.

7. Revelation 21:5.

respect to its having any outcome at all. We must ask, in all deliberate naiveté:[8] *How different? What* does the gospel promise?

The whole of Christian theology can be understood as the attempt to answer this question. A systematic theology's proposal will therefore not emerge only in a final section thematically devoted to it. This work's offering became explicit within the first few chapters: the gospel promises inclusion in the triune community by virtue of union with Christ and just so in a perfected human community.

That is, the gospel promises what this work has described in various connections and called deification, following the example of the fathers. So Basil the Great: the final result of the Spirit's work in us is "endless joy in the presence of God, becoming like God, and . . . becoming God."[9] We should note the dialectics of Basil's vision: we will be simultaneously *with* God and so other than he, *like* God in sanctity and righteousness, and *personally identified* with God. Or let us again quote Martin Luther, to dispel any suspicion that interpretation of salvation as deification may be an Eastern peculiarity: "Our shame is great, that we were the devil's children. But the honor is much greater, that we are children of God. For what greater fame and pride could we have . . . than to be called the children of the Highest and to *have all he is and has?* [emphases added]"[10]

It is the fact of God's Trinity which requires that his concluding gift to us, should he make one, must be inclusion in his own life, the gift not of something other than God but of "all he is." The *triune* God does not and indeed cannot beneficently affect us causally; for him, causal action, with its intrinsic distancing, would mean exclusion from himself and so cursing rather than blessing. The goal of all the biblical God's ways is the glory of God.[11] Were an otherwise biblical God—contrary of course to possibility—monadic, his intention of his own glory would be a sort of omnipotent egocentricity, and the reality of God would be a universal moral disaster. But God's glorification of himself is instead supreme blessing because the *triune* God can and does include creatures in that glory.

Yet there remains matter for the traditionally concluding part of a systematic theology. While our answer to the eschatological question is already before us, it raises a series of very difficult new questions. Even so, this part of the work is the shortest of all, for many also of these have already been discussed. In this work, eschatology makes the briefest explicit section not because it is an afterthought but because most of what has often indeed appeared as an eschatological afterthought has dominated this work from the beginning.

If the proposition "In union with Christ, we will be included in the triune life" is to be further developed or unpacked, a first such further question is immediately at hand: How is this unpacking to be managed? The bald assertion that

---

8. If what undid modernity's eschatological courage can be regarded as sophistication, then this is the famous "second naiveté."

9. *On the Spirit*, 9.32.

10. *Festpostil*, WA 17/II, 324, 8–15.

11. Pp. 17–20.

we will be included in the divine life summons no vision and just so is inappropriate to its own intent. But where are more descriptive evocations of the creature's perfection in God to be obtained, and by what standard is their truth to be judged?

There are two great funds of eschatological description in the Bible: the Old Testament's prophetic writings and the apocalyptic parts of the New Testament. In this connection it is vital to remember that faith in the God of Israel became fully eschatological, and indeed apocalyptic, before the appearance of the church. We could develop the gospel's eschatology entirely as extended "spiritual" exegesis of any one of a large number of Old Testament texts.[12] And we will in fact begin by taking, more or less at random, one such text to be a paradigm of certain key formal aspects of appropriate eschatological description.

In the eleventh chapter of Isaiah, the first thing promised, which enables all else, is the presence of the Messiah.[13] Description of the Messiah himself is quite straightforwardly propositional, despite some tropic decoration: he will be a descendent of David, God's Spirit will rest on him, he will worship the true God, and he will judge justly. But his justice transcends the possibilities of this age, and just at that point the description turns to more purely poetic diction: "He will strike the earth with the rod of his mouth. . . . Righteousness shall be the belt around his waist."[14]

Description of the perfected state itself is at one point again propositional: there will be no more violence.[15] But the peace that replaces violence is evoked solely in a brilliant play of figures: "The wolf shall live with the lamb. . . . The nursing child shall play over the hole of the asp."[16] The final sentence of the passage shows an abrupt but fine change of dictions: the cause of universal peace is propositionally stateable as universal worship of jhwh, quite in Augustine's sense; but this universality itself can only be invoked with simile, "as the waters cover the sea."[17]

Two points are to be observed. First is the alternation of dictions. About the person of the Messiah, and about the need and conditions for peace, direct propositions are possible and necessary. But description of eschatological peace itself, as a state of creatures, shifts immediately to metaphor and simile. We must, of course, remember that this distinction is itself modern; it belongs to our analysis of the prophet's language and not to the conceptual repertoire of the prophet.

Second is the relation between negative and affirmative in the passage's central evocation of eschatological fulfillment. Isaiah prophesied to a community

---

12. Philip Melanchthon, *Loci praecipui theologici* (1559), 926–929, does just that, taking Old Testament texts for all his interpretation of the resurrection life.

13. Since the blessings brought by the promised king transcend the possibilities of this age, it is in fact *the* Messiah of which the text speaks, whatever may have been the occasion of Isaiah's prophesying.

14. Isaiah 11:1–5.

15. Isaiah 9a.

16. Isaiah 6–8.

17. Isaiah 9b.

whose dominantly experienced evil was violence simply as such: repeated military battering and imperial brigandage and rape, the almost equally destructive violence of the defense, and in their train both internal communal struggle and the relapse of husbandry to nature's tooth and claw. "They shall not hurt or destroy"[18] is the negative proposition to which the affirmative eschatological vision of the poem corresponds.

It is both predictable in itself and observable throughout Scripture: positive poetic invocation of salvation appears as the contrary of experienced and propositionally describable damnation. What humanity finally hopes for—in cultures that hope for anything finally[19]—is what it intolerably lacks; nor need this be unworthy or futile, if the hopes can be construed by the gospel. A certain agreement with Feuerbach[20] will be observed: our eschatological visions are indeed "projections." As our creations they are therefore implicated in idolatry; but like our other religious notions they can become true when broken and reinterpreted by the gospel. So a first of those mentioned nineteenth-century eccentrics and modernity's most interesting christologian, Isaac Dorner: "In reference to the future, believers are not limited to . . . wishing. Christians are a prophetic race, they know of the end . . . of the divine work begun."[21] We have a second principle of eschatological description, further developed in the following section.

Finally on this line, we must note that we should assign the New Testament's apocalyptic scenarios to the poetic rather than the propositional side of Scripture's eschatological language. The Revelation, the "synoptic apocalypse,"[22] Paul's apocalyptic assurances to the Thessalonians,[23] and other New Testament bits and pieces plot sequences of events. But each of these events, looked at for itself, must in fact be the whole End; nor could the various scenarios be jointly carried out. Moreover, all share one fatal flaw as prediction. Friedrich Nitzsch, a compendiast of nineteenth-century dogmatics, made the decisive observation: we can hardly construct our doctrine by recurring to primal Christianity's plans of the last days, since a determining feature of them all, the chronologically speedy return of Christ, proved wrong.[24]

18. Ibid. 9a.
19. Isaac A. Dorner, *A System of Christian Doctrine*, tr. Alfred Cave, J. S. Banks (Edinburgh: T. & T. Clark, 1980) 4:374: "It is only where personal moral duties spring into consciousness . . . that not merely are ideas of a future separation of the good and bad . . . formed, but the future of the world as a whole is also gradually placed under an ethical point of view. Most . . . religions . . . do not reach the thought of a goal of the world, but remain entangled in an alternation between periods of triumph now on the part of the . . . beneficent powers, and now on the part of the dark . . . powers."
20. 1:52–57.
21. *Christian Doctrine*, 377.
22. Mark 13:2–27parr.
23. I Thessalonians 4:16–17; II Thessalonians 2:3–12.
24. *Lehrbuch der evangelischen Dogmatik* (Freiburg: J. C. B. Mohr, 1896), 591.
The two chief occasions of truly baseless conjecture are, of course, I Thessalonians 4:13–18 and Revelation 20.

The final advent of Christ and the final collapse of this world's system and the final advent of the Kingdom must be understood as one event. Schleiermacher, and much of Neo-Protestantism following him, were surely insofar right, that they founded Christian hope strictly "on believers' communion with Jesus," so that the notion of sequenced eschatological events chronologically related to his advent is overcome.[25] So another of those nineteenth-century outsiders, Gottfried Thomasius: what the church hopes for "is no other good thing beyond or beside [Christ]; in hope for him her entire hope for the future is contained."[26] At least in this, such thinkers undoubtedly captured the heart of the New Testament's eschatology: "and so we will be with the Lord forever."[27]

III

How then do eschatological visions appear? Earlier, this work argued that the historical variability and scope of Christian ethics appears as the gospel makes an interpreting way through history. When the gospel penetrates a period or territory, it does not find it religiously or morally empty; the gospel's ethics emerge as it interprets the hopes and fears by which people at a time and place already live.[28] The key to our present question is to observe that this interpretation cannot go one way only.

As the promise interprets the antecedent hopes and fears of some community, these in turn necessarily interpret the promise. To a community destroyed by violence, the prophet rightly promised the peace to be made by Messiah's rule, which will be both recognizable after the fact as the fulfillment of their longings and beyond anything they could otherwise have envisioned. For those able to think only of the next meal a vision of the Son's Wedding-Banquet is neither unspiritual nor "pie in the sky." To a Rome that still remembered its founding dream of republic but had forgotten its meaning Augustine proclaimed the coming Polity of God. Eschatological descriptions emerge as the other side of the same event of interpretation in which the gospel's ethics emerge.

Here is another place where historical profusion is a character of Christian discourse, so that theology can do no more than state the principle, and then perhaps display an instance. We will develop as our illustrative case an eschatological

---

Chiliasm, one version of which locates the saints' penultimate rule, "the millenium," between Christ's advent and the final Kingdom, has been condemned by both Roman Catholicism and the Reformation. To the former—with a good quick history, Estêvâo Bettencourt, "Chiliasmus," *Sacramentum Mundi*, ed. Karl Rahner, Adolf Darlap (Freiburg: Herder, 1967), 1:716–720. The fundamental Reformation Augsburg Confession, XVII, condemns the opinion "that before the Resurrection of the dead the righteous will enjoy a wordly kingdom."

25. Pannenberg, *Systematische Theologie*, 3:576.

26. *Christi Person und Werk: Darstellung der evangelisch-lutherischen Dogmatik vom Mittelpunkte der Christologie aus* (Erlangen: Andreas Deichert, 1888) 2:550.

27. I Thessalonians 4:17.

28. Pp. 209–210.

vision that may emerge in conversation with America's dream of economic free-dom—a dream that is becoming paradigmatic for the rest of the world also. Obvi-ously, the case is not, at the time and place of this writing, chosen at random.

America is the nation invented by Enlightenment philosophers; just so it is the paradigmatic capitalist nation. Capitalist theories, which elsewhere have func-tioned as hypotheses to be followed when they work, have in America the status of founding and inviolable myth. Thus what elsewhere is only description of cer-tain ways of participating in the market comes in America to carry moral and even religious weight: entrepreneurship or accumulation of wealth are seen as goods in themselves. What hope and what damnation lurk in this mythology?

In the Enlightenment itself, the economic notion of "the free market" was integral with the political vision of liberal government. Ideologists of capitalism sometimes still claim that the two are inseparable, that where the market is set free, political liberty must follow. But contrary experiments in many "develop-ing" states, most fatefully in a China again fallen to barbarian rule, have surely now falsified the claim. Indeed, in the United States itself the last decades have simultaneously seen a resurgence of economic direction by newly unfettered markets and precipitous decay of political institutions and participation. It is precisely in the separability of free markets and free polities, in the possibility of the market asserting itself as the communal good in its own right, that a specific damnation appears.

What hopes decisively direct and move Americans? It is contrary to much rhetoric but observably the case: they are not hopes for the American commu-nity itself, that is, they are not political hopes. America is instrumental in its citi-zens' dreams; thus, except perhaps in remnants of the romantic South, Americans do not find it "sweet and beautiful to die for one's country."[29] The "American dream" is not of a better America as such but of "a better life" for one's family and therein for oneself; the larger community and its polity are understood as means to enable and protect this. The linking of family and self is to be noted: Americans tend in moral practice to identify community with the smallest natu-ral community, but they just so have not aspired to be the moral atoms of mere individualism. The familial and personal good life is the compound of economic viability, inner mutual love, and solidarity over against the outside world.

The fears that direct and move Americans are of course contraries of the dream. Thus Americans in their own ways fear disease, impoverishment, and violence, as in one mode or another all peoples do. But they fear equally, as they show when roused to vote or petition, encroachment on the autonomy of linked family and self. And therein is the possibility of evil. For as Americans isolate the good life from the polity and the civil society, the American dream resolves to mere economics and acquires the quality of simple greed. And greed dissolves the communal structures for the good life itself. The dreamers become the moral

---

29. When American troops are put in harm's way, the concern is no longer that they accom-plish their mission and honor the nation but simply that there be no casualties.

atoms they did not intend to be and become themselves the enemies of familial-personal fulfillment.

The free market is in modernity an entirely necessary device, an enormous computer regulating a transactional field too complex for any imaginable central direction. Just so, the existence of the market has a moral-political value of primary importance: the attempt to direct modern economic life without it inevitably becomes socially and politically tyrannous.

Nevertheless the market itself has no conscience. "Gangster capitalism" is just as possible as more civil varieties; and the market will arrange optimal supply and price for cocaine or terrorist weapons as happily as for tomatoes—and probably will dictate that the tomatoes be tasteless. When the market becomes a communal good in its own right, this moral vacuum tends to drain the community of moral and aesthetic substance. The communal context of American hopes and dreams is, with painful irony, proving especially vulnerable.

The American dream's postmodernity is the subliminally haunting recognition that an economically defined life cannot be good. Socially, it is the dissolution of the family itself by unacknowledged moral atomism. Americans then tend to flee to any "spirituality" at hand to compensate for "emptiness." And they redefine "family" and civilize divorce and detach sexual intimacy from public obligation and both from procreation, hoping to carry remembered familial goodness into whatever constellation of human atoms they find themselves hurled into.

The last point is complexly ironic. Late- and postmoderns dare not be aware that when they redefine the relations that constitute the family, to accommodate their own or others' curved-in autonomy, or consent to a practice of abortion on demand to enable this, or take to crystal-gazing to transcend it all, they are moved by nothing grander than greed, that their liberalism and "spirituality" are nothing but hypertrophic capitalism. They dare not know that the danger threatening the American good life is they themselves and their efforts to obtain or keep it. Nor can they admit that as they retreat into families and imitation families, abandoning the mediating communities of religion and art and sociability, they become themselves the destroyers of these small communities also. But they do know and experience that "consumerism" and "the collapse of the family" and the "celebrity" of riches are a damnation.[30]

The first promise of the gospel to persons moved by these hopes and terrified by this damnation is that the difference of the economy from the polity will at the End disappear, because all apparent independence of short-term continuities from the long-term continuity of God's teleology will be unmasked. In the Kingdom, humanity will be subject to no mechanistic continuities, also not those of the economy. Or we may put it so: in our life together in God, there will no longer be any difference between our interests and the common good. The polity is not an emergency measure in view of sin; but the economy is.

---

30. And so there is an endless series of "movements" to combat them; recently "Promise Keepers" has been in the news, presenting scenes of thousands of men in tears, resolving not to be the economically controlled atoms that they are.

In encounter with the American dream, the gospel's promise should be interpreted as the promise of human flourishing. Grasping for economic viability is answered by the promise of death's overcoming and reappears transformed in the vision of the great Celebration's relaxation and pleasure. Longing for the mutuality now possible only in the family, and rare enough there, is answered by the promise of union with Christ; it then reappears in a vision of all humanity bound together by bonds as inward as those between parent and child and as ecstatic as those of sexual union. Recourse to solidarity over against the indeed threatening outside is answered by the promise of participation in a life whose only "outside" is the triune love.

Even the sheer drive to possess reappears, in the promised possession of nothing less than God. And the American damnation is banished: when we will be consumed by *God* and consume *him*, just so life will be freed from all need to consume; when my family is the Trinity and all humanity in him, my family cannot collapse; and the celebrity of divine riches *deserves* our love.

IV

So far a brief illustrative venture into interpretation of the gospel promise by a community's hopes and fears and of the mix of propositions and tropes proper to such interpretation. It is plain that fantasy and linguistic ingenuity are decisively at work in such evocations. Our final question in this section must be: What prevents such eschatological envisioning from becoming arbitrary play? There are several limiting controls.

The first is the doctrine of Trinity itself. Since created fulfillment is inclusion in the triune life, no vision of fulfillment can be true if what it depicts could not fit into that life. Thus, for example, the vision of *nirvana* is great and noble, but since its enabling aspect is the abolition of personality, it cannot describe that for which the church hopes. For the church hopes for fulfillment by inclusion in a *perichoresis* of irreducible personalities.

Pietist ethicists of the simpler sort used to ask such questions as "Could you invite Jesus into a bar with you?" Whatever the answer to that question, and whatever such questions' general status within ethics, they had a right idea in eschatological context. It is indeed a limitation of our fantasy: Could you invite Jesus into your envisioned Fulfillment? Or rather, Can you imagine Jesus taking you with him into it? Believers will enter the triune life only as members of the *totus Christus*; Christ will enjoy whatever we enjoy. A Quranic vision of many concubines can no more suit than can a popular "Christian" vision of disembodied spiritual bliss.

Second, we must here note that the New Testament, and that very much in the train of the Old Testament, does provide a dominating eschatological concept and set of metaphors. Scripture is dominated by one sort of language for fulfillment, the language of politics—and indeed this work's standard quick way of referring to Fulfillment has been "the Kingdom." Mark sums up Jesus' mission: "Jesus came . . . proclaiming the good news of God, and saying, 'The time is fulfilled, and the kingdom of God has come near; repent, and believe'";[31] and everything in all the Gospels verifies this summary. When, after all the drama, the Revelation finally comes to depict the Fulfillment itself, we first are shown "a great white throne and the one who sat on it,"[32] and then a "holy city,"[33] by the light of which "the nations" shall walk and into which "the kings of the earth will bring their glory."[34]

There are two reasons why the "the heart of Christian hope" is the "future of the Kingdom of God."[35] The first is that as the gospel and the whole biblical story are the story of God's acts with and for other persons than himself, the fulfillment of that story must be the achievement of his moral ends for them: "Everything else . . . is the consequence of God's own coming to perfect his rule over his creation."[36] The second is that the achieving of this God's moral ends is indeed a political achievement, a perfecting of "his rule," for his story is the story of his action with and in community. He is the triune God, whose own life is communal, and the partner—since he has one—of his action is therefore a community of other persons.

No eschatological vision, therefore, can be appropriate that does not begin and end with God and *his* purposes for his community of creatures. Our "blessedness" is always to be defined by the moral will of the Lord. And no eschatological vision can be right that abstracts the blessed from their communal reality as the people, the temple, the polity, the joint body, and the communion of God.

Just so, a third control is the Ten Commandments, already adduced in this very connection. These stipulate God's intention for human community, and God will not contradict himself. Whatever we will be with this God and each other when taken into him, we will therein be worshipful and mutually honoring and honest and chaste and selfless.

We may at once summarize these considerations and lay a metaphysical basis for all that follows by recalling and slightly amplifying a teaching of the first volume:[37] as entry into the life of the triune God, Fulfillment is entry into his specific infinity. And this infinity is neither time that goes on forever nor time's cancellation in a still point at the center of a temporal wheel. The triune God's infinity is rather the inexhaustibility of a particular event, the Advent of Christ, that is, the interpretation and appropriation by and to Jesus of all that precedes his final coming.

Jesus' life is indeed that of a particular person: it is one sequence of events and not another, and it is made definite by his death. But the plot of that sequence is self-giving to others. When the Father knows himself in this Son, just so this

31. Mark: 1:14–15.
32. Revelation 20:11.
33. Revelation 21:2.
34. Revelation 21:24.
35. Pannenberg, *Systematische Theologie*, 3:569.
36. Ibid.
37. 1:219.

consciousness extends without limit. And as the Spirit is the Spirit of the particular person Jesus, he is just so the Spirit who transcends all particular limits.

Thus the Eschaton is the inexhaustible event of the triune God's interpretation of created history by the life of the one creature Jesus. The Eschaton is infinite created life, made infinite in that it is the life of creatures seen by the Father as one story with the story of the Son and enlivened by the Spirit who is the Telos of that story.

V

It follows in several ways from all the preceding that we cannot predict what visions of Fulfillment the gospel's history may yet conceive, though we can say quite definitely what actually entertained visions are *not* proper. Nevertheless, as the previous few paragraphs also establish, all possible descriptions of fulfillment in the triune God must have a logical product: "Love never ends."[38] "Love" is the New Testament's and the church's single word for the future the gospel holds out, whether for this age or for the End. It could not be otherwise. The Spirit is the agent of love in the triune life, and the Spirit is the agent of eschatological perfection. Therefore love must be the summary reality of all that blessed creatures can have in God.

Humanity's End is a perfectly mutual community between differentiated persons, foundationally enacted by the Spirit as the love of the Father and the incarnate Son. So the American Edwardsean Samuel Hopkins, with reference to John 17: "The three persons in the godhead form an infinitely high, holy and happy society; . . . and the society of the redeemed . . . will be an eternal imitation and image of the infinitely high and perfect society of the Three-One."[39]

We will live in this love as we are together the Body of the Son; therefore this same love must be the being also of our human community with one another. We will be as different from one another as the Father is different from the Son; just as such we will be perfectly united to one another by the Spirit. Indeed, in analogy of the triune identities, there will be nothing to any one of us but what she or he uniquely is from and for all the rest of us, and just so each of us will be absolutely and primally personal. The myth that my self-identity is constituted in a substance other than lived dramatic coherence will no longer be necessary.

Since our communion with one another will be established by our inclusion in the communion of Father, Son, and Spirit, it will be shaped by the "processions" and "missions" that make that communion. The Father will look on us as he looks on his Son. He will know what he is as God by seeing what he has made of us; and we will know him and ourselves as the outcome of the utter joyous Freedom that he is. As the Son offers himself in obedience to the Father the church will be both the self, the "body" that he offers, and participant in the act of offer-

---

38. I Corinthians 13:8.
39. *The Works of Samuel Hopkins* (Boston: Doctrinal Tract and Book Society, 1865), 2:58.

ing. And it is the very freedom of God as the Spirit that will be our freedom in this fellowship.

Thus love is the Johannine Christ's single "new commandment," the giving of which is John's theological equivalent for Luke's Ascension-stories.[40] The commandment is eschatological: "See what love the Father has given us, that we should be called children of God. . . . When he is revealed, we will be like him."[41] But the key New Testament passage is the address of Paul to the Corinthians with which we began this section.

According to Paul, the difference between love and all other gifts of the Spirit is that love "abides" eschatologically.[42] But so do also, as suddenly appears in the last verse of the chapter, the two other members of a perhaps conventionally referenced trio[43] of faith, hope, and love. Yet Paul's whole argument has been that only love never ends, that precisely therefore love is superior to all other gifts, explicitly including faith.[44] How are we to reconcile these positions? Doubtless Paul intends to tell us by saying that of the three abiding virtues love is "the greatest." In this context that must mean that faith and hope are present in the Fulfillment just and only as they are fulfilled in love.

Insofar as in Paul's discourse faith is to be distinguished from love,[45] the object of faith is the crucified one. The gospel is identical with "the message about the cross,"[46] so that Paul "decided to know nothing" among his hearers "except Jesus Christ, and him crucified."[47] Thus faith, in this context, is directed externally and to a past event. In love, however, the difference between internal and external relations is transcended, and the lovers are wholly present in each other.

Insofar as hope is to be distinguished from love, hope is the strictly eschatological relation. We hope for "the glory of God,"[48] which is precisely "what we do not see."[49] Also hope, in this context, is externally directed, to a future event. In love this separation also is transcended.

Yet there seems to be a difference between faith and hope, just in the present connection. When faith is fulfilled, when the one I know and trust confirms my trust and so earns my love, I trust him or her all the more. But when a specific hope is fulfilled by the advent of what is hoped for, how can this hope then continue? And if the whole of life is invested in a specific hope, when such hope is fulfilled must not all hope cease? But would not a life without hope be damna-

---

40. John 13:31–14:7.

41. I John 3:1–2.

42. I Corinthians 13:13. For the arguments about interpretation of *nyni . . . menei*, Hans Conzelmann, *I Corinthians*, tr. James Leitch (Philadelphia: Fortress, 1975), 229–231.

43. Ibid., 229–230.

44. I Corinthians 13:2.

45. Which it usually should not be, except dialectically as here.

46. I Corinthians 1:17–18.

47. Ibid., 2:2.

48. Romans 5:2.

49. Ibid., 8:25.

tion rather than salvation? We have arrived again at what this work has called the antinomy of hope.

VI

The antinomy of hope is the underlying reason of the dialectical theology's supposition that eschatological promise can have no content. If a promise stipulates a describable fulfillment, it appears that when the promise is fulfilled this content becomes present and is no longer future. Then the *promise* apparently must drop away. But is a creature ever related to the biblical God otherwise than by promise? The dialectical theology's solution to this quandary was to empty the gospel's eschatological promise of describable content.

The first step away from this dead end is to remember: believers' hope is in specific persons, the triune persons and one another; it is not hope for love as a general possibility to be fulfilled by anyone at large. When my hope to love and be loved by some specified person is fulfilled, what then? The remarkable phenomenon that must be observed at this point is that experienced love is itself hope for new opportunity of love. Persons live just as they are capable of surprising.[50] To love some person is to accept in advance the surprises he or she will bring to me, as revelations of my own proper good. Therefore when love comes, hope comes with it.

Hope for specific love is hope for a recognizable event. If I hope to love and be loved by someone, and this hope is fulfilled, I will know that it is. The love of a person or persons is thus a specifiable object of hope. And yet in the case of *this* specifiable object of hope, the seeming tautology does not hold, that when a specific hope is fulfilled that hope ceases. On the contrary, the fulfillment of hope is in this case its own beginning.

If I hope to be loved by and to love someone and to my joy find this hope fulfilled, the very same hope has then its true beginning, for the hope is identified not by impersonal benefits but by the personhood of the beloved. And when that hope is just so again fulfilled, it has again its true beginning, and so on, in concept, forever. Just so with the gospel's promise of love at the end, of the triune persons for each other, of Christ for us and we for Christ, of the triune persons' love for us in Christ and of our love for them in Christ, and of our love for everyone another.

---

50. 1:219–220.

THIRTY-TWO

The Last Judgment

I

We will at the end be taken into God. But according to the teaching here pro-posed, God creates by accommodating in himself, and the church consists now in communion with God. We already live, move, and have our being in God even as rebellious creatures, and in the church with willing personal participa-tion. Before the Great Entrance of the Byzantine liturgy, the choir sings, "We represent, hiddenly, the cherubim. . . . Let us lay by all earthly cares, to receive the King of the universe, whom legions of angels hiddenly accompany."[1] How much more may creatures live in God than they do where such songs can be truly sung?

What will be different in the Kingdom? Something must be; throughout the New Testament, the Kingdom is not yet come, however definitely it may be among us. And if our present state, also in the church, is human perfection, perfected humanity leaves much to be desired. But what exactly do we await beyond what we have?

The question is urgent for the system here offered, which construes more continuity between creation and human fulfillment, and then between the church and the Kingdom, than do some others. Such tendencies are of course far from new or peripheral in the tradition. When Irenaeus wrote, "Out of the greatness of his love he was made what we are, that he might bring us to be what he is,"[2] or when Athanasius laid down his famous dictum "He became man so that we could

1. Metropollitan Augoustinos, "Die göttliche Eucharistie als Opfer und ihr Priestertum in der orthodoxen Theologie und Praxis," *Bonn Document*, 104, cites this in illustration of his showing that the Christian liturgy is the "re-presentation in act" of the whole economy of salvation, but especially of the Eschaton.
2. *Against All Heresies*, v.praef.

become God,"[3] they did not distinguish qualitatively between what believers are becoming in this age and what they will be in the Eschaton, or indeed between what humanity is created to be and what it will then be.

Nor have only Greek fathers spoken so. Martin Luther did not distinguish qualitatively between ultimate and penultimate sanctification when he preached: "Everything [Christ] is and does is present in us and there works with power, so that we are utterly deified, so that we do not have some piece or aspect only of God, but his entire fullness."[4] Some also of those more eccentric nineteenth-century systems replicated such teaching. So Gottfried Thomasius: "In communion with Christ, the believer already possesses the true life, which is in its nature divine and therefore eternal. This is the divine-human life of Christ, which was introduced into the believer by baptism, which the believer has appropriated by faith, and which has become the active principle of his own personhood."[5]

Since believers' present deification is their habitation of the gate of heaven, it is the difference between the church and the Kingdom that must be grasped. A first step is to remind ourselves that the church is what she is, and believers in the church are what they are, only in anticipation, and so in separation from their own truth. The people of God cannot yet assemble. This people is the temple of the Holy Spirit precisely in her longing for a sanctity she now constantly loses hold of. The polity of God still battles with other principalities and powers and is invaded by them. The church is now the body of Christ only in that within herself she confronts the body of Christ as an other than herself. Believers' existing communion in the Trinity is the painful intrusion there of a plurality of still decidedly self-centered persons. And perhaps most decisively, the church of Jews and gentiles is still a separate community from Israel according to the flesh.

Thomasius brought the church's separation from her anticipated self to a formula: "What . . . separates [the church] from her goal, is double. On the one side, it is her own subjective condition," the continued intrusion of sin and death. "On the other side it is the removal of her Head from this world. For although his separation from the world does not withdraw his personal fellowship of life and love from the church . . . the congregation has him only in faith, not yet in seeing."[6] "Therefore the congregation awaits a Last Judgment."[7]

It is this Last Judgment we have here to consider, as the line between our participation in God as sinful creatures and as believers and our participation in him as fulfilled saints. Removal of the church's separation from Christ and relegation of sin and evil to the past are the same event.

3. *On the Incarnation*, 54.

4. *Predigt* (1525), WA 17/I:438. Note the date of this sermon: at the very moment of his chief theological decisions.

5. *Christi Person und Werk: Darstellung der evangelisch-lutherischen Dogmatik vom Mittelpunkte der Christologie aus*, 3rd ed., ed. F. J. Winter (Erlangen: Andreas Deichert, 1888), 2:553.

6. Ibid., 2:549.

7. Ibid., 2:551.

II

It is perhaps already plain that the "Last Judgment" here to be described is not quite the same as that which has dominated much popular piety and iconography. Since the expectation of final judgment comes very directly from Scripture, it is Scripture's concept that must control ours; and Scripture does not conceive judgment, divine or otherwise, as a sorting of satisfactory and unsatisfactory human specimens. Michelangelo's Sistine altar piece is magnificent, and theologically sophisticated perhaps beyond late modern deciphering, but it and its thousands of lesser cognates do not well depict the biblical Judgment.

Almost any Old Testament scene in which the verb regularly translated "to judge"[8] is used can display what Scripture means by judgment. The confrontation between Sarah and Abraham does so splendidly: "Then Sarai said to Abram, 'May the wrong done to me be on you! I gave my slave girl to your embrace, and when she saw that she had conceived, she looked on me with contempt. May the Lord judge between you and me!'"[9] A wrong has been done, by which the mutual order of the community, its righteousness, has been deranged. Judgment is the act that restores the community to its right order, done by the one competent in a particular case.[10] Here that can only be the Lord, since in the clan there is no law but Abraham's. But so soon as Israel becomes a national polity, judgment is the regular work of officers of the community; already Moses had deputies.[11]

In this matter as in others, the outcome of Israel's history with God is recognition of her hopes' eschatological character. Right judgment was as scarce in Israel as elsewhere, and in Israel this was an eschatological offense, since Israel possessed God's own *torah*. Thus it was very much because her judges "do not judge for[12] the fatherless, and the widow's cause does not come to them" that the Lord destroys Israel's national state.[13] And just so the messianic restoration and transformation will be done by one who "shall not judge by what his eyes see[14] . . . but with righteousness he shall judge the poor, and decide with equity for the meek."[15] The last judgment is fully described by Ezekiel: "I myself will judge between the fat sheep and the lean sheep. Because you pushed with flank and shoulder, and butted at all the weak animals . . . until you scattered them far and wide, I will save the flock, and they shall no longer be ravaged; and I will judge between sheep and sheep. I will set up over them one shepherd, my servant David."[16] The *last* judgment will simply be the appearance of this Messiah, after which another judgment will not be needed.

---

8. *Shtp.*

9. Genesis 16:6.

10. For justification of these generalizations, Johannes Pedersen, *Israel*, tr. A. Møller (London: Oxford University Press, 1926), 2:336–351.

11. Exodus 18:13–16.

12. The New Revised Standard Version "defend" badly obscures the point of the accusation.

13. Isaiah 1:23.

14. That is to say, by first appearances of respectability, etc.

15. Isaiah 11:3–4.

16. Ezekiel 34:22–23.

Insofar as judgment in Scripture concerns individuals, it is thus not primally a matter of rewarding or punishing them according to some general rule of their deserts but of rectifying their injustices against one another; Sarah calls for judgment "between" Abraham and herself. Insofar as individuals are in such actions punished or rewarded, it is because the members of living communities constantly give and take, in imperfect communities often unjustly, so that intervention to restore community must take from some and give to others. The recently famous "biblical option for the poor," which appears in our cited passages, rests on the certainty that when "the rich" and "the poor" have become social categories, there must be much to be made up between them.

This is as true of ultimate as of penultimate judgment; the expectation of final judgment is hope for a divine act that will truly do what penultimate judgments pervert or at best accomplish partly and temporarily. When history is taken into the Kingdom, all its accumulated mutual wrongs must be rectified. As Jonathan Edwards wrote, there are many "causes and controversies that must be decided by the supreme Judge" before the human community can be righteous; some are individuals' violation of our "union . . . in society," some are "causes between one nation and another," and some are even between one generation and another, so "that men that live now on the earth may have action against those that lived a thousand years ago." As an instance of the last sort, he gives the case between the Spanish and the Amerindians![17] The question of final judgment's consequences for individuals will be postponed to the penultimate chapter; it is the final intervention itself and its consequences for community that here concern us.

The New Testament's one addition to Scripture's understanding of judgment is an identification of the judge: judgment will be conducted by Jesus the Christ[18] with his disciples[19] around him, that is to say, by this human judge with a human court. What difference this identification makes depends on Christology; we here encounter another matter in which standard Western Christology fails to sustain the burden.

According to the standard teaching, which we will here describe as it appears in Thomas Aquinas, divine judicial power[20] belongs to the Son, as he is the subsistent wisdom of the Father.[21] But since it is "accordingly as he is a man" that Christ will be judge, the question is how the man Jesus participates in the Son's power. According to Thomas, Jesus will judge with only the authority that belongs to human nature, raised in his case to universality and supremacy[22] by created grace,[23] not by a communication of properly divine attributes. The participation of Jesus' human judicial power in the Son's divine power is then that the

17. *Miscellanies*, 1007.
18. Acts 10:42.
19. I Corinthians 6:21.
20. *Potestas judicialis.*
21. *Summa theologiae*, iii.59.1.
22. Ibid., 2.
23. Ibid., 8.5.

latter provides the standard of the former and that Jesus is "imbued" with that standard as others are not.[24]

Thus the standard by which the world is to be judged is not itself, according to usual teaching, defined by the Incarnation. And as Christ judges he does so by supernatural enhancement of a power belonging to all humanity. The vision is ineluctably that of a human judge writ large, judging by abstract principles of divine law; and this vision is surely partly to blame for the superstition and fear with which most believers, in contradiction to their faith, anticipate the Judgment—unless indeed they have persuaded themselves not to anticipate it at all. But what if we were to construe Christ's power of judgment by the Christology of this work's first volume?

Then we would say that the power of final judgment belongs to Christ "accordingly as he is a man" simply in that this man and the divine Son are one personal identity. Then Christ is himself the truth by which he judges. There is no standard of judgment that is what it would have been without the Cross and Resurrection.

The Last Judgment will be according to the law that unites the *totus Christus* and that is as such the *torah* that the Son is for the Father. It will be by a human "judicial power" that is as such the power that the Father exercises over all creation through the Son and in the freedom of the Spirit. It will be judgment by the Son of his Spouse, according to the law of their union. In sum, the Final Judgment will be the rectification of the community of God's people by bringing them into exact concert with the triune community and its righteousness, as this is defined by Christ's death and Resurrection.

Or in the language of that nineteenth century to which in this chapter we like to recur, a Last Judgment is needed because "Christianity cannot always remain merely a historic principle *alongside* the absolutely opposite principle . . . as though the two were of equal authority."[25] Sooner or later, "a permanent division" must be "effected . . . when the powers hostile to the kingdom of God are . . . consigned to the past."[26] The negative side of final judgment is "the excision of everything evil from the kingdom of Christ"; the positive side is "the revelation of the full power of redemption."[27]

III

Citations scattered through the previous sections provide a list of the evils whose removal will make the difference between the Kingdom and this age. That is, they state what the Last Judgment consigns to the past. First on the list is death.

24. Ibid., 59.2.
25. Citing another of those nineteenth-century eccentrics, Isaac Dorner, *A System of Christian Doctrine*, vol. IV, tr. Alfred Cave, J. S. Banks (Edinburgh: T. & T. Clark, 1890), 416.
26. Ibid., 417.
27. Ibid., 415.

Death is hard to conceive, and not just because we are reluctant to face it. Late modernity has generally supposed it brave to say that death is the simple cessation of the person; and apart from the gospel this supposition would doubtless be the part of valor.[28] Historically, however, humanity has found the sheer cessation of a person literally unthinkable, for death so conceived is the termination of consciousness, and that turns out to be an impossible thought.

I can of course affirm and as a matter of mere language understand the proposition, "My consciousness will some day cease." But if I try to summon experiential content[29] for this prediction, all I can conjure is a consciousness of darkness and emptiness or the strange consciousness of sleep, which of course are still consciousness. Moreover, the present nothingness of a consciousness would be constituted by memory: I, the erstwhile such-a-one, am nothing. Thus when I try to think my own death simply as cessation, the best I can do is to think of myself as remembering that I used to be and so being conscious that I now am nothing and am conscious of nothing. To the concept of truly vanished consciousness, no projected experience can correspond.[30]

There is perhaps one way in which I can think the cessation of my consciousness: I can try to think general nonexistence, by dwelling with the negative part of Heidegger's question, "Why not rather just nothing?" For to abolish consciousness, we must abolish not only Augustine's immediate present perception, but memory and anticipation as well. With respect to any particular consciousness, its extinction is therefore *exactly* the same as there never having been or being or being going to be anything at all; nor does this merely mean that for that consciousness it is the same *as if* there had been nothing at all. The vanishing of a consciousness is insofar the—even retrospective!—nonexistence of the world.

At this point one cannot refrain from asking: if all consciousness ceased, would anything then exist or indeed ever have existed or be going to exist?[31] A particular tree in the forest is doubtless there when no one perceives it, but is a universe? Moreover, does it matter whether or not *all* consciousness is extinguished? Does not the extinction of even one consciousness make all reality dubious? However one may finally work out these questions, which some have considered the key questions of metaphysics and others found hopelessly muddled, it should anyway be clear: humankind's universal inability to think death as mere cessation is not mere fear or egocentricity.

28. This part is taken, it should be noted, by few. The repristination in postmodernity of primitive or superstitious denials of death is pitiable to behold.

29. I use this term as yet another attempted translation of Hegel's *Vorstellung*. We can entertain a *Begriff* of consciousness's cessation but can pair it to no *Vorstellung*.

30. We have here a *Begriff* without a *Vorstellung*; the epistemological impossibility of such a concept is much of the truth of idealism.

31. This element of truth in idealism recurs in the strangest places; so the Max-Planck Institut cosmologist Frank Tipler, unpublished paper marked "Delivered at the Vatican Observatory Conference on Science Philosophy and Theology," September 1987: "This brings to the age-old philosophical problem of whether a universe which has no observers in it . . . can possibly be said to exist. My own inclination would be to say no."

The closest historically achieved approach to a notion of death as personal extinction, notably shared with archaic Greece by preexilic Israel,[32] is the image of the dead as shadows—negative images!—of former selves, resident in the grave as a realm of what precisely *used to be*.[33] In Israel, this conception left what Gerhard von Rad called a "theologically strange vacuum" in her interpretation of reality, a negative fact not interpreted by Exodus or creation, and so not within the Lord's domain:[34] a psalmist could presume that "those who go down to the Pit . . . [are] those whom you remember no more, for they are cut off from your hand."[35] This psalmist's question "Is your steadfast love declared in the grave, . . . or your saving help in the land of forgetfulness?"[36] was intended as bitter rhetoric—though it is open to a different answer than his, which in time was given.

Nor is expectation of endless consciousness necessarily happy. On the contrary, the thought sheerly in itself is horrifying: that I should go on, and on, and on, and . . .[37] The infinity that here opens before consciousness is the empty infinity of nihilism, in which because there is no end nothing has any point. The greatest nonbiblical religions are devoted to the hope that consciousness may after all be dissolved, by aeons of willed and at the last moment unwilled paradox.

The idea of "life after death" becomes an object of hope only when a content is promised for it. Thus in Socratic theology human immortality becomes an attractive notion when humanity persuades itself that consciousness's endless continuance is in fact participation in divine timelessnesss, so that death can be escape into the gods' eternal pleasures.

We saw in the first volume why and how Israel could not finally let death remain theologically unthought, nor yet think it in Socratic fashion.[38] Insofar as death then becomes an explicit feature *within* Israel's faith, it can only appear as the *enemy* of the Lord; and then the Lord's final triumph must be death's abolition. So "the Isaiah apocalypse,"[39] from the last period of canonical Israel's prophecy, proclaims that on "the day" when the Lord undoes the present scheme of things and enthrones himself on Zion as manifest universal king, he "will destroy . . . the shroud that is cast over all peoples . . . he will swallow up death forever."[40] As death has swallowed humankind, now the Lord will turn the tables, and the

32. Pedersen, *Israel*, 1–2:462.

33. A detailed and nuanced description of Israel's relation to death is provided by Hans Walter Wolff, *Anthropology of the Old Testament*, tr. anon. (reprint, Mifflinton: Sigler Press, 1966), 99–118.

34. *Theologie des alten Testaments* (Munich: Chr. Kaiser, 1965), 2:371–372.

35. Psalm 88:4–5.

36. Psalm 88:11–12.

37. I remember sitting in church as a child and trying to make sense of the preacher's talk of eternity and of the difference between an eternity of pleasure and an eternity of punishment. I decided that there was in any case little difference between the two, both being terrifying.

38. 1:64–74.

39. To the form and dating of this part of Isaiah, and to the exegesis of our passage, Hans Wildberger, *Jesaja*, in *Biblischer Kommentar Altes Testament*, ed. Siegfried Herrmann, Hans Walter Wolff (Neukirchen-Vluyn: Neukirchener Verlag des Erziehungsvereins, 1978), 885–1026.

40. Isaiah 25:7.

universal death-shroud will be lifted. This victory is identical with the Lord's vindication of his people and of his promises to them: the parallel construction continues, "and the disgrace of his people he will take away."[41]

But what will the overcoming of death mean for the nevertheless dead? The first volume of this work construed "the Ezekiel-question" as the effective conclusion of the Old Testament: "Mortal, can these bones live?"[42] For "the house of Israel" as a nation, Ezekiel himself already receives the hint of resurrection: "I am going to open your graves, . . . O my people; and I will bring you back to the land of Israel."[43] Yet this is still not victory over death, the restoration of dead Israel to a life not again terminated by death; nor is it the vindication of Abraham and Sarah and Moses and the legions of righteous dead. The promise of such resurrection appears only in the Old Testament's extreme genre, apocalypse, and then hesitantly: "Many of those who sleep in the dust of the earth shall awake, some to everlasting life."[44] And only at the very edge even of this vision does the promise at last become personal: "But you, go your way and rest, you shall rise for your reward at the end of the days."[45]

For Jesus and his disciples, with the Pharisees and against the Sadducees, a final resurrection belonged to the assured substance of Jewish faith.[46] And the church is the community that believes the Lord has answered his own question to Ezekiel by raising Jesus. The church thus lives in certainty of what Israel learned to hope at the very end of her canonical history with God.

In the church, therefore, any suggestion that "there is no resurrection of the dead" makes her faith simply vain.[47] Indeed, believers' resurrection follows necessarily from the eschatologically lively Spirit's habitation in the church: "If the Spirit of him who raised Jesus from the dead dwells in you, he who raised Christ from the dead will give life to your mortal bodies also, through his Spirit that dwells in you."[48]

Thus the hope entertained by the church is not for the mitigation or evasion of death but for its undoing. The church does not hope for the survival of some part of the human person, not even an "essential" or "central" part, or for a redefinition of death as liberation from the material world. When the Lord raises his people from the dead, he does not rescue them from a neutral if unfortunate circumstance or reach an adjustment with another power; he conquers an enemy.

Just here we encounter a subsidiary but real theological puzzlement. On the one hand, since death is the enemy of God and so of his people, it seems that death cannot belong to humanity as God wills it, and therefore that an unfallen humanity would not have been mortal. Moreover, Scripture seems to support this suppo-

41. Isaiah 25:8.
42. Ezekiel 37:3.
43. Ezekiel 37:11–12.
44. Daniel 12:2.
45. Daniel 12:13.
46. Mark 12:18–27parr; Acts 4:1–4.
47. I Corinthians 15:12–19.
48. Romans 8:11.

sition. In Genesis' second creation narrative, death is the sanction of the Lord's prohibition to Adam of the one tree.[49] Accordingly, death appears in Paul's teaching as the consequence of Adam's violating the prohibition: "As sin came into the world through one man and death through sin."[50] Following this line, Augustine formulated what would be traditional teaching: "The death of the body results from sin. Therefore if Adam had not sinned, he would not have died in the body."[51]

Yet on the other hand, must not creatures and so humanity have a temporal end? Whatever may be true of consciousness? And what could we call such an end but death? There has been a minority, in the modern period perhaps a majority, that is cautiously willing to attribute mortality to humanity's created nature. We may cite Karl Barth as its most distinguished representative: "It *also* belongs to humankind's nature, it *also* is God's creation, . . . that we are mortal."[52]

Moreover, there is scriptural reason also for this minority position. Paul's teaching rests on one chapter of Genesis, and indeed on one construal of it, and the theological majority's on the passage in Paul. It is therefore the more remarkable that the rest of Genesis, and the Old Testament generally, know no such doctrine. In the rest of Genesis the finitude of our days belongs simply to our difference from the Creator: "My spirit shall not abide in mortals forever . . . their days shall be one hundred twenty years," not because they are sinful but simply because "they are flesh."[53] It is in faithfulness to this aspect of the matter that Barth inserts his "also" and that even Augustine qualifies the attribution of immortality to created humanity. According to Augustine's fuller teaching, apart from sin the embodied human "is mortal insofar as he *can* die, and immortal insofar as he does not *need* to die. . . . The first human was . . . immortal because he was provided from the tree of life, and not by his natural constitution."[54]

Creatures have their end in God. In the human case, is that conceivable without death or something very like it? Martin Luther supposed that had Adam not sinned he would have been "rapt" into his final end in God "without death, after he had lived . . . to satiety."[55] But what difference is there between this posited rapture after a life that needs no more time to be complete, and the death, for example, of Jacob, who, satiated with years, reunited with his children and grandchildren, and with his mission accomplished, tucked his legs up in bed, "breathed his last, and was gathered to his people?"[56] Particularly since we know what Jacob did not, that Jacob's people are in fact gathered to God?

---

49. Genesis 2:17.
50. Romans 5:12.
51. *De Genesi ad litteram*, vi.23.
52. *Kirchliche Dogmatik*, III/2:765–770. Pannenberg, *Systematische Theologie* (Göttingen: Vandenhoeck & Ruprecht, 1993), 3:603, argues that death and finitude must be separable, since the risen Jesus will not die and yet remains a finite human. But this will not do; the finitude precisely of the risen human Jesus is constituted in the fact that his life is made a whole by his death.
53. Genesis 6:3.
54. *De Genesi ad litteram*, 25. Just so Thomas Aquinas, *Summa theologiae*, i–ii.85.5–6.
55. *Ennaratio In Genesis*, 79.
56. Genesis 49:33.

There is this one difference between Jacob's death and what Luther posited for an unfallen Adam: as Jacob was taken to his ancestors he was simultaneously taken *from* those gathered around his bed and from all the great coming family of Israel. What makes death the Lord's enemy, and fearful for us, is that it separates lovers. Were my death simply my affair, the old maxim might hold, that since my death will never be part of my experience I have no need to fear it. But death will take my loves from me and me from them, and that is the final quite objective horror, for it decrees the *present* emptiness of all human worth, constituted as it is by love. Having no more being would be no evil were being not mutual.

A human end that was not what we know as death is a might-have-been. And the might-have-been is of the sort we have had so often to leave theologically empty. There would have been an undying humanity only in a created history that did not contain the cross, and under a God whose second identity was not the crucified Jesus. But precisely the crucified Jesus, and the law of his relation to the Father, constituted in his death and Resurrection, will be the standard of the Judgment, the norm of what will be committed to the past. Thus also Augustine could not actually conceive creatures' fulfillment except as *death and* resurrection, and held that those saints who are alive at Christ's return will experience both as they are rapt to him.[57]

At this point above all we must cling to the rule that has appeared at several junctures: humanity has no other actual end than its supernatural end, nor is that end, as actually set, otherwise achievable than by Jesus' death and Resurrection. Therefore a humanity that would not have needed to die is a posit contrary to irreducible fact, which we may conceptually isolate by abstraction from God's actual history with us but about which we can say nothing material. Could there have been a humanity that was like us except that it did not die? Because Adam had not sinned? We must presume that God could have lived such a history with such a humanity, but this mere abstract possibility is the only thing we can affirm.

God's overcoming of death is not, therefore, only his overcoming of something intruded into his creation. It is simultaneously his transformation of creatures' natural temporal finitude, and just so his achieving of his original end for the creation in one of its defining aspects.

IV

Friedrich Nitzsch again: "The state of blessedness will consist in an intensification of those anticipatory joys that already in this life are joined to communion with God, only that every limitation through sin and death fall away."[58] We have considered death, now we must consider sin.

---

57. *De civitate Dei*, xx.20.
58. Friedrich Nitzsch, *Lehrbuch der Evangelischen Dogmatik* (Freiburg: J. C. B. Mohr, 1896), 606.

Sin is broken in believers by the agency of Christ within their persons. Yet short of the Kingdom, other agencies are also effective there, and sin therefore remains actual.

Insofar as we are one with Christ, sin is impossible. Thus Paul argues in the sixth chapter of Romans that the baptized *should* not continue to sin because in fact they *cannot* sin, being "dead" to it; and that they are dead to sin because they have been joined with Christ Jesus, whose death is behind him.[59] In this respect, nothing will change at the Eschaton; as Dorner observed, "the essential . . . unity of the soul with Christ" simply "continues."[60] The famous Augustinian charac-terization of the saints' condition as *non posse peccare*, being "unable to sin," applies both in the church and the Kingdom, insofar as in either the saints live in Christ and he in them.[61]

This inability to sin does not infringe human freedom, whether in this life or the Kingdom. As we have seen, created wills' freedom occurs precisely in rapture by God.[62] We may here simply recall earlier discussions of the relation between divine and human free initiative, and cite Augustine to apply them to the condi-tion of the saints: "Nor do they lack free will because they are unable to delight in sin. On the contrary, their will is so fully freed from delight in sinning that it is liberated to an unswervable delight in not sinning."[63]

The saints' freedom from sin lies in union with Christ, in belonging to the *totus Christus*. The fact that in this age they nevertheless sin lies in their continu-ing determination by other communities. Also of the church herself it must be said that insofar as she harbors sin, it is because of her inevitable entanglement with other polities of this world.[64] When the Lord ascended and left his disciples behind, what he left them behind *in* was their home towns and the Roman Em-pire and the economic arrangements of Palestine and all their other entangle-ments in communities of the *libido dominandi*. According to Paul, even marriage, the very "mystery" of believers' union with Christ, is as a structure of this age an entanglement potentially separating believers from Christ.[65]

Nor does this teaching dilute personal responsibility for sin. It only reiter-ates a point made over and over in various connections: personhood itself is a communal phenomenon. As the doctrine of original sin insists, my sin and the

---

59. Romans 6:1–14.
60. *Dogmatics*, 3:411.
61. The Wesleyan tradition has appeared too little in this work, owing to my ignorance of it. Its sizeable moment of truth at this point must at least be recognized.
62. Pp. 107–108.
63. *De civitate Dei*, xxii.30: "Nec ideo liberum arbitrium non habebunt, quia peccata eos delectare non poterunt. Magis quippe erit liberum a delectatione peccandi usque ad delectationem non peccandi indeclinabilem liberatum."
64. Thomasius, *Christi Person und Werk*, 2:551: "Entire blessedness is only possible for [the church] when the powers and elements enemy to God, that still are powerful in her midst . . . are finally cast out from her. Therefore the congregation awaits a Last Judgment."
65. I Corinthians 7.

sin of my communities, as these are extended both diachronically and synchronically, cannot be disentangled. If we follow Martin Luther's phenomenology, according to which sin is always some form of incurvature into oneself, we may say: the communities and collectives of this world all at the last fail their members, and just so abandon them to find themselves in themselves; that is, the communities and collectives of this world bind their members to sin.

In the Kingdom, there will be only the one community. Our inner division will therefore vanish. Saints in the church still live in other and opposed communities and so are ever and again driven to find their coherence and meaning in themselves, as the only thing bridging their various communities, and just thereby to sin. Saints in the Kingdom bring their divided selves into the perfectly coherent one triune community and so are every instant liberated anew from incurvature into themselves.

In this connection also we must not reify an abstract possibility. Saints in the Kingdom will not be as if they had not sinned, but rather the last clause of the previous paragraph is precise: their blessedness will be eternally actual liberation from each their specific burden of sin. The head of the *totus Christus*, as whom they enjoy the sinless community of the Kingdom, is the Jesus whose very life is defined as death for their sin. The memory of their sins will be joy to them, since precisely these bind them to Christ; in the Kingdom the proposition will be *true* which in this age must be rejected, that sin only occasions greater grace.[66]

V

Liberation from death and liberation from sin together liberate for love, for community constituted in utter mutuality. Here we again reach the line where analysis and speculation must for a moment become poetry. There will be a community whose whole life will be a feast given by God, who "will make for all peoples a feast of rich food, a feast of well-aged wines."[67] There will be a universal community of all who have beaten "their swords into plowshares, and their spears into pruning hooks."[68] There will be a community, "the holy city, the new Jerusalem," that will come "down out of heaven from God, prepared as a bride adorned for her husband."[69]

Death undoes love. To love is to live from hopes invested in the other; to love is to learn what is my good from what the other in fact does for me. But when I must look forward to death, I face the emptiness of hopes and expectations, and so of love. The New Testament thus thinks of the futurity of death as the key of our bondage to sin: we are "those who all their lives were held in slavery by the fear of death."[70]

---

66. Romans 6:1.
67. Isaiah 25:6.
68. Isaiah 2:4.
69. Revelation 21:2.
70. Hebrews 2:15.

The marriage promise, our closest approach to God's self-commitment to Jesus and so to us, does not for mere hyperbole's sake commit us "till death do us part." To love is unconditionally to accept the will of the other, which may indeed kill—this is what all romanticism knows. The antinomy of love, a variant of the antinomy of hope, is that when love thus fulfills itself in its extreme possibility, it separates the lovers and undoes itself. Only love that has undergone death for the other and just thereby lives anew can be sure in itself. The perfect community of the Kingdom is and can only be a community of the resurrected.

Also sin undoes love; indeed it is simply love's opposite. More specifically to our present point, sin in its character as idolatry undoes polity, undoes the structure of community in which we find each other. Christ's final judgment will commit idolatry to the past. It will leave us with no alternative communities united by devotion to other gods. It will establish the sole dominion of the polity of God. Just so it will make love inevitable.

As for the pseudopersonification of sin, the loveless liar, he will be cast "into the lake of fire and sulfur,"[71] and that will be that. What his mode of nonbeing thereafter will be need not concern us; the universe will be rid of him.

VI

Paired with sin and death, as the church's difference from the Kingdom, "is the removal of her Head from this world." This is dramatically portrayed by Luke's picture of the disciples staring up after the ascending Christ and having their worst suspicions angelically confirmed in the guise of comfort: "This Jesus, who has been taken up from you."[72] The church now possesses her Lord sacramentally only, that is, actually and truly but still in faith and not by "sight." Indeed, the eschatological separation is constituted in the sacramental relations themselves: the church, the community of disciples, is now the presence of Christ only in that within her that same Christ is present as an other than she, and there only as a sign signified by other signs.

When the Lord comes "in the same way" as he departed,[73] his presence to faith will be transformed into a presence as directly apprehended as is humans' presence now to each other—or rather, far more directly. This will be the great blessedness of the saints. In this chapter, however, we are concerned with his coming insofar as it is Judgment. What does the transcending of the Lord's sacramental presence in the church relegate to the past?

The following suggestion is perhaps initially surprising but on reflection seems inevitable. That even after his Resurrection the Lord is present to faith and not to sight constitutes the church's character as an eschatological detour; it is because the Lord has come but nevertheless is yet to come that the church's life is sacramental. The Lord's return will restore his people to the main road, ending

---

71. Revelation 20:10.
72. Acts 2:10–11.
73. Acts 1:11.

the detour. But that is to say, his return will terminate the separation between the church and Israel according to the flesh. Perhaps we may even say: the church does not now see her Lord in the flesh because he is a Jew according to the flesh and the church is separated from Judaism according to the flesh. As judgment in the present respect, what the Lord's coming will dismiss is the generic ungodliness of the church's dominating gentiles and continuing Judaism's disbelief.

Throughout the church's history her greatest puzzlement and temptation has been the existence of another continuation of Israel close by her, which consists of Jews by right of descent and perdures in despite of the Resurrection. Paul's confrontation with this mystery, in Romans, perhaps lacks conceptual coherence, but remains the canonical challenge and example.[74] Paul was sure, if of anything, that "the calling of God" is "irrevocable."[75] Compelled therefore to believe that "all Israel"—and he clearly is not quite sure what he means by that—must somehow finally be saved, he seems to have constructed another apocalyptic scenario to accommodate the event.[76] We need not reproduce the scheme, if indeed there was one. But we surely must adopt Paul's hope.

What we now know as Judaism is a continuation of Israel very specifically "according to the flesh": it understands Israel as the "children of an original ancestral couple, Abraham and Sarah."[77] Moreover, this Judaism emerged to enable this Israel's continued coherence in the absence of the Temple, has its religious entity in the study of torah, especially insofar as torah separates Israel from the nations, and consciously exists in a pause of history, between the destruction of the Temple—contemporaneous with the first flourishing of the gospel's mission!—and the advent of Messiah.[78] Thus this Judaism and the church are mirror images of one another—and indeed they were born and developed in historical lock step.[79] What the Lord will undo at his coming is their separation; he will fit the reverse images to one another. They shall both "look on him whom they have pierced."[80]

Much recent theology has been determined to overcome "supersessionism."[81] Those most thematically involved have commonly supposed that their effort is incompatible with belief that the advent of Jesus Christ definitely fulfills the promises to Israel.[82] Since the identity of Christ as the Son is the same fact as his finality in God's history with his people, this supposition further implies that

---

74. The most convincing exegesis of Romans 9–11 known to me is James D. G. Dunn, *The Theology of Paul the Apostle* (Grand Rapids: Eerdmans, 1998), 499–532.

75. Romans 11:29.

76. Romans 11:25–26.

77. Jacob Neusner, *Rabbinic Judaism: Structure and System* (Minneapolis: Fortress, 1995), 124.

78. Ibid., 169–191.

79. Ibid., 169–238.

80. It will be seen that my position converges, from the Christian side, with the teaching of Franz Rosenzweig, *Der Stern der Erlösung* (Frankfurt am Main: Suhrkamp, 1988).

81. Pp. 190–195.

82. Also the otherwise very helpful work of R. Kendall Soulen is slightly bent by this assumption; e.g., "Karl Barth and the Future of the God of Israel," *Pro Ecclesia* 6 (1997):413–428.

supersessionism can only be avoided by repristinating a Christology in which Jesus is not quite identical with the Son, that is, by repristinating Arianism or Nestorianism.[83] But after the decisions of the councils, such a withdrawal amounts to retreat from the faith; if the common supposition were correct, then the church to be faithful would in fact have to teach that after Christ's Resurrection no Judaism could have a further role in God's history with his people. The common supposition, however, is wrong.

The time of the church occurs *within* the advent of Christ to fulfill the Old Testament. Thus until the Last Judgment and our resurrection, Christ has *not* yet come in the way that fully consummates Israel's history. It is this in itself rather obvious point that is jointly forgotten by Christian supersessionism and by most attempts to overcome it.

When Christ's advent has been accomplished in such fashion as to make further coming superfluous, there will indeed be no more role for Judaism as a community separate from the church, *or* for the church as a community separate from Israel; both will be superseded in these roles. As the Kingdom is present in heaven, the "one hundred forty-four thousand . . . of the people of Israel" and the "great multitude . . . from every nation" are one church in the praise of the Lamb.[84] The risen Jesus, the head of the *totus Christus*, is, after all, one of the hundred and forty-four thousand.

In the time of the church until the Judgment, the Judaism of Israel according to the flesh must continue. It must continue precisely because Israel did not believe as a historically identifiable continuing community,[85] lest "the gifts and the calling of God" prove after all revocable.[86] And, since the church is thus doomed to be mostly gentile, this Judaism must continue lest God's *torah* be forgotten. For within the perfected polity of God it will eternally be the role of the hundred and forty-four thousand to remember every one of God's commands[87] and lead in the praise of God for them.

VII

The Last Judgment is in all these ways a closure of the human narrative. Closure is demanded by the very character of God's creation: he creates not a cosmos that goes on forever or perhaps just stops but a history that is a creation because its closure makes it a whole. The Last Judgment is therefore the very model of what late and postmodernity abhor: any and every curtailment of our going on and on

---

83. So, notably, Paul M. Van Buren, in numerous books and articles.

84. Revelation 7.

85. There are those whom also this position will not satisfy, because it regards Judaism's defining disbelief in Jesus' Resurrection as a failure to do something that should have been done. But Christianity cannot deny this without denying itself. Some will then hold that orthodox Christianity is thereby shown to be intrinsically "anti-Jewish"; surely at this point the accusation has become quite meaningless, except perhaps in the mouths of those who do not themselves believe.

86. Romans 11:25–29.

87. The Talmud's "session in heaven" can continue its debates.

and . . . , of our self-transcendence into a future. Every closure is for this sensibility premature and is experienced as repression.[88] And to be sure, the Judgment does just that; it finally represses our simple ongoing. Whether this is experienced as deliverance or as final frustration will depend on faith or unfaith. Dramatic closure must be experienced as repression by those who do not apprehend their lives dramatically. The question is: Can those who understand themselves undramatically understand themselves at all?

---

88. Postmodernity abhors closure even when it recognizes the horror of going on and on and on; Faustus is by no accident its hero.

THIRTY-THREE

The Great Transformation

I

The advent of Christ in judgment, in his "alien work," will consign to the past sin, death, and all division of God's people from each other and so from him. In its own positive meaning, it will establish and constitute the new reality of the Kingdom, that is, a new and final participation in the triune life. This new participation in God is the Kingdom, and the resurrection, and accomplishes all the transformations embraced in the promise of "a new heaven and a new earth." But again, *what* is to happen?

An enigmatic bit of Pauline apocalyptic has always seemed to suggest the enabling core of eschatological transformation, if only we could understand him: "Then comes the end, when [Christ] hands over the kingdom to God the Father . . . [so] that God may be all in all."[1] And perhaps we can grasp a little of his intention, enough to be going on with. For however Paul may have envisioned the decisive change, it is at least clear that he locates it in the triune life itself. Whatever of Paul's theologoumenon may be lost to us or whatever of his apocalyptic scenario we would reject if we could make it out, this much is surely sufficiently arresting.

The triune God is too intimately involved with his creation for its final transformation to be founded in anything less than an event of his own life. The future that the Spirit is for the Father and the Son is a real future which must *come* to pass. Moreover, insofar as the Spirit is also the future for creation, the heavenly presence of this future for God is, as we have seen, God's anticipation of it, and what is anticipated must be *going to* happen. It belongs to the "whither" of the triune life that it truly has a "whence."

---

1. I Corinthians 15:24.

Thus even what we have called the antinomy of hope is real for God; indeed, as his time is the possibility of ours, so the reality of the antinomy for him is the necessity of its reality for us. The antinomy is solved in God as he solves it for us: in that the coming future is love. We need not again trace the dialectics of love and hope. The difference of course is that God's future is not cut off from him; the Spirit is the same one God as is the Father or the Son. Therefore "hope" is perhaps not quite the word. Indeed, the triune life is itself the solution, also for us, of the antinomy: the triune life is the unity of love among the divine identities, including the relations in which each of them is an object of expectation for the others.

Nevertheless, God's life does have a "whither" and a "whence": the Father's expectation for the missions on which he sends the Son and the Spirit is genuine expectation and so must *come to* fulfillment. It belongs to God's life that the fulfillment of the missions is in contingent but ineluctable fact the love between the Father and the Son as that love *comes to be* the love between the Father and the *totus Christus*, when Judgment shall have purified the church of all involvement with sin and of all separation from her head.

The discourse of this book has regularly skirted the edges of what language can do; in this ultimate part and penultimate chapter, the risks are especially great. Nevertheless we must venture: the triune life in which the Kingdom is present differs from that for which it is future, in that each of the divine identities arrives at new relations to the others.

Christ will know himself as his people with no more reservation; he will be the head of a body that he does not need to discipline. Thus he will eternally adore God *as* the one single and exclusive person of the *totus Christus*, as those whom the Father ordained for him and whom the Spirit has brought to him. The Spirit will no more bring and join the Son's people to him, for they will be with and joined to him. Thus the Spirit will be Freedom with no burden, Freedom to play infinitely with the possibilities of love between the Father and the embodied Son. And the Father will no more *exert* power but simply rule and love and be loved.

II

What will this event mean for humans in their relation to God? A first step is to note that Paul's teaching must at least mean that Christ's domination of rebellious creation will end because the rebellion is ended. So Jonathan Edwards, who in these chapters has returned as a guide:[2] "Christ . . . is now made head over all things to the church. That is . . . he rules all events, every change and part of the universe so as to conduce to the good of his church, and to bring to pass the ends of his mediation. . . . But when the end shall be entirely accomplished and the church is brought to the consummation of glory, there will be no more need this governing and ordering of all things to this end."[3]

2. Having rather dropped out in the part on ecclesiology!
3. *Miscellanies*, 86.

Moreover, the change in Christ's role between the world and the Father must involve a transformation also in his role between the church and the Father. So long as the church is herself still embroiled with the powers of this world and therefore with what the risen Christ must dominate, Christ must have an agency as Lord *of* the church that is other than his agency *as* the church. A passage of Goeffrey Preston's remarkable ecclesiological meditations surely captures some part of Paul's intent: when "God . . . is all in all, then . . . Christ will no longer be the *vis-à-vis* of the Church but will stand together with the Church before the Father in the Holy Spirit."[4]

It has been a slogan of this book: in this age the church is the presence of Christ in the world only in that within her Christ is present to her as an other. She is the body of Christ only because in her gathering the very same body of Christ is an object given to her from beyond her. The great eschatological trans-formation, in all its aspects, has this at its center: the dialectic of Christ's pres-ence to and by the church will end, the people of God will directly be Christ's availability also for her members, and Christ will be directly our availability to each other. In the perfected Community, I will intend the body of God by in-tending the Community. And to do that I will not need to be turned from my fellows to other things among us. And I will intend my brothers and sisters by intending the Son. Also in this latter movement I will not need other mediations; the same event that will be our resurrection will be our "revealing" to one an-other as "the children of God."[5]

Here is perhaps the innermost point where our discourse must change from propositions to poesy: How are we to speak of human experience as the experi-ence of those from whom the second identity of God does not distinguish him-self? Let us say: there will be a burst of absolute love embracing all the events of created time, which can as such only be the event of God but which the redeemed will know as their own active eros. Let us say: there will be a universally encom-passing liturgy, with the Father as the bishop enthroned in the apse and the apostles as the presbyters around him and the redeemed of all times as the con-gregation and the angel-driven creation as the organ and orchestra, and the tomb of all martyrs as the altar, and the Lamb visibly on the altar, and the Spirit as the Lamb's power and perception,[6] and the music and drama and sights and aromas and touches of the liturgy as themselves the Life who is worshipped. Let us say: there will be a political community whose intimacy is such that from the vantage of this world it could only be called delirium but which just so will be perfectly ordered because the delirium's dynamism will be the perichoresis of the triune life.[7]

Having been driven to such flights, we must quickly return to propositional restrictions. Plainly, the logic of the previous paragraphs is that of "deification."

4. *Faces of the Church* (Grand Rapids: Eerdmans, 1997), 153.
5. Romans 8:19.
6. Revelation 4; 6:9–11.
7. The opposition of "Dionysian" and "Apollonian" will be transcended!

Three specifications of this concept are needed just here—and some may think them overdue.

A definition by Anastasius of Sinai, often quoted in Eastern theology,[8] provides the one: "Deification is elevation to a higher plane, not an enlargement or transformation of nature."[9] Because we become God, we do not cease to be creatures; we will be those creatures who are indissolubly one with the creature God the Son is.

This leads to the second qualification. Athanasius's aphorism, "He became man in order that we might become God," while indeed true just as it stands, can be misleading out of its context. Irenaeus can supply the needed precision: the God who becomes what we are is the God-man; what he becomes is what we actually are, "fallen and passible man, condemned to death"; and we become what he is, humans so united with God as to "receive and bear God."[10]

An assymetry observable in Irenaeus's doctrine points to the third needed qualification: the God-man becomes one of us, but the redeemed do not become additional God-humans. Rather they become participants in the one God-man, members of the *totus Christus*; they are God-bearers communally and not otherwise.

Within the way of understanding presented throughout this book, it must often be a question: In the Kingdom, what will be the difference between the Son and the rest of us? Perhaps we may now give one answer to that question by supposing another scene contrary to possibility. Were I, within the eschatologically perfected *totus Christus*, to say "I am God," the first person singular would remove me from the union, so that the sentence would be false. It would after all be the "old man" talking, the person not yet one with Christ and so still implicated in the communities of domination. But Christ has no old man; and if we can imagine him within the triune-human community saying "I am God," it would be a simple and humble observation of fact.

III

There is an alternative interpretation of final transformation, which is sometimes thought to be the Western alternative to a supposedly Eastern eschatology of deification: the saints' final blessedness is constituted in the *visio dei*, in seeing God. So Philip Melanchthon: "Eternal life will be perpetual adoration."[11] Thomas Aquinas is more specific: the first gift of eternal glory is "the vision of God in his essence."[12] Seeing seems to involve a certain distance between creatures who see

---

8. I must put it this way, since it is how I know of Anastasius and his definition.

9. *The Guide*, PG lxxxix.36.

10. The point is established by Douglas Farrow, "St. Irenaeus of Lyons," *Pro Ecclesia* 4 (1995): 333–353.

11. *Loci praecipui theologici* (1559), 927.

12. *De articulis fidei et ecclesiae sacramentis*, 257a–b. The *Summa theologiae* could of course be quoted at length to this point.

and God who is seen, while deification suggests the overcoming of such distance; thus the two interpretations are sometimes thought to be polar.

In fact, however, the two are but different evocations of the same expectation. This can be seen in a theologian whose thought is a chief root of both lines of tradition, Origen of Alexandria: those united to God by union with the Son "will do one thing only, know God. They will be transformed by knowing the Father, to become properly the Son, as now only the Son knows the Father."[13] In this original unified thought, it is union with God that enables knowing him and vice versa knowing God that transforms into identity with the Son. At least one side of the theologoumenon goes back very far, to at least the Elder John: "We will be like him, for we will see him as he is."[14] And it has continued, notably and most powerfully in Gregory Palamas: "The deifying Gift of the Spirit" is precisely that "light of hyper-glory which the saints behold."[15]

Seeing God, what would one see? *If* one abstracts from his Trinity, one must suppose one would not see a visible something but the Illumination by which other things become visible. In the *visio dei* so taken, God is seen as the sun is seen and not seen by those it bathes with its light when they look toward the source of that light and so stare into it. And this outpouring of illumination from God, received by a consciousness that judgment has made able to endure it, must itself be the power of deification. So far, we may perhaps say, so good. But we cannot be content with the abstraction.

There is, moreover, a problem between East and West, which is related to such abstraction on both sides. According to Thomas, the redeemed will see the divine essence. This appears to be emphatically and directly denied by Palamas: even the redeemed cannot see God "according to his—hyperessential—essence [*hyperousian ousian*],[16] but only according to his deifying . . . energy." For being seen is a relation, but "God's *ousia* has no relations" and "transcends everything in God that can be shared."[17]

We have already regretted Palamas's doctrine at this point,[18] which supposes that in order to honor God *himself* we must abstract from the triune life and posit a divine *ousia* devoid of relations and participations, that is to say, of everything that in Scripture constitutes the reality of God. Eastern understanding is in this matter still far too uncritically implicated in Pseudo-Dionysius's barely Christianized Neoplatonism,[19] in which as we stare toward the One we see only light precisely because we do *not* see its source, because the One does not and cannot

13. *Commentary on John*, 1.16.92.
14. I John 3:2.
15. *Triads*, iii.1.6.
16. It must be remembered that Gregory knows no other divine *ousia* that is not hyperessential.
17. *Triads*, iii.1.29.
18. 1:152–153.
19. For a one-sidedly negative presentation of Pseudo-Dionysius's influence, Paul Rorem, *Pseudo-Dionysius: A Commentary on the Texts and an Introduction to Their Influence* (New York: Oxford University Press, 1993).

"stoop to contact with humans"[20]—or indeed anything else, including its own immediate self.

In any case of this judgment about Palamas, Thomas does not suppose the redeemed will know the divine essence that Palamas says is intrinsically unknowable, since Thomas does not suppose there is such an essence. In Thomas's metaphysics, the divine essence is simply "what [God] is," *quid sit*, and he knows no *hyperousia* beyond this. Therefore the divine essence is not immune to the personal relation of being known by another—or indeed of being desired or enjoyed by another. Only so, after all, can God himself be the goal of the Augustinian restlessness.[21]

For Thomas, what is knowable is what actually exists;[22] and God is essentially actual, since his essence is his existence, since what he is determines that he is.[23] Therefore God in his essence is precisely the supremely knowable reality. Thomas notes the Dionysian possibility, that the excess of God's knowability to our power of knowing might make him enduringly inaccessible to creatures, as nocturnal animals cannot see the sun because they cannot bear to look at it, but rejects this as contrary to the faith: "If the created intellect could not at all see the essence of God, either it could not at all attain beatitude or its beatitude would consist in something other than God." For the Augustinian restlessness of our hearts cannot find fulfillment in the mere knowledge that we *have* a first cause and reason; it is the "natural desire"[24] of a mind that knows something has a cause "to know *what* that cause *is*."[25]

Thus in direct contradiction of a cited passage from Dionysius,[26] Thomas says that God is "beyond existence" not because he is "not at all an existent" but on the contrary because he is his own existence.[27] His transcendence of existence does not, therefore, remove him from being known but is the very thing that makes him paradigmatically knowable.

In this life, we indeed cannot know God in his essence.[28] This is because in this life the soul sees only what bodily senses bring to it,[29] that is, "sensible" creatures.[30] And all such creatures are "effects of God that are inadequate to their cause."[31] From the creation, therefore, we can discover only that the creation,

---

20. An Arian maxim cited from its use at 1:100.

21. *Summa theologiae*, i/ii.4.3: "Ad beatitudinem ista tria concurrere: scilicet visionem, quae est cognitio perfecta intelligibilis finis; comprehensionem, quae importat presentiam finis; delectationem vel fruitionem, quae importat quietationem rei amantis in amato."

22. For this paragraph, compendiously, *Summa theologiae*, i.12.1.

23. 1:212–214.

24. Which we must always remember is in Thomas a "nature" established by grace.

25. *Summa theologiae*, i/ii.3.3.

26. Presented of course as Dionysius's real meaning.

27. Inquantum est suum esse.

28. *Summa theologiae*, i.12.11: "ab homine pura Deus videri per essentiam non potest, nisi ab hac vita mortali separatur."

29. Ibid.

30. Ibid., i.12.12.

31. Ibid.

including ourselves, does have a first cause and reason, and discover those things which must pertain to" this cause because it is that[32]—we have returned to the matter of a previous chapter.[33] Such knowledge "is not vision of his essence,"[34] of *quid est*. It is always rather—as we saw in that chapter—knowledge of how he differs from his effects, of "what he is not."[35]

But this limitation is not, according to Thomas, founded in the essential relation between God and created minds and can therefore be transcended in the Kingdom. Indeed, in itself the relation between God and created minds not only satisfies the conditions for vision but does so paradigmatically.

> Two things are required for seeing:[36] . . . the power of sight, and union of the seen reality with sight, for there cannot be the act of sight unless the reality seen is somehow in the one who sees. . . .[37] Now if there were a single reality that was at once the source of the power of seeing and the thing to be seen, one who saw *this* reality would derive simultaneously the power of seeing and the forming of the mind in which sight occurs.[38]

And God, of course, is just this reality.

In the same passage we discover also why knowledge of God from creatures, his "effects," cannot be knowledge of his essence, and why the blessed nevertheless can have such knowledge. A sensible object obviously cannot itself enter the mind, only its sensory image.[39] But there can be no sensory image of God, and therefore sensible creatures, even though they are God's effects and therefore must mediate some knowledge of him, do not mediate vision of what God is. But *God can* enter the mind himself, there to form it to himself,[40] if he lifts its capacities beyond themselves to receive him;[41] and just that is what constitutes beatified saints' vision.

Thus also for Thomas deification and the beatific vision coincide. We will see God precisely because he has "entered" us to become the very form of our persons. We will see God because our justification and sanctification, as we earlier drew their description from Luther, are complete.

And yet there is nevertheless a difference between Palamas and Thomas. With respect to our knowledge of God in this life, their positions are for all religious purposes the same: we know that God is and how he must differ from creatures

32. Ibid., i.12.12.

33. Pp. 36–37.

34. *Summa theologiae*, i.12.11.

35. Robert W. Jenson, *The Knowledge of Things Hoped For* (New York: Oxford Univiversity Press, 1969), 58–79.

36. English providing no verb "to vision," we are compelled to translate *visio* and its cognates with "seeing" and its cognates throughout this passage.

37. See pp. 295–296.

38. *Summa theologiae*, i.12.2.

39. *Phantasm*.

40. *Summa theologiae*, i.12.2.

41. Ibid., i.12.4–5.

in order to be God.[42] With respect to the vision of God by perfected saints, however, the difference between the two points to a real alternative. Life in the Kingdom will according to Palamas much less differ from saints' life in this world than it will according to Thomas, since for Palamas the fundamental restriction of our relation to God is the same in both cases, the intrinsic inaccessibility of God himself. Here we must decide for Thomas.

A further difference between Thomas and Palamas, and perhaps generally between West and East, will emerge in the next chapter; and on that matter we will decide for Palamas. But now it is time to undo abstraction from God's triunity also as it appears in Thomas.

Thomas speaks simply of "God" entering and forming the blessed person, to enable and constitute beatifying vision. This is insufficient. It is specifically the Son who is one with believers and beatified saints and forms their persons. And it is the Spirit who turns them in the Son to the Father, in the Freedom and Love the Spirit is.

Moreover, Thomas with much of the tradition presumes seeing as the paradigm of knowing. The Son, however, is primally God's *uttered* Word; and therefore this work has at every step insisted that *hearing* must be the paradigm of knowing. How does that work out here? Within this system, what are we to make of the indeed biblical and ecumenical promise that while we now know God by faith, and so by hearing, we shall then see him "face to face"?[43]

Surely the solution to the last two questions—and to much next to be discussed—must be that in the Kingdom the difference between hearing and seeing will be transcended, so that while we now live by hearing and *not* by sight, the hearing of the redeemed will be itself a seeing. The redeemed will not cease to be created by the address of God. Yet the Son is "begotten, not made"; he hears the Father's Word only as he *is* that Word, so that his hearing has the immediate presence that in created time we call sight. And insofar as the blessed share his relation to the Father, their hearing too will be an immediate and fulfilled apprehension.

The finitude of created time is constituted in the possibility of its disruption; the burden of created time is constituted in the actuality thereof. Created time differs from God's time in that the extent of the specious present is uncontrollable, in that pieces of temporal reality can get away from us, in that the future can be merely threatening and the past fixed and dead. Created time should have been integrated by congruence with triune time, but the incurvation of fallen humanity on what we possess, that is, on the present, prevents this, by alienating past and future. "Through the self-seeking of the Ego the moment of its presence is estranged from subsequent moments; and then the future comes to us as alien."[44]

42. To their agreement, 1:227–228.
43. I Corinthians 13:12.
44. Wolfhart Pannenberg, *Systematische Theologie* (Göttingen: Vandenhoeck & Ruprecht, 1993), 3:606.

On the other side of Judgment no such incurvature is any longer possible, and blessed creatures' union with the Son will make their time congruent with the Trinity's time. Then the alienation of past and present from the future, which in this life constitutes sight's difference from hearing, will not obtain. Caught up in the infinitely swift triune *perichoresis*, the redeemed will see what they hear. The word will precisely *present* them with their futures.

Finally in this section, we must simply recall a decisive way in which deification and vision come together: both are participation in a *life* with whose activity we cannot keep pace.[45] Also when God is all in all, his ways with us will surprise us. As knowers of God we will eternally discover that each new revelation presents an infinity of unforeseen questions. As sharers in God, each new influx of being will expand us for what we could not before accommodate. We have cited it before: "The good that is in the creatures comes forever nearer . . . to an identity with that which is in God" without ever reaching it.[46]

Thus also in this context we must acknowledge the hiddenness of God, here precisely as an aspect of the saints' blessedness. God, we have said, is unknowable in two senses: first, when we know God, we embark on an act that can never achieve rest, since it is finite knowledge of an infinite object; second, the very completeness of his revelation hides him. When God is all in all, these come together. God will be more more and more unknowable for being so intimately known. In God, we will know that he is infinitely beyond us. And this experience will be precisely the experience of his glory and of our participation in it. Or as Henri de Lubac summed up Eastern patristic teaching: "God . . . would only be found, even in the light of eternal beatitude, by being forever sought"[47]—and at *this* point, the verb "sought" can be right.

IV

If life were simply to continue after death, in whatever fashion, those raised would not be identified by their lives lived toward death and made whole entities by it. And that is to say, their death would not in fact have been their death, and their new life would not be God's victory over death. The creedal "resurrection" of precisely the *dead persons*, as the whole persons they were, is a determining necessity of the gospel's eschatology. The life that will be appropriated into God is the life that ends in death: "For all of us must appear before the judgment seat of Christ, so that each may receive recompense for what has been done in the body."[48]

The New Testament's dominant language for the End is indeed the language of the "Kingdom of God." But death is "the last enemy to be destroyed,"[49] the

45. 1:216–236.
46. Jonathan Edwards, *Miscellanies*, 1099.
47. Henri de Lubac, *The Mystery of the Supernatural*, tr. R. Sheed (New York: Herder & Herder, 1967), 55. Or, indeed, see Thomas Aquinas, *Summa theologiae*, i.12.7.
48. I Corinthians 5:10.
49. I Corinthians 15:26.

last barrier to God's rule, so that death's destruction and the achieving of God's final reign are the same. God is "God not of the dead, but of the living";[50] just so his eschatological rule must encompass only the living.

We have just seen that the human content of the Kingdom, deification and the vision of God, are communal at their enabling center. A conclusion seems to follow and this work will draw it: the first and enabling subject of the resurrection is communal, the *totus Christus*. There is even a sense in which Christ, *insofar* as his body the church is still an association also and not purely a community, possesses his risen body only in anticipation; thus the Lord's own resurrection awaits a future also. Removal of the interim separation between the members of Christ and their Head, which appears in the sacramental character of his presence with them, is the heart of the resurrection.

In beginning our discussion in this way, this work opposes an imbalance of the theological tradition: its tendency to start with and orient its propositions by "individual eschatological hope and . . . the last judgment, toward which each individual moves."[51] Where a misleading tendency is so deeply embedded in piety and homiletics and iconography as this one is, and where the matter anyway constantly threatens to drive language beyond its capabilities, systematic theology— and assuredly a single work of systematic theology—can do no more than propose a few first corrections. But a beginning must be made.

How is the *totus Christus* embodied when the Father is all in all? That is the proper first question about resurrection, rather than questions about the strayed molecules of organic bodies, space for all those people, and the like. For all such questions presuppose that the resurrection will take place within the present structure of reality, which begs the very question at issue.

We must draw on discussions scattered through the whole previous work: the personal body is availability to others and to oneself; the personal body is the reality of the person's history up to any moment; the personal body is what is seen; the personal body is the person as an occupant of space. How are these conditions satisfied for and within the body of Christ, when it is taken wholly into God? The list itself suggests a first insight: it is the coincidence of precisely these characters as determinants of one phenomenon that must guide us.

The Spirit as the divine future is the same God as the Father and the Son. Therefore, we said, in triune time speaking is itself showing, hearing itself seeing; the Son is first the Word of God and just so the Image of God. The same vectored identities must hold for the redeemed, insofar as their time is made congruent with the triune time. Therefore when the redeemed hear the Father, this will itself be their seeing of the Son and so of each other. But what is visible is available. Therefore the *totus Christus* needs nothing more to be embodied than full congruence with the eternal *perichoresis* of the triune life.

Can such propositions as those of the last paragraph mean anything to us? Yes and no. They are in themselves exterior descriptions of a life we still stand

50. Mark 12:27.
51. Pannenberg, *Systematische Theologie*, 3:571.

outside of, much as we can produce true descriptions of the life of animals while not knowing what it is like. Yet that comparison goes too far, for the life of the church anticipates the life of the Kingdom, so that participation in her liturgy, and in her life of witness and charity, does provide intimations of this immortality. What might it be to *see* precisely in that and because we *hear*? The improvisations of a great organ during the offertory, or the blessing of someone helped in Jesus' name, rescue the identification from experiential vacuity. And there is anyway nothing for it but to plunge on.

The body is the availability of the person to date, of his or her history as it any moment presents itself. The redeemed histories are complete in their deaths. And they are brought into the history of God as those for whom the Son died; they appear in God's life because and as Jesus' love infinitely interprets them. They are brought into God as the *interpretandum* of the inner dialogue of the Son's actual triune life. Therefore the reality in God of all the redeemed's past, and its mutual availability between each of them and Christ and so between all of them, again need nothing more then full congruence with the eternal *perichoresis* of the triune life.

Finally, as sight apprehends what is present in space, the identities we have traced mean that also the space of the redeemed's embodiment is established by the congruence of their time with the triune time. The space between the Father and Christ at his right hand accommodates the embodiment of the *totus Christus.*

But are not all these analyses circular? As the "embodiment" of the final community has been described, wherever the Father looks to see the Son or the Son to offer his body to the Father, or the saints to see themselves in the Son, all that is there is some nexus of their mutual communication. Does there not need to be "something" there for a body to be there? Indeed, does there not have to be some *matter* there? We have arrived at the final topic of this chapter.

V

A body in the new creation must indeed be a something, and a material something. But we learned from the Byzantines: to be something is to be posited in a *freedom.*[52] It has been a further key position of this work: to be something is to be *mentioned* by that Freedom.[53] And we learned from Jonathan Edwards: the specific materiality of something is an inertia or solidity intended by God in relation to other such inertias; there is a material world when God in any way he chooses brings creatures to each other as other than one another.[54]

The same triune event that will be the resurrection will be also the creation of a new material world, of a new heaven and a new earth; the achievement of God's reign will be the "end of the world" and the beginning of another. "Because the realism of the biblical tradition tied full realization of the divine will

52. P. 96.
53. 1:210. In this volume, pp. 3–15.
54. Pp. 39–42.

for justice . . . to the overcoming of the power of sin in the behavior of all humans to each other, therefore hope for the Kingdom of God is connected in Jewish expectation with the notion[55] of an overturn of the natural boundaries of human existence: nothing less is required than a new heaven and a new earth."[56] The final topic of this chapter is cosmic transformation.

A first insight must be: the new creation will be an event in that "widest connection" of God's history with his creation, of which the natural history of this aeon, with its continuities and predictabilities, and for all its seemingly so colossal spans of time and space, is but one aspect. The cosmos's final transformation and the laws and boundary conditions of the event are therefore as unpredictable by the laws deriving from the "big bang" as was that singularity itself. Natural laws are in any case the regularities of God's intentions, and so will be those of the new creation, but now they will be the thoughts of that God whose *Logos* is the personally unitary *totus Christus*.

It is that aspect of cosmic transformation in which it is the *end* of cosmic history as we now experience it that recently seems to pose the greatest problems: How can the catastrophe of biblical apocalyptic fit into the future of the universe as now predicted? It is sometimes hoped to alleviate the difficulties by finding analogies between cosmological predictions of the universe's collapse and apocalyptic predictions that "the . . . stars will be falling, . . . and the powers in the heavens will be shaken."[57] But cosmologists go back and forth between predictions of collapse and those of endless cosmic expansion, in a cycle that suggests caution about exploiting their findings. And in either case of these predictions the problem remains the same: an endless or very long *continuation* of cosmic history *after* the end of human history, whether the latter occurs by the collapse of the solar system, other natural catastrophe, or an appearance of God in the style of biblical apocalyptic. The judgment is surely correct: "The Bible's eschatology of the world, which reckons with its imminent end—even if without chronological commitment—is not congruent with scientific extrapolations about the world's possible end."[58]

One can, to be sure, cast a few reconciling scenarios. We might simply assert[59] that the universe must contain enough mass to cause its eventual collapse into final singularity. And we might then point out that the lapse between the death of the last human and this "end of the world"—however unimaginably long the lapse may be—only poses a universalized version of a problem we already have and must anyway deal with: the problem of the so-called intermediate state between believers' death and the End.

55. *Vorstellung.*

56. Pannenberg, *Systematische Theologie*, 3:629.

57. Mark 13:24–25parr.

58. Pannenberg, *Systematische Theologie*, 3:635. There have in fact been few attempts actually to work out alleged congruence. The most notorious recent proposal, by Frank J. Tipler, e.g., "The Omega Point as Eschaton," unmarked paper delivered to the American Academy of Religion, fails quickly, since it depends upon a physicalistic reduction of consciousness.

59. Since this is an assertion that could hardly be permanently disposed of.

Or one might posit an End for humanity while the cosmos simply kept going and argue that such a continued cosmic history would be meaningless and just therefore theologically irrelevant; the universe would have served its purpose. Or one might even say that God will then have his own other purposes with it, that it will be in fact that universe without Christ and without humanity about whose possible meaning for God we earlier speculated.

Perhaps the theologically most plausible of such scenarios is that the universe's predicted future will simply break off when the End comes. We should not, it might be argued, expect that the predicted future of the universe would accommodate the Bible's expected cosmic transformation, since what is to be transformed are the very laws by which the predictions are made. And indeed it must be a chief part of the truth we are seeking: the "revealing of the children of God" *is* the *telos* of creation,[60] so that when this happens all other predictions about creation's future are off, however justified in themselves. We must remember: it is the eschatological plot of universal history, not cosmological or political or other such history, that is the encompassing reality.

Yet all such scenarios share two fatal flaws, for the systematic theology developed in this work. First, they are projected from the viewpoint of an observer not wholly taken into the triune life. What when there are no such observers? What can be the meaning of propositions about a history of the universe after all possible observers are otherwise engaged?[61] Second, they depend on the supposition that created time is a reality independent of triune time, that created history can simply go on its way after God is all in all. By the maxims of this book, the supposition must be false.

A solution possible within the framework of thought this work has developed must be something like the following. When the redeemed are, as we have seen they will be, themselves a communal agent in the triune life, they will themselves think the movements of matter and energy, not as we may now trace a few of God's intentions after him but with God as he thinks and just so determines them. The history of the universe will not proceed externally to the mutual human story; cosmic history after the End will not be abstractable from human history. As the universe is the stage for the story of God with his people, so the universe after the End will be the stage for the fulfillment of that story, for the eternal event of the interpretation of all lives by the life of Jesus.

We may thus even allow that predictions of what the universe will be doing after all humans have died may not be simply inaccurate or meaningless. But just as modern science's general account of the universe, which brackets out teleology and freedom, must be an abstraction from what is actually going on, so eschatological predictions made with the same exclusions cannot display the reality of the events they predict. Indeed the gap between ateleological explanation

---

60. Romans 8:20.
61. Note that modern cosmology itself poses this problem, in that it predicts the vanishing of cosmologists before the vanishing of the cosmos.

and the truth must be even greater than it is for the present age, for the devil and his angels will have been finally expelled from the world to be described, which is to say there will be no teleological gaps or disruptions to give purchase to ateleological explanation.

We can enter only a little way into the situation just described, into the saints' experience of their universe. Perhaps we can best do this by adapting a passage from this work's doctrine of creation,[62] as follows.

The universe precisely in its immensity and complexity is counterpart to the *perichoresis* that is the infinite God and merely in itself is there for his sheer enjoyment. When our time is fully congruent with his, we may enjoy the material universe as he does, because we will not merely follow along in the triune music and delight but be improvisers and instigators within it. What the saints will do with continuously generating star clusters and black holes, *or* with a final rush back into singularity if such a thing occurs, will—at least—be to play with them close at hand.

The chief thing remains to be said, or anyway drawn out. The End, human *and* cosmic, will be the great triumph of the Spirit, that is, of freedom and love. If the more immediately foregoing paragraphs are false and this sentence true, little is lost.

VI

We conclude by returning to the question of *material* embodiment, which provoked the previous section. Will the new heaven and earth be matter? Will the *totus Christus* be a material body? And will the plural bodies of the redeemed be material bodies? And what can we mean by "body" in such questions? What can be said conceptually is quickly said.

The material world is what God intends in order to intend a community of persons who can intend others as distinct from themselves and so be enabled for community with one another. Therefore the embodiment of resurrection must be material. But therefore also what is denoted by "matter," the means and constraints of separation and relation, must be malleable to any fundamental changes in God's intention of community. Jonathan Edwards supposed the saints "will be able to see from one side of the universe to the other," since they will not see "by such slow rays of light that are several years travelling."[63] And Isaac A. Dorner wrote, "Matter will have exchanged its darkness, hardness, heaviness, immobility and impenetrableness for clearness, radiance, elasticity and transparency."[64] Such things having been said, the rest must be poetry.

The material of New Jerusalem's walls and streets, of the divine-human community's *place*, will be jasper, sapphire, agate, emerald, onyx, carnelian,

---

62. P. 129.

63. *Miscellanies*, 926.

64. Isaac A. Dorner, *A System of Christian Doctrine*, vol. IV, tr. Alfred Cave, J. S. Banks (Edinburgh: T. & T. Clark, 1890), 429.

chrysolite, beryl, topaz, chrysoprase, jacinth, amethyst, pearls, and "gold, transparent as glass."[65] We are to take this information with the desperate seriousness that transcends the registering of prose. After all, will there be no jewelers or goldsmiths in the Kingdom? And will the achievement of their lives provide no matter for eternal interpretation by Jesus' love? That feast of "rich food . . . of well-aged wines strained clear,"[66] will it have no taste? Will there be no cooks or vintners in the Kingdom? Or even connoisseurs?

We can conclude this section and chapter in no better way than by another and longer citation from Edwards, the first master of "second naiveté":

> How ravishing are the proportions of the reflections of rays of light, and the proportions of the vibrations of the air! And without doubt, God can contrive matters so that there shall be other sort of proportions, that may be quite of a different kind . . . that shall be vastly more ravishing and exquisite. And to all probability, the abode of the saints after the resurrection will be so contrived by God, that there shall be external beauties and harmonies altogether of another kind from what we perceive here, and probably those beauties will appear chiefly on the bodies of the man Christ Jesus and of the saints.[67]

---

65. Revelation 21:18–21.
66. Isaiah 25:6.
67. *Miscellanies*, 182.

THIRTY-FOUR

The Saints

I

There are several remaining matters that can be grouped under this title, each an aspect of the eschatology of individuals. The first is the resurrection of individuals within the *totus Christus*. Why must dead individuals be raised and not just the community? That is, why is it not enough that those of God's people present at Messiah's final coming be transformed into an eternal polity? It is vital to understand that the question is genuine: Israel's hope for rescue from death is first and fundamentally hope for the *community*'s resurrection, and initially this simply meant eternal reconstitution of the people, enabled by a general transformation of reality. It would even be possible to regard Christ's Resurrection and the formation of the church as already the needed reconstitution.

The promise of death's overcoming emerged in Israel as a condition of the fulfillment of the promise to Abraham. So long as the nation is replenished generation by generation, its mere continuance can seem enough to make the promises' fulfillment possible. But when the same end has come upon Israel as upon other nations relegated to the past by history, when "the whole house of Israel" lies picked clean and dried in the valley,[1] Israel's hope must be dead too, if death is the last word. The exilic prophets see that the Lord's promise must fail under the conditions of this age and that a key among impeding conditions is the universality of death.[2]

In similar fashion, the promise of individuals' resurrection appears as in turn it is seen that a promise of Israel's restoration from death cannot be fulfilled if the great dead who define Israel are left in the grave. So long as the diachronic

---

1. Ezekiel 37:11.
2. 1:63–74.

self-identity of Israel is constituted simply in historical continuity itself, Abraham, Moses, Miriam, Ruth, David, and the rest continue to belong to Israel. But if that continuity is cut off, and Israel is then brought to new life while these remain in the grave, they are excluded. What, however, would a living Israel be, to which the great carriers of the promise did not belong?

And what, moreover, would the righteousness of a renewed Israel be, in which judgment had not rectified the injustice suffered by the not so great, because they were not there for judgment to be rendered? It is at least arguable that the "hope for resurrection appears in Israel first in connection with those for whom the balance . . . has not worked out in this life."[3] The Enlightenment's insistence on "immortality" because only in "a future life" could God's moral governance be fulfilled[4] in fact captured an essential logic of this last step in Israel's hope, however inappropriate the Enlightenment's conceptual repertoire.

Thus biblical hope for resurrection is not what too much piety and teaching have made of it, individuals' hope to "be saved," "to get into heaven." The resurrection of individuals is needed for the sake of the restored life of the community. Insofar as I hope for myself, faith's hope is to join and contribute to the *totus Christus* that will live God's life and to see the injustice in which I am involved rectified. But once this character of individual believing hope is secured, we must indeed proceed to consider its fulfillment, that is, the resurrection of individuals.

The diachronically constituted community cannot be raised without its past members. Nor are we to become identical with one another, or melt into one monadic superperson, even one named *totus Christus*. The redeemed life will be congruent with and moved by the divine life, and this is the mutual life of irreducible personal identities. Because the church finds its ground and pattern in the life of the Trinity, it is a *communion* of persons and a communion of communions; and the Kingdom is what the church anticipates. The hope of Israel and the church is thus irremediably antithetical to hope for dissolution into abstract divinity or for rescue from the wheel of karma or for reincarnation or soul transmigration, or any other state that represses personhood; the gospel can be true or the promises of such fulfillments can be true but not both.

II

The life of the Kingdom, we have said, is an infinite act of interpretation, of all history by the love enacted as the life and death of Jesus. The Lord knows himself as the one who lived for his sisters and brothers and whose life has this definiteness in that it was closed by a specific appropriate death; it is by this completed story that he interprets the life of other humans and it is in this interpretation that he possesses his own life. Clearly, only someone who has died can do this

---

3. Wolfhart Pannenberg, *Systematische Theologie* (Göttingen: Vandenhoeck & Ruprecth, 1993), 3:591.
4. The archetype of such argument is of course Immanuel Kant's *Religion innerhalb der Grenzen der blossen Vernunft*.

and so only someone who is risen. But the event requires both sides: if the redeemed are to bring each his or her unique past to the eternal act of this mutual interpreting, reading the Crucified's love by that past and offering it to him to read by his love, they too must individually rise.

We have made one small step toward understanding "the resurrection of the body" as the creeds confess it and as it applies to the redeemed individually. The personal body, we have seen, is the presence of the past. In the *perichoresis* of triune time the saints' pasts will be there for them, to interpret with Christ and together as that for which Christ died. Just so the redeemed will live with and in Christ.

And we can make a second step: the redeemed will therefore be available to one another; they will be able to intend one another in love. The personal body is, we have said throughout this work, personal availability. And then a third step: to intend one another they must be able to locate one another. The personal body is personal location. Somehow the redeemed will have their space.

But how are we to understand the space of the redeemed community and the saints' mutual availability in it? The needed insight is that the community in which the redeemed will locate Christ and one another is the community anticipated by the church. We therefore may say: the redeemed will locate one another in a spatiality that is anticipated by the spatiality of the Eucharist. The redeemed will each be mutually located for each in the way in which the Lord is now eucharistically located for all.

Here we may a last time call on Johannes Brenz and his colleagues.[5] According to their interpretation of eucharistic presence, and that of this work, all the universe is one place for the Father and for the incarnate Son at his right hand, so that where we within that place are to find the incarnate Son depends only on his intention to be found. When the created time of the redeemed is made fully congruent with Christ's inner-triune time, so is their present tense made coherent with his; and so then is their space made coherent with his space. When their future is no longer alienated from their present, even while remaining the "whither" of that present, then their mutual spatial otherness will not impose travel as a condition of mutual presence any more than it now does for the risen Christ. Also for the saints, mutual location will be determined solely by mutual determination to find one another in one configuration of personal loves rather than another.

We again encounter the threat of circularity, as in the previous chapter.[6] There must surely be *something* to do what the loaf and cup do in Eucharist: be *there* and so direct the redeemed to their Head and to each other. We encounter again the question of the saints' *material* embodiment, now in respect of their and their Lord's mutual individual availability.

There is, moreover, a closely related aspect of personal embodiment, to which we have before paid little explicit attention but which is implicit in all the aspects we have noted: both others and myself *recognize* me by recognizing my body. There is a material object by which the diachronic identity of the person con-

---

5. First invoked 1:204–206.
6. P. 348.

fronted with one previously encountered is itself known. And here is a mystery, for the diachronic self-identity of a *person* is of course very much a matter of virtues and other habits, of what we call character. It must indeed be, as Gottfried Thomasius said, much in the style of late romanticism, that "in the earthly body the spiritual special character of the person to some extent expresses itself."[7]

But then must it not be so also in the Kingdom? Or rather, must it not be more so? Thomasius continues, "so the new spiritual body will be much more the transparent expression of the sanctified person, the bright mirror of his inner purity and moral beauty."[8] Somehow, the redeemed will be morally and historically recognizable by one another, from their *appearance* to one another.

The *matter* of personal bodies is of course no other than the matter of the universe, and whatever happens with the materiality of heaven and earth must happen also with the materiality of the redeemed. So Augustine: "By the great . . . cosmic conflagration of corruptible elements, the attributes which congregate in our corruptible bodies will be burned away; and the substantial bodies will have attributes appropriate to bodies which by a miraculous change are immortal."[9]

But here there is a reversal, and observing it provides as much further understanding as this effort will achieve. We have claimed that the material entities of the universe are, in that "substance" just instanced by Augustine,[10] inertial vectors thought by God.[11] And we argued in the previous chapter that when God is all in all, the redeemed will themselves think the movements of matter and energy;[12] the process of the new heaven and the new earth will not be other than the process of their discourse together.[13] But that means that for the materiality of the saints' bodies nothing more will be necessary and constitutive than their own loving intentions to be available to one another. We may paraphrase another passage of the previous chapter, its concluding citation: God can indeed "contrive matters" so that the bodies of "the saints after the resurrection" will be material by "harmonies altogether of another kind."[14] Thomas Aquinas lists four such: "impassibility, . . . clarity, . . . agility, . . . and subtlety."[15]

III

Where in the foregoing paragraphs prose became poetry is hard to say; perhaps the problematic conceptual coherence of Thomas's "impassibility" and "agility"

---

7. *Christi Person und Werk: Darstellung der evangelisch-lutherischen Dogmatik vom Mittelpunkt der Christologie aus*, 3rd Aufl., ed. F. J. Winter (Erlangen: Andreas Deichert, 1888), 588.

8. Ibid.

9. *De civitate Dei*, xx.16.

10. And in the temporary sense allowed by Jonathan Edwards.

11. Pp. 39–41.

12. Pp. 350–351.

13. Augustine, *De civitate Dei*, xix.4: "Quid autem facere volumus, cum perfici volumus finem summi boni, nisi ut caro adversus spritum non concupiscat, nec sit in nobis hoc vitium, contra quod spiritus concupiscat?"

14. P. 352.

15. *De articulis fidei et ecclesiae sacramentis*, 257B.

marks the spot. It can only be hoped that wherever the two meet, some under-standing of "the resurrection of the body" does emerge. Two specific questions must still be considered, and they provide tests of the direction that understand-ing will go.

The first is sexual differentiation. That we are humans only in that we are male or female humans is a decisive fact of our created embodiment;[16] as Jesus interprets Scripture in Matthew, God "made them at the beginning . . . male and female."[17] Will we be thus differentiated in the Kingdom? And if so, will that make any difference there? The answer will go far to determine our sense of what resur-rected embodiment is.

A saying of Jesus recorded in the synoptic Gospels may seem to require nega-tive answers to these questions: "For when they rise from the dead, they neither marry nor are given in marriage, but are like angels in heaven."[18] Presumably angels are not sexually differentiated and so do not marry. But theology's per-haps most vigorous defender of sexuality's created good, Karl Barth,[19] points out that the passage says not that the redeemed *are* angels but that they are *like* them.[20] What then is the point of comparison?

The Pharisees had asked Jesus how levirate marriages would be sorted out in the resurrection, supposing of course that they could not be. Levirate marriage was ordained to assure that one chief purpose of marriage, the bearing and nur-ture of children within diachronically identifiable families, was maintained even in the frequent circumstance of early male death.[21] And it is indeed obvious: "To the . . . church's consummation belongs . . . a cessation of reproduction, which continually gives the church a new world to subdue."[22] However the woman of the Pharisees' question will in the resurrection be related to her seven husbands, she will have no levirate obligation to them.

From which it does not follow that the fact that she as a woman was united to them as men will be missing from the story she gives to Christ's eternal interpretation: its delights to be examined in ever new ways and its miseries and problematics transformed into ever new instances of mercy. And since this eter-nal event of interpretation is the substance of created life as it is caught up in the triune life, the fact that she is a woman and not a man, and that there are men, will somehow belong to the dance of that life. Humanity's sexuality turns us to each other in *two* ways, of which only the turning to unborn generations must end with this age.

Therefore—though sometimes with a bit of reluctance, stemming from the inheritance of pagan antiquity's misogyny—the Western theological tradition has

16. P. 89.

17. Matthew 19:4.

18. Mark 12:25parr.

19. To the following, *Kirchliche Dogmatik* (Zürich: Evangelischer Verlag, 1948), III/2:355–358.

20. Ibid., 356.

21. Deuteronomy 25:5–6.

22. Isaac A. Dorner, *A System of Christian Doctrine*, vol. IV, tr. Alfred Cave, J. S. Banks (Edinburgh: T. & T. Clark, 1890), 381.

held with Augustine that "The one who created both sexes will restore both."[23] And Barth, once he has banished the possibility of eschatological sexlessness, evokes the sexuality of risen humanity with nothing less than the Song of Solomon, which he interprets as an "eschatological" song of eroticism freed from burdens and sin.[24] Perhaps there is another reason why the saints do not marry: the root identity of personal and communal being, a hint of which we in this age experience only in married sexuality, will in the Kingdom be an encompassing bond.

The second is the embodiment of the *visio dei*. Is the resurrection of the body relevant to the saints' capacity to behold God? Will the redeemed see God with the eyes of the new body? What we mean by "body" in "resurrection of the body" must again depend in considerable part on the answer.

Gregory Palamas is drastic in the affirmative: "God . . . is invisible to creatures but is not invisible to himself. He will then be the one who sees himself through us, through our souls but also through our bodies. . . . Therefore we will then see the divine and inaccessible light through bodily organs."[25] And in this matter, Augustine agrees, though with less theological gusto: "The spirit will use . . . those bodily eyes. . . . [Their] power will be more excellent not merely for them to see more sharply . . . but for them to see spiritual realities."[26]

In this eschatology, union with God will be an embodied union; only within this union will we see God, with God who sees himself; and therefore we will see God with the eyes of the risen body. The vision of God will not be a vision from no perspective, or unaffected by the particular history I am, or by my location in the network of the saints' mutual availability.

Thomas Aquinas votes in the negative. He poses a *quaestio*, "Can the essence of God be seen by bodily eyes?" And answers: God "can be seen neither with the senses nor with the imagination, but only with the intellect." Then he continues, with the most interesting part of the article: "Therefore . . . when it is written 'In my flesh I will see God my Savior,'[27] this is not to be interpreted that [Job] will see God with the eye of the flesh, but that he, who indeed will exist in flesh after the resurrection, will see God."[28] The saints' vision of God will be, in this eschatology, a purely intellectual apprehension, independent of the fact that after the resurrection these souls are also embodied.

One is in fact tempted to interpret Thomas: the saints will after the resurrection see God in *spite of* their embodied state. Whatever may be the legitimacy of such an interpretation of Thomas, his and other Western understanding of the body's eschatological place does pose the question, Why would pure souls, absorbed in their sheerly intellectual vision of God, want bodies anyway? At this point the question is diagnostic: if Thomas's distinction seems right, we have one

---

23. *De civitate Dei*, xxii.17.
24. *Kirchliche Dogmatik*, III/2:355.
25. *Triads*, i.3.37.
26. *De civitate Dei*, xxii.29.
27. Job 19:26.
28. *Summa theologiae*, i.12.3.

understanding of "the resurrection of the body," which this system of theology deprecates; if it seems wrong, we have another understanding, which this system promotes.

IV

The second matter of this chapter is the destiny of individuals. When Christ sets right the injustices of history, what will that mean for particular believers? For particular unbelievers? For the good and evil persons of general human history? May some human creatures not enter the Kingdom at all? That is, fail utterly of humanity's only purpose? If so, what then of them?

Some matters within this general area can be rather quickly handled because the decisions to be made are quite clear, though they may be in fact the theologically more important. Because judgment means putting history right, also those must face it who in baptismal union with Christ will surely enter the Kingdom. We should remember, for example, that Paul's vehement exposition of judgment according to each one's works in the second chapter of his letter to Rome was addressed to the *congregation* there.[29] Quite apart from any question of final exclusion, believers's hope for Christ's final advent must include a certain trembling; as the writer of Hebrews concludes a fulmination on the matter, "It is a fearful thing to fall into the hands of the living God."[30]

Moreover, since it is precisely the life that has passed through such judgment the interpretation of which will make each one's life in the Kingdom, the saints' blessedness will not be identical bliss. According to Paul the Judgment will test each one's works "with fire" to see what they are. If I have built with precious materials, so that my work "survives," I will "receive a reward"—and it appears that my works' survival will itself be the reward. But if "the work is burned up, the builder will suffer loss; the builder will be saved, but only as through fire."[31] "The . . . person is saved indeed, but empty-handed of the mementos . . . of past times,"[32] like someone saved from a burning home. Even a tale of shoddy works will be turned to joy in the Kingdom, interpreted as it will be by Christ's death just on account of them, but someone with many or only such works will nevertheless be differently placed within the community of *totus Christus* than will be, for example, the martyrs.

Another perspective on this matter is proposed by Jonathan Edwards. Because "the saints will be progressive in knowledge and happiness to all eternity,"[33] they will at no one moment of eternity be simply equivalent in knowledge and happiness.[34] The redeemed will "press on," in Paul's favorite racing metaphor,

29. James D. G. Dunn, *The Theology of Paul the Apostle* (Grand Rapids: Eerdmans, 1998), 490–491.

30. Hebrews 10:31.

31. Corinthians 3:10–15.

32. Dunn, *Theology*, 491.

33. *Miscellanies*, 435.

34. Ibid., 430.

from different starting places and with different abilities; there will be gradations of achievement and authority also in the Kingdom. But since this race also is an aspect of the eternal exercise of mutual love, "the exaltation of some in glory above others will be so far from diminishing . . . the perfect . . . joy of the rest . . . that they will be the happier for it."[35]

The life of the Kingdom will thus little resemble the "heaven" of popular imagination. Cartoons of identically clad and identically harp-equipped saints are of course intended mockingly, but in fact they betray a sense deeply ensconced in piety, of "heaven" as the place where nothing happens anymore, because there are no mutual differences and so no mutual challenges. On the contrary, the Kingdom will be a life of mutual and so differentiated challenge and of triumphantly differing achievement, in a way of which all the frenzies of this world can provide at most a pale negative image.

V

A set of in fact spiritually less weighty questions is both more usually agitated and much harder to decide. The resurrection confessed in the creed is the resurrection of believers, as ingredient to translation of God's people into the Kingdom, to the removal of the last separation between Christ and his body. Does that mean that unbelievers are excluded from the Kingdom, from humanity's only true goal? Or baptized persons who do not live by their baptism? If some are excluded, what will become of them?

There would seem to be overwhelming biblical opinion on one side of these questions. The most straightforward theologoumenon is in Paul's second letter to Thessalonica: "Those who do not obey the gospel of our Lord Jesus . . . will suffer the punishment of eternal destruction, separated from the presence of the Lord."[36] In this Paul continues a tradition of Old Testament apocalyptic: "Many of those who sleep in the dust of the earth shall awake, some to everlasting life, and some to shame and everlasting contempt."[37] But then we may remember that according to this same Paul in Romans, precisely the Israel that does *not* "obey the gospel" nevertheless must eventually be saved.[38] We may also note, for later reference, that Paul says this as *comfort* to the Thessalonican congregation—that his judgment is pronounced on third parties who when the letter is read will not be there to hear.

Thus also the view customarily labeled "universalism" can appeal to New Testament theologoumena. The logic especially of Paul's own soteriology can never stop short of universal affirmations: "Therefore just as one man's trespass led to condemnation for all, so one man's act of righteousness leads to justifica-

---

35. Ibid., 431.
36. II Thessalonians 1:6–8.
37. Daniel 12:2.
38. Romans 11:26.

tion and life for all."[39] Nor can Paul's hope for Israel be supported otherwise than with the same universals: "And so all Israel will be saved. . . . For God has imprisoned all in disobedience so that he may be merciful to all."[40] There is therefore an intellectually and spiritually impressive minority tradition of those prepared to agree with Origen, the first great universalist, that "God's goodness through Christ may recall all his creatures to their one end."[41] Even the Origenistic vision of a *cosmic* christological *apokatastasis panton*, "restoration of all things," finds its beginning in the New Testament: "God was pleased to reconcile to himself all things, whether on earth or in heaven";[42] God's plan "for the fullness of time" is "to gather up all things in him, things in heaven and things on earth."[43]

Indeed, two chief interlocutors of this work belong to the tradition that expects a universal restoration, though one of them is reluctant to affirm it directly. Gregory of Nyssa grounds his affirmation of "the restoration of all" on the unquenchable longing for God which God has implanted in each human creature as its very nature, and in the infinity of the future in which this longing can be realized.[44] Karl Barth, in a famous passage,[45] rejects Gregory's doctrine but in a very strange way.

The tendency of Barth's thinking, centered in his doctrine of predestination, is apparent. He sums up hundreds of pages on the doctrine of individual election:[46] "We know God's graceful election, whether as the election of Jesus Christ or as the election of his congregation or of individuals, in no other way than as a choice made by his *mercy*." He sees where this must lead but protests that a doctrine of universal salvation is "a proposition, which out of respect for the freedom of God's grace one may not venture." Barth is undoubtedly right to say, "One . . . may not derive a right or obligation from grace." But one may nevertheless affirm universal salvation simply as a fact; and his grounds for not doing so betray that his teaching leads to it: "As the merciful God need not choose or call a single human person, so also not the whole of humanity."[47] Just so; and since God has certainly chosen and called at least that one single person, what does this equivalence suggest? If God is free to take all in, what must it mean that his decision is always merciful?

All humans are of course not in the same position before the entrance of the Kingdom, and we must reckon with that. We begin with the baptized.

---

39. Romans 5:18.

40. Romans 11:26–32.

41. *First Principles*, i.6.1. The bases for Origen's universalism were complex. Primary was surely his trust in "God's goodness," here cited. His more speculative basis, in a posited original bliss for all souls, which must be restored on the principle that the end must recapitulate the beginning, we need not share—which is good, since he is condemned a heretic for it.

42. Colossians 1:20.

43. Ephesians 1:10.

44. *The Life of Moses*, 2. Gregory's position thus differs from Origen's, though it may well have been the influence of Origen that led him to take it.

45. *Kirchliche Dogmatik*, II/2:462.

46. *Kirchliche Dogmatik*, II/2:336–563.

47. Ibid.

A believer's baptism is God's own promise of the Kingdom, sealed personally. Paul nevertheless warns the Corinthian baptized to take heed lest they "fall";[48] exclusion is evidently a possibility. Yet if the promise of God cannot fail for the Israel that does not obey the gospel, as Paul also insists, how can it fail for those to whom God has addressed his baptismal promise and who in baptism have in fact obeyed the gospel?

If I am baptized, should I fear exclusion? Paul apparently thinks I should, and in the referenced passage puts this fear into me. And yet were this fear to determine any part of my believing life, all would be undone. For to hear and believe the gospel and simultaneously to fear exclusion from the Kingdom is impossible. So Catholic-Reformation dialogue: having defined faith as "the giving over of oneself to God and God's word of promise," the parties agreed, "No one can in this . . . sense believe, and simultaneously suppose that God in his word of promise is unreliable. In this sense, Luther's dictum holds: . . . faith is certainty of salvation."[49]

Such second-person threatening as Paul's to the Corinthians can therefore only be understood as addressed to believers insofar as they do not believe, that is, insofar as they are still involved in communities of the *libido dominandi*, insofar as "the old man" still lives. But it is addressed to them precisely to remind them that they no longer *are* this old man, that they are dead to the allurements that attract him.[50] That is, the threat of exclusion is made precisely to turn us away from entertaining it. So again, if I am baptized, should I fear exclusion? Perhaps the confessor's proper answer is "Since you ask, No."

The third-person proposition, "It is possible for the baptized to be lost," can, it seems, only function as just that, a proposition about a third person not there to be addressed. It has no context in which to be actual.

The children of Israel have the promise even more surely then the baptized; it is, after all, their Kingdom that is promised. Yet often in the Old Testament it is only a "remnant" for whom the promise continues to hold. So Isaiah can be explicit that on "that day" of the great restoration, "only a remnant . . . will return."[51] Whom then, on that day, when Messiah comes finally, will he leave in then irreversible exile? Modern secular Jews? All those idolatrous Judean kings? Caiaphas? The question is not a particularly Jewish question; but within the Christian question about the universality or particularity of salvation it is a key question.

Perhaps for Christian theology's own purposes we can only suppose that the dialectic traced for the baptized applies first for the children of Abraham. Scripture certainly supposes that it is possible for descendants of Abraham to be unfaithful to the covenant in such fashion as to be outside the remnant, and so does

---

48. I Corinthians 10:1–13.
49. Ökumenischer Arbeitskreis evangelischer und katholischer Theologen, *Lehrverurteilungen— kirchentrennend?* ed. Karl Lehmann, Wolfhart Pannenberg (Freiburg: Herder, 1986), 62.
50. Romans 6, of course.
51. Isaiah 10:20–22.

Paul;[52] moreover, for Paul and the rest of the New Testament the rejection of Jesus was an eschatological unfaithfulness. Yet the one thing obvious to Paul is that the members of Israel according to the flesh, whatever else must be said about them, do not need to be grafted into God's olive tree.[53]

Also in the case of Israel, as it seems, the dialectics cannot be brought to rest in any simple proposition. It is anyway certain that no child of Abraham will be excluded because she or he is not baptized—having said that, it must also quickly be said that the church must regard the baptism of those Jews whom the Father grants her as a vital element of her own life.[54] Which is to say: the church has no message to Jews about exclusion.

There remain all those who do not worship the God of the gospel at all, who are neither of Abraham's many seeds nor of his one seed.[55] If we cannot quite teach categorically that all the baptized or all Jews will enter the Kingdom, we must also refrain from asserting that all others will be excluded. The second Vatican Council had much tradition on its side when among those who "can attain eternal salvation" it listed "Mohammedans . . . who with us adore one God, the merciful, the judge of all men on the last day," those who "in shadows and images seek the unknown God," and morally striving pagans "who by no fault of their own do not know Christ and his church."[56]

The council's doctrine is to be sure indefinite enough; "can" is not "will" or any other very helpful auxiliary verb. And there is at least one very necessary restriction on conclusions that might be drawn from the council's teaching.

As we have seen, attaining the salvations offered by the religions would be in some instances incompatible with entry into the Kingdom and in others irrelevant to it.[57] For example, insofar as the "illumination" cultivated by many Asian religions is a possible experience in this life, it is surely compatible with entry into the Kingdom but is also only contingently relevant thereto. But insofar as "illumination" denotes final arrival at personal nothingness, one could not attain both it and the Kingdom.

The point in this context: if followers of other religions enter the Kingdom proposed by the gospel, this is not because they have arrived at the salvations proposed by their religions. Quite apparently, all religions are not "different ways to the same place." On the contrary, if there is a commonality between religions, and particularly between other religions and biblical religion, it is not because they converge at the goal but because they coincide along the way.[58]

52. Romans 9.

53. Romans 11.

54. E.g., p. 71.

55. Galatians 3:16.

56. *Lumen gentium*, 16.

57. To this, Joseph-Augustine DiNoia, *The Diversity of Religions* (Washington, D.C.: Catholic Univesity Press, 1992).

58. DiNoia, *Diversity of Religions*, 61. "A theology of religions that assumes the religious unity of humankind by dissolving rather than resolving . . . differences seeks prematurely to enjoy an eschatological promise whose fulfillment will come only as a stunning and marvelous gift."

How then would, for example, a shamanist enter the Kingdom? Here an affirmative rule must be observed with equal strictness: the same way as anyone else, by incorporation in Christ. We can speculate a bit into how that might happen, though our speculations cannot take us far.

All humans are addressed by God, and all prayer, audible or visible, is response to the address of God, however misaddressed the response. No human creature, therefore, lives otherwise than as participant in a dramatic dialogue the outcome of which is "Enter into the joy of your Lord"; all are in fact on the way into Christ. In the somewhat slippery formulation of the second Vatican Council, there are "those who without the gospel seek a righteous life" and "whatever of goodness or of the truth is found among them, is considered by the church as a preparation for the gospel and as given by him who enlightens all that they may have life."[59]

God creates all humans, as humans, by his continual moral address; and we will take this to be the council's "preparation for the gospel." The problem is, of course, that preparation for the gospel is not itself the gospel. It does not make descendants of Abraham on any principle or believers in Christ however "anonymous." Nor can striving for goodness and truth—that is, good works—justify unbelievers anymore than it does believers. Also of the council's good and striving unbelievers we must therefore say that they "have not completed the history from reprobation to election."[60] Will some of them? Or all of them? And what of unbelievers who do not notably strive?

If a partial or complete *apokatastasis* of those outside the people of God is to take place, it can only be by an eschatological address of the gospel, about the circumstances of which it would be entirely useless to make guesses. Will God give those who have not at their death been converted all eternity for this to happen? Or in some eschatological dialogue, will he give them so to hear the gospel that none can say No? Which, as we have seen, he can do in such fashion as precisely to enable the freedom of their response?

We can therefore say no more than that, without violence to the plot of his saving history, God can bring all to the Kingdom, but that he may not. "All or some heathen may be excluded" must be accepted as a true proposition. But then we must also note that here is again a third-person proposition, and that actual second-person threats of exclusion do not seem to have played a role in the apostolic kerygma to gentiles. So Paul summarized the message with which he come to Thessalonica: he had called the gentiles to turn "to God from idols, to serve a living and true God, and to wait for his Son from heaven, whom he raised from the dead—Jesus, who rescues us from the wrath that is coming."[61] Wrath appears, but again only for someone else. "You individually are headed for eternal torment, believe lest you enter it" does not seem to have belonged to the apostolic missionary repertoire.

59. *Lumen gentium*, 16.
60. P. 178.
61. I Thessalonians 1:9–10.

As this work's possible contribution to understanding, it offers the following observation: with respect to the baptized, the children of Israel, and those simply outside the covenant, in each case differently, "Exclusion is possible" is a true theological, that is, second-level, proposition, to which, however, no first-level believing discourse corresponds. So far as the present work sees, this is a unique situation. The church must think that damnation is possible but is not to make it an article of faith, proclaim it, or threaten it except in such fashion as to obviate the threat. What sort of truth does "Damnation is possible" then have? Perhaps God does not wish us to know.

As to the nature of damnation, should any incur it, we can proceed as briskly as we did with the devil. If there are to be the damned, they will be teleological entities with no *telos*. Augustine's definition captures the contradiction: damnation "will be a permanent dying, when the soul can neither live, since it does not have God, nor escape, . . . by dying."[62] What would it be, to exist by virtue of a purpose with which there was no more connection?

Isaac Dorner summarizes the two interpretations of this situation that have competed in the tradition: there are the "church teachers who make freedom and reason, and especially consciousness of God, to be extinguished forever in the damned," as in Augustine's teaching just cited; and there are the more speculative "advocates of the [sheer] annihilation of the ungodly." And then he makes the judgment that this work will share and with which we will close the subject: "Both views . . . approach very near to each other."[63] What difference indeed would there be between a terminated consciousness—remembering the problems of that notion—and the extinguishing of freedom, reason, and the consciousness of God?

VI

Between the death of the redeemed and their resurrection, there is an interim. This would be the case also apart from the stay of Christ's final advent; Abraham and Moses have been long in the grave. The expectation of the Lord's chronologically immediate return at first hid the problem for the primal church, but as deaths of the baptized became a regular phenomenon the question had to arise: What of our sisters and brothers who are no longer here to greet the Lord? In what situation are they? Have they permanently joined the dead in Sheol?[64]

When Paul encounters the problem, his response is for the most part a simple reiteration of the message of resurrection, with application to the dead sisters and brothers: "We do not want you to be uninformed . . . about those who have died. . . . For since we believe that Jesus died and rose again, even so, through Jesus, God will bring with him those who have died. . . . [W]e who are alive, who

---

62. *De civitate Dei*, xxi.3: "Sempiterna mors erit, quando nec vivere animus poterit Deum non habendo, nec doloribus corporis carere muriendo."

63. *System of Christian Doctrine*, 426.

64. For a general survey of solutions, Pannenberg, *Systematische Theologie*, 3:618–621.

are left until the coming of the Lord, will by no means precede those who have died."[65]

One clause of this passage, however, strikes a different note: if God is to "bring with him" those who have died, they must somehow be with him now. Thus when Paul confronts the possibility that he may himself become one of "those who have died," he can think of prospective death as departing "to be with Christ" and even as from a selfish point of view desirable.[66]

But what is the nature of this interim being with Christ? Here Paul is at a loss, displayed by a remarkable passage in II Corinthians.[67] Paul uses a rather Socratic or even gnostic image: of the body as a "tent" or "dwelling." In the present "tent . . . we groan, longing to be clothed with our heavenly dwelling." So far, we have simply a drastic version of hope for the resurrection. But then Paul notices the time between "taking off" this body and being "clothed" with a spritual body at the resurrection, and we see that he does not in fact think like Socrates: "if indeed, when we have taken it off we will not be found naked." He does not seem to know how to feel about the prospect; nakedness is not a comforting image, and he may even be thinking of the third chapter of Genesis. What indeed, by biblical lights, could a person with no body be? If Israel's old conception of shadows lost even to the Lord can no longer obtain? Paul's desperate image of a naked personhood is in a way precise, but its precision only points the problem.

One rather obvious solution appears early and continues in the tradition: "The death of saints is rather sleep than death."[68] Sleep is at once unconsciousness and bliss, and maintains the continuity of the person. And indeed we cannot dispense with the requiem prayers: *Dona eis requiem*, "Give them rest." Yet neither can the picture of saints "with" the Lord, and there sound asleep, fully satisfy.

It is unsurprising that Christian theology took early and eagerly to the Socratic concept of the soul as a spiritual substance essentially independent of embodiment. "The reception of the notion[69] of the immortal soul . . . is an indication of the resurrection-notion's own inner problematic. . . . This is located in the question, how someone awakened from the dead in the more or less distant future can be identical with a human person who now lives."[70] That is indeed the problem, and in isolation the Socratic notion of the soul provides a solution to it: I am now an embodied soul; after I die I will be a disembodied soul; after the resurrection I will be a better-embodied soul; and all along, I am the same soul.

The solution, however, fits badly within Christian theology and has been an irritant foreign body throughout its career there. The continuity between death

65. I Thessalonians 4:13–15.
66. Philippians 1:21–24.
67. II Corinthians 5:3–10.
68. John of Damascus, *The Orthodox Faith*, 88.25–26.
69. *Vorstellung.*
70. Pannenberg, *Systematische Theologie*, 3:637.

and resurrection is that the person is "with Christ" in the resurrection and before it. But being with Christ comprises the whole content of the Fulfillment: if a disembodied person can be awake and with Christ, all further developments must be wholly superfluous. A theologoumenon that makes the resurrection superfluous falls, however, under severe condemnation: faith determined by it is "vain."[71]

What the theologoumenon of the immortal soul in fact suggests, whatever may creedally be confessed, becomes apparent in more unguarded utterances. We may hear, at random, the Edwardsean Samuel Hopkins: "When the spirits of the just are separated from the body, the world which to us is invisible opens to their view. They find themselves unconfined. . . . They are set at liberty, to range without restraint in the regions of bliss . . . while their views, exercises and enjoyments are high and increased . . . far beyond our conception. They are . . . like a bird liberated from a cage . . . [that] now flies and sports unconfined in the open light and air."[72] This is very good Socrates, but what then is the point of getting a body again? Hopkins's teacher Edwards felt the problem: "The spirits of just men made perfect will . . . have inexpressible, inconceivable happiness and perfect contentment, but yet part of their happiness will consist in hope of what is to come."[73] Exactly, but how can equipment with a body be an object of such a being's hope?

The conceptual and spiritual dissonance sometimes emerges when the restraints of dogma are relaxed. Thus Neo-Protestantism, in those strains committed both to biblical conceptions and to idealist metaphysics, made bizarre hybrids of "soul" and "body," so as to retain the notion of the immortal soul while less devaluing the body. Richard Rothe thought of a "Holy-Spiritual natural organism,"[74] a "soul-body," which in the life of faith "ripens" under "the material garment, which it here still wears." The resurrection is then simply that this "organism," once ripened, casts off its then unneeded material body and "exists as pure spirit."[75] As for saints now with the Lord, they are already ripened and so already in fact risen.[76] The teaching is preposterous, but we see why Rothe is driven to it.

Hans Urs von Balthasar, Catholic theologian of this century,[77] provides the cleansing negation from which to start: "Between the death of a human being, which is by definition the end from which he cannot return, and what we term 'resurrection' there is no common measure."[78] Neither a true escape-soul nor some Christian hybrid, nor any other posited anthropological entity, can bridge

---

71. I Corinthians 15:14.
72. *The Works of Samuel Hopkins* (Boston: Doctrinal Tract and Book Society, 1865), 2:43.
73. *Miscellanies*, 371.
74. *Heiliggeistigen Naturorganismus* (!).
75. *Dogmatik* (Heidelberg: J. C. B. Mohr, 1870, posthum.), 3:104.
76. Ibid., 103.
77. Von Balthasar is much too little cited in this work. The reason is simply that I have never been able to get sufficiently into his thinking.
78. *Mysterium Paschale*, tr. Aidan Nichols (Edinburgh: T. & T. Clark, 1990), 50.

the gap. It can be bridged not by anything humans are in themselves but only by and in God. Perhaps indeed we cannot now envision the saints without the myth of the soul, but behind and constraining it must be far more biblical understanding.

The key insight is a simple one: a saint now in heaven is not an otherwise constituted entity who anticipates resurrection; God's anticipation of the saint's resurrection *is* the heavenly reality of the saint. For God's anticipation of creation's life in the Kingdom, of our deification and our vision of his glory, is the whole being of heaven. The saints' present reality is in no way attenuated by this doctrine; what God anticipates indeed belongs to the "whither" of his life but is just so accessible to him and so real in its own mode.

Moreover, the saints now themselves actively anticipate their resurrection, rejoice in Edwards's "hope of what is to come" as their present being. For the life of the saints that God anticipates is the life they will lead in him when their time is made congruent with his; therefore what subsists in his anticipation is precisely their lively sharing in his life, including his anticipation of them. Heaven is the Kingdom itself in a particular mode of being, a mode sustained by the perfect intimacy of future and present in the triune *perichoresis*.

Can we then, as we earlier inquired, talk to the saints? It would seem we can, if we can talk to God. For the saints' living present-tense occurs within God's presence to us from his heaven. We are, to be sure, returned to a position and caution earlier made: therefore the saints are not our way to God; he is our way to them. If believers solicit the saints' prayers, they do this not otherwise than as in the Eucharist they pray together and for one another in the community constituted by God's presence.

The church's fellowship with members already "with Christ" is thus in fact intrusion into the community of the Kingdom itself, into creatures' life within God when he is all in all. Our address to the saints and their prayer for us is not an event within a preliminary stage of the Eschaton; it is an event in the Kingdom itself. The saints' side of the matter we have already interpreted. Our side is also intelligible: after all, the church's addresses to the saints also belong to that history, the eternal christological interpretation of which *is* the actuality of the Kingdom. What we say in the church will be interpreted as the life of the Kingdom; if we say a word to St. Ann, her answer will be part of that interpretation; and both our word and hers are now anticipated by God, to make his heaven.

The root form of the church's verbal fellowship with the saints in heaven is therefore some such communal cry as "With angels and archangels, and with *all* [emphasis added] the company of heaven, we laud and magnify your glorious name."[79] That may also be the last word of this chapter.

---

79. The transition to the Sanctus in several Western rites.

THIRTY-FIVE

Telos

God will reign: he will fit created time to triune time and created polity to the *perichoresis* of Father, Son, and Spirit. God will deify the redeemed: their life will be carried and shaped by the life of Father, Son, and Spirit, and they will know themselves as personal agents in the life so shaped. God will let the redeemed see him: the Father by the Spirit will make Christ's eyes their eyes. Under all rubrics, the redeemed will be appropriated to God's own being.

The last word to be said about God's triune being is that he "is a great fugue."[1] Therefore the last word to be said about the redeemed is Jonathan Edwards's beautiful saying, cited at the end of the first volume[2] to the converse point: "When I would form an idea of a society in the highest degree happy, I think of them . . . sweetly singing to each other."[3]

The point of identity, infinitely approachable and infinitely to be approached, the enlivening *telos* of the Kingdom's own life, is perfect harmony between the conversation of the redeemed and the conversation that God is. In the conversation God is, meaning and melody are one.[4]

The end is music.

1. 1:236.
2. 1:235.
3. *Miscellanies*, 188.
4. 1:236.

Index of Topics

This index, like that in volume 1, is not exhaustive. It lists a few topics that perhaps some readers may want to locate and that are not listed in or are not fully located by the table of contents. Most of theology's key matters are not included.

Index of Names